STUDY GUIDE

for

Julie Dahlquist

University of Texas at San Antonio

Pearson Prentice Hall

Boston San Francisco New York
London Toronto Sydney Tokyo Singapore Madrid
Mexico City Munich Paris Cape Town Hong Kong Montreal

Acquisitions Editor: Tessa O'Brien
Editorial Project Manager: Melissa Pellerano
Associate Production Project Manager: Alison Eusden
Senior Manufacturing Buyer: Carol Melville

Copyright© 2012, 2009, Pearson Education, Inc., 75 Arlington Street, Boston, MA 02116. Pearson Prentice Hall. All rights reserved. Printed in the United States of America. This publication is protected by copyright and permission should be obtained from the publisher prior to any prohibited reproduction, storage in a retrieval system, or transmission in any form or by any means, electronic, mechanical, photocopying, recording, or likewise. For information regarding permission(s), write to: Rights and Permissions Department.

This work is protected by United States copyright laws and is provided solely for the use of instructors in teaching their courses and assessing student learning. Dissemination or sale of any part of this work (including on the World Wide Web) will destroy the integrity of the work and is not permitted. The work and materials from it should never be made available to students except by instructors using the accompanying text in their classes. All recipients of this work are expected to abide by these restrictions and to honor the intended pedagogical purposes and the needs of other instructors who rely on these materials.

Pearson Prentice Hall™ is a trademark of Pearson Education, Inc.

Prentice Hall
is an imprint of

www.pearsonhighered.com

1 2 3 4 5 6 OPM 15 14 13 12 11

ISBN-13: 978-0-13-214833-7
ISBN-10: 0-13-214833-1

Contents

Chapter 1	Corporate Finance and the Financial Manager	1
Chapter 2	Introduction to Financial Statement Analysis	11
Chapter 3	Time Value of Money: An Introduction	27
Chapter 4	Time Value of Money: Valuing Cash Flow Streams	39
Chapter 5	Interest Rates	63
Chapter 6	Bonds	79
Chapter 7	Stock Valuation	101
Chapter 8	Investment Decision Rules	117
Chapter 9	Fundamentals of Capital Budgeting	135
Chapter 10	Stock Valuation: A Second Look	159
Chapter 11	Risk and Return in Capital Markets	173
Chapter 12	Systematic Risk and the Equity Risk Premium	189
Chapter 13	The Cost of Capital	209
Chapter 14	Raising Equity Capital	221
Chapter 15	Debt Financing	235
Chapter 16	Capital Structure	245
Chapter 17	Payout Policy	263
Chapter 18	Financial Modeling and Pro Forma Analysis	277
Chapter 19	Working Capital Management	295
Chapter 20	Short-Term Financial Planning	313
Chapter 21	Option Applications and Corporate Finance	325
Chapter 22	Mergers and Acquisitions	339
Chapter 23	International Corporate Finance	353

© 2012 Pearson Education, Inc. Publishing as Prentice Hall

Chapter 1
Corporate Finance and the Financial Manager

■ Key Learning Objectives

- Grasp the importance of financial information in both your personal and your business lives
- Understand the important features of the four main types of firms and see why the advantages of the corporate firm have led it to dominate economic activity
- Explain the goal of the financial manager and the reasoning behind that goal, as well as understand the three main types of decisions a financial manager makes
- Know how a corporation is managed and controlled, the financial manager's place in it, and some of the ethical issues financial managers face
- Understand the importance of financial markets, such as stock markets, to a corporation and the financial manager's role as liaison to those markets
- Recognize the role that financial institutions play in the financial cycle of the economy

■ Chapter Synopsis

1.1 Why Study Finance?

Financial decisions are made in both personal lives and in business. The **Valuation Principle** shows how to compare the costs and benefits of these decisions. Learning to apply this principle will allow you to make knowledgeable decisions as a consumer and as a manager.

1.2 The Four Types of Firms

There are four major types of firms: sole proprietorships, partnerships, limited liability companies, and corporations. First, a **sole proprietorship** is a business owned and run by one person; these firms are usually very small. The owner of the business has unlimited personal liability for any of the firm's debt. It is difficult to transfer ownership of a sole proprietorship.

Second, a **partnership** is owned and run by more than one person. Since all partners are liable for the firm's debt, a lender can require any partner to repay all of the firm's outstanding debt. A **limited partnership** has two kinds of owners, general partners and limited partners. General partners oversee the firm's activities and have unlimited liability. Limited partners have limited liability; their liability is limited to their investment. These limited partners cannot legally be involved in the managerial decision making for the business.

Third, a relatively new form of business in the United States is the **limited liability company (LLC)**. These companies have multiple owners who have limited liability.

Fourth, a **corporation** is a legally defined, artificial being, separate from its owners. The corporation is solely responsible for its obligations. There is no limit to the number of owners a corporation can have; these owners are called shareholders, stockholders, or equity holders. Since a corporation is a separate legal entity, a corporation's profits are subject to taxation separate from its owners' tax obligations. Corporations are responsible for 85% of the business revenue in the United States.

1.3 The Financial Manager

The financial manager makes the financial decisions of the business for the stockholders. The financial manager has three main tasks:

1. Make investment decisions

2. Make financing decisions

3. Manage cash flow from operating activities

The investment decisions shape what the firm does and whether it will add value for its owners. When making investment decisions, the financial manager must weigh the costs and benefits of each investment or project and decide which qualify as good uses of stockholders' money. After deciding what investments to make, the financial manager must decide how to pay for them. If the corporation needs to raise additional money to fund a large investment, the financial manager must decide whether to raise more money from new and existing owners by selling more shares of stock or to borrow the money. In addition, the financial manager must make sure that the firm has enough cash on hand to meet its obligations as they come due.

The goal of the financial manager is **to maximize the wealth of the owners.** The owners of the company have put their money at risk when they buy stock in the corporation. The financial manager is the caretaker of the stockholders' money; it is the job of the financial manager to make decisions that are in the best interest of the shareholders.

1.4 The Financial Manager's Place in the Corporation

The shareholders are the owners of the corporation, but they rely on others to actively manage the corporation. The shareholders elect a **board of directors** who have the ultimate decision-making authority in the corporation. The board of directors makes rules on how the corporation should be run, sets policy, and monitors the performance of the company. The board of directors delegates most of the day-to-day decision making and running of the company to its management. The **chief executive officer (CEO)** is in charge of running the corporation by instituting the rules and policies that the board of directors has set. In some cases, the chairman of the board of directors is also the CEO.

A management team, separate from the owners, runs a corporation. The managers are hired to act as the agents of the shareholders. The temptation of the managers to put their own self-interest ahead of the interests of the shareholders is known as the **agency problem.** Often, compensation packages of top managers are designed to ensure that the managers' interests are in line with the shareholders' interests.

1.5 The Stock Market

Companies initially sell their stock in the **primary market.** A public corporation has many owners and its shares trade in a **stock market.** When the existing owners trade their shares of stock, this is being done in the **secondary market.** The secondary market allows stockholders to sell their shares to turn their investment into cash. The largest stock market in the world is the New York Stock Exchange (NYSE). There are other stock exchanges in the United States, such as the American Stock Exchange (AMEX) and NASDAQ (National Association of Security Dealers Automated Quotation). The biggest stock exchanges outside the United States are the London Stock Exchange (LSE) and the Tokyo Stock Exchange (TSE).

Some stock markets, like the NYSE, are physical locations where **market makers** (known as **specialists** on the NYSE) match buyers and sellers. Other markets, such as the NASDAQ, are not a physical location where dealers and market makers meet. Instead, the dealers and market makers are connected by a computer network and telephones. The market makers post two prices for every stock they make a market in. The **bid price** is the price at which they are willing to buy the stock; the **ask price** is the price for which they are willing to sell the stock. The ask price is higher than the bid price and the difference is called the **bid–ask spread.** The bid–ask spread is a **transaction cost** that investors must pay.

1.6 Financial Institutions

In the financial cycle, (1) people invest and save their money; (2) that money, through loans and stock, flows to companies who use it to fund growth through new products, generating profits and wages; and (3) the money then flows back to the savers and investors. Financial institutions help money move through the financial cycle; they also help money move through time. For example, you need money today to buy a house; you do not have the money today, but will earn it over time as you work at your job. A bank lends you money today so that you can buy the house and you pay the money back to the bank in the future as your earn it. Financial institutions also assist in spreading out risk in the financial markets.

■ Selected Concepts and Key Terms

Sole Proprietorship

A sole proprietorship is a business owned by one individual who has unlimited liability. The business itself pays no taxes; the owner is responsible for paying taxes on the company's profits.

Partnership

A partnership is similar to a sole proprietorship (unlimited liability and the owners are taxed) but there is more than one owner.

Limited Liability

Limited liability means that the financial liability of an owner is limited to his or her investment in the company.

Limited Liability Company (LLC)

A limited liability company has multiple owners who have limited liability. An LLC is typically taxed like a sole proprietorship or partnership.

Corporation

A corporation is a legal entity separate from its owners, who have limited liability. Ownership in a corporation is divided into shares of **stock** and the owners are referred to as **stockholders, shareholders, or equity holders.** A corporation meeting certain restrictions, such as having fewer than 100 stockholders, can elect to be treated as an **S corporation** and taxed like a partnership. Otherwise, the corporation is a **C corporation** and must pay corporate taxes on its profits. A corporation can distribute its after-tax profits to the stockholders by making **dividend payments.** Since individuals must pay personal income taxes on these dividends, shareholders in a **C corporation** effectively must pay tax twice.

Board of Directors

The shareholders of a corporation elect a **board of directors** who have the ultimate decision-making authority in the corporation. This board of directors makes rules on how the corporation should be run, sets policy, and monitors the performance of the company. The **chief executive office (CEO)** institutes the rules and policies set by the board of directors.

Agency Problem

Managers of a corporation are hired to work for the owners. Although managers are hired as the agents of the shareholders, managers are tempted to put their own self-interests ahead of the interests of the shareholders. This is known as an **agency problem.**

Hostile Takeover

A **hostile takeover** occurs when an individual or organization purchases a large fraction of a corporation's stock and gets enough votes to replace the board of directors and CEO. The threat of losing their jobs as a result of a hostile takeover motivates boards of directors and CEOs to make good decisions.

Stock Market

A **stock market** (also known as a **stock exchange** or a **bourse**) is an organized market in which owners of public corporations can trade their shares of stock. The stock market determines the market price for shares and provides liquidity. A stock is **liquid** if it is easy for owners to sell shares for a price close to what they could contemporaneously buy it.

Primary and Secondary Markets

Companies originally sell their stock in the **primary market;** the primary market is the market in which companies raise capital. Once investors own these existing shares they can sell them in the **secondary market.** The secondary market provides liquidity for investors.

Market Makers

Market makers (known as **specialists** on the NYSE) match buyers and sellers. The specialists are willing to buy the stock at the **bid** price and sell the stock at a higher price called the **ask** price. The difference between these two prices is known as the **bid–ask** spread. This bid–ask spread is profit for the specialists and a **transaction cost** to investors. A transaction cost is a cost that investors have to pay in order to trade.

Financial Cycle

In the basic **financial cycle**, money flows from savers and investors to companies and entrepreneurs with ideas, and then back to the savers and investors in the form of profits and interest. All financial institutions play some role in this cycle. Financial institutions also help move money through time (e.g., loans against future wages) and spread risk across large investor bases.

■ Concept Check Questions and Answers

1. What is a limited liability company (LLC)? How does it differ from a limited partnership?

    All of the owners of a limited liability company have limited liability and can actively run the business. A limited partnership has two types of owners: general partners and limited partners. The general partners run the business and are personally liable for the firm's debt obligations. The limited partners cannot run the business and their liability is limited to their investment in the company.

2. What are the advantages and disadvantages of organizing a business as a corporation?

The advantages of organizing as a corporation are: (1) limited stockholder liability, (2) easy transfer of ownership, (3) unlimited life of the corporation, and (4) future business prospects are the only limitation for outside funding. The disadvantage of a corporation is double taxation; the corporation pays taxes on its profits and then shareholders pay taxes on the profits that are distributed to them.

3. What are the main types of decisions that a financial manager makes?

The financial manager makes the financial decisions of the business for the stockholders. The financial manager makes investment decisions, makes financing decisions, and manages cash flow from operating activities.

4. What is the goal of the financial manager?

A financial manager is a caretaker of the stockholders' money. The financial manager's job is to make decisions that are in the best interests of the shareholders. The financial manager compares the costs and benefits of a decision to determine which will maximize the wealth of the stockholders.

5. How do shareholders control a corporation?

The shareholders of a corporation elect the board of directors. This board of directors has the ultimate decision-making authority in the corporation. If the board of directors is not making decisions that are in the best interests of the shareholders, the shareholders will vote to replace the board.

6. What types of jobs would a financial manager have in a corporation?

Financial managers can be found working in the treasury department of firms, in capital budgeting, risk management and credit management, or for the controller in the accounting or tax divisions.

7. What ethical issues could confront a financial manager?

Managers are hired to be caretakers of the shareholders' money. Their job is to make decisions that add wealth for the owners. Managers face the ethical dilemma of whether to adhere to their responsibility to put the interests of the shareholders first when it conflicts with their own self-interests.

8. What advantage does a stock market provide to corporate investors? To financial managers?

A stock market allows investors to easily sell their shares in the corporation when they want to turn their investment into cash. The stock market provides liquidity and determines the market price for the shares.

The analysis and trading of participants in a stock market provides feedback to managers about their decisions. For example, if market participants like the decisions that the managers are making, they will want to buy more of the stock and this will drive up the stock price. If they think the managers are making poor decisions, they will sell their stock, and the stock price will fall.

9. What are the main differences between the NYSE and NASDAQ?

The NYSE is an auction market; prices are set through direct interaction between buyers and sellers. NASDAQ is an over-the-counter, or dealer, market. On the NYSE, each stock has only one market maker, but a stock can have multiple market makers competing against each other in a dealer market such as NASDAQ.

10. **What is the basic financial cycle?**

    The financial cycle consists of (1) people saving and investing their money; (2) that money flowing to companies who use it to fund growth, generating profits and wages; and (3) the money flowing back to savers and investors.

11. **What are three main roles financial institutions play?**

    Financial institutions help move money through the financial system and help move money through time. They also help in spreading out risk in the financial markets.

■ Examples with Step-by-Step Solutions

1.1 **Problem:** You own stock in Hill Country Corporation. The corporation earns $8 per share before taxes. After it has paid taxes, it will distribute the rest of its earnings to you as a dividend. The dividend is income to you, so you will then pay taxes on these earnings. The corporate tax rate is 35% and your tax rate on dividend income is 20%. How much of the corporate earnings is paid in taxes and how much do you get to keep?

   Solution

   Plan: We have the following information:
   Earnings before Taxes: $8
   Corporate Tax Rate: 35%
   Personal Dividend Tax Rate: 20%

   First, we need to calculate the corporation's earnings after taxes by subtracting the taxes paid from the pretax earnings of $8. The taxes paid will be 35% (the corporate tax rate) of $8. Since all of the after-tax earnings will be paid to you as a dividend, you will pay taxes of 20% on that amount. The amount left over is what you get to keep after all taxes are paid.

   Execute: $8 per share × 0.35 = $2.80 in taxes at the corporate level. This leaves $8 − $2.80 = $5.20 in after-tax earnings per share to distribute.

   You will pay $5.20 × 0.20 = $1.04 in taxes on that dividend. This leaves $4.16 ($5.20 − $1.04) for you to keep.

   Evaluate: As a shareholder you keep $4.16 of the original $8 in earnings; the remaining $2.80 + $1.04 = $3.84 is paid as taxes. Thus, the government is effectively taxing at a rate of $3.84/$8.00 = 0.48 = 48%.

Taxation of S Corporation Earnings

1.2 **Problem:** Rework Example 1.1 assuming that Hill Country Corporation has elected Subchapter S treatment and your tax rate on non dividend income is 35%.

   Solution

   Plan: We have the following information:
   Earnings before Taxes: $8
   Corporate Tax Rate: 0%
   Personal Tax Rate: 35%

In this case, the corporation pays no taxes on the $8 per share that it earned. In an S corporation, all income is treated as personal income to you, whether or not the corporation chooses to pay dividends to distribute earnings or to retain the earnings. As a result, you must pay a 35% tax rate on those earnings.

Execute: Your income taxes are 0.35 × $8 = $2.80, leaving you with $8 − $2.80 = $5.20 in after-tax earnings.

Evaluate: The $2.30 in taxes that you pay is substantially lower than the $3.84 paid in Example 1.1 As a result, you are left with $5.20 per share after all taxes instead of $4.16. However, note that in a C corporation, you are only taxed when you receive the income as a dividend, whereas in an S corporation, you pay taxes on the income immediately regardless of whether the corporation distributes it as a dividend or reinvests it in the company.

■ Questions and Problems

1. You own stock in Cormier Concrete Corp. (CCC). CCC earned $6 per share before taxes. After paying taxes, CCC will distribute the rest of the earnings to you in the form of a dividend. If CCC is in the 30% tax bracket and your tax rate on dividend income is 20%, how much of the corporate earnings is paid in taxes and how much do you get to keep?

2. What would happen if CCC in the previous problem elected Subchapter S treatment and your tax rate on non dividend income is 35%? How much is paid in taxes and how much do you get to keep?

■ Solutions to Questions and Problems

1. $6 × 0.30 = $1.80 is paid in corporate taxes. You receive $4.20 in the form of a dividend. You pay $0.84 to the government in taxes. After all taxes are paid, you get to keep $3.36.

2. You will pay $6 × 0.35 = $2.10 in taxes. You will get to keep the remaining $3.90.

■ Self-Test Questions

1. Which of the following is true about a limited partnership?
   a. A limited partnership is limited to 10 partners.
   b. Owners of a limited partnership pay taxes twice, once at the partnership level and once at the personal level.
   c. A limited partner cannot legally be involved in the managerial decisions of the business.
   d. The financial liability of a limited partnership is limited to the limited partners.

2. Which of the following business structures faces double taxation?
   a. S Corporation
   b. C Corporation
   c. Limited Partnership
   d. Limited Liability Company

3. The financial manager
   a. makes investment decisions.
   b. makes financing decisions.
   c. manages cash flow from operating activities.
   d. All of the above.

4. The goal of the financial manager is to
   a. maximize wealth for the shareholders.
   b. maximize cash flow.
   c. maximize sales.
   d. maximize the number of shareholders.

5. Although managers are hired as the agents of the shareholders, managers are tempted to put their own self-interests ahead of the interests of the shareholders. This is known as:
   a. The bid–ask spread
   b. Liquidity
   c. Limited liability
   d. An agency problem

6. The price at which a market maker is willing to buy a stock is known as the _____ and the price the market maker is willing to sell the stock is known as the _____.
   a. Ask price; bid price
   b. Ask price; liquidity price
   c. Liquidity price; bid price
   d. Bid price; ask price

7. A(n) _____ occurs when an individual or organization purchases enough of a corporation's stock to replace the board of directors and CEO.
   a. Liquidation
   b. Hostile takeover
   c. S corporation
   d. Agency problem

8. The price of a corporation's stock is determined
   a. by the CEO.
   b. by the board of directors.
   c. in the stock market.
   d. by the IRS.

9. What is the largest stock market in the world?
   a. The New York Stock Exchange
   b. The American Stock Exchange
   c. NASDAQ
   d. The Tokyo Stock Exchange

10. Most of the day-to-day running of a corporation is delegated to the:
    a. Shareholders
    b. Limited partners
    c. Management
    d. Board of directors

11. In an auction market, such as the NYSE, price is set by
    a. the board of directors of the listed companies.
    b. the interaction between buyers and sellers.
    c. the limited partners of the listed companies.
    d. the Securities & Exchange Commission.

12. Which of the following best describes the financial cycle?
    a. People save and invest money, businesses use that money to expand, businesses earn profits and return the money to the investors.
    b. Businesses invest in new products and earn profits, the government taxes the businesses, the government uses the tax revenue to give benefits to households.
    c. People spend money, businesses invest money, financial institutions lend money.
    d. The money that the government invests is given to businesses to create profits so that households have more money to spend.

Answers to Self-Test Questions

1. c
2. b
3. d
4. a
5. d
6. d
7. b
8. c
9. a
10. c
11. b
12. a

Chapter 2
Introduction to Financial Statement Analysis

■ Key Learning Objectives

- Know why the disclosure of financial information through financial statements is critical to investors
- Understand the function of the balance sheet
- Use the balance sheet to analyze a firm
- Understand how the income statement is used
- Analyze a firm through its income statement, including using the DuPont Identity
- Interpret a statement of cash flows
- Know what management's discussion and analysis and the statement of stockholders' equity are
- Understand the main purpose and aspects of the Sarbanes-Oxley reforms following Enron and other financial scandals.

■ Chapter Synopsis

Financial statements allow managers to assess the success of their own firm and compare it to competitors. These statements are also a way in which the firm communicates its information to investors.

2.1 Firms' Disclosure of Financial Information

U.S. companies with publicly traded securities are required to file financial statements with the Securities & Exchange Commission (SEC) on a quarterly basis on form **10-Q** and annually on form **10-K**. Financial statements must also be included in the **annual report** provided for shareholders. These financial statements must conform to the Financial Accounting Standards Board's (FASB's) **Generally Accepted Accounting Principles (GAAP)**. A neutral third party, known as an **auditor,** checks the financial statements to ensure they are prepared according to GAAP. The four financial statements a public company is required to provide are: the balance sheet, the income statement, the statement of cash flows, and the statement of stockholders' equity.

2.2 The Balance Sheet

The **balance sheet** is divided into two parts: (1) **assets** and (2) **liabilities and stockholders' equity.** The assets (on the left side of the balance sheet) show how the firm uses its capital. These assets are divided into two categories: **current assets** and **long-term assets.** Current assets include cash and assets that can be converted into cash within one year, such as, marketable securities, accounts receivable, and inventory. The long-term assets include assets such as machinery or real estate that will produce tangible benefits for more than one year. Each year, **depreciation** is deducted from the value of long-term assets. Depreciation is not a cash expense; it represents the wear and that occurs as the long-term assets are used and takes into consideration that these assets are less valuable as they become older. The **book value** of an asset equals the price paid for the asset minus the accumulated depreciation.

The right side of the balance sheet shows the firm's obligations to creditors as well as stockholders' equity. The obligations to creditors include both **current liabilities** and **long-term liabilities.** Current liabilities are obligations that will be paid within one year, such as accounts payable, notes payable, and deferred expenses. Long-term liabilities include loans longer than one year. **Stockholders' equity** is the difference between the firm's assets and liabilities. It is an accounting measure of the firm's net worth. It is important to remember the balance sheet identity:

$$\text{Assets} = \text{Liabilities} + \text{Stockholders' Equity}$$

Stockholders' equity on the balance sheet does not reflect the amount investors are willing to pay for the equity. The market value of a stock does not depend on the historical cost of the firm's assets; instead, it depends on what investors expect those assets to produce in the future. The total market value of a firm's equity equals the market price per share times the number of shares.

2.3 Balance Sheet Analysis

Although the book value of a firm's equity is not a good estimate of the company's true value as an ongoing firm, it is sometimes used as an estimate of the liquidation value of the firm. The liquidation value is what would be left if all of the assets were sold and liabilities paid. Comparing the book value of a firm to its market value will give us the market-to-book ratio (also called the price-to-book [P/B] ratio):

$$\text{Market-to-Book Ratio} = \frac{\text{Market Value of Equity}}{\text{Book Value of Equity}}$$

While this ratio will vary across firms, for most successful firms the market-to-book ratio substantially exceeds 1. A ratio greater than 1 indicates that the value of the firm's assets as they are currently being used exceeds their historical cost (or liquidation value). Analysts often classify firms with low market-to-book ratios as **value stocks,** and those with high market-to-book ratios as **growth stocks.**

Another important piece of information that we can learn from a firm's balance sheet is the firm's leverage, or the extent to which it relies on debt as a source of financing. The debt-equity ratio is calculated as

$$\text{Debt-Equity Ratio} = \frac{\text{Total Debt}}{\text{Total Equity}}$$

The **enterprise value** of a firm assesses the value of the underlying business assets, unencumbered by debt and separate from any cash and marketable securities. The enterprise value is how much it would cost to take over the business; in other words, it is how much it would cost to buy all of a company's equity and pay off its debts. We compute it as:

$$\text{Enterprise Value} = \text{Market Value of Equity} + \text{Debt} - \text{Cash}$$

Comparing a firm's current assets and current liabilities gives an indication of whether the company has sufficient working capital to meet its short-term needs. This can be done using the current ratio or the quick ratio ("acid-test" ratio). These ratios are calculated as:

$$\text{Current Ratio} = \frac{\text{Current Assets}}{\text{Current Liabilities}}$$

$$\text{Quick Ratio} = \frac{\text{Current Assets} - \text{Inventory}}{\text{Current Liabilities}}$$

The higher the current ratio and the quick ratio, the less risk the firm has of experiencing a cash shortfall in the near future.

2.4 The Income Statement

The **income statement** lists the firm's revenues and expenses over a period of time. Whereas the balance sheet shows the firm's assets and liabilities at a given point in time, the income statement shows the flow of revenues and expenses generated by those assets and liabilities between two dates. The first line of the income statement shows the revenues from sales of products, and the second line shows the costs incurred to make and sell the products. The third line is **gross profit,** the difference between sales revenues and the costs. The next group of items is operating expenses. These are expenses from the ordinary course of running the business that are not directly related to producing the goods or services being sold. They include administrative expenses and overhead, salaries, marketing costs, and research and development expenses. The third type of operating expense, depreciation and amortization (a charge that captures the change in value of acquired assets), is not an actual cash expense but represents an estimate of the costs that arise from wear and tear or obsolescence of the firm's assets. The firm's gross profit minus operating expenses is called operating income. Next we include other sources of income or expenses (such as cash flows from the firm's financial investments) that arise from activities that are not the central part of a company's business. After adjusting for these other sources of income or expenses, we have the firm's earnings before interest and taxes, or **EBIT.** From EBIT, we deduct the interest paid on outstanding debt to compute pretax income, and then we deduct corporate taxes to determine the firm's net income.

The last or "bottom" line of the income statement shows the firm's **net income.** Net income represents the total earnings of the firm's equity holders. It is often reported on a per share basis as the firm's **earnings per share (EPS),** which we compute by dividing net income by the total number of shares outstanding:

$$EPS = \frac{\text{Net Income}}{\text{Shares Outstanding}}$$

2.5 Income Statement Analysis

The income statement provides useful information regarding the profitability of a firm's business and how it relates to the value of the firm's shares. Three profitability ratios are: **gross margin, operating margin,** and **net profit margin:**

$$\text{Gross Margin} = \frac{\text{Gross Profit}}{\text{Sales}}$$

$$\text{Operating Margin} = \frac{\text{Operating Income}}{\text{Total Sales}}$$

$$\text{Net Profit Margin} = \frac{\text{Net Income}}{\text{Total Sales}}$$

The gross margin simply reflects the ability of the company to sell a product for more than the sum of the direct costs of making it. The firm's other expenses of doing business are reflected in the calculation of the operating margin. The net profit margin shows the fraction of each dollar in revenues that equity holders get to keep after the firm pays interest and taxes.

By combining information in the firm's income statement and balance sheet, we can gauge how efficiently a firm is utilizing its assets. A broad measure of efficiency is **asset turnover:**

$$\text{Asset Turnover} = \frac{\text{Sales}}{\text{Total Assets}}$$

Low values of asset turnover indicate that the firm is not generating much revenue (sales) per dollar of assets. Since total assets includes assets like cash that are not directly involved in generating sales, we might want to consider the relationship between sales and fixed assets by looking at the **fixed asset turnover:**

$$\text{Fixed Asset Turnover} = \frac{\text{Sales}}{\text{Fixed Assets}}$$

Another important consideration is how the firm is managing its working capital. We can express the firm's accounts receivable in terms of the number of days' worth of sales that it represents, called the **accounts receivable days, average collection period,** or **days sales outstanding:**

$$\text{Accounts Receivable Days} = \frac{\text{Accounts Receivable}}{\text{Average Daily Sales}}$$

A significant unexplained increase in this number could be a cause for concern because it indicates that the firm is doing a poor job collecting from its customers. To look at how efficiently the firm converts inventory into sales, we calculate the **inventory turnover ratio:**

$$\text{Inventory Turnover} = \frac{\text{Sales}}{\text{Inventory}}$$

Lenders often assess a firm's leverage by computing an **interest coverage ratio,** also known as a **times interest earned (TIE) ratio;** dividing earnings by interest shows how easily the firm can cover its interest payments.

Analysts and financial managers often evaluate the firm's return on investment by comparing its income to its investment using ratios such as the firm's **return on equity (ROE)** or its **return on assets (ROA):**

$$\text{Return on Equity} = \frac{\text{Net Income}}{\text{Book Value of Equity}}$$

$$\text{Return on Assets} = \frac{\text{Net Income}}{\text{Total Assets}}$$

Knowing a firm's ROE is not enough; we need to know the drivers behind ROE. High margins, efficient use of assets, or even simply high leverage can all lead to a higher ROE. A common tool for looking more closely at the drivers behind a company's ROE is the **DuPont Identity:**

$$\text{ROE} = \frac{\text{Net Income}}{\text{Sales}} \times \frac{\text{Sales}}{\text{Total Assets}} \times \frac{\text{Total Assets}}{\text{Total Equity}}$$

The **price-earnings ratio (P/E)** compares the market value of a company's stock with its earnings.

$$\text{P/E Ratio} = \frac{\text{Market Capitalization}}{\text{Net Income}}$$
$$= \frac{\text{Share Price}}{\text{Earnings per Share}}$$

2.6 The Statement of Cash Flows

The **statement of cash flows** uses information from the income statement and balance sheet to determine how much cash a firm has generated and how that cash has been allocated. The statement of cash flows is divided into three sections: operating activities, investment activities, and financing activities. The first section, operating activity, starts with net income from the income statement. It then adjusts this number by adding back all non cash entries related to the firm's operating activities. The next section, investment activity, lists the cash used for investment. The third section, financing activity, shows the flow of cash between the firm and its investors.

2.7 Other Financial Statement Information

In the **management discussion and analysis (MD&A)** the company's management discusses the recent year providing a background on the company and any significant events that may have occurred. Management must also discuss any important risks that the firm faces and issues that may affect the firm's liquidity or resources. Any **off-balance sheet transactions,** which are transactions or arrangements that can have a material impact on the firm's future performance yet do not appear on the balance sheet, and must also be disclosed.

The **statement of stockholders' equity** breaks down the stockholders' equity computed on the balance sheet into the amount that came from issuing new shares versus retained earnings. Companies provide extensive notes with further details on the information provided in the financial statements. The information in these notes is often very important to interpret fully the firm's financial statements.

2.8 Financial Reporting in Practice

A firm's financial statements are of critical importance to investors and financial managers. Safeguards such as GAAP and auditors are in place to help ensure that the information is reliable and accurate. Unfortunately, as evidenced by the well-known Enron accounting scandal, even with these safeguards, abuses sometimes take place.

Seeing the importance to investors of accurate and up-to-date financial statements, Congress passed the **Sarbanes-Oxley Act** (SOX) in 2002. The intent of this legislation was to improve the accuracy of information given to both boards and to shareholders. SOX attempted to achieve this goal in three ways: (1) by overhauling incentives and independence in the auditing process, (2) by stiffening penalties for providing false information, and (3) by forcing companies to validate their internal financial control processes.

■ Selected Concepts and Key Terms

Financial Statements

Every public company is required to produce four **financial statements:** the **balance sheet,** the **income statement,** the **statement of cash flows,** and the **statement of stockholders' equity.** These statements give creditors and investors information about a firm's past performance.

Balance Sheet

The **balance sheet** lists the firm's assets and liabilities at one point in time. The asset (left side) of the balance sheet lists the cash, inventory, property, plant and equipment, and other investments the company has made. Liabilities, or the firm's obligations to creditors, appear on the right side. Stockholders' equity is the difference between the firm's assets and liabilities, and is an accounting measure of the firm's net worth. According to the **balance sheet identity** assets must equal liabilities plus stockholders' equity.

Income Statement

The income statement lists the firm's revenues and expenses over a period of time. The last line of the income statement shows the firm's net income, which is a measure of its after-tax profitability during the period.

Statement of Cash Flows

The statement of cash flows measures the change in cash over a period of time. It is divided into three sections: operating activities, investment activities, and financing activities. In the operating activities section, net income is adjusted by adding back all non cash entries related to the firm's operating activities. The investment activities section lists the net cash used for investment. The financing activities section shows the flow of cash between the firm and its investors.

Book Value

The book value of a long-term asset is equal to its acquisition cost less accumulated depreciation. Depreciation is not an actual cash expense; it is a way of recognizing that buildings and equipment wear out and become less valuable the older they get. For example, net property, plant, and equipment is equal to the total book value of a firm's long-term assets after subtracting the depreciation from previous years. The **book value of equity (stockholders' equity** or **net worth)** is the difference between total assets and total liabilities.

Market Capitalization

The total market value of equity is known as **market capitalization.** It equals the market price per share times the number of shares. Market capitalization does not depend on the historical cost of the firm's assets; instead it depends on what investors expect those assets to produce in the future. The book value of equity should not be confused with the market value of equity; the market value of equity may be different because the book value of assets does not perfectly match the market value of the assets and because many of the firm's intangible assets are not captured on the balance sheet.

■ Concept Check Questions and Answers

1. What is the role of an auditor?

    An auditor is a neutral third party hired by the corporation to check the annual financial statements, ensure they are prepared according to the generally accepted accounting principles (GAAP), and verify that the information is reliable.

2. What are the four financial statements that all public companies must produce?

    All public companies must produce the balance sheet, the income statement, the statement of cash flows, and the statement of stockholders' equity.

3. What is depreciation designed to capture?

    Depreciation measures the decline in an asset's value because of its increasing age and usage.

4. The book value of a company's assets usually does not equal the market value of those assets. What are some reasons for this difference?

    Many of the assets listed on the balance sheet are valued based on their historical cost rather than their true value today. Also, many of the firm's valuable assets, such as the firm's reputation in the marketplace, are not captured on the balance sheet.

5. What does a high debt-to-equity ratio tell you?

   A high debt-to-equity ratio means that a company is using a lot of debt to finance its assets. In other words, the company is using a lot of financial leverage.

6. What is a firm's enterprise value?

   The enterprise value of a firm assesses the value of the underlying business assets, unencumbered by debt and separate from any cash and marketable securities.

7. What do a firm's earnings measure?

   Earnings measure how much is left over for the shareholders after all expenses have been paid.

8. What is dilution?

   A growth in the number of shares in a corporation is referred to as dilution because there will be more total shares to divide the same earnings.

9. How can a financial manager use the DuPont identity to assess the firm's ROE?

   The DuPont Identity allows a manager to look at the drivers of net income: profit margin, asset turnover, and equity multiplier.

10. How do you use the price-earnings (P/E) ratio to gauge the market value of a firm?

    The P/E ratio is the ratio of the stock price to the firm's earnings per share. It is a measure that is used to assess whether a stock is over, under, or fairly valued based on the idea that the value of a stock should be proportional to the level of earnings it can generate for its shareholders. P/E ratios tend to be higher for firms with high growth rates.

11. Why does a firm's net income not correspond to cash earned?

    Net income does not correspond to cash earned for two reasons. First, there are non cash expenses on the income statement, such as depreciation and amortization. Second, certain uses of cash, such as the purchase of a building, are not reported on the income statement.

12. What are the components of the statement of cash flows?

    The statement of cash flows is divided into three sections: operating activities, investment activities, and financing activities.

13. Where do off-balance sheet transactions appear in a firm's financial statements?

    Off-balance sheet transactions are disclosed on the management discussion and analysis (MD&A). Even though off-balance sheet transactions do not appear on the balance sheet, they can have a material impact on the firm's future performance.

14. What information do the notes to the financial statements provide?

    The notes to the financial statements provide information such as the accounting assumptions that were used in preparing the statements. Also, details of acquisitions, spin-offs, leases, taxes, and risk management activities are shown in these notes.

15. Describe the transactions Enron used to increase its reported earnings.

    Enron sold assets at inflated prices to other firms and promised to buy back those assets at even higher prices in the future. Thus, Enron received cash today in exchange for a promise to pay more cash in the future. Enron recorded the incoming cash as revenue and hid the obligation to buy the assets back in a variety of ways.

16. What is the Sarbanes-Oxley Act?

    In 2002, Congress passed the Sarbanes-Oxley Act. This act requires, among other things, that CEOs and CFOs certify the accuracy and appropriateness of their firm's financial statements and increases the penalties against them if their financial statements later prove to be fraudulent.

■ Examples with Step-by-Step Solutions

Problems using the concepts in this chapter generally involve understanding the basic format used in simple financial statements. For example, you should be able to identify which statements would be affected by specific events and what effect the events would have on variables such as earnings per share and book value of equity. You may also have to calculate ratios based on the financial statement information. The example problems below refer to Martinez Manufacturing Corp. Martinez's 2010 balance sheet and income statement are shown below.

Martinez Manufacturing Corporation
Balance Sheet
December 31, 2010

Assets			Liabilities and Stockholders' Equity	
Current Assets			Current Liabilities	
Cash	18.7		Accounts payable	31.4
Accounts receivable	22.3		Notes payable/short-term debt	5.8
Inventories	16.5		Total current liabilities	37.2
Total Current Assets	57.5			
			Long-Term Liabilities	
Long-Term Assets			Long-term debt	114.1
Net property, plant, and equipment	115.2		Total long-term liabilities	114.1
Total long-term assets	115.2		Total Liabilities	151.3
			Stockholders' Equity	21.4
Total Assets	172.7		Total Liabilities and Stockholders' Equity	172.7

Martinez Manufacturing Corporation
Income Statement for the Year Ended December 31, 2010

Total sales	184.9
−Cost of sales	−146.3
Gross profit	38.6
−Selling, general and administrative expenses	−13.9
−Research and development	−6.2

Continued

Martinez Manufacturing Corporation
Income Statement for the Year Ended December 31, 2010

−Depreciation and amortization	−1.4
Operating income	17.1
+Other income	0
Earnings before interest and taxes (EBIT)	17.1
+Interest income (expense)	−8.2
Pretax income	8.9
−Taxes	−2.67
Net Income	6.23

Market versus Book Value

2.1 Problem: Suppose Martinez Corp. has 2.5 million shares outstanding, and these shares are trading for a price of $20 per share, what is Martinez's market capitalization? How does the market capitalization compare to Martinez's book value of equity?

Solution

Plan: Market capitalization is equal to the price per share times the number of shares outstanding. We can find Martinez's book value of equity at the bottom right side of its balance sheet.

Execute: Martinez's market capitalization is (2.5 million shares) × ($20/share) = $50 million. This market capitalization is significantly higher than Martinez's book value of equity of $21.4 million.

Evaluate: Martinez must have sources of value that do not appear on the balance sheet. The company might have opportunities for growth, a high-quality management team, or valuable relationships with suppliers and customers.

Computing Enterprise Value

2.2 Problem: On December 31, 2010, what was Martinez's enterprise value?

Solution

Plan: We will solve the problem using the equation: Enterprise value = market capitalization + debt − cash. We computed market capitalization in Example 2.1; the market capitalization is $50 million. The amount of cash ($18.7 million) and the amount of debt ($119.9 million) are shown on the balance sheet.

Execute:
Enterprise value = market capitalization + debt − cash
Enterprise value = $50 million + $119.9 million − $18.7 million
Enterprise value = $151.20 million

Evaluate: It would cost $151.20 million to take over Martinez. It would cost $50 million + $119.9 million = $169.9 million to buy all of the company's equity and pay off its debts. Because we would acquire $18.7 million in cash, the net cost to purchase Martinez would be $151.20 million.

DuPont Analysis

2.3. Problem: Using the information in Martinez's balance sheet and income statement, use the DuPont Identity to compute the company's ROE. Compare Martinez's ROE to Bradfield Fabrication Inc.'s ROE. You are given the following information about Bradfield:

Profit Margin: 3%

Asset Turnover: 1.62

Equity Multiplier: 5.99

Solution

Plan: To use the DuPont Identity to compute the ROE, we need to determine the company's profit margin, asset turnover, and equity multiplier. Multiplying these three numbers will give us the company's ROE. We already have the three components for the DuPont equation for Bradfield. We simply need to multiply them together to get the ROE. We need to complete the table below:

	Profit Margin Net Income/Sales	Asset Turnover Sales/Total Assets	Equity Multiplier Total Assets/Equity	ROE NI/Equity
Martinez				
Bradfield	0.03	1.62	5.99	

Execute:

	Profit Margin Net Income/Sales	Asset Turnover Sales/Total Assets	Equity Multiplier Total Assets/Equity	ROE Net Income/Equity
Martinez	6.23/184.9 0.0337	184.9/172.7 1.0706	172.7/21.4 8.0701	0.2911
Bradfield	0.03	1.62	5.99	0.2911

(*Note:* Multiplying 0.0337 × 1.0706 × 8.0701 for Martinez results in 0.2912 rather than 0.2911; this slight difference is due to the rounding error that exists when each individual ratio is calculated.)

Evaluate: Both Martinez and Bradfield have an ROE of 29.11%. However, we can see a difference in the way the two companies earn their ROE. The profit margin for both companies is 3%. Bradfield has a much higher asset turnover than Martinez; this means that Bradfield is much better at using its assets to generate sales. While its asset turnover is much lower, Martinez is able to attain the same ROE as Bradfield because its equity multiplier is much higher than Bradfield's. This means that Martinez is using proportionately more debt to purchase its assets.

Computing Profitability and Valuation Ratios

2.4. Problem: Given the balance sheet and income statements for Martinez and that the company has 2.5 million shares outstanding selling at $20 per share, calculate the operating margin, net profit margin, P/E ratio, and the ratio of enterprise value to operating income and sales for Martinez.

Solution

Plan: We need to compute the following ratios given the inputs provided in Martinez's balance sheet and income statement. The enterprise value was calculated as $151.20 million

Operating Margin = Operating Income/Sales

Net Profit Margin = Net Income/Sales

P/E ratio = Price/Earnings

Enterprise value to operating income = Enterprise Value/Operating Income

Enterprise value to sales = Enterprise Value/Sales

Execute:

Operating Margin = 17.1/184.9 = 9.25%

Net Profit Margin = 6.23/184.9 = 3.37%

P/E ratio = $20/($6.23 million/2.5 million shares) = $20/2.49 per shares = 8.032

Enterprise value to operating income = $151.20/17.1 = 8.84

Enterprise value to sales = $151.20/184.9 = 0.82

Evaluate:

Computing profitability and valuation ratios for Martinez allows us to compare the company with other companies that may be very different in size.

The Impact of Depreciation on Cash Flow

2.5. **Problem:** Suppose Martinez had an additional $1 million depreciation expense in 2010. If Martinez's tax rate on pretax income is 30%, what would be the impact of this expense on Martinez's earnings? How would it impact Martinez's cash at the end of the year?

Solution

Plan: Depreciation is an operating expense, so Martinez's operating income, EBIT, and pretax income would be affected. With a tax rate of 30%, Martinez's tax bill will decrease by 30 cents for every dollar that pretax income is reduced. In order to determine how Martinez's cash would be impacted, we have to determine the effect of the additional depreciation on cash flows. Recall that depreciation is not an actual cash outflow, even though it is treated as an expense, so the only effect on cash flow is through the reduction in taxes.

Execute: Martinez's operating income, EBIT, and pretax income would fall by $1 million because of the $1 million in additional operating expenses due to depreciation.

This $1 million decrease in pretax income would reduce Martinez's tax bill by 0.30 × $1 million = $0.30 million. Therefore, net income would fall by 1 − 0.30 = $0.70 million. These changes would result in Martinez's income statement looking like this:

Martinez Manufacturing Corp.
Income Statement for the Year Ended December 31, 2010

Total sales	184.9
−Cost of sales	−146.3
Gross profit	38.6
−Selling, general and administrative expenses	−13.9
−Research and development	−6.2
−Depreciation and amortization	−2.4
Operating income	16.1
+Other income	0
Earnings before interest and taxes (EBIT)	16.1
+Interest income (expense)	−8.2
Pretax income	7.9
−Taxes	−2.37
Net Income	5.53

On the statement of cash flows, net income would fall by $0.70 million, but we would add back the additional depreciation of $1 million because it is a non cash expense. Thus, cash from operating activities would rise by −0.70 + 1 = $0.30 million. Thus, Martinez's cash balance at the end of the year would increase by $0.30 million, the amount of the tax savings that resulted from the additional depreciation deduction.

Evaluate: The increase in cash balance comes completely from the reduction in taxes. Because Martinez pays $0.30 million less in taxes, even though its cash expenses have not increased, the company has $0.30 million more in cash at the end of the year.

■ Questions and Problems

1. On October 2, 2005, Starbucks had a book value of equity of $2 billion, 768 million shares outstanding, and a market price of $30 per share. Starbucks also had cash of $207 million, and total debt of $1.4 billion.
   a. What was Starbucks' market capitalization? What was Starbucks' market-to-book ratio?
   b. What was Starbucks' book debt-equity ratio? What was its market debt-equity ratio?
   c. What was Starbucks' enterprise value?

2. Consider the following potential events that might have occurred to Martinez on December 31, 2010. For each one, indicate which line items on Martinez's balance sheet would be affected and by how much. Also, indicate the change to Martinez's book value of equity if the event occurred.
   a. Martinez uses $1 million of its available cash to purchase new machinery for its assembly line.
   b. Martinez issues $3 million in new long-term debt. The company will use the cash it has raised to purchase a new building in several months.
   c. A fire destroys an uninsured $2 million building.
   d. Martinez sells $1 million of its inventory to one of its customers on credit.

3. California Tile has cash of $6.12 million, current assets of $16.75 million, and current liabilities of $15.48 million. It also has inventories of $1.25 million.
   a. What is California's current ratio?
   b. What is California's quick ratio?
   c. If Monterey Tile has a current ratio of 1.08 and a quick ratio of 0.98, what can you say about the asset liquidity of California relative to Monterey?

4. Suppose a firm's tax rate is 40%.
   a. What effect would a $100 million operating expense have on this year's net income? What effect would it have on next year's net income?
   b. What effect would a $100 million capital expense have on this year's earnings, if the capital is depreciated at a rate of $20 million per year for 5 years? What effect would it have on next year's earnings?

5. You are analyzing the leverage of two firms and you note the following (all values are in millions of dollars):

	Debt	Book Equity	Market Equity	Operating Income	Interest Expense
Firm A	500	300	400	100	50
Firm B	100	40	50	9	7

   a. What is the market debt-to-equity ratio of each firm?
   b. What is the book debt-to-equity ratio of each firm?
   c. What is the interest coverage ratio of each firm?
   d. Which firm will have more difficulty meeting its debt obligations?

6. You are analyzing two companies, Anderson and Bailey. You have collected the following information about these two companies:

	Sales (Income Statement)	Accounts Receivable (Balance Sheet)	Inventory (Balance Sheet)
Anderson	348,920	27,540	34,290
Bailey	58,109	5987	6199

   a. What is each company's Accounts Receivable Days?
   b. What is each company's Inventory Turnover?
   c. Which company is managing its accounts receivable and inventory more efficiently?

Solutions to Questions and Problems

1. a. Market capitalization = 768 million × $30 = $23 billion
      Market-to-book ratio = $23 billion/$2 billion = 11.5
   b. Book debt-equity ratio = 1.4/2 = 0.70
      Market debt-equity ratio = 1.4/23 = 0.06
   c. Enterprise value = Market Value of Equity + Debt − Cash = 23 + 1.4 − 0.207 = $24.193 billion

2. a. Cash would decrease by $1 million and net plant, property, and equipment would increase by $1 million. There would be no change in equity.
   b. Cash would increase by $3 million and long-term debt would increase by $3 million. There would be no change to equity.
   c. Net plant and equipment would fall by $2 million and the book value of equity would fall by $2 million.
   d. Inventory would decrease by $1 million and accounts receivable would increase by $1 million. There would be no change to equity.

3. a. Current ratio = 16.75/15.48 = 1.08
   b. Quick ratio = (16.75 − 1.25)/15.48 = 1.00
   c. Monterey and California have the same current ratio. However California's quick ratio is higher than Monterey's. Therefore, Monterey must have proportionately more inventory than California.

4. a. A $100 million operating expense would be immediately expensed, increasing operating expenses by $100 million. This would lead to a reduction in taxes of 40% × $100 million = $40 million. Thus, earnings would decline by 100 − 40 = $60 million. There would be no effect on next year's earnings.
   b. Depreciation of $20 million would appear each year as an operating expense. Thus, net income would change each of the next 5 years by −$20(1 − 0.40) = −$12 million.

5. a. Market debt-to-equity for Firm A is 500/400 = 1.25 and for Firm B is 100/50 = 2.0.
   b. Book debt-to-equity for Firm A is 500/300 = 1.67 and for Firm B is 100/40 = 2.5.
   c. Interest coverage ratio for Firm A is 100/50 = 2.0 and for Firm B is 9/7 = 1.29.
   d. Firm A will have an easier time making its interest payments; its operating income is 2 times as large as its interest payments and Firm B's is only 1.29 times larger.

6. a. Anderson's accounts receivables days is 27,540/(348,920/365) = 28.81 and Bailey's is 5,987/(58,109/365) = 37.61.
   b. Anderson's inventory turnover is 348,920/34,290 = 10.18 times; Bailey's is 58,109/6,199 = 9.37 times.
   c. Anderson is managing its accounts receivables and its inventory more efficiently. Anderson collects its money on average in 28.81 days while Bailey takes on average 37.61 days. Anderson turns over its inventory more often; this means that items sit in Anderson's inventory for a shorter period of time.

■ Self-Test Questions

1. Which of the following is a list of current assets?
   a. Cash, accounts payable, accounts receivable
   b. Cash, inventory, sales revenue
   c. Cash, accounts receivable, inventory
   d. Sales revenue, depreciation, cash

2. Market capitalization
   a. equals the market price per share times the number of shares.
   b. is the book value of equity.
   c. depends on historical cost of the firm's assets.
   d. All of the above.

3. Analysts often classify firms with low market-to-book ratios as _____ and those with high market-to-book ratios as _____.
   a. Growth stocks; value stocks
   b. Liquidation stocks; value stocks
   c. Growth stocks; high enterprise value stocks
   d. Value stocks; growth stocks

4. Which of the following might be used to measure a firm's leverage?
   a. Current ratio
   b. Debt-equity ratio
   c. Quick ratio
   d. Operating margin

5. Cardinal Construction has $30 million in debt and $2 million in cash on its balance sheet. Cardinal's market capitalization is $50 million. The company's enterprise value is
   a. $18 million
   b. $22 million
   c. $78 million
   d. $82 million

6. Kelly Computer Corp. has a gross margin of 60%. This means that if Kelly sells a $100 product,
   a. the direct cost of the product is $40.
   b. the direct cost of the product is $60.
   c. the direct cost of the product is $140.
   d. the direct cost of the product is $160.

7. Donalson Development Corp. is interested in knowing how efficiently it is managing its net working capital. Which of the following ratios would tell the company something about its working capital management?
   a. Fixed asset turnover
   b. Operating margin
   c. Accounts receivable days
   d. Return on equity

8. Which of the following would lead to a higher ROE?
   a. A higher profit margin
   b. A higher asset turnover
   c. A higher equity multiplier
   d. All of the above

9. Which of the following is a TRUE statement?
   a. Net income does not correspond to cash earned because non cash entries such as depreciation appear as expenses on the income statement.
   b. The statement of cash flows is divided into three sections: assets, liabilities, and shareholders' equity.
   c. Increases in inventory are recorded as an expense on the income statement even though it does not represent an actual cash outflow.
   d. Purchases of new property, plant, and equipment are reported in the "operating activity" portion of the statement of cash flows.

10. The Sarbanes-Oxley Act attempts to improve the accuracy of information given to both boards and shareholders by
    a. overhauling incentives and independence in the auditing process.
    b. stiffening penalties for providing false information.
    c. forcing companies to validate their internal financial control processes.
    d. All of the above.

11. To calculate a firm's book value, you would need
    a. Only the firm's balance sheet.
    b. Both the firm's balance sheet and income statement.
    c. Both the firm's balance sheet and the current market price of the stock.
    d. The firm's balance sheet, income statement, and the current market price of the stock.

12. Natalie wants to learn more about Corinth Enterprises but the only information she has about the company is its balance sheet. With only this information, which of the following can Natalie calculate?
    a. The firm's enterprise value
    b. The firm's current ratio
    c. The firm's total asset turnover
    d. The firm's book value

Answers to Self-Test Questions

1. c
2. a
3. d
4. b
5. c
6. a
7. c
8. d
9. a
10. d
11. a
12. b

Chapter 3
Time Value of Money: An Introduction

■ Key Learning Objectives

- Identify the roles of financial managers and competitive markets in decision making
- Understand the Valuation Principle, and how it can be used to identify decisions that increase the value of the firm
- Assess the effect of interest rates on today's value of future cash flows
- Calculate the value of distant cash flows in the present and of current cash flows in the future

■ Notation

r	interest rate
PV	present value
FV	future value
C	cash flow
n	number of periods

■ Chapter Synopsis

3.1 Cost-Benefit Analysis

The job of a manager is to make decisions on behalf of the firm's owners. The decisions that the managers make should increase the value of the firm. Decisions in which the value of the benefits is greater than the value of the costs will increase the value of the firm. In order to make decisions that make the firm's investors better off, managers must:

1. Identify the costs and benefits of a decision.

2. Quantify the costs and benefits.

When quantifying the costs and benefits of a decision, we must value all of the options in the same terms—cash today. Suppose, for example, that Travis offers to trade you his accounting book for your statistics book. First, identify the costs and benefits of the decision. The cost of the trade to you (what you are giving up) is your statistics book. The benefit to you (what you are gaining) is an accounting book. Second, quantify these costs and benefits. If you could sell your statistics book to the university bookstore for $40, the cost of the decision is $40. If you could buy the accounting book at the university bookstore for $50, the benefit of the decision is $50. Therefore, your net benefit of making the trade is $50 − $40 = $10. Because the net value of the decision is positive, you should accept the trade.

3.2 Market Prices and the Valuation Principle

To make good decisions, managers follow the **Valuation Principle.** This principle is: The value of a commodity or an asset to the firm or its investors is determined by its competitive market price. The benefits and costs of a decision should be evaluated using those market prices. When the value of the benefits exceeds the value of the costs, the decision will increase the market value of the firm.

Deciding whether it was worthwhile to trade your statistics book for an accounting book was easy to evaluate: you were able to use current prices to convert them into equivalent cash values. Note that you did not have to decide whether you thought the accounting book was better than the statistics book; your personal preferences and opinions were not important. The price determined the value of the good. Whenever a good trades in a competitive market, one in which the good can be bought and sold at the same price, it is easy to quantify the value of the good by using the market price.

3.3 The Time Value of Money and Interest Rates

When we considered trading your statistics book for an accounting book, we were looking at a decision in which the costs and benefits occurred at one point in time. For most business decisions, however, costs and benefits occur at different points in time. Typically, a project will have an upfront cost but will provide benefits at a future point in time. Consider, for example, an investment that costs $250,000 today but will pay you $275,000 in one year. While both the cost, $250,000, and the benefit, $275,000, are expressed in dollar terms, the cost and benefit are not directly comparable. We must also consider the timing of the costs and benefits. We need to consider the time value of money to value this decision.

According to the time value of money, a dollar today is worth more than a dollar in one year. This is because money received today can be invested to grow to have a larger value in the future. Suppose that you can deposit money into a savings account and earn 8%. If you invest $1 today, you can convert this $1 into $1.08 in one year. The **interest rate, r,** for a given period is the interest rate at which money can be borrowed or lent over that period. In this example, you can exchange $1 today for $(1 + 0.08)$ dollars in the future. We refer to $(1 + r)$ as the **interest rate factor** for cash flows.

Let's consider the example of an investment that costs $250,000 today but will pay you $275,000 in one year. If the interest rate is 8%, the cost of the investment can be expressed as:

$$\text{Cost} = (\$250,000 \text{ today}) \times (1.08 \text{ \$ in one year/\$ today})$$
$$= \$270,000 \text{ in one year}$$

Using the Valuation Principle, we can compute the investment's net value by subtracting the cost of the investment from the benefit in one year:

$$\$275,000 \text{ in one year} - \$270,000 \text{ in one year} = \$5000 \text{ in one year}.$$

In other words, we come out $5000 ahead by making the investment than simply putting the $250,000 in the bank today and earning 8%. Because the value of the investment is measured at a future point in time, the measurement is called the **future value.**

Alternatively, we could compute the value of the investment today. To do so, we must convert the benefit that we will receive in one year ($275,000) to the value of that benefit today:

$$\text{Benefit} = (\$275,000 \text{ in one year})/(1.08 \text{ \$ in one year/\$ today})$$
$$= \$254,629.63 \text{ today}$$

We then subtract the cost of the investment today from the benefit of the investment today:

$$\$254,629.63 \text{ today} - \$250,000 \text{ today} = \$4629.63 \text{ today}$$

Because this number is calculated as a value today, it is known as the **present value**.

Often, it is helpful to visualize when cash flows occur by putting the cash flows on a **timeline.** For example, suppose your parents agree to give you $5000 in 1 year and another $5000 in 2 years to help cover your college expenses. We represent this information on a timeline as follows:

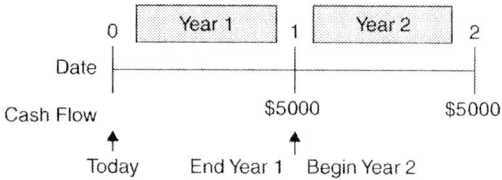

Date 0 represents the present. Date 1 is one year from now; it represents the end of the first year (and the beginning of the second year). The $5000 cash flow below Date 1 is the payment you will receive at the end of the first year. Date 2 is two years from now; it represents the end of the second year. The $5000 cash flow below Date 2 is the payment you will receive at the end of the second year.

In this example, both cash flows are inflows. In many cases, however, a financial decision will involve both inflows and outflows. To differentiate between the two types of cash flows, we assign a different sign to each: Inflows are positive cash flows and outflows are negative cash flows.

3.4 Valuing Cash Flows at Different Points in Time

When financial decisions require us to compare or combine cash flows that occur at different points in time, we must follow three important rules:

Rule 1: Comparing and Combining Values

It is only possible to compare or combine values at the same point in time. A dollar today and a dollar in one year are not equivalent. Having money now is more valuable than having money in the future; if you have the money today you can earn interest on it. To compare or combine cash flows that occur at different points in time, you first need to convert the cash flows into the same units by moving them to the same point in time.

Rule 2: Compounding

To calculate a cash flow's future value, we must compound it. Suppose you have $100 today, and you want to determine the equivalent amount one year from today. If the current market interest rate is 7%, you can use that rate as an exchange rate, meaning the rate at which we exchange money today for money in one year. That is,

($100 today) × (1.07 $ in one year/$ today) = $107 in one year

In general, if the market interest rate for the year is r, then we multiply by the interest rate factor, $(1 + r)$, to move the cash flow from the beginning to the end of the year. This process of moving forward along the timeline to determine a cash flow's **future value** is known as **compounding.**

Rule 3: Discounting

To calculate the present value of a future cash flow, we must discount it. Suppose you will receive a $100 prize in one year. If the current market interest rate is 7%, you can compute the value of this price today:

$$\frac{\$100 \text{ in one year}}{1.07 \text{ \$ in one year/\$ today}} = \$93.46 \text{ today}$$

To move the cash flow back along the timeline, we divide it by the interest rate factor, $(1 + r)$. The process of finding the **present value** of a future cash flow is known as **discounting.**

In general, to compute the present value of a cash flow C that comes n periods from now, we must discount it by the n intervening interest rate factors. If the interest rate r is constant, this yields

$$PV = C \div (1+r)^n = \frac{C}{(1+r)^n}$$

Applying the Rules of Valuing Cash Flows

The rules of cash flow valuation allow us to compare and combine cash flows that occur at different points in time. Here is a summary of these three rules:

Rule	Formula
1. Only values at the same point in time can be compared or combined.	None
2. To calculate a cash flow's future value, you must compound it.	Future Value of a Cash Flow $FV_n = C \times (1+r)^n$
3. To calculate the present value of a future cash flow, we must discount it.	Present Value of a Cash Flow $PV = C \div (1+r)^n = \frac{C}{(1+r)^n}$

■ Selected Concepts and Key Terms

Cost-Benefit Analysis

To evaluate a decision, we must value the incremental costs and benefits associated with that decision. A good decision is one for which the value of the benefits exceeds the value of the costs. To compare costs and benefits that occur at different points in time, in different currencies, or with different risks, all of the costs and benefits must be put into common terms. Typically, we convert costs and benefits into cash today.

Arbitrage

Arbitrage is the process of trading to take advantage of differing prices of equivalent goods in different markets. If equivalent goods or securities trade simultaneously in different competitive markets, they will trade for the same price in each market.

Valuation Principle

The value of an item is determined by its competitive market price. A good decision is one for which the value of the benefits exceeds the value of the costs using market prices.

Interest Rates and Time Value of Money

The **time value of money** is the idea that the value of a dollar differs depending on when it is received. Cash received in the future is worth less than cash received today. If you had the small amount of cash today, you could invest it so that it would equal the larger amount in the future. It is only possible to compare cash flows occurring at different times by bringing them to the same point in time. The **interest rate, r,** is the rate at which money can be borrowed or lent without risk. The **interest rate factor, $(1 + r)$** defines how we convert cash flows across time. The **present value (PV)** of a cash flow is its value in terms of cash today.

Valuing Cash Flows at Different Points in Time

There are three rules to follow when valuing cash flows:

1. Only cash flows that occur at the same point in time can be compared or combined.

2. To calculate a cash flow's **future value,** you must **compound** it. This is done using the formula:

$$FV = C \times (1 + r)^n$$

3. To calculate a cash flow's **present value,** you must **discount** it.

$$PV = \frac{C}{(1 + r)^n}$$

■ Concept Check Questions and Answers

1. When costs and benefits are in different units or goods, how can we compare them?

   When costs and benefits are in different units or goods, we must quantify their values in equivalent terms—cash today.

2. If crude oil trades in a competitive market, would an oil refiner that has a use for the oil value it differently than another investor would?

   No, the oil refiner would not value the crude oil differently than any other investor would. The oil refiner would value the crude oil based upon the market price of the crude oil.

3. How does investors' profit motive keep competitive market prices correct?

   If an item, such as gold, were trading in one market for a price that was lower than in another market, investors would have the incentive to make a profit by purchasing the item in the low price market and selling it in the high price market. This action would drive the price up in the low price market and the price down in the high price market until the price was identical in the two markets.

4. How do we determine whether a decision increases the value of the firm?

   First, we must identify the costs and benefits of a decision. Second, we must quantify the costs and benefits. If the benefits exceed the costs, then the decision adds value.

5. How is an interest rate like a price?

   The interest rate is like a price because it is the cost of borrowing money or the amount that we will be paid when we lend money.

6. Is the value today of money to be received in one year higher when interest rates are high or when interest rates or low?

   The value of money to be received in one year is higher when interest rates are lower because it is not being discounted at as high of a rate.

7. Can you compare or combine cash flows at different times?

   No, you cannot compare or combine cash flows that occur at different times because a dollar today and a dollar at another point in time are not equivalent.

8. What do you need to know to compute a cash flow's present or future value?

   To compute a cash flow's present or future value you need to know the interest rate and the number of time periods for discounting or compounding.

■ Examples with Step-by-Step Solutions

Comparing Costs and Benefits

3.1 **Problem:** You work for a wholesale food company. You can purchase 5000 pounds of flour for $1800 today plus $150 in shipping costs. A retailer is willing to purchase the 5000 pounds of flour from you at a price of $0.50 a pound today, including shipping. Will taking this opportunity increase the value of your company?

Solution

Plan: To determine whether this opportunity will increase the value of the company, we must compare the costs and the benefits using market prices. The market price purchasing the flour is $1800 plus $150 in shipping costs. The market price at which we can sell the flour for is $0.50 per pound.

Execute:
The benefit of this opportunity is 5000 × $0.50 = $2500. The cost of this opportunity is $1800 + $150 = $1950. Thus, the benefit is $2500 − $1950 = $550 greater than the cost.

Evaluate: The opportunity contributes $550 to the value of the firm. The opportunity should be taken.

Competitive Market Prices Determine Value

3.2 **Problem:** Suppose your employer offers you a choice between a $20,000 bonus and 30 ounces of gold. Whichever one you choose will be awarded today. Gold is trading today at $500 per ounce. Ignoring income tax implications:
   a. Which form of the bonus should you choose?
   b. What do you tell your broker, who advises you to take the gold because he predicts that the price of gold is going to double in value this year?

Solution
Plan: Determine the value of each option in today's dollars.
Execute:
Value of bonus = $20,000

$$\text{Value of the gold} = 30 \left[\frac{\$500}{1 \text{ ounce of gold}} \right]$$

$$= \$15,000$$

Evaluate:
a. The value of the gold ($15,000) is less than the value of the bonus ($20,000); you should take the cash bonus.
b. The reason you can compare the two options is because gold trades in a competitive market and you can buy it and sell it for the same price. Thus, if you want to hold gold, you would be better off taking the bonus and buying 30 ounces of gold for $15,000; you would still have $5000 left over.

Applying the Valuation Principle

3.3 Problem: Due to an existing contract, you have the ability to purchase 500 ounces of gold and 500 ounces of silver for a price of $610,000. The current market price for gold is $1200 an ounce, and the current market price for silver is $18 an ounce. As a jewelry manufacturer, you are not sure that you will need 500 ounces of both gold and silver, so you are wondering whether you should take the opportunity to purchase the gold and silver. How valuable is this opportunity?

Solution

Plan: We need to quantify the costs and benefits using market prices. We are comparing $610,000 with 500 ounces of gold at $1200 an ounce and 500 ounces of silver at $18 an ounce.

Execute:
Using the competitive market prices we have:

500 ounces of gold × $1200/ounce today = $600,000

500 ounces of silver × $18/ounce today = $9000

The value of the opportunity is the value of the gold and silver today minus the cost of the opportunity, or $600,000 + $9000 − $610,000 = −$1000 today. Because this value is negative we should **not** take the opportunity. The decision should be not to take the opportunity even if we believed that the value of gold would rise over the next month; only the current market prices, not our expectation or opinion of future market prices; should enter into our decision.

Evaluate: If we did need 500 ounces of gold and silver, it would be cheaper to purchase them at the current market prices than to purchase them together for $610,000.

Comparing Revenues at Different Points in Time

3.4 Problem: You are going to graduate from college in one year. Your grandparents have promised to give you a graduation gift of $4000 on the day you graduate. They know that you are trying to buy a car now, so they make an offer of giving you $3750 today instead of the $4000 when you graduate. The interest rate is 4% and there are no income tax effects. Should you take the money today?

Solution

Plan: Determine the value of each option in today's dollars.

Option A: Receive $4000 in 1 year

Option B: Receive $3750 today

Interest Rate: 4%

Execute:

Option A: Present value of receiving $4000 in one year = $4000/(1 + 0.04) = $3846.15

Option B: Present value of receiving $3750 today = $3750

Evaluate: The present value of receiving $4000 one year from now exceeds the $3750. Therefore, waiting one year for the $4000 is a better choice.

Present Value of a Cash Flow

3.5 **Problem:** Your brother has offered to pay you $5000 a year from today if you will lend him $4700 today. Suppose the interest rate is 6%. Should you make this loan to your brother?

Solution
Plan:

Cash Flows Today	In One Year
−$4700	$5000

Interest: 6%

The cost of $4700 is already in PV terms. The benefit, however, is in terms of dollars in one year. We must convert it to a present value using the interest rate and then compare it to the cost. If the present value of the cost is less than the present value of the benefit, then we should make the loan.

Execute: First, convert the future benefit to a present value at the interest rate:

PV(Benefit) = ($5000 in one year) ÷ (1.06 $ in one year/$ today) = $4716.98 today

The value of the opportunity is the difference between the present values of the benefits and the costs:

$4716.98 − $4700.00 = $16.98 today

Evaluate: The value is positive, so making the loan is a good deal.

■ Questions and Problems

1. Metropolitan Zoo is considering changing its pricing structure. Currently, the zoo charges an entrance fee of $8 per person. The zoo estimates that 500,000 people (200,000 adults and 300,000 children) will visit the zoo over the next year if it continues the existing pricing policy. An alternative policy would be to increase the fee for adults to $10 per adult but lower the fee for children to $5 per child. Under this alternative policy, the zoo estimates that the adult attendance will drop to 180,000 over the next year but children's attendance will increase to 330,000. If the change in the attendance is the only consequence of this decision, what are its costs and benefits? Is the alternative policy a good idea?

2. As your prize as a game show contestant, you are offered the choice between (a) one ton of olive oil or (b) a trip to Italy, including an airline ticket, seven nights' lodging, and a rental car for one week. You have always wanted to go to Italy and know that you could never use one ton of olive oil. Currently, olive oil is selling for $5400 a ton, an airline ticket to Italy costs $1500, lodging in Italy is $200 per night, and it costs $300 to rent a car for a week in Italy. Which prize will make you better off?

3. Suppose the interest rate is 5.5%.
   a. Having $100,000 today is equivalent to having what amount in 1 year?
   b. Having $100,000 in 1 year is equivalent to having what amount today?

4. Your firm has identified three potential investment projects. All of the projects would use the same tract of land, so you can only select one of them. In addition, all of the projects would generate risk-free cash flows and the interest rate is 5%.
   - Project 1 costs $1 and pays $1 million in 1 year
   - Project 2 costs $10 million and pays $12 million in 1 year
   - Project 3 has a cash inflow of $10 million today but a cash outflow of $9 million in 1 year

   Which project will best serve the goal of increasing the firm's value?

5. First State Bank is willing to trade U.S. dollars for Mexican pesos at a rate of $1 = 10 pesos. Second National Bank is willing to trade U.S. dollars for euros at a rate of $1 = 0.71 euros. Third State Bank is willing to trade euros for pesos at a rate of 1 euro = 16 pesos. What arbitrage opportunity is available?

6. Your grandparents have offered to give you either $8000 today or $10,000 in three years. If the interest rate is 4% per year, which option is preferable?

7. Marco just received a $2000 bonus at work. He decided to place the money in a savings account that pays 6% interest. How much money will be in the savings account when Marco retires in 40 years if he does not add any money or withdraw any money over that time period?

■ Solutions to Questions and Problems

1. The zoo's cost of the new pricing policy is the revenue it would have had under the old plan or 500,000 × $8 = $4,000,000. The benefit of the new pricing policy is the revenue that will be received or (180,000 × $10) + (330,000 × $5) = $1,800,000 + $1,650,000 = $3,450,000.

   The alternative pricing policy is not a good idea. The costs of the decision exceed the benefits of the decision.

2. You should choose the olive oil. You can sell the olive oil for $5400, buy the airline ticket ($1500), pay for your lodging ($200 × 7), rent a car ($300), and still have $2200 left over. The fact that you cannot personally use all of the olive oil is irrelevant; since you can sell it, the value of the olive oil is the current market price.

3. a. Having $100,000 today is equivalent to having 100,000 × 1.055 = $105,500 in 1 year.
   b. Having $100,000 in 1 year is equivalent to having 100,000/1.055 = $94,787 today.

4. Projects 2 and 3 are equally as valuable—select either one.

$$NPV_1 = -\$1 + \frac{\$1,000,000}{1.05} = \$952,380$$

$$NPV_2 = -\$10,000,000 + \frac{\$12,000,000}{1.05} = \$1,428,571$$

$$NPV_3 = \$10,000,000 + \frac{-\$9,000,000}{1.05} = \$1,428,571$$

5. You can take $1 to Second National Bank and exchange it for 0.71 euros. Then, go to Third State Bank and exchange the 0.71 euros for 11.36 pesos. Then, take the 11.36 pesos to First National Bank and exchange the pesos for $1.136.

6. The $10,000 three years from today is preferable because it has a present value of $10,000/(1.04)^3 = \$8889.96$.

7. The future value is $2000 \times (1 + 0.06)^{40} = \$20,571.44$.

■ Self-Test Questions

1. Which of the following is true of a competitive market?
   a. A good can be bought and sold at the same price.
   b. Arbitrage will ensure that the buying price is higher than the selling price.
   c. Arbitrage will ensure that the selling price is higher than the buying price.
   d. Arbitrage opportunities are more likely to exist in competitive markets than in noncompetitive markets.

2. In general, a dollar received today
   a. is equivalent to a dollar received tomorrow.
   b. is worth less than a dollar received tomorrow.
   c. is worth more than a dollar received tomorrow.
   d. not related in value to a dollar received tomorrow.

3. The rate at which you can exchange money today for money in the future by borrowing is the
   a. current market interest rate.
   b. present value.
   c. future value.
   d. cost-benefit difference.

4. If the interest rate is 8%, then $100 today is equivalent to
   a. $92 a year from today.
   b. $100 a year from today.
   c. $108 a year from today.
   d. $116 a year from today.

5. When making an investment decision, a manager should take the alternative
   a. with the lowest costs.
   b. with the highest benefits.
   c. with the lowest future value of costs.
   d. which increases the value of the firm today the most.

6. According to the Valuation Principle, the value of an asset is
   a. determined by its competitive market price.
   b. greater to an owner than to an investor.
   c. greater to a seller than to a buyer.
   d. irrelevant in deciding whether it should be sold.

7. Kevin sees that gold is selling for $260 an ounce in London and $270 an ounce in New York. Kevin quickly buys gold in London and sells it in New York. Kevin is practicing
   a. the time value of money.
   b. arbitrage.
   c. commodity conversion.
   d. insider trading.

8. Laura has the opportunity to trade 200 ounces of silver for 10 ounces of gold. Which of the following is most relevant to her decision to make the trade?
   a. Her projection of the price of gold one year from now.
   b. Her projection of the price of silver one year from now.
   c. The price of silver and gold today.
   d. Her preference for silver over gold.

9. A decision will increase the market value of a firm when
   a. the costs are lower than the current market interest rate.
   b. no money is borrowed to take on the project.
   c. the value of the benefits of the decision exceeds the cost.
   d. investment prices are used, rather than market prices, in evaluating the project.

10. To calculate the present value of a cash flow that occurs in five years, you must
    a. compound it.
    b. consider its arbritrage value.
    c. discount it.
    d. multiply it by the current market interest rate.

11. On a timeline, today is represented as
    a. Date 0
    b. Time Period 1
    c. $(1 + n)$
    d. Time Period $n - 1$

12. To move a cash flow back in time on a timeline, you
    a. multiply it by the interest rate factor to discount it.
    b. divide it by the interest rate factor to discount it.
    c. multiply it by the interest rate factor to compound it.
    d. divide it by the interest rate factor to compound it.

Answers to Self-Test Questions

1. a
2. c
3. a
4. c
5. d
6. a
7. b
8. c
9. c
10. c
11. a
12. b

Chapter 4
Time Value of Money: Valuing Cash Flow Streams

■ Key Learning Objectives

- Value a series of many cash flows
- Value a perpetual series of regular cash flows called a *perpetuity*
- Value a common set of regular cash flows called an *annuity*
- Value both perpetuities and annuities when the cash flows grow at a constant rate
- Compute the number of periods, cash flow, or rate of return of a loan or investment

■ Notation

C	cash flow
C_n	cash flow at date n
FV	further value
FV_n	further value on date n
g	growth rate
N	date of the last cash flow in a stream of cash flows
P	initial principal or deposit, or equivalent present value
PV	present value
r	interest rate or rate of return

■ Chapter Synopsis

Many business decisions require the valuation of cash flows that occur at different points in time. This chapter builds on the tools used to value cash flows occurring at different time periods used in Chapter 3. In addition to the general technique, we will develop short cuts for valuing **annuities** and **perpetuities.**

4.1 Valuing a Stream of Cash Flows

Most investment opportunities have multiple cash flows that occur at different points in time.

Consider a **stream of cash flows:** C_0 at Date 0, C_1 at Date 1, and so on, up to C_N at Date N. These cash flows will look like this on a timeline:

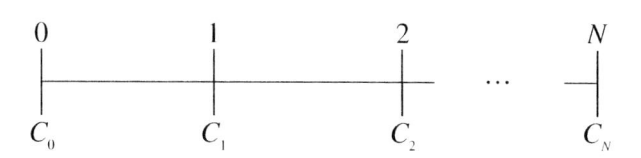

```
  0        1        2              N
  |────────|────────|────── ... ───|
  C_0      C_1      C_2            C_N
```

Using the rules of cash flow valuation, we compute the present value of this cash flow stream in two steps. First, we compute the present value of each individual cash flow. Then, once the cash flows are in common units of dollars today, we can combine them by adding them together:

$$PV = C_0 + \frac{C_1}{(1+r)} + \frac{C_2}{(1+r)^2} + \cdots + \frac{C_N}{(1+r)^N}$$

4.2 Perpetuities

When cash flows follow a regular pattern, we can take some shortcuts for valuing them.

Perpetuities

A **perpetuity** is a stream of equal cash flows that occur at regular intervals and last forever.

Here is the timeline for a perpetuity:

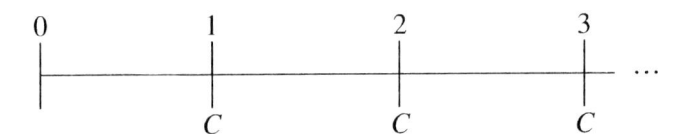

```
0        1        2        3
|--------|--------|--------|---  ...
         C        C        C
```

Note from the timeline, note that the first cash flow does not occur immediately; *it arrives at the end of the first period*. This timing is sometimes referred to as payment *in arrears* and is a standard convention in loan payment calculations.

The present value of a perpetuity with payment C and interest rate r is:

$$PV = \frac{C}{(1+r)} + \frac{C}{(1+r)^2} + \frac{C}{(1+r)^3} + \cdots$$

To find the value of a perpetuity one cash flow at a time would take forever—literally! Luckily, there is a shortcut. We can value this perpetuity using the equation:

$$PV(C \text{ in perpetuity}) = \frac{C}{r}$$

4.3 Annuities

An **annuity** is a stream of N equal cash flows paid at regular intervals. The difference between an annuity and a perpetuity is that an annuity ends after some fixed number of payments. Most car loans, mortgages, and some bonds are annuities. The cash flows of an annuity look like this on a timeline:

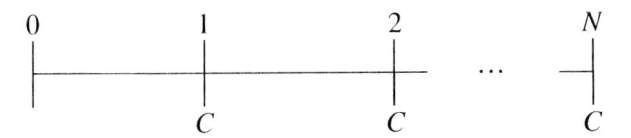

```
0        1        2              N
|--------|--------|---  ...  ----|
         C        C              C
```

Note that just as with the perpetuity, we adopt the convention that the first payment takes place at Date 1, one period from today. The present value of an N-period annuity with payment C and interest rate r is:

$$PV = \frac{C}{(1+r)} + \frac{C}{(1+r)^2} + \frac{C}{(1+r)^3} + \cdots + \frac{C}{(1+r)^N}$$

We calculate the present value of an annuity by calculating the present value of each of the cash flows and then adding them all together. This can become tedious and time consuming; luckily, we can use this shortcut formula:

$$\text{PV(annuity of } C \text{ for } N \text{ periods with interest rate } r) = C \times \frac{1}{r}\left(1 - \frac{1}{(1+r)^N}\right)$$

Using this shortcut formula for the present value of an annuity, it is easy to find a simple formula for the future value. If we want to know the value N years in the future, we move the present value N periods forward on the timeline. When we compound the present value for N periods at interest rate r, the result is:

$$\text{FV(annuity)} = \text{PV} \times (1+r)^N$$

$$= \frac{C}{r}\left(1 - \frac{1}{(1+r)^N}\right) \times (1+r)^N$$

$$= C \times \frac{1}{r}((1+r)^N - 1)$$

4.4 Growing Cash Flows

A **growing perpetuity** is a stream of cash flows that occur at regular intervals and grow at a constant rate forever. Suppose that you will receive a payment every year. The payment for the first year will be $100 and the payment will grow by 3% each year after that. This is shown on the following timeline:

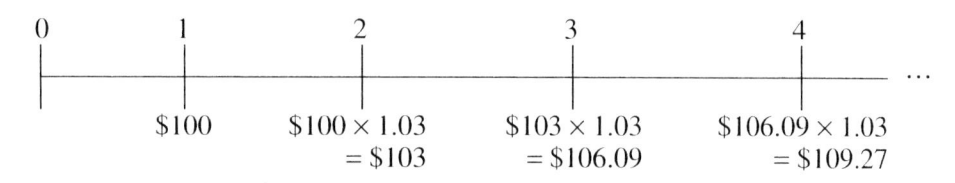

0	1	2	3	4	...
	$100	$100 × 1.03 = $103	$103 × 1.03 = $106.09	$106.09 × 1.03 = $109.27	

To calculate the present value of this perpetuity, we use the shortcut formula:

$$\text{PV(growing perpetuity)} = \frac{C}{r - g}$$

A **growing annuity** is a stream N growing cash flows, paid at regular intervals. In other words, a growing annuity is a growing perpetuity that eventually comes to an end. To calculate the present value of a growing annuity, we use the formula:

$$PV = C \times \frac{1}{r - g}\left(1 - \left(\frac{1+g}{1+r}\right)^N\right)$$

4.5 Solving for Variables Other Than Present Value or Future Value

Solving for the Cash Flows

Sometimes we are interested in calculating a variable other than present value or future value. For example, suppose you borrow $20,000 from your parents to help cover your college expenses. You agree to make equal annual payments for the next 10 years and will pay an interest rate of 6%. The time line looks like this:

Date (Years)	0	1	2	...	10
Cash Flow	$20,000	−C	−C		−C

The cash flows must have a present value of $20,000 when discounted using a 6% interest rate. Using the formula for the present value of an annuity,

$$\$20{,}000 = C \times \frac{1}{0.06}\left(1 - \frac{1}{1.06^{10}}\right)$$
$$= C \times 7.36$$

Solving this equation for C gives:

$$C = \frac{20{,}000}{7.36}$$
$$= \$2717.39$$

You will need to make 10 annual payments of $2717.39 today in exchange for your parents giving you $20,000 today.

We can use this same idea to solve for the cash flows when we know the future value rather than the present value. For example, suppose you plan to go to graduate school in 5 years. You would like to have $50,000 saved to help cover graduate school expenses. If you can earn 8% per year on your savings, how much do you need to save each year to meet your goal?

The timeline for this example is:

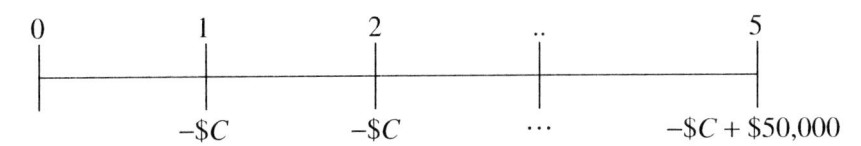

```
0         1         2        ..        5
|---------|---------|---------|---------|
         -$C       -$C       ...   -$C + $50,000
```

That is, you plan to save some amount C per year, and then withdraw $50,000 from the bank in five years. You need to find the annuity payment that has a future value of $50,000 in five years. Using the formula for the future value of an annuity:

$$\$50{,}000 = FV(annuity)$$
$$= C \times \frac{1}{0.08}(1.08^5 - 1)$$
$$= C \times 5.8666$$
$$= 8522.82$$

Rate of Return

In some situations, you know the present value and cash flows of an investment opportunity but you do not know the interest rate that equates them. The **rate of return** on an investment opportunity is the rate at which the present value of the benefits exactly offsets the cost of the investment. Suppose that you are offered an investment that costs $4000 but promises to pay you $1000 a year for five years beginning one year from today. For example, suppose that you place a $1000 investment in a bank today and will be able to withdraw $2000 in six years. On a timeline this appears as:

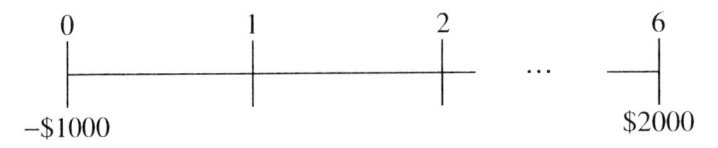

```
     0          1         2                  6
     |----------|---------|---------...------|
   -$1000                                  $2000
```

You want to know what interest rate the bank is paying you. Another way of analyzing this is to ask the question: What interest rate, r, would you need so that the NPV of this investment is zero?

$$NPV = -1000 + \frac{2000}{(1+r)^6} = 0$$

Rearranging this gives:

$$1000 \times (1+r)^6 = 2000$$

That is, r is the interest rate you would need to earn on your $1000 to have a future value of $2000 in six years. We can solve for r as follows:

$$1 + r = \left(\frac{2000}{1000}\right)^{1/6} = 1.1225$$

or $r = 12.25\%$. This rate is the IRR of this investment opportunity. Making this investment is like earning 12.25% per year on your money for six years.

Solving for the Number of Periods

In addition to solving for cash flows or the interest rate, we can solve for the amount of time it will take a sum of money to grow to a known value. In this case, the interest rate, present value, and future value are all known. We need to compute how long it will take for the present value to grow to the future value.

Suppose we invest $10,000 in an account paying 10% interest, and we want to know how long it will take for the amount to grow to $20,000.

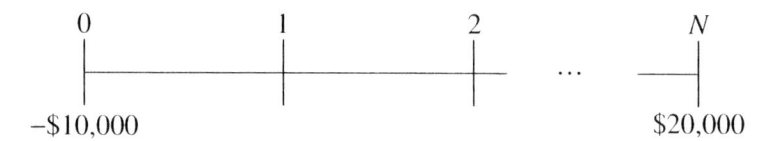

```
0           1           2                    N
|-----------|-----------|------ ... --------|
-$10,000                                  $20,000
```

We want to determine N.

In terms of our formulas, we need to find N so that the future value of our investment equals $20,000:

$$FV = \$10{,}000 \times 1.10^N = \$20{,}000 \tag{4.1}$$

One approach is to use trial and error to find N. For example, with $N = 7$ years, $FV = \$19{,}487$, so it will take longer than 7 years. With $N = 8$ years, $FV = \$21{,}436$, so it will take between 7 and 8 years.

Alternatively, this problem can be solved with a financial calculator or Excel. In this case, we solve for N:

	N	I/Y	PV	PMT	FV	Excel Formula
Given:		10.00%	−10,000	0	20,000	
Solve for:	7.27					=NPER(RATE,PMT,PV,FV) = (0.10, 0,−10,000,20,000)

It will take about 7.3 years for our savings to grow to $20,000.

■ Selected Concepts and Key Terms

Time Value of Money

The **time value of money** is the idea that the value of a dollar differs depending on when it is received. Cash received in the future is worth less than cash received today. If you had the small amount of cash today, you could invest it so that it would equal the larger amount in the future. It is only possible to compare cash flows occurring at different times by bringing them to the same point in time.

Valuing Cash Flows at Different Points in Time

There are three rules to follow when valuing cash flows:

1. Only cash flows that occur at the same point in time can be compared or combined.

2. To calculate a cash flow's **future value**, you must **compound** it. This is done using the formula:

$$FV = C \times (1 + r)^n$$

3. To calculate a cash flow's **present value**, you must **discount** it.

$$PV = \frac{C}{(1+r)^n}$$

Valuing a Stream of Cash Flows

To calculate the present value of a **stream of cash flows,** calculate the present value of each cash flow and add them together:

$$PV = C_0 + \frac{C_1}{(1+r)} + \frac{C_2}{(1+r)^2} + \cdots + \frac{C_N}{(1+r)^N}$$

Net Present Value of a Stream of Cash Flows

The **net present value** of an investment opportunity is the PV(benefits − costs). The benefits are the cash inflows. The costs are the cash outflows.

Perpetuities, Annuities, and Other Special Cases

A **perpetuity** is a constant cash flow C paid every period, forever. The present value of a perpetuity is:

$$PV(C \text{ in perpetuity}) = \frac{C}{r}$$

An **annuity** is a constant cash flow C paid every period for N periods. The present value of an annuity is:

$$C \times \frac{1}{r}\left(1 - \frac{1}{(1+r)^N}\right)$$

In a **growing perpetuity**, the cash flows grow at a constant rate g each period. The present value of a growing perpetuity is:

$$\frac{C}{r - g}$$

Solving for Variables Other Than Present Value or Future Value

The annuity and perpetuity formulas can be used to solve for the annuity payments when either the present value or the future value is known. The **internal rate of return** (IRR) of an investment opportunity is the interest rate that sets the NPV of the investment opportunity equal to zero. The annuity formulas can be used to solve for IRR, the payment, or the number of periods it takes to save a fixed amount of money.

■ Concept Check Questions and Answers

1. How do you calculate the present value of a cash flow stream?

   To calculate the present value of a cash flow stream, you must calculate the present value of each cash flow and then add these values together.

2. How do you calculate the future value of a cash flow stream?

   To calculate the future value of a cash flow stream, you must calculate the future value of each cash flow and then add these values together.

3. What are some examples of perpetuities?

   The perpetual bonds issued in the seventeenth century by the *Hoogheemraadschap Lekdijk Bovendams* are perpetuities that are still paying interest today. A common example of a perpetuity would be providing the money for an endowment that would allow an institution to spend money on a particular event every year forever.

4. What is the intuition behind the fact that an infinite stream of cash flows has a finite present value?

   While an infinite stream of cash flows pays a cash flow forever, the very distant cash flows have very little value today (due to the time value of money). Thus, the stream of payments of a perpetuity can be replicated using a finite amount of money.

5. What are some examples of annuities?

   A lottery that pays $20,000 a year for ten years to the winner would be an example of an annuity. Another example of an annuity would be saving $200 a month for 30 years in a retirement savings account.

6. What is the difference between an annuity and a perpetuity?

   An annuity ends at some point in time while a perpetuity continues into infinity.

7. How can an infinitely growing stream of cash flows have a finite value?

   While an infinitely growing stream of cash flows pays a cash flow forever, the very distant cash flows have very little value today (due to the time value of money). Thus, the stream of payments of a growing perpetuity can be replicated using a finite amount of money.

8. What is an example of a growing perpetuity?

   An example of a growing perpetuity would be donating an amount of money that would fund a $10,000 scholarship next year and then a scholarship that increases at a rate of 4% each year to keep up with inflation forever.

9. How do you calculate the cash flow of an annuity?

   The present value of an annuity of C for n periods with interest rate r is:

   $$PV(\text{annuity of } C \text{ for } N \text{ periods}) = C \times \frac{1}{r}\left(1 - \frac{1}{(1+r)^N}\right)$$

10. How do you calculate the rate of return on an investment?

    The rate of return on an investment is the interest rate that sets the net present value of the cash flows equal to zero. You can guess the rate of return and manually calculate its value. An easier solution is to use a spreadsheet or calculator to automate the guessing process.

■ Examples with Step-by-Step Solutions

Present Value of a Stream of Cash Flows

4.1 **Problem:** Wayne has just graduated from college and wants to open his own business, Wayne's Web Design. He needs some money to get started. His older brother has agreed to lend him the money if Wayne will pay him 6% interest and pay him back within five years. Wayne thinks that he could make enough money from the business to pay his brother back $500 in one year and $1000 two years from now. After that, he thinks the business will really take off and that he will be able to pay his brother $3000 a year for the next three years. How much would Wayne be able to borrow from his brother?

Solution

Plan: The cash flows Wayne can give to his brother are:

Date (Years)	0	1	2	3	4	5
Cash Flow		−$500	−$1000	−$3000	−$3000	−$3000
	PV = ?					

How much money should Wayne's brother be willing to give Wayne in return for his promised payments? He should be willing to give him an amount that is equivalent to these payments in present value terms. This is the amount of money that it would take him to produce these same cash flows. We need to calculate the present value of each of the future cash flows using the formula PV = C/(1 + i)^n.

Execute: We can calculate the PV as follows:

$$PV = \frac{\$500}{(1+.06)^1} + \frac{\$1000}{(1+.06)^2} + \frac{\$3000}{(1+.06)^3} + \frac{\$3000}{(1+.06)^4} + \frac{\$3000}{(1+.06)^5}$$

PV = $471.70 + $890.00 + $2518.86 + $2376.28 + $2241.77

PV = $8498.61

Evaluate: Wayne's brother should be willing to lend him $8498.61 in exchange for Wayne's promised payments. This amount is less than the total amount Wayne will pay him due to the time value of money.

Computing the Future Value

4.2 Problem: You have been offered the following investment opportunity: If you invest $5000 today, you will receive $2000 at the end of each of the next 3 years. If you could otherwise earn 4% per year on your money, should you undertake the investment opportunity?

Solution

Plan: Start with a timeline. We denote the $5000 investment as a negative cash flow (because it is money we need to spend) and the money we receive as positive cash flows.

Date (Years)	0	1	2	3
Cash Flow	−5000.00	2000.00	2000.00	2000.00

To decide whether we should accept this opportunity, we will need to compute the NPV by computing the present value of the stream.

Execute: The NPV is:

$$NPV = -\$5000 + \frac{\$2000}{(1+0.04)^1} + \frac{\$2000}{(1+0.04)^2} + \frac{\$2000}{(1+0.04)^3}$$

$$NPV = -\$5000 + \$1923.08 + \$1849.11 + \$1777.99$$

$$NPV = \$550.18$$

Evaluate: Because the NPV is positive, the benefits exceed the costs and you should make the investment. Indeed, the NPV tells us that taking this opportunity is equivalent to getting an extra $550.18 that you can spend today.

Endowing a Perpetuity

4.3 Problem: You want to provide money for your local no-kill animal shelter to care for a dog. It costs the shelter $200 to care for one dog for a year. You want to provide the shelter with enough money to care for one dog every year forever. Therefore, you want to give the shelter enough money today that it will be able to spend $200 a year forever. If the animal shelter earns 7% on its investments, how much will you need to donate to endow the dog care? (Assume that the shelter spends the first $200 one year from today.)

Solution

Plan: The timeline of the cash flows you want to provide is:

Date (Years)	0	1	2	3	...
Cash Flow		200	200	200	...

This is a standard perpetuity of $200 per year. The funding you would need to give the shelter is the present value of this cash flow stream.

Execute: From the formula for a perpetuity,

$$PV = C/r = \$200/0.07$$
$$= \$2857.14$$

Evaluate: If you donate $2857.14 today, and if the shelter invests it at 7% per year forever, then $200 will be available each year for the care of a dog.

Present Value of a Lottery Prize Annuity

4.4 **Problem:** You are the lucky grand prize winner of a $20 million drawing. You can take your prize money either as (a) 20 payments of $1 million per year (starting today), or (b) $12 million paid today. If the interest rate is 8%, which option should you take?

Solution

Plan: Option (a) provides $20 million in prize money but paid over time. To evaluate it correctly, we must convert it to a present value. Here is the timeline:

Date (Years)	0	1	2	3	...	19
Cash Flow	$1 million	$1 million	$1 million	$1 million	...	$1 million

Because the first payment starts today, the last payment will occur in 19 years (for a total of 20 payments). The $1 million at Date 0 is already stated in present value terms, but we need to compute the present value of the remaining payments. Fortunately, this case looks like a 19-year annuity of $1 million per year, so we can use the annuity formula.

Since Option (b) is already in today's dollar terms, we do not need to do any calculations to determine its value.

Execute: Using the annuity formula:

$$PV(\text{19-year annuity of \$1 million}) = \$1 \text{ million} \times \frac{1}{0.08}\left(1 - \frac{1}{1.08^{19}}\right)$$

$$= \$1 \text{ million} \times 9.604$$

$$= \$9.604 \text{ million today}$$

In Option (a), you get $1 million today plus an annuity that is worth $9.604 million today. Since these are both now in today's dollars, we can combine them. Option (a) is worth $1 million + $9.604 million = $10.604 million.

Alternatively, to find the present value of the annuity, we can put the following values into a financial calculator:

	N	I/Y	PV	PMT	FV
Given:	19	8		1,000,000	
Solve for:			−9,603,599		

The present value of receiving $1 million a year for each of the next 19 years is $9,603,599. We would need to add the $1 million received today to this amount to get the total value of $10.604 million.

As shown in the appendix, Excel can also be used to find the present value of an annuity.

Evaluate: Option (b), $12 million upfront, is more valuable—even though the total amount of money paid is much less than with Option (a).

Chapter 4 Time Value of Money: Valuing Cash Flow Streams 49

Savings Plan Annuity

4.5 **Problem:** Max and Colleen want to save money for son Jake's college education. Today is Jake's fourth birthday. They plan to begin putting $2000 in a savings account earning 5% interest on Jake's fifth birthday. They will continue placing $2000 in the savings account each year on his birthday. How much will be in his account when he turns 18?

Solution

Plan: As always, we begin with a timeline. In this case, it is helpful to keep track of both the dates and Jake's age:

Jake's Age	4	5	6	7	...	18
Date (Years)	0	1	2	3	...	14
Cash Flow		2000	2000	2000	2000	2000
						FV = ?

This college savings plan looks like an annuity of $2000 per year for 14 years. To determine the amount that will be in the account when Jake turns 18, we will need to compute the future value of this annuity.

Execute: Using the formula to calculate the future value, we have:

$$FV = \$2000 \times \frac{1}{0.05}(1.05^{14} - 1)$$
$$= \$2000 \times 19.5986$$
$$= \$39,197.20$$

Alternatively, you can place the known variables in a financial calculator ($N = 14$, $I/YR = 5$, $PMT = 2000$), and have the calculator calculate the FV of $39,197.26. The key strokes would look like:

	N	I/Y	PV	PMT	FV
Given:	14	5		2000	
Solve for:					−39,197.26

A third approach to find the future value is to use the financial functions in Excel. This approach is described in the appendix.

Evaluate: By investing $2000 per year for 14 years and earning interest at 5%, $39,197.20 will be available for Jake's college education when he turns 18.

Endowing a Growing Perpetuity

4.6 **Problem:** In Example 4.3, you planned to donate money to the animal shelter to fund the annual care of a dog. Given an interest rate of 7% per year, the required donation was PV = $200/0.07 = $2857.14.

Before accepting the money, however, the animal shelter has asked that you increase the donation to account for the effect of inflation on the cost of dog care in future years. Although $200 is adequate for a dog's care next year, the animal shelter estimates that dog care costs will rise by 3% per year thereafter. To satisfy their request, how much do you need to donate now?

Solution

Plan: The cost of the dog care next year is $200, and the cost then increases 3% per year forever. First, we need to develop a timeline:

Date (Years)	0	1	2	3	...
Cash Flow		200	200(1 + 0.03)	200(1 + 0.03)^2	...

From the timeline, we recognize the form of a growing perpetuity and can value it that way.

Execute: To finance the growing cost, you need to provide:

$$PV = \frac{C}{r-g} = \frac{200}{0.07-0.03} = \$5000$$

Evaluate: Instead of providing $2857.14, you need to provide $5000 (almost double the original amount) to fund the increasing cost of dog care.

Retirement Savings with a Growing Annuity

4.7 Problem: Rachel is 23 years old and is planning for retirement in 45 years. She is considering saving 10% of her salary each year for her retirement. Her current salary is $50,000; so under this plan, she would save $5000 for retirement this year. She thinks that her salary will increase by 4% every year, allowing her to increase the amount she saves for retirement by 4% each year. If she follows this plan and can earn 9% per year on her savings, how much will she have in her retirement account in 45 years when she is 68 years old?

Solution

Plan: Her retirement savings plan is represented by the following time line:

Age	23	24	25	...	68
Time	0	1	2	...	45
		$5000	$5200	...	$28,083

This example involves a 45-year growing annuity, with a growth rate of 4% and an initial cash flow of $5000. First, we solve for the present value of this growing annuity. Then, we calculate the future value.

Execute: The present value of Rachel's growing annuity is given by:

$$PV = \$5000 \times \frac{1}{0.09-0.04}\left(1-\left(\frac{1.04}{1.09}\right)^{45}\right) = \$5000 \times 17.5827 = \$87,913.50$$

Rachel's savings plan is equivalent to having $87,913.50 in the bank today. To determine how much she will have in the bank when she retires in 45 years, we need to move this amount forward 45 years:

$$FV = \$87,913.50 \times (1.09)^{45} = \$4.249 \text{ million in 45 years}$$

Evaluate:
Rachel will have $4.249 million at the age of 68 when she retires using this savings plan.

Computing a Loan Payment

4.8 Problem: You want to buy a $200,000 home. The bank offers you a 30-year loan with equal annual payments and an interest rate of 7% per year. The bank requires that you pay 10% of the purchase price as a down payment, so you can borrow only $180,000. What is the annual loan payment?

Solution

Plan: We start with the timeline (from the bank's perspective):

Date (Years)	0	1	2	3	...	30
Cash Flow	−180,000	C	C	C	...	C

We want to solve for an annuity payment. The equation we will use is:

$$C = \frac{P}{\frac{1}{r}\left(1 - \frac{1}{(1+r)^N}\right)}$$

We can solve for the loan payment, C, given $N = 30$, $r = 7\%$, and $P = \$180{,}000$.

Execute: The annuity payment (cash flow) is:

$$C = \frac{P}{\frac{1}{r}\left(1 - \frac{1}{(1+r)^N}\right)}$$

$$= \frac{180{,}000}{\frac{1}{0.07}\left(1 - \frac{1}{(1+0.07)^{30}}\right)}$$

$$= 14{,}505.55$$

A second approach to find the annuity payment is to use a financial calculator. To do so we would use the following key strokes:

	N	I/Y	PV	PMT	FV
Given:	30	7	−180,000		
Solve for:				14,505.55	

A third approach to find the annuity payment is to use the financial functions in Excel. Using Excel to solve problems is described in the appendix.

Evaluate: You will need to pay $14,505.55 each year to repay the loan. The bank is willing to accept these payments because the PV of 30 annual payments of $14,505.55 at 7% interest rate per year is exactly equal to the $180,000 it is giving you today.

Computing the Rate of Return with a Financial Calculator

4.9 Problem: Blake is retiring and has been offered two options by his pension plan: take either (a) $500,000 lump-sum payment immediately, or (b) 10 payments of $75,000 per year starting one year from today. How high of a rate of return would Blake need to be able to earn investing on his own in order to prefer the $500,000 payout?

Solution

Plan: Blake has the option of receiving $500,000 today or an annuity. We need to solve for the rate of return that makes the two offers equivalent. Anything above that rate of return would make the present value of the annuity lower than the $500,000 lump-sum payment; anything above that rate of return would make the present value of the annuity higher than the $500,000 lump-sum payment.

Execute: First, we set the present value of Option (b) equal to Option (a), which is already in present value since it is an immediate payment of $500,000:

$$\$500,000 = \$75,000 \text{ X}$$

Using a financial calculator to solve for the interest rate:

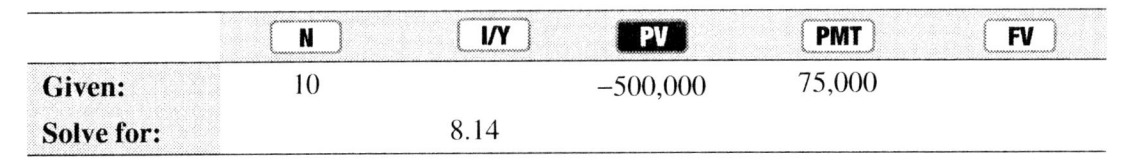

	N	I/Y	PV	PMT	FV
Given:	10		−500,000	75,000	
Solve for:		8.14			

The rate of return equating the two options is 8.14%.

Evaluate:

8.14% is the rate of return that makes giving up the $500,000 payment today and taking the 10 installments of $75,000 an even trade in terms of present value. If Blake could earn more than 8.14% investing on his own, then he should take the $500,000 today, invest it, and generate 10 installments that are more than $75,000 each. If he could not earn at least 8.14%, he should choose the ten $75,000 payments because he could not replicate this by investing $500,000 today on his own.

Solving for the Number of Periods in a Savings Plan

4.10 Problem: Your goal is to save $50,000 for a down payment on a house. You have $9450 today to put in your savings account. You will make additional payments of $5000 a year beginning one year from today. If you can earn 7% on your savings, how long will it be before you have $50,000 in your account?

Solution

Plan: The timeline for this problem is:

Date (Years)	0	1	2	3	...	N
Cash Flow	−9540	−5000	−5000	−5000	...	−5000 50,000

We need to find N so that the future value of your current savings plus the future value of your planned additional savings (which is an annuity) equals your desired amount of $50,000. There are two contributors to the future value: the initial lump sum of $9450 that will continue to earn interest, and the annuity contributions of $5000 per year that will earn interest as they are contributed. Thus, we need to combine the future value of the lump sum and the future value of the annuity and solve for N.

Execute: Mathematically, we can solve for N as follows:

$$9540 \times 1.07^N + 5000 \times \frac{1}{0.07}(1.07^N - 1) = \$50{,}000$$

$$1.07^N \left(9540 + \frac{5000}{0.07}\right) - \frac{5000}{0.07} = \$50{,}000$$

$$1.07^N (80{,}968.57) = 121{,}428.57$$

$$1.07^N = 1.4997$$

$$N = \frac{\ln(1.4997)}{\ln(1.07)} = \frac{0.405265}{0.067659} = 6 \text{ years}$$

We could also solve for N using a financial calculator. To do this, we would use the following key strokes:

	N	I/Y	PV	PMT	FV
Given:		7	−9450	−5000	50,000
Solve for:	6				

Evaluate: It will take 6 years to save the down payment of $50,000.

■ Questions and Problems

1. Your daughter is currently 8 years old. You anticipate that she will be going to college in 10 years. You would like to have $100,000 in a savings account at that time. If the account promises to pay you a fixed interest rate of 3% per year, how much money do you need to put into the account today to ensure that you will have $100,000 in 10 years?

2. Your grandparents have offered to give you either $8000 today or $10,000 in three years. If the interest rate is 4% per year, which option is preferable?

3. Congratulations! You have just sold the rights to your first novel. Your publisher has offered to pay you $15,000 today or $3000 a year for 10 years (with the first payment made one year from today). If you can earn 5% on your investments, which offer should you take?

4. Your friend, Zeke, just signed a $6 million contract with the New York Giants. However, he will not receive the entire $6 million today. He will receive $1 million today, $1.5 million a year from today, $2 million two years from today, and $1.5 million three years from today. Since he never took a finance class, he has asked you to figure out how much this contract is really worth today. If he can earn 11% on his investments, how much is this contract worth today?

5. Your have been offered the following investment opportunity: if you invest $10,000 today, you will receive $2000 two years from now, $4000 four years from now, and $6000 six years from now.
   a. What is the PV of the opportunity if the interest rate is 7% per year? Should you take the opportunity?
   b. What is the PV of the opportunity if the interest rate is 3% per year? Should you take the opportunity?

6. You have determined that you will need $3,000,000 when you retire in 40 years. You plan to put aside a series of payments each year in an account yielding 12% per year to reach this goal. You will put the first payment in the account 1 year from today. How large does each annual payment need to be for you to have $3,000,000 in the account when you retire?

7. You want to fund an annual $5000 scholarship for your alma mater. If the university can earn 9% on the money you give, how large of a donation would you need to make to endow this gift?

8. After thinking more about the gift that you wanted to endow in Problem 7, you realized that the scholarship amount should increase annually to keep up with tuition costs. If you want the scholarship to be $5000 the first year but increase by 4% every year, how large would your donation need to be to endow this scholarship if the university can earn 9%?

9. Your grandparents just gave you a gift of $15,000 that you have put in a savings account which earns 5% interest. You are planning to use this money to fund an annual vacation as long as the money lasts. If you withdraw $1600 a year to take a vacation (beginning one year from today), how many vacations can you take before the money is depleted?

10. You are considering purchasing a $230,000 home. If you make a 20% down payment, the bank is offering to make you a 20-year loan that requires annual payments and has an interest rate of 8% a year. What will your annual payment be if you sign up for this mortgage?

11. You bought a painting five years ago for $550. Today, you sell the painting for $790. What was the rate of return on your investment in this painting?

12. Your child needs to get braces. The orthodontist will provide orthodontic services if you pay $3000 today or if you make four annual payments of $1000 (with the first payment made one year from today). What interest rate is the orthodontist offering (what is the rate of return)?

13. Sandra has decided to cut costs as much as possible during her four years of college. One way she does this is by minimizing her textbook costs by buying old textbook editions online and by not purchasing study guides. She estimates that she has saved $1000 a year with this strategy. However, even without all of the required course materials, Sandra is a good enough student to maintain a 3.2 GPA. Her friend Heather takes a different strategy and purchases all up-to-date textbooks and study guides; with all of this additional help, Heather is able to maintain a 3.5 GPA. Upon graduation, Sandra is offered a job making $30,000 a year. With her higher GPA, Heather gets a job offer that pays 10% more. Assume that Heather continues to earn $3000 a year more than Sandra for the next 40 years. Assuming a 7% discount rate, what is the NPV of Heather's decision to spend the money on her course materials? (For simplicity, assume that all cash flows occur at the beginning of the year in which they occur.)

■ Solutions to Questions and Problems

1. $FV = \$100,000 = PV(1 + .03)^{10}$

   $PV = \$100,000/1.3439 = \$74,409.39$

2. The $10,000 three years from today is preferable because it has a present value of $10,000/(1.04)^3 = \$8,889.96$.

3. You should take the $3000 a year for 10 years because the present value of this is $23,165.20.

Chapter 4 Time Value of Money: Valuing Cash Flow Streams   55

4. The present value of the contract is $5.07 million.

5. a. PV = −$1203; do not take the opportunity
   b. PV = $464; take the opportunity

6. $3911

	N	I/Y	PV	PMT	FV
Given:	40	12			3,000,000
Solve for:			−3910.88		

7. $5000/0.09 = $55,556

8. $5000/(0.09 − 0.04) = $100,000

9. 13 years

	N	I/Y	PV	PMT	FV
Given:		5	15,000	−1600	0
Solve for:	12.96				

10. $18,741

	N	I/Y	PV	PMT	FV
Given:	20	8	184,000		
Solve for:				−18,740.81	

11. 7.5%

	N	I/Y	PV	PMT	FV
Given:	5		−550		790
Solve for:		7.5			

12. 12.6%

	N	I/Y	PV	PMT	FV
Given:	4		−3000	1000	
Solve for:		12.6			

13. The present value (at the beginning of college) of spending the extra $1000 a year while in college is $3624. The present value (at the beginning of college) of earning $3000 more a year is $32,648. Therefore, the NPV of investing in the extra course materials is (32,648 − 3624) = $29,024.

Self-Test Questions

1. Your insurance company promises to pay you $20,000 a year for the next 30 years. This promise would be called a(n)
   a. perpetuity.
   b. annuity.
   c. rate of return.
   d. compounded present value.

2. A stream of equal cash flows that occur at regular intervals and last forever is known as
   a. net present value.
   b. IRR.
   c. a perpetuity.
   d. compounding.

3. The **rate of return** on an investment opportunity is
   a. the compounded future value of the investment.
   b. the rate at which the present value of the benefits exactly equals zero.
   c. also known as the present value of the investment opportunity.
   d. the rate at which the present value of the benefits exactly offsets the cost of the investment.

4. The present value of a perpetuity
   a. calculated by dividing the cash flow by the interest rate, or C/r.
   b. is infinite because a perpetuity goes into infinity.
   c. cannot be calculated because you would be dividing by zero.
   d. is equivalent to the future value multiplied by the interest rate, or FV $*$ r.

5. ABC Corporation has issued perpetual bonds that will pay interest of $1000 a year forever. Using a 5% discount rate, what would you be willing to pay for this bond?
   a. $10,000
   b. $20,000
   c. $30,000
   d. Cannot calculate a price because the interest payments continue forever.

6. Raul has decided to start saving for retirement by placing $10,000 a year in a savings account which earns 15% interest. He will continue to place $10,000 in the savings account each year until the account balance is at least $1,000,000. How many years will Raul be putting money in this account?
   a. 18 years
   b. 20 years
   c. 22 years
   d. 25 years

7. You just bought a house for $275,000. If the house appreciates at a rate of 4% a year, how much will the house be worth in 20 years?
   a. $570,240
   b. $602,559
   c. $752,340
   d. $877,560

8. You want to fund a scholarship that will pay one student's tuition to State U. every year beginning one year from today. The tuition next year will be $7000. The university expects tuition to increase at a rate of 6% a year. If the initial money that you provide to endow this scholarship is placed in a fund that earns 8% a year, how much will you need to provide to fund this scholarship?
   a. $50,000
   b. $92,750
   c. $116,667
   d. $350,000

9. Your parents have agreed to help finance the rest of your college education by giving you $10,000 today, $15,000 one year from today, and $18,000 two years from today. Using a 5% discount rate, the present value of your parents' promise is:
   a. $30,612
   b. $38,775
   c. $40,612
   d. $44,775

10. You are considering buying a house today for $270,000. You think that you can rent the house for $20,000 a year for the next three years. Assume that you would receive the entire rent for the year at the end of each year; therefore, the first time you would receive the rental money would be one year from today. At the end of three years, you would be able to sell the house for $325,000. If the discount rate is 8%, what is the PV of this rental property investment?
    a. $20,430
    b. $39,537
    c. $43,440
    d. $72,000

11. Your brother offers to give you $1000 today if you will give him $3000 in 20 years. What is the minimum interest rate you would need to be able to earn for you to agree to this offer?
    a. 3.00%
    b. 5.65%
    c. 8.65%
    d. 11.00%

12. You just won a contest and your prize is that you will receive $100 a year, beginning one year from today, for 50 years. If the interest rate is 6%, how much is your prize worth?
    a. $182.44
    b. $282.44
    c. $1576.19
    d. $1670.76

Answers to Self-Test Questions

1. b
2. c
3. d
4. a
5. b
6. b
7. b
8. d
9. c
10. b
11. b
12. c

■ Appendix: Using a Financial Calculator

The two most commonly used financial calculators are the HP-10BII and the TIBAII Plus Professional. These financial calculators automate some of the arithmetic required to work the problems in this chapter. The basic operation of these calculators is the same, but each has some unique keystrokes necessary to perform financial calculations. This appendix will provide you with an overview of how to use both of these calculators for financial calculations.

Specifying Decimal Places

Make sure you have plenty of decimal places displayed!

HP-10BII

TI BAII Plus Professional

Toggling between the Beginning and End of a Period

You should always make sure that your calculator is in *end-of-period* mode.

HP-10BII

Chapter 4 Time Value of Money: Valuing Cash Flow Streams

TI BAII Plus Professional

Set the Number of Periods per Year

You will avoid a lot of confusion later if you always set your periods per year "P/Y" to 1:

HP-10BII

TI BAII Plus Professional

General TVM Buttons

HP-10BII

TI BAII Plus Professional

Solving for the Present Value of a Single Future Cash Flow (Example 3.5)

You are considering investing in a savings bond that will pay $15,000 in ten years. If the competitive market interest rate is fixed at 6% per year, what is the bond worth today? [Answer: $8375.92]

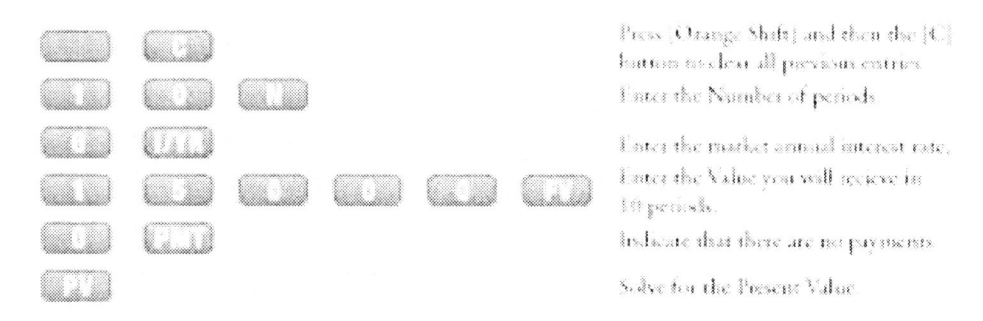

HP-10BII

TI-BAII Plus Professional

© 2012 Pearson Education, Inc. Publishing as Prentice Hall

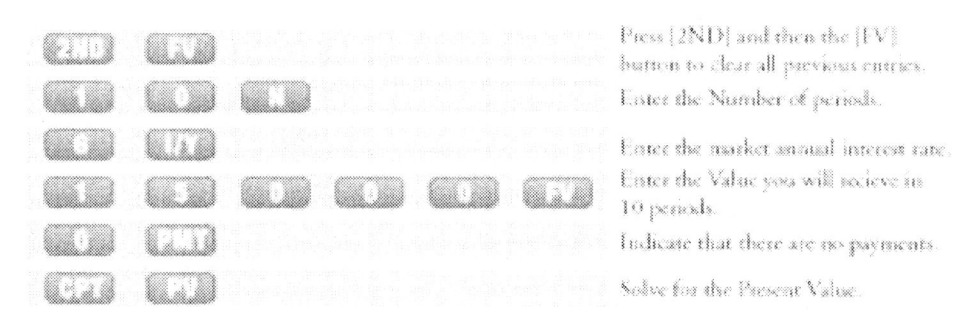

Solving for the Future Value of an Annuity (Example 4.5)

Ellen is 35 years old, and she has decided it is time to plan seriously for her retirement. At the end of each year until she is 65, she will save $10,000 in a retirement account. If the account earns 10% per year, how much will Ellen have saved at age 65? [Answer: $1,644,940]

HP-10BII

Press [Orange Shift] and then the [C] button to clear all previous entries.
Enter the Number of periods.
Enter the market annual interest rate.
Enter the Payment amount per period.
Indicate that there is no initial amount in the retirement account.
Solve for the Future Value.

TI-BAII Plus Professional

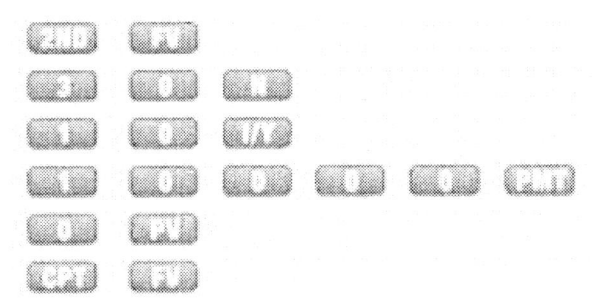

Press [2ND] and then the [FV] button to clear all previous entries.
Enter the Number of periods.
Enter the market annual interest rate.
Enter the payment amount per period.
Indicate that there is no initial amount in the retirement account.
Solve for the Future Value.

Solving for the Rate of Return

If you have an initial cash outflow of $2000 and one cash inflow per year for the following four years of $1000, $400, $400, and $800, what is the rate of return on the project per year (sometimes called the Internal Rate of Return or IRR on the TI Calculator? [Answer: 12.12%]

HP-10BII

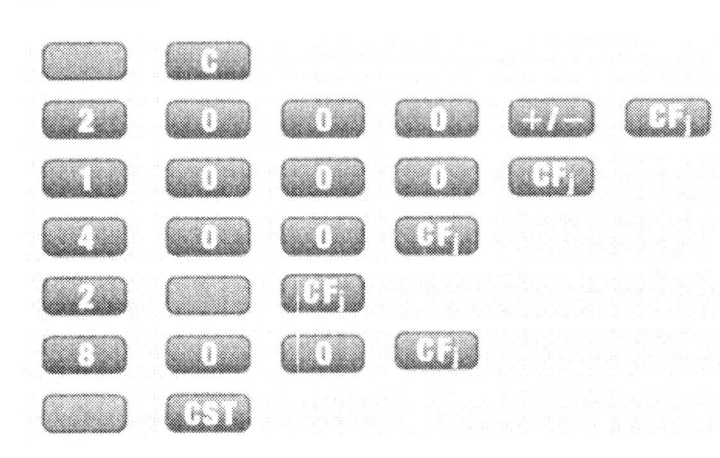

Press [Orange Shift] and then the [C] button to clear all previous entries.
Enter the initial cash outflow.
Enter the first cash inflow.
Enter the second cash inflow.
Enter the number of consecutive periods the second cash inflow occurs.
Enter the fourth cash inflow.
Press [Orange Shift] and then the [CST] button to calculate the IRR/year.

Chapter 4 Time Value of Money: Valuing Cash Flow Streams 61

TI-BAII Plus Professional

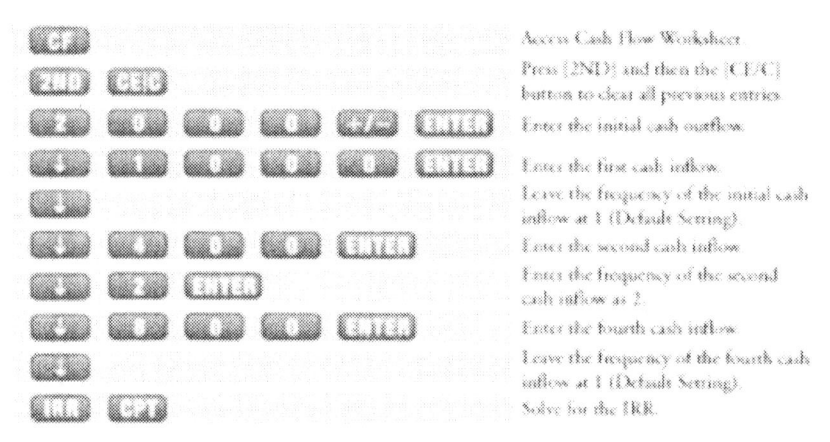

The Appendix in your book covers how to calculate TVM problems using a financial calculator. Here, we give several examples using Excel.

Using Excel to Calculate PV and FV

Microsoft Excel has time value of money functions based on the variables introduced in this chapter. The notation in Excel is: N = NPER, r = RATE, PV = PV, C = PMT, and FV = FV. You must input four of these variables and Excel will calculate the fifth variable for you. Suppose, for example, you invest $2000 at 8% for 10 years and you want to know what you will have in the future. On a timeline, this will look like:

Date (Years)	0	1	2	3	…	10
Cash Flow		−2000	−2000	−2000	…	−2000
						?FV

In this case, NPER = 10 and RATE = 8%. PV will be 0. (Nothing occurs on the timeline today.) PMT is −2000. The variable that you do not know is FV.

The screen shot of an Excel spreadsheet in Figure 4.1 below shows an example of how to use Excel to calculate FV for this example problem.

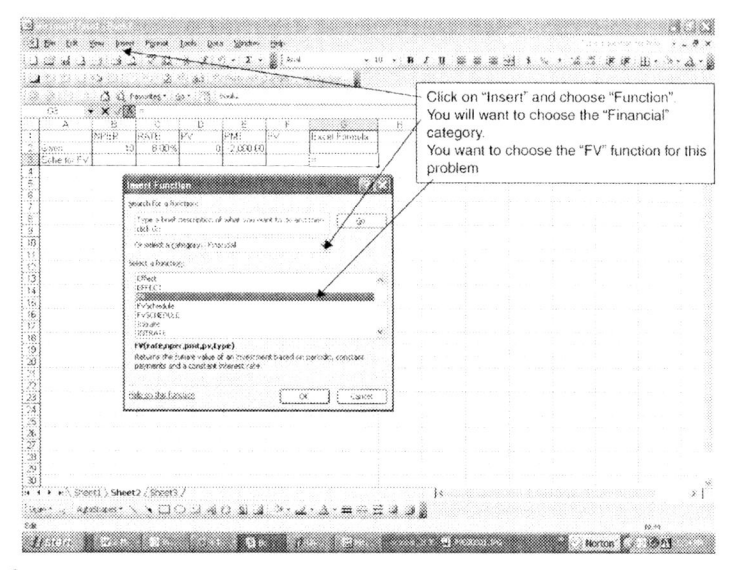

Figure 4.1

© 2012 Pearson Education, Inc. Publishing as Prentice Hall

A box, such as the one shown in Figure 4.2 below, will pop up so that you can put in the values for the various variables. For example, you will put the rate (8.00%) for "RATE" and the number of time periods (10) for "NPER." In the example below, "c2" is placed in the RATE box; this will cause the number that is placed in Column C, Row 2 in the spreadsheet to be used for the interest rate. Alternatively, the number 0.08 could be placed in this box.

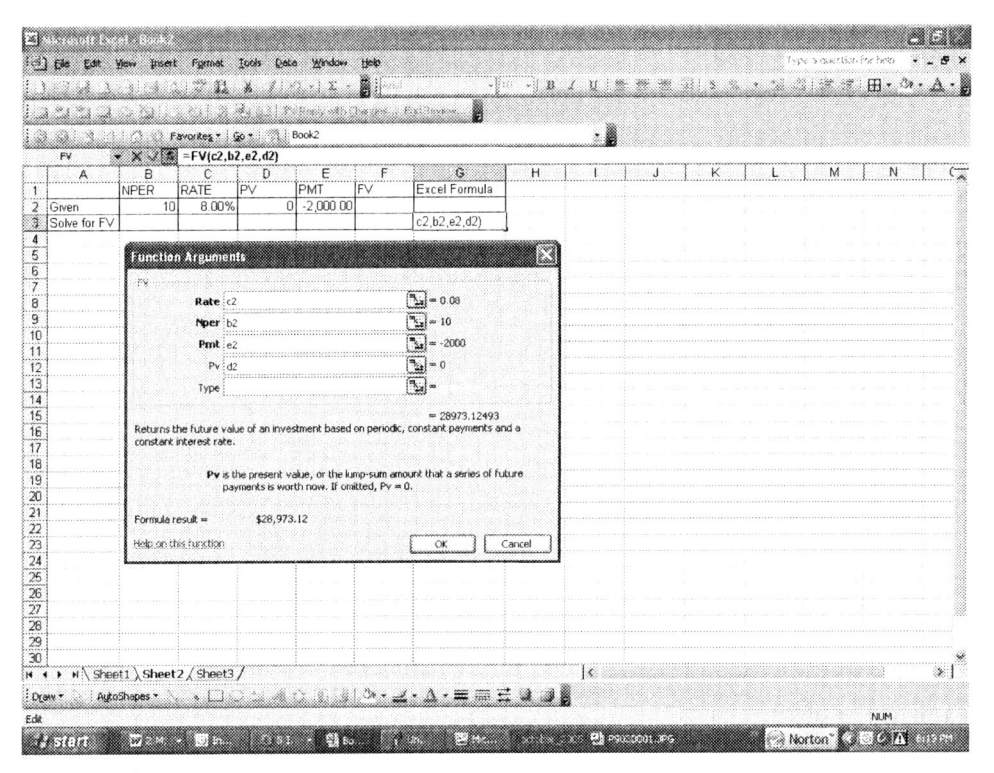

Figure 4.2

This function will return the FV of $28,973.12. Thus, we will have a result that looks like the following:

	NPER	RATE	PV	PMT	FV	Excel Formula
Given:	10	0.08	0	−2000		
Solve for FV:					28,973.1249318197	=FV(C2,B2,E2,D2)

The advantage of placing the cell references for the variables in the Excel formula is that we can easily change any of the variables and determine the new future value with very little additional work. For example, suppose that you change your mind and decide that you would like to save $3000 a year rather than only $2000 a year. You would simply change the value in the cell for PMT (cell e2 in our sample spreadsheet). Without any further changes, the FV function will return the future value of $43,459.69.

	NPER	RATE	PV	PMT	FV	Excel Formula
Given	10	0.08	0	−3000		
Solve for FV:					43,459.6873977295	=FV(C2,B2,E2,D2)

Chapter 5
Interest Rates

■ Key Learning Objectives

- Understand the different ways interest rates are quoted
- Use quoted rates to calculate loan payments and balances
- Know how inflation, expectations, and risk combine to determine interest rates
- See the link between interest rates in the market and a firm's opportunity cost of capital

■ Notation

APR	annual percentage rate
APY	annual percentage yield
C	cash flow
C_n	cash flow that arrives in period n
EAR	effective annual rate
FV	future value
m	number of compounding periods per year
n	number of periods
N	date of the last cash flow in a stream of cash flows
PV	present value
r	interest rate or discount rate
r_n	interest rate or discount rate for an n-year term

■ Chapter Synopsis

In this chapter, we consider the factors that affect interest rates and discuss how to determine the appropriate discount rate for a set of cash flows. We will look at the way interest is paid, the way interest rates are quoted, and how to calculate the effective interest paid in one year given different quoting conventions. We also consider some of the main determinants of interest rates—namely, inflation and economic growth. Because interest rates tend to change over time, investors will demand different interest rates for different investment horizons based on their expectations and the risk involved in longer time horizons.

5.1 Interest Rate Quotes and Adjustments

An interest rate is the price of using money. Just like any other price, interest rates are set by market forces, in particular, the supply and demand of funds. When the supply (savings) is high and the demand (borrowing) is low, interest rates are low, other things being equal. Interest rates are also influenced by expected inflation, risk, and tax consequences.

Interest rates can differ as to how often interest is paid. Interest rates can also differ depending on the investment horizon. Interest rates can also vary due to risk or tax consequences. Because interest rates may be quoted for different time intervals, such as monthly, semiannual, or annual, it is often necessary to adjust the interest rate to a time period that matches that of our cash flows.

Interest rates are often reported as an **effective annual rate (EAR)** or **annual percentage yield (APY)**, which indicates the total amount of interest that will be earned at the end of one year. If interest is earned for periods other than a year, we need to convert the discount rate. We can convert a discount rate of r for one period to an equivalent discount rate for n periods using the following formula:

$$\text{Equivalent } n\text{-Period Discount Rate} = (1 + r)^n - 1$$

In this formula, n can be larger than 1 (to compute a rate over more than one period) or smaller than 1 (to compute a rate over a fraction of a period). **When computing present or future values you should adjust the discount rate to match the time period of the cash flows.**

The most common way to quote interest rates is in terms of an **annual percentage rate (APR),** which indicates the amount of **simple interest** earned in one year, that is, the amount of interest earned without the effect of compounding. To compute the actual amount that you will earn in one year, the APR must be converted to an effective annual rate. The effective annual rate corresponding to an APR is given by the conversion formula:

$$1 + EAR = \left(1 + \frac{APR}{m}\right)^m$$

(m = number of compounding periods)

The EAR increases with the frequency of compounding because of the ability to earn interest on interest sooner.

5.2 Application: Discount Rates and Loans

Many loans, such as mortgages and car loans, have monthly payments and are quoted in terms of an APR with monthly compounding. These types of loans are **amortizing loans,** which means that each month you pay interest on the loan plus some part of the loan balance. Each monthly payment is the same, and the loan is fully repaid with the final payment. Your loan payment each month includes interest and repayment of part of the principal, reducing the amount you still owe. Because the loan balance (amount you still owe) is decreasing each month, the interest that accrues on that balance is decreasing.

The outstanding balance on an amortizing loan is different each month. The amount you owe at any point in time must equal the present value of your future obligations on the loan. So, the outstanding balance, also called the outstanding principal, is equal to the present value of the remaining future loan payments, again evaluated using the loan interest rate.

5.3 The Determinants of Interest Rates

Interest rates are determined by market forces based on the relative supply and demand of funds. This supply and demand is determined by individuals', banks', and firms' willingness to borrow, save, and lend. Nominal interest rates indicate the rate at which your money will grow if invested for a certain period. The real interest rate is the growth in purchasing power after adjusting for inflation. The real rate of interest is calculated using the formula:

$$\text{real rate} = \frac{\text{nominal rate} - \text{inflation rate}}{1 + \text{inflation rate}}$$
$$\approx \text{nominal rate} - \text{inflation rate}$$

The interest rate will vary, depending on the horizon, or term, of the investment or loan. The relationship between the investment term and the interest rate is called the **term structure** of interest rates. We can plot this relationship on a graph called the **yield curve.** Most of the time the yield curve will be moderately upward sloping. A sharply increasing (*steep*) yield curve, with long-term rates much higher than short-term rates, generally indicates that interest rates are expected to rise in the future. A decreasing (*inverted*) yield curve, with long-term rates lower than short-term rates, generally signals an expected decline in future interest rates.

5.4 The Opportunity Cost of Capital

The discount rate that we should use to evaluate cash flows is the investor's **opportunity cost of capital** (or more simply, the **cost of capital**), which is *the best available expected return offered in the market on an investment of comparable risk and term to the cash flow being discounted.*

The opportunity cost of capital is the return the investor forgoes when the investor takes on a new investment. For a risk-free project, it will typically correspond to the interest rate on U.S. Treasury securities with a similar term. But the cost of capital is a much more general concept that can be applied to risky investments as well.

■ Selected Concepts and Key Terms

Amortizing Loan

An **amortizing loan** is a loan in which each month you pay interest on the loan plus some part of the loan principal, or amount borrowed. Each monthly payment is the same, and the loan is fully repaid with the final payment. Since the loan balance declines over time, the interest portion of the payment declines over time while the principal repayment portion increases.

Annual Percentage Rate (APR)

The **annual percentage rate (APR)** is the periodic interest rate, r, times the number of compounding periods per year. Because it does not include the effect of compounding, the APR quote is less than the actual amount of interest that will be received if there is more than one compounding period in a year.

Effective Annual Rate (EAR)

The **effective annual rate (EAR)** is the amount of interest that will be earned over a year. The more compounding periods there are, the greater the EAR will be for a given APR.

Opportunity Cost of Capital

The **opportunity cost of capital** is the best available expected return offered in the market on an investment of comparable risk and term to the cash flow being discounted. The cost of capital is the return the investor forgoes when making a new investment. For a risk-free project, it will typically correspond to the interest rate on U.S. Treasury securities with a similar term. For risky projects, it will include a risk premium.

Nominal Interest Rate

The **nominal interest rate** is the rate at which money will grow. It is the rate quoted in the financial markets.

Real Interest Rate

If prices in the economy are increasing because of inflation, the nominal interest rate does not represent the increase in purchasing power that will result from investing at the nominal rate. The **real interest rate** is the rate of growth of purchasing power after adjusting for inflation. It is approximately equal to the nominal interest rate minus the rate of inflation.

Term Structure

The **term structure** is the relationship between an investment's term and its interest rate. A graph of this relationship is called the **yield curve.**

■ Concept Check Questions and Answers

1. What is the difference between an EAR and an APR quote?

    An annual percentage rate (APR) is the rate that interest earns in one year before the effect of compounding. An effective annual rate (EAR) is the rate that the amount of interest actually earns at the end of one year. Because the APR does not include the effect of compounding, it is typically less than the EAR.

2. Why can't the APR be used as a discount rate?

    Because the APR does not reflect the true amount you will earn in one year, the APR itself cannot be used as a discount rate.

3. How is the principal repaid in an amortizing loan?

    The principal is repaid over the life of the loan in an amortizing loan. When each payment is made, some of the payment goes toward principal and some toward interest.

4. Why does the part of your loan payment covering interest change over time?

    Each time a payment is made, the outstanding balance on the loan is reduced. Since the interest is calculated on the outstanding balance, the amount of interest owed decreases over time.

5. What is the difference between a nominal and real interest rate?

    The nominal interest rate is the rate quoted by banks and other financial institutions, whereas the real interest rate is the rate of growth of purchasing power, after adjusting for inflation. The real interest rate is approximately equal to the nominal rate less the rate of inflation.

6. How are interest rates and the level of investment made by businesses related?

   When the costs of an investment precede the benefits, an increase in the interest rate will decrease the investment's PV. All else being equal, higher interest rates will therefore tend to shrink the set of positive-PV investments available to firms.

7. What is the opportunity cost of capital?

   The opportunity cost of capital is the best available return offered in the market on an investment of comparable risk and term to the cash flow being discounted.

8. Can you ignore the cost of capital if you already have the funds inside the firm?

   No, you cannot ignore the cost of capital if you already have funds inside the firm. These funds still have an opportunity cost and investors expect a return on these funds.

■ Examples with Step-by-Step Solutions

Valuing Monthly Cash Flows

5.1 **Problem:** Suppose your bank account pays interest monthly with an effective annual rate of 10%. What amount of interest will you earn each month? Also, if you have no money in the bank today, how much will you need to save at the end of each month to accumulate $20,000 in 10 years?

Solution

Plan: To convert the EAR to a monthly rate in the first part of the question, we can use the equation:

$$\text{Equivalent } n\text{-Period Discount Rate} = (1 + r)^n - 1$$

The second part of the question is a future value of an annuity question. It is asking how big of a monthly annuity we would have to deposit in order to end up with $20,000 in 10 years. However, in order to do this problem, we need to write the timeline in terms of *monthly* periods because our cash flows (deposits) will be monthly:

Date (Month)	0	1	2	3	...	120
Cash Flow		−C	−C	−C	...	−C
						20,000

That is, we can view the savings plan as a monthly annuity with 10 × 12 = 120 monthly payments. We have the future value of the annuity ($20,000), the length of time (120 months), and we will have the monthly interest rate from the first part of the question. We can then use the future value of an annuity formula to solve for the monthly deposit.

Execute: A 10% EAR is equivalent to earning $(1.1)^{\frac{1}{12}} - 1 = .7974\%$ per month.

The exponent in this equation is 1/12 because one month is 1/12 of a year.

To determine the amount to save each month to reach the goal of $20,000 in 120 months, we must determine the amount of the monthly payment, C, that will have a future value of $20,000 in 120 months, given an interest rate of 0.7974% per month. Now that we have all of the inputs in terms of months (monthly payment, monthly interest rate, and total number of months), we use the future value of annuity to solve this problem:

$$FV(\text{annuity}) = C \times \frac{1}{r}[(1+r)^n - 1]$$

$$C = \frac{FV(\text{annuity})}{\frac{1}{r}[(1+r)^n - 1]} = \frac{\$20{,}000}{\frac{1}{0.007974}\left[(1.007974)^{120} - 1\right]} = \frac{\$20{,}000}{199.8619} = \$100.07$$

We can also compute this result using a financial calculator:

	N	I/Y	PV	PMT	FV
Given:	120	.7974			20,000
Solve for:				100.07	

Evaluate: Thus, if we save $100.07 per month and we earn interest monthly at an effective annual rate of 10%, we will have $20,000 in 10 years. Notice that the timing in the annuity formula must be consistent for all of the inputs. In this case, we had a monthly deposit, so we needed to convert our interest rate to a monthly interest rate and then use the total number of months (120) instead of years.

Converting the APR to a Discount Rate

5.2 **Problem:** You are purchasing a new computer. You can purchase the computer for an upfront cost of $2,500, or you can pay $75 a month for 36 months. Your firm can borrow at an interest rate of 8% APR with monthly compounding. Should you purchase the computer outright for $2500 or should you pay the $75 a month for three years?

Solution
Plan: The timeline for making the $75 a month payments is:

Date (Month)	0	1	2	3	...	36
Cash Flow		−75	−75	−75	...	−75

We need to compute the present value of these monthly payments using the annuity formula. First, we need to compute the discount rate that corresponds to a period length of one month. To do so, we convert the borrowing cost of 8% APR with monthly compounding to a monthly discount rate.

We will need to compare the present value of the monthly payments to the cost of paying $2500 for the computer today.

Execute: The 8% APR with monthly compounding really means 8%/12 = 0.6667% every month. The 12 comes from the fact that there are 12 monthly compounding periods per year. Now that we have the monthly rate corresponding to the stated APR, we can use that discount rate in the annuity formula to compute the present value of the monthly payments:

$$PV = 75 \times \frac{1}{0.006667}\left(1 - \frac{1}{1.006667^{36}}\right)$$

$$= 75 \times \frac{1}{0.006667}(0.21275) = \$2393.32$$

We can also compute this result using a financial calculator:

	N	I/Y	**PV**	PMT	FV
Given:	36	8/12		75	
Solve for:			2393.39		

Evaluate: Thus, paying $75 a month for 36 months is equivalent to paying $2393.32 today. (The slightly different answer of $2393.39 we get using the calculator is due to rounding differences.) This cost is lower than paying $2500 for the computer today. Therefore, it is better for you to make the $75 a month payments rather than pay the $2500 today.

Computing Monthly Loan Payments

5.3 **Problem:** Suppose you borrow $180,000 to buy a new house. Your 30-year mortgage loan has a 9% APR, compounded monthly. What will your monthly mortgage payments be?

Solution

Plan: The timeline for this mortgage looks like:

Date (Month)	0	1	2	3	...	360
Cash Flow	+180,000	−C	−C	−C	...	−C

First, we need to compute the discount rate that corresponds to a period length of 1 month. To do so, we convert the borrowing cost of 9% APR with monthly compounding to a monthly discount rate. Then we will use the present value of an annuity formula to solve for the monthly mortgage payment.

Execute: The 9% APR with monthly compounding really means 9%/12 = 0.75% every month. The 12 comes from the fact that there are 12 monthly compounding periods per year. Now that we have the monthly rate corresponding to the stated APR, we can use that discount rate in the annuity formula to compute the monthly payments:

$$\$180,000 = C \times \frac{1}{0.0075}\left(1 - \frac{1}{1.0075^{360}}\right)$$

$$= C \times \frac{1}{0.0075}(0.9321)$$

$$C = \$180,000 \times \frac{0.0075}{0.9321}$$

$$= \$1448.34$$

We can also calculate this using a financial calculator:

	N	I/Y	**PV**	PMT	FV
Given:	360	9/12	180,000		
Solve for:				1448.32	

Evaluate: You will need to make a monthly payment of $1448.34 for 360 months to pay off the $180,000 mortgage. Using the financial calculator resulted in a slightly different answer ($1448.32) because of rounding differences. We were rounding to only four decimal places as we worked the problem. The financial calculator uses more decimal places.

Computing the Outstanding Loan Balance

5.4 **Problem:** Now, let's say that you are 10 years into your $180,000 mortgage loan from Example 3.5 and you decide to sell your house. When you sell the house, you will need to pay whatever the remaining balance is on your mortgage loan. After 120 months of payments, how much do you still owe on your mortgage?

Solution

Plan: We have already determined that the monthly payments on the loan are $1448.34. The remaining balance on the loan is the present value of the remaining 20 years, or 240 months, of payments. Thus, we can just use the annuity formula with the monthly rate of 0.75%, a monthly payment of $1448.34, and 240 months remaining.

Execute:

$$PV = \$1448.34 \times \frac{1}{0.0075}\left(1 - \frac{1}{1.0075^{240}}\right)$$

$$= \$1448.34 \times \frac{1}{0.0075}(0.8336)$$

$$= \$160,978.16$$

We can also calculate this using a financial calculator:

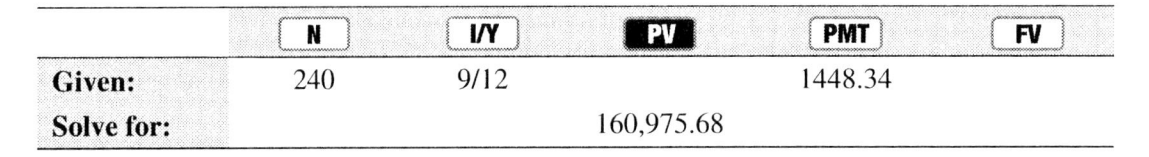

	N	I/Y	PV	PMT	FV
Given:	240	9/12		1448.34	
Solve for:			160,975.68		

Evaluate: After 10 years, you owe $160,978.16. At any point in time, including when you first take out the loan, the present value of your remaining payments must equal the balance of the loan. Recall that when the bank gave you the $180,000 in the first place, it was willing to take 360 monthly payments of $1448.34 in return only because the present value of those payments was equivalent to the cash it was giving you. Any time that you want to end the loan, you must pay the bank a lump sum equal to the present value of what it would receive if you continued making your payments as planned.

Calculating the Real Interest Rate

5.5 **Problem:** If the short-term U.S. government bond rate is 5.5% and the rate of inflation is 2.9%, what is the real interest rate?

Solution

Plan: The bond rate tells us the nominal rate. Given the nominal rate and inflation for each year, we can use the following equation to calculate the real rate of interest:

$$\text{real rate} = \frac{\text{nominal rate} - \text{inflation rate}}{1 + \text{inflation rate}}$$

Chapter 5 Interest Rates

Execute:

$$\text{real rate} = \frac{\text{nominal rate} - \text{inflation rate}}{1 + \text{inflation rate}}$$

$$= \frac{0.055 - 0.029}{1 + 0.029} = 2.5\%$$

The real rate of interest is 2.5% (which is approximately equal to the difference between the nominal rate and inflation: 5.5% − 2.9% = 2.6%).

Evaluate: If you earn 5.5% interest on an investment when the rate of inflation is 2.9%, then your purchasing power is really increasing by 2.5%.

Using the Term Structure to Compute Present Values

5.6 **Problem:** Assume that the current yield curve shows the following rates on securities with one to five years to maturity.

Term	Rate
1	1.20%
2	1.27%
3	1.29%
4	1.35%
5	1.52%

Compute the present value of a risk-free 5-year annuity of $1000 per year, given the yield curve.

Solution

Plan: The timeline of the cash flows of the annuity is:

Date (Year)	0	1	2	3	4	5
Cash Flow		1000	1000	1000	1000	1000

With these cash flows and the interest rates given in the chart we can calculate the present value.

Execute: To compute the present value, we discount each cash flow by the corresponding interest rate:

$$PV = \frac{1000}{1.012} + \frac{1000}{1.0127^2} + \frac{1000}{1.0129^3} + \frac{1000}{1.0135^4} + \frac{1000}{1.0152^5}$$

$$= 988.14 + 975.08 + 962.28 + 947.77 + 927.35 = 4800.62$$

Evaluate: The present value of receiving $1000 each year for the next five years is $4800.62. The yield curve tells us the market interest rate per year for each different maturity. In order to calculate the PV of cash flows from five different maturities correctly, we need to use the five different interest rates corresponding to those maturities. We cannot use the annuity formula here because a different interest rate is used to discount each cash flow.

Long-Term vs. Short-Term Loans

5.7 **Problem:** You work for a bank that has just made two loans. In one, you loaned $5000 today in return for $5300 in 1 year. In the other, you loaned $5000 today in return for $16,035.68 in 20 years. The difference between the loan amount and repayment amount is based on an interest rate of 6% per year. Imagine that immediately after you make the loans, news about economic growth is announced that increases inflation expectations so that the market interest rate for loans like these jumps to 8%. Loans make up a major part of a bank's assets, so you are naturally concerned about the value of these loans. What is the effect of the interest rate change on the value to the bank of the promised repayment of these loans?

Solution

Plan: Each of these loans has only one repayment cash flow at the end of the loan. They differ only by the time to repayment:

Loan Today	1
−5000	+5300

Loan Today	1 ... 19	20
−5000	0	+16,035.68

The effect on the value of the future repayment to the bank today is just the PV of the loan repayment, calculated at the new market interest rate of 8%.

Execute:

For the 1-year loan: $PV = \dfrac{\$5300}{(1.08)^1} = \$4907.41$

For the 20-year loan: $PV = \dfrac{\$16,035.68}{(1.08)^{20}} = \$3440.43$

Evaluate: The value of the 1-year loan decreased by $5000 − $4907.41 = $92.59 or 1.85%. The value of the 20-year loan decreased by $5000 − $3440.43 = $1559.57 or 31.19%. The small change in market interest rates, compounded over a longer period, resulted in a much larger change in the present value of the loan.

The Opportunity Cost of Capital

5.8 **Problem:** Suppose your friend Matthew offers to pay you $800 a year from today if you will lend him $750 today. Looking in the market for other options for investing your money, you find your best alternative option for investing the $750 that you view as equally risky as lending to your friend has an expected return of 7%. What should you do?

Solution

Plan: Your decision depends on what the opportunity cost is of lending your money to Matthew. If you lend him the $750, then you cannot invest it in the alternative with a 7% expected return. Thus, by making the loan, you are giving up the opportunity to earn a 7% expected return. Therefore, you can make your decision by using your 7% opportunity cost of capital to value the $750 in one year. In other words, if you put the $750 in the alternative investment, how much would you have in one year? You know that if you lend the $750 to Matthew that you will have $800 in one year.

Execute: The value of the $750 in one year is its present value, compounded at 7%:

$$PV = \$750 \times (1.07)^1 = \$802.50$$

Evaluate: You should place the $750 in the alternative investment option with the 7% expected return. You expect to receive $802.50 in one year which is greater than the $800 Matthew offered to pay you in one year.

The Valuation Principle tells us that we can determine the value of an investment by using market prices to value the benefits net of the costs. As this example shows, market prices determine what our best alternative opportunities are, so that we can decide whether an investment is worth the cost.

■ Questions and Problems

1. You won $1 million in the lottery. The prize is paid out in equal, semiannual payments over 50 years with the first payment made immediately. GenexCapital.com has offered to buy the ticket for $250,000 in cash today. In the contract, they claim to be using an 8% APR with semiannual compounding. Are they indeed using an 8% APR with semiannual compounding?

2. You have a $15,000 balance on your credit card. The interest rate on the credit card is 18% APR. If you make a monthly payment of $400 a month (and make no new charges on your credit card), how long will it take you to pay off your credit card?

3. You have decided to refinance your mortgage. You plan to borrow whatever is outstanding on your current mortgage. The current monthly payment is $2200, and there are exactly 22 years left on the loan. The mortgage interest rate on your existing loan is 8% APR. How much do you owe on the mortgage today?

4. If you refinance your mortgage in Problem 3 to a mortgage that has a 6% APR, what will your monthly payments be. Assume that you finance the entire outstanding balance for 22 years.

5. You want to save $20,000 to purchase a new car. You place $700 a month in a special savings account earning 6% interest. How long will it be before you have saved $20,000?

6. Samantha places $4 a day in a savings account that earns 3%, compounded daily. How much will she have in the account after 4 years?

7. Tristan just took out a mortgage to pay for a new house; the interest rate on his mortgage is 5% and the inflation rate is 2%. When Tristan's parents bought their house, the interest rate on their mortgage was 11% and inflation was 9.5%. Did Tristan or his parents pay a higher real rate of interest?

8. You are considering opening a savings account and have found the following options:

    Bank A offers 6.2% APR compounded annually

    Bank B offers 6.1% APR compounded quarterly

    Bank C offers 5.8% APR compounded monthly

    Bank D offers 5.75% APR compounded weekly

    In which bank would you prefer to put your money?

9. Auto Finance Corp. is offering a 48-month car loan with a 5.75% APR (monthly compounding). If you borrow $20,000 to buy a new car, how much will your monthly car payments be?

■ Solutions to Questions and Problems

1. If they are paying 8% APR (4% per six months), then the PV of the annuity payments at this rate must be $250,000.

$$PV = \$10,000\left[\frac{1}{0.04} - \frac{1}{0.04(1.04)^{99}}\right] + 10,000$$
$$= \$254,852 > \$250,000$$

Discounting the annuity payments at a rate of 8% APR results in a PV that exceeds $250,000, a slightly higher discount rate must be used to equate the annuity payments with the $250,000 offered today.

The actual rate is:

$$\$10,000\left[\frac{1}{r} - \frac{1}{r(1+r)^{99}}\right] + 10,000 = \$250,000 \Rightarrow APR = 8.175\%$$

2. This is a present value of an annuity problem in which you must solve for N:

$$\$400\left[\frac{1}{0.015} - \frac{1}{0.015(1.015)^{N}}\right] = \$15,000$$

$$N = 55.5 \text{ months}$$

We can also compute this result using a financial calculator:

	N	I/Y	PV	PMT	FV
Given:		1.5	15,000	−400	
Solve for:	55.5				

3. You owe the present value of the $2200 monthly annuity payment for 22 years (264 months) discounted at a rate of 8%:

$$PV = \frac{2200}{0.00667}\left(1 - \frac{1}{(1.00667)^{264}}\right)$$
$$= \$272,806$$

You can also compute this result using a financial calculator:

	N	I/Y	PV	PMT	FV
Given:	264	.667		2.200	
Solve for:			272,806		

4. To calculate the monthly payment:

$$272,806 = C\left[\frac{1}{0.005} - \frac{1}{0.005(1.005)^{264}}\right] \Rightarrow \$1863$$

Chapter 5   Interest Rates   75

We can also compute this result using a financial calculator:

	N	I/Y	PV	PMT	FV
Given:	264	.5	272,806		
Solve for:				1863.47	

5. You use the FV of an annuity formula:

$$FV(annuity) = C \times \frac{1}{r}\left[(1+r)^n - 1\right]$$

Since your goal is to have $20,000, that is your future value. $700 will be your monthly cash flow, or C. You need to put your interest rate in monthly terms; r is .06/12 = 0.005. You solve for n.

It will take 27 months of depositing $700 into the account to have $20,000 saved. We can also compute this result using a financial calculator:

	N	I/Y	PV	PMT	FV
Given:		.5		−700	20,000
Solve for:	26.77				

6. Again, you will use the FV of an annuity formula. Now, $C = \$4$, $r = 0.03/365 = 0.00008219$, and $n = 4 \times 365 = 1460$. Samantha will have $6204.58 in four years. You can also compute this result using a financial calculator:

	N	I/Y	PV	PMT	FV
Given:	4X365	3/365		4	
Solve for:					6204.58

7. Tristan pays a real interest rate of approximately 5% − 2% = 3%. His parents paid a real interest rate of approximately 11% − 9.5% = 1.5%. Therefore, Tristan pays a higher real interest rate.

8. You need to calculate the EAR at each of the banks using the formula:

$$1 + EAR = \left(1 + \frac{APR}{m}\right)^m$$

$$\text{Bank A EAR} = \left(1 + \frac{0.061}{4}\right)^4 - 1 = 6.2\%$$

$$\text{Bank B EAR} = \left(1 + \frac{0.061}{4}\right)^4 - 1 = 6.24\%$$

$$\text{Bank C EAR} = \left(1 + \frac{0.058}{12}\right)^{12} - 1 = 5.96\%$$

$$\text{Bank D EAR} = \left(1 + \frac{0.0575}{52}\right)^{52} - 1 = 5.92\%$$

You would prefer to put your money in Bank B which is offering the highest EAR. For every $100 you place in Bank B you will earn $6.24 in interest in one year.

9. We can use the PV of an annuity formula to calculate the monthly payment:

$$\$20{,}000 = C \times \frac{1}{0.0048}\left(1 - \frac{1}{1.0048^{48}}\right) = C \times 208.33(1 - 0.7947) = C \times 42.7701$$

So, C = $467.62.

We can also compute this result using a financial calculator:

	N	I/Y	PV	PMT	FV
Given:	48	5.75/12	20,000		
Solve for:				467.41	

Using the formula results in a slightly different number ($467.62) than the calculator ($46,741) due to rounding errors. We rounded the numbers to four decimal places when using the equation.

■ Self-Test Questions

1. Cambridge State Bank is paying 7% interest on its one-year certificates of deposit. If the inflation rate is 4%, which of the following is the best approximation for the real rate of interest that Cambridge State Bank is paying?
    a. 4/7%
    b. 3%
    c. 1¾%
    d. 11%

2. A steeply upward-sloping yield curve indicates that
    a. interest rates are expected to rise in the future.
    b. there is a negative real interest rate.
    c. the real rate of return is low.
    d. the real rate of interest is relatively high.

3. Brenda borrows $3000 from Mountain View State Bank. The interest rate on the loan is 8% interest, compounded quarterly. The EAR on the loan is:
    a. 2.00%
    b. 7.76%
    c. 8.24%
    d. 8.31%

4. Which of the following statements about an amortizing loan is TRUE?
    a. Each month you pay only interest on the loan and you repay the principal balance at the end of the loan.
    b. The loan balance increases each month as you make more payments.
    c. Each monthly payment becomes smaller because the interest on the balance is decreasing.
    d. Although the payment is the same each month, the interest that accrues each month decreases.

5. If the supply of savings is high
   a. and the demand for loans is low, interest rates will be low.
   b. and the demand for loans is low, interest rates will be high.
   c. the yield curve will be downward sloping.
   d. the real interest rate will be negative.

6. Tony has taken out a $15,000 student loan. If the interest rate on this loan is 5%, compounded monthly, and the term of the loan is 10 years, how much will Tony's monthly payments on the student loan be?
   a. $125.34
   b. $159.10
   c. $161.88
   d. $752.16

7. Candi is saving for retirement by placing $1000 in a savings account twice a year. The savings account pays 12% interest compounded semiannually. If Candi continues to do this for 30 years, how much will she have saved?
   a. $241,333
   b. $482,665
   c. $533,128
   d. $7,471,641

8. Justin is considering an investment that will pay him $5000 a year for the next 20 years. Which of the following should Justin use to discount these future cash flows to the present?
   a. the APR divided by the EAR.
   b. the rate of inflation.
   c. the rate of amortization.
   d. the opportunity cost of capital.

9. Your parents want to place money in an account so that you can withdraw $200 a week for the next four years while you finish college and graduate school. If they place the money in an account that earns 4% interest, compounded weekly, how much do they need to place in the account so that the funds will be depleted in four years? (Assume that you will make the first withdrawal one week from today.)
   a. $28,329
   b. $29,971
   c. $34,847
   d. $38,429

10. Titan State Bank offers to pay you 6% interest, compounded quarterly. The 6% interest rate is known as
    a. the real rate of interest.
    b. the EAR.
    c. the rate of inflation.
    d. the nominal interest rate.

11. The _____ is a graphical representation of the term structure of interest rates.
    a. yield curve
    b. time line
    c. real interest rate curve
    d. opportunity cost of capital line

12. You just loaned $1000 to Harry who promised to pay you $1276.28 in five years. You also made a $1000 loan to Margaret who promised to pay you $2653.30 in 20 years. Both of these repayment amounts are based on a 5% annual interest rate. If right after you make these loans, the market interest rates rise to 8%, which of the following is true?
    a. The value of the short-term loan will decrease by more than the value of the long-term loan due to the increase in the market interest rate.
    b. The value of the long-term loan will decrease by more than the value of the short-term loan due to the increase in the market interest rate.
    c. The value of both loans will increase by the same amount due to the increase in the market interest rate.
    d. The value of the short-term loan will decrease and the value of the long-term loan will increase due to the increase in the market interest rate.

Answers to Self-Test Questions

1. b
2. a
3. c
4. d
5. a
6. b
7. c
8. d
9. d
10. d
11. a
12. b

Chapter 6
Bonds

■ Key Learning Objectives

- Understand bond terminology
- Compute the price and yield to maturity of a zero-coupon bond
- Compute the price and yield to maturity of a coupon bond
- Analyze why bond prices change over time
- Know how credit risk affects the expected return from holding a corporate bond

■ Notation

CPN	coupon payment on a bond
FV	face value of a bond
n	number of periods
P	initial price of a bond
PV	present value
y	yield to maturity
YTM	yield to maturity
YTM_n	yield to maturity on a zero-coupon bond with n periods to maturity

■ Chapter Synopsis

Governments and companies issue bonds to finance long-term projects. The price investors pay to buy these bonds acts as a loan to the issuer. The Valuation Principle implies that the price of a security in a competitive market should be the present value of the cash flows an investor will receive from owning it. Therefore, pricing bonds gives us an opportunity to apply what we have learned in the last three chapters about valuing cash flows using market rates.

6.1 Bond Terminology

Bonds are securities sold by governments and corporations to raise money from investors today in exchange for promised future payments. The terms of the bond are described as part of the **bond certificate,** which indicates the amounts and dates of all payments to be made. Payments on the bond are made until a final repayment date called the **maturity date** of the bond. The time remaining until the repayment date is known as the **term** of the bond.

Bonds typically make two types of payments to their holders: interest payments known as **coupons** and the **face value** (or **par value**) that is paid at maturity. The amount of each coupon payment, CPN, is:

$$CPN = \frac{\text{Coupon Rate} \times \text{Face Value}}{\text{Number of Coupon Payments per Year}}$$

6.2 Zero-Coupon Bonds

A **zero-coupon bond** is a bond that does not make coupon payments. The only cash payment the investor receives is the face value of the bond on the maturity date. Prior to its maturity date, the price of a zero-coupon bond is always less than its face value. That is, zero-coupon bonds always trade at a discount (a price lower than the face value), so they are also called **pure discount bonds.** Although the bond pays no "interest" directly, as an investor you are compensated for the time value of your money by purchasing the bond at a discount to its face value.

The IRR of an investment in a bond is given a special name, the **yield to maturity (YTM)** or just the *yield*. The yield to maturity of a bond is the discount rate that sets the present value of the promised bond payments equal to the current market price of the bond.

Suppose a one-year, risk-free, zero-coupon bond with a $1000 face value sells for $960. We can calculate the yield to maturity on this bond as:

$$960 = \frac{1000}{1+\text{YTM}_1} \Rightarrow 1+\text{YTM}_1 = \frac{1000}{960} = 1.0417$$

Therefore, the yield to maturity for this bond is 4.17%. The formula to find the yield to maturity on an *n*-year zero-coupon bond is:

$$1+\text{YTM}_n = \left(\frac{\text{Face Value}}{\text{Price}}\right)^{1/n}$$

6.3 Coupon Bonds

In addition to paying investors their face value at maturity, coupon bonds make regular coupon interest payments. The return on a coupon bond comes from two sources: (1) any difference between the purchase price and the principal value, and (2) its periodic coupon payments. To compute the yield to maturity of a coupon bond, we need to know all of its cash flows. The yield to maturity is the single discount rate that equates the present value of the bond's remaining cash flows to its current price, as shown in the following timeline:

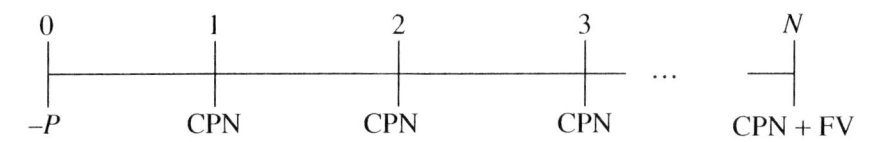

```
0           1           2           3     ...     N
|           |           |           |             |
-P         CPN         CPN         CPN        CPN + FV
```

Because the coupon payments represent an annuity, the yield to maturity is the interest rate *y* that solves the following equation:

$$P = \underbrace{\text{CPN} \times \overbrace{\frac{1}{y}\left(1-\frac{1}{(1+y)^N}\right)}^{\text{Annuity Factor using the YTM }(y)}}_{\text{Present Value of all of the periodic coupon payments}} + \underbrace{\frac{FV}{(1+y)^N}}_{\substack{\text{Present Value of the} \\ \text{Face Value repayment} \\ \text{using the YTM }(y)}}$$

Trial and error must be used to solve for yield to maturity. The yield we find will be a rate per coupon interval. This yield is typically stated as an annual rate by multiplying it by the number of coupons per year, thereby converting it to an APR with the same compounding interval as the coupon rate.

6.4 Why Bond Prices Change

Most issuers of coupon bonds choose a coupon rate so that the bonds will initially trade at, or very close to, par. However, once it is issued, the market price of a bond generally changes over time.

For a bond to sell at par, the interest rate it pays (the coupon rate) must be exactly equal to the yield to maturity demanded by investors. As interest rates in the economy fluctuate, the yields that investors demand to invest in bonds will also change. As interest rates rise, investors demand a higher yield to maturity. Since they apply a higher discount rate for a bond's remaining cash flows, the present value of the cash flows is reduced and the bond price falls. Therefore, *as interest rates and bond yields rise, bond prices will fall, and vice versa. Interest rates and bond prices always move in the opposite direction.*

As the next payment from a bond grows nearer, the price of the bond increases to reflect the increasing present value of that cash flow. Immediately after a coupon payment is made, the bond price will fall because the purchaser of the bond will not receive that coupon payment. This pattern—slowly rising as a coupon payment nears and then dropping abruptly after the payment is made—continues for the life of the bond.

While the effect of time on bond prices is predictable, unpredictable changes in interest rates will also affect bond prices. Further, bonds with different characteristics will respond differently to changes in interest rates—some bonds will react more strongly than others. Longer-term bonds will respond more to a given change in interest rates than a shorter-term bond will. Bonds with higher coupon rates—because they pay higher cash flows upfront—are less sensitive to interest rate changes than otherwise identical bonds with lower coupon rates. Bond traders are more concerned about changes in the bond's price that arise due to changes in the bond's yield, rather than these predictable patterns around coupon payments. As a result, they often do not quote the price of a bond in terms of its actual cash price, which is also called the **dirty price** or **invoice price** of the bond. Bonds are usually quoted in terms of a **clean price**, which is the bond's cash price less an adjustment for accrued interest, the amount of the next coupon payment that has already accrued:

$$\text{Clean Price} = \text{Cash (dirty) Price} - \text{Accrued Interest}$$

$$\text{Accrued Interest} = \text{Coupon Amount} \times \left(\frac{\text{days since last coupon payment}}{\text{days in current coupon period}} \right)$$

6.5 Corporate Bonds

Corporate bonds are bonds issued by corporations. There is a chance that the bond issuers may default; that is, the corporation may not pay back the full amount promised in the bond prospectus. This risk of default is known as the **credit risk** of the bond. While corporations may default, there is virtually no chance that the U.S. government will fail to pay interest and default on U.S. Treasury securities. To compensate for the risk that companies may default, investors demand a higher interest rate on corporate bonds than the rate on U.S. Treasuries. Therefore, investors pay less for bonds with credit risk than they would for an otherwise identical default-free bond.

The yield to maturity of a defaultable bond is not equal to the expected return of investing in the bond. The promised cash flows used to determine the yield to maturity are always higher than the expected cash flows investors use to calculate the expected return. As a result, the yield to maturity will always be higher than the expected return of investing in the bond. *Moreover, a higher yield to maturity does not necessarily imply that a bond's expected return is higher.*

Standard & Poor's and Moody's rate bonds, provide assistance to investors in assessing the creditworthiness of a particular bond issue. Bonds in the top four categories are referred to as **investment-grade bonds** because of their low-default risk. Bonds in the bottom five categories are called **speculative bonds, junk bonds,** or **high-yield bonds** because their likelihood of default is high.

■ Selected Concepts and Key Terms

Coupons, Coupon Rate

Coupons are periodic interest payments on a bond. The amount of each coupon payment is determined by the **coupon rate** of the bond. By convention, the coupon rate of the bond is expressed as an APR, so the amount of each coupon payment equals:

$$\text{CPN} = \frac{\text{Coupon Rate} \times \text{Face Value}}{\text{Number of Coupon Payments per Year}}$$

Zero-Coupon Bonds

A **zero-coupon bond** makes no coupon payments, so the only payment the investor receives is the face value of the bond on the maturity date. These bonds are called **pure discount bonds** because their market price will always be lower than their face value.

Treasury Bills, Notes, and Bonds

Treasury securities are issued by the U.S. Treasury. **Treasury bills** have original maturities less than one year and are zero-coupon bonds that are sold at a discount. **Treasury notes** have original maturities from one to ten years, and **Treasury bonds** have original maturities of more than ten years. Typically, Treasury notes and bonds make semiannual coupon payments.

Corporate Bonds

Corporate bonds are issued by corporations. When a bond issuer does not make a bond payment in full, the issuer has **defaulted**. The risk that default can occur is called **default** or **credit risk**. The expected return of a corporate bond, which is the firm's debt cost of capital, equals the **risk-free rate of interest** plus a **risk premium**. The difference between yields on Treasury securities and yields on corporate bonds is called the **credit spread** or **default spread**.

The **expected return** on a corporate bond is less than the bond's **yield to maturity** because the yield to maturity of a bond is calculated using the promised cash flows, not the expected cash flows.

Bond Ratings

Bond ratings summarize the creditworthiness of bonds for investors. **Investment-grade bonds** are rated BBB and above by Standard & Poor's or Baa and above by Moody's; these bonds have low-default risk. **High-yield** or **junk bonds** have relatively high-default risk; they are rated below BBB by Standard & Poor's or below Baa by Moody's.

Maturity Date

A bond repays its face value on the **maturity date.**

Face Value

The **face value** or **par value** of a bond is the amount the bond pays at is maturity date. If a bond is selling at a price greater than its face value, it is said to be selling at a **premium.** If a bond is selling at a price less than its face value, it is said to be selling at a **discount.**

Yield to Maturity (YTM)

A bond's **yield to maturity** is the discount rate that sets the present value of the promised bond payments equal to the current market price of the bond. This is the bond's internal rate of return.

Why Bond Prices Change

A bond will trade at a **premium** if its coupon rate exceeds its yield to maturity. It will trade at a **discount** if its coupon rate is less than its yield to maturity. If a bond's coupon rate equals its yield to maturity, it trades at **par**. As a bond approaches maturity, the price of the bond approaches its face value.

When interest rates rise, bond prices fall, and vice versa. Long-term zero-coupon bonds are more sensitive to changes in interest rates than are short-term zero-coupon bonds. Bonds with low coupon rates are more sensitive to changes in interest rates than similar maturity bonds with high coupon rates.

■ Concept Check Questions and Answers

1. What types of cash flows does a bond buyer receive?

   The cash flows that a bond buyer receives are the coupon payments and the par value at maturity.

2. How are the periodic interest payments on a bond determined?

   The periodic interest payments on a bond are determined by multiplying the coupon rate by the bond's par value, and dividing by the number of coupon payments per year.

3. Why would you want to know the yield to maturity of a bond?

   The yield to maturity of a bond is the internal rate of return that an investor earns on the bond by holding the bond to maturity.

4. What is the relationship between a bond's price and its yield to maturity?

   The bond's price and yield to maturity are inversely related.

5. What cash flows does a company pay to investors holding its coupon bonds?

   Companies pay bond investors regular coupon payments and the par value at maturity.

6. What do we need in order to value a coupon bond?

   In order to value a bond, we need to know the cash flows that will occur and the interest rate to use to discount those cash flows. For a coupon bond, the coupon rate multiplied by the face value of the bond gives us the periodic cash flows and the face value of the bond will occur at the bond's maturity.

7. Why do interest rates and bond prices move in opposite directions?

   Bond prices and interest rates move in opposite directions because the interest rates are used to discount the future cash flows of the bond. Thus, when interest rates increase, the present value of the cash flows decreases.

8. **If a bond's yield to maturity does not change, how does its cash price change between coupon payments?**

   The accrued interest changes as a bond moves from one coupon payment to the next. It is this accrued interest that causes a bond's price to increase between coupon payments, even if the yield to maturity stays constant.

9. **What is a junk bond?**

   A junk bond, also known as a speculative bond, is a bond rated BB or lower by Standard and Poor's or Ba or lower by Moody's.

10. **How will the yield to maturity of a bond vary with the bond's risk of default?**

    The yield to maturity will increase as a bond's risk of default increases, as investors want to be compensated for taking additional risk with their investment.

■ Examples with Step-by-Step Solutions

Yields for Different Maturities

6.1 Problem: Suppose the following table summarizes prices of zero-coupon U.S. Treasury securities per $100 of face value. Determine the corresponding yield to maturity for each bond.

Maturity	1 Year	2 Years	3 Years	4 Years
Price	$98.04	$93.35	$86.38	$79.21

Solution

Plan: The table gives the prices and number of years to maturity and the face value is $100 per bond. We can solve for the YTM of the bonds using the formula:

$$1 + YTM_n = \left(\frac{\text{Face Value}}{\text{Price}}\right)^{1/n}$$

Execute: Solving for YTM for each of the four securities, we get:

$$1 + YTM_1 = \left(\frac{100}{98.04}\right)^{\frac{1}{1}} = 1.02 \Rightarrow YTM_1 = 2.0\%$$

$$1 + YTM_2 = \left(\frac{100}{93.35}\right)^{\frac{1}{2}} = 1.035 \Rightarrow YTM_2 = 3.5\%$$

$$1 + YTM_3 = \left(\frac{100}{86.38}\right)^{\frac{1}{3}} = 1.050 \Rightarrow YTM_3 = 5.0\%$$

$$1 + YTM_4 = \left(\frac{100}{79.21}\right)^{\frac{1}{4}} = 1.060 \Rightarrow YTM_4 = 6.0\%$$

Evaluate: The YTM is the internal rate of return of buying the bond. For example, for the security that matures in four years, discounting a $100 cash flow that will occur in four years at a discount rate of 6% results in a present value of $79.21.

Chapter 6 Bonds   85

Computing the Price of a Zero-Coupon Bond

6.2 Problem: If the yield to maturity is 6%, what is the price of a three-year risk-free zero-coupon bond with a face value of $1000?

Solution

Plan: We can compute the bond's price as the present value of its face amount. The discount rate is the bond's yield to maturity.

Execute: $P = 1000(1.06)^3 = 839.62$

Evaluate: We calculate the price of a zero-coupon bond by computing the present value of the face amount using the bond's yield to maturity. An investor who pays $839.62 for three-year zero-coupon bond with a face value of $1000 will have a yield to maturity of 6%.

The Cash Flows of a Coupon Bond or Note

6.3 Problem: Suppose it is February 15, 2009 and the U.S. Treasury has just issued bonds with a February 2013 maturity, $10,000 par value, and a 6% coupon rate with semiannual coupons. The first coupon payment will be paid on August 15, 2009. What cash flows will you receive if you hold this bond until maturity?

Solution

Plan: The description of the bond should be sufficient to determine all of its cash flows. The phrase "February 2013 maturity, $10,000 par value" tells us that this is a bond with a face value of $10,000 and 4 years to maturity. The phrase "6% coupon rate with semiannual coupons" tells us that the bond pays a total of 6% of its face value each year in two equal semiannual installments. Finally, we know that the first coupon is paid on August 15, 2009.

Execute: The face value of this bond is $10,000. Because this bond pays coupons semiannually, you will receive a coupon payment every 6 months of CPN = $10,000 × 6/2 = $300. Here is the timeline based on a 6-month period.

Date	Feb 15 2009	Aug 15 2009	Feb 15 2010	Aug 15 2010	Feb 15 2011	Aug 15 2011	Feb 15 2012	Aug 15 2012	Feb 15 2013
Period	0	1	2	3	4	5	6	7	8
Cash Flow		300	300	300	300	300	300	300	300 + 10,000

Note that the last payment occurs four years (8 six-month periods) from now and is composed of both a coupon payment of $300 and the face value payment of $10,000.

Evaluate: Since a bond is just a package of cash flows, we need to know those cash flows in order to value the bond. The description of the bond contains all of the information we would need to construct its cash flow timeline.

Computing the Yield to Maturity of a Coupon Bond

6.4 Problem: Consider the four-year, $10,000 bond with a 6% coupon rate and semiannual coupons described in Example 6.2. If this bond is currently trading for a price of $10,358.51, what is the bond's yield to maturity?

Solution

Plan: We worked out the bond's cash flows in Example 6.2. From the cash flow timeline, we can see that the bond consists of an annuity of eight payments of $300, paid every 6 months, and one lump-sum payment of $10,000 in four years (eight six-month periods). The problem states that the price of the bond is $10,358.51. We can use the following equation to solve for the yield:

$$P = CPN \times \frac{1}{y}\left(1 - \frac{1}{(1+y)^N}\right) + \frac{FV}{(1+y)^N}$$

We must use six-month intervals consistently throughout the equation.

Execute: Because the bond has eight remaining coupon payments, we compute its yield y by solving:

$$\$10,358.51 = 300 \times \frac{1}{y}\left(1 - \frac{1}{(1+y)^8}\right) + \frac{10,000}{(1+y)^8}$$

Solving by trial-and-error, we find that $y = 2.5\%$. Because the bond pays coupons semiannually, this yield is for a 6 month period. We convert it to an APR by multiplying by the number of coupon payments per year. Thus, the bond has a yield to maturity equal to $2.5\% \times 2 = 5\%$ APR with semiannual compounding.

We can also solve for the yield using a financial calculator.

	N	I/Y	PV	PMT	FV
Given:	8		−10,358.51	300	10,000
Solve for:		2.5			

We must remember that the 2.5% that the calculator shows is for a six month period. We must convert it to an APR by multiplying by the number of periods within each year. This bond has a yield to maturity of $2.5\% \times 2 = 5\%$ APR with semiannual compounding.

Evaluate: As the equation shows, the yield to maturity is the discount rate that equates the present value of the bond's cash flows with its price. This bond is selling for a premium above par. The coupon rate exceeds the yield to maturity of the bond.

Computing a Bond Price from Its Yield to Maturity

6.5 Problem: Consider again the four-year, $10,000 bond with a 6% coupon rate and semiannual coupons in Example 6.2. Suppose you are told that its yield to maturity has increased to 7% (expressed as an APR with semiannual compounding). What price is the bond trading for now? What is the effective annual yield on the bond?

Chapter 6 Bonds

Solution

Plan: A 7.0% APR is equivalent to a semiannual rate of 3.5%. The cash flows of this bond are an annuity of eight payments of $300, paid every six months, and one lump-sum cash flow of $10,000 paid in four years (eight six-month periods). We can solve for the price of the bond using the equation:

$$P = CPN \times \frac{1}{y}\left(1 - \frac{1}{(1+y)^N}\right) + \frac{FV}{(1+y)^N}$$

To calculate the effective annual yield using the bond's yield to maturity expressed as an APR we use the formula:

$$\text{Effective Annual Yield} = \left(1 + \frac{APR}{n}\right)^n - 1$$

Execute: Using the equation and the 6-month yield of 3.5%, the bond price must be:

$$P = 300 \times \frac{1}{.035}\left(1 - \frac{1}{(1+.035)^8}\right) + \frac{10,000}{(1+.035)^8}$$

$$= 2062.19 + 7594.12 = 9656.31$$

The price of the bond can also be calculated using a financial calculator:

	N	I/Y	PV	PMT	FV
Given:	8	3.5		300	10,000
Solve for:			9656.30		

The effective annual rate is:

$$\text{Effective Annual Yield} = \left(1 + \frac{0.07}{2}\right)^2 - 1 = 7.12\%$$

Evaluate: The bond's price is $9656.31 (the penny difference when using the financial calculator is due to rounding differences) when the cash flows the investor will receive are discounted at a 7% APR. This bond is selling at a discount from par. The coupon rate is below the yield to maturity.

Determining the Discount or Premium of a Coupon Bond

6.6 Problem: Consider three 20-year bonds with annual coupon payments. One bond has a 9% coupon rate, one has a 7% coupon rate, and one has a 5% coupon rate. If the yield to maturity of each bond is 7%, what is the price of each bond per $100 face value? Which bond trades at a premium, which trades at a discount, and which trades at par?

Solution

Plan: From the description of the bonds, we can determine their cash flows. Each bond has 20 years to maturity and pays its coupons annually. Therefore, each bond has an annuity of coupon payments, paid annually for 20 years, and then the face value paid as a lump sum in 20 years. They are all priced so that their yield to maturity is 7%, meaning that 7% is the discount rate that equates the present value of the cash flows to the price of the bond. The coupon payment will vary for each bond; the coupon payment will be 100 multiplied by the coupon rate.

We will use the following equation to solve for the price of each bond:

$$P = CPN \times \frac{1}{y}\left(1 - \frac{1}{(1+y)^N}\right) + \frac{FV}{(1+y)^N}$$

Execute: For the 9% coupon bond, the annuity cash flows are $9 per year (9% of each $100 face value). Similarly, the annuity cash flows for the 7% and 5% bonds are $7 and $5 per year. We use a $100 face value for all of the bonds.

Using these cash flows, the bond prices are:

$$P(9\% \text{ coupon bond}) = 9 \times \frac{1}{.07}\left(1 - \frac{1}{(1+.07)^{20}}\right) + \frac{100}{(1+.07)^{20}}$$
$$= 95.35 + 25.84$$
$$= 121.19$$

$$P(7\% \text{ coupon bond}) = 7 \times \frac{1}{.07}\left(1 - \frac{1}{(1+.07)^{20}}\right) + \frac{100}{(1+.07)^{20}}$$
$$= 74.16 + 25.84$$
$$= 100$$

$$P(5\% \text{ coupon bond}) = 5 \times \frac{1}{.07}\left(1 - \frac{1}{(1+.07)^{20}}\right) + \frac{100}{(1+.07)^{20}}$$
$$= 52.97 + 25.84$$
$$= 78.81$$

The prices for these bonds can also be calculated using a financial calculator:

9% bond:

	N	I/Y	PV	PMT	FV
Given:	20	7		9	100
Solve for:			121.19		

7% bond:

	N	I/Y	PV	PMT	FV
Given:	20	7		7	100
Solve for:			100.00		

5% bond:

	N	I/Y	PV	PMT	FV
Given:	20	7		5	100
Solve for:			78.81		

Evaluate: The 9% coupon bond trades at a premium, the 7% coupon bond trades at par, and the 5% coupon bond trades at a discount. The prices reveal that when the coupon rate of the bond is higher than its yield to maturity, it trades at a premium. When its coupon rate equals its yield to maturity, it trades at par. When its coupon rate is lower than its yield to maturity, it trades at a discount.

The Effect of Time on the Price of a Bond

6.7 Problem: Suppose you purchase a 25-year, zero-coupon bond with a yield to maturity of 8%. For a face value of $100, the bond will initially trade for:

$$P(25\text{ years to maturity}) = \frac{100}{1.08^{25}}$$
$$= 14.60$$

If the bond's yield to maturity remains at 8%, what will its price be 10 years later? If you purchased the bond at $14.60 and sold it 10 years later, what would the IRR of your investment be?

Solution

Plan: If the bond was originally a 25-year bond and 10 years have passed, then it has 15 years left to maturity. If the yield to maturity does not change, then we can compute the price of the bond with 15 years left exactly as we did for 25 years, but using 15 years of discounting instead of 25.

Once we have the price in 10 years, we can compute the IRR of the investment. The cash flows that we would have from the investment would be the initial cash outflow of 14.60 and then the cash inflow that we would receive in Year 10 when we sold the bond.

Period	0	1	2	3	4	5	6	7	8	9	10
Cash Flow	−14.6										+ price of bond in Year 10

Execute: First, we calculate the price of the bond in Year 10; remember the bond still has 15 years until maturity.

$$P(15\text{ years to maturity}) = \frac{100}{1.08^{15}}$$
$$= 31.52$$

If you purchased the bond for $14.60 and then sold it after five years for $31.52, the IRR of your investment would be:

$$\left(\frac{31.52}{14.60}\right)^{\frac{1}{10}} - 1 = 8\%$$

Evaluate: Your IRR is exactly the same as the yield to maturity on the bond. The bond price is higher, and hence the discount from its face value is smaller, when there is less time to maturity. The discount shrinks because the yield has not changed, but there is less time until the face value will be received. This example illustrates a more general property for bonds. If a bond's yield to maturity does not change, then the IRR of an investment in the bond equals its yield to maturity even if you sell the bond early.

The Interest Rate Sensitivity of Bonds

6.8 **Problem:** Consider a five-year coupon bond with 10% annual coupons with a $1000 face value. How much will the price of the bond change if its yield to maturity decreases from 5% to 4%? What is the percentage change in the price?

Solution

Plan: We need to compute the price of the bond for each yield to maturity and then calculate the percentage change in the prices. The cash flows are $100 per year for 5 years and then the $1000 face value is repaid at maturity. The timeline for this problem looks like this:

Period	0	1	2	3	4	5
Cash Flow		100	100	100	100	100 + 1000

First, we need to discount these cash flows using a 5% discount rate to get the price the bond will sell for if the yield to maturity is 5%. Next, we need to discount these cash flows using a 4% discount rate to get the price the bond will sell for if the yield to maturity is 4%. Once we have these two prices, we can calculate the percentage change in the two prices.

Execute: We calculate the price of the bond with a 5% yield to maturity as:

$$P(\text{at a } 5\% \text{ YTM}) = 100 \times \frac{1}{.05}\left(1 - \frac{1}{(1+.05)^5}\right) + \frac{1000}{(1+.05)^5}$$

$$= 432.95 + 783.53$$

$$= 1216.48$$

Or using a financial calculator:

	N	I/Y	PV	PMT	FV
Given:	5	5		100	1000
Solve for:			1216.47		

We calculate the price of the bond with a 4% yield to maturity as:

$$P(\text{at a } 4\% \text{ YTM}) = 100 \times \frac{1}{.04}\left(1 - \frac{1}{(1+.04)^5}\right) + \frac{1000}{(1+.04)^5}$$

$$= 445.18 + 821.93$$

$$= 1267.11$$

Or using a financial calculator:

	N	I/Y	PV	PMT	FV
Given:	5	4		100	1000
Solve for:			1267.11		

The price of the bond increases from $1216.48 to $1267.11 if its yield to maturity decreases from 5% to 4%. This is a percentage change of:

$$\% \text{change} = \frac{1267.11 - 1216.48}{1216.48}$$
$$= \frac{50.63}{1216.48}$$
$$= 4.16\%$$

Evaluate: A lower yield to maturity resulted in a higher bond price. When the yield to maturity decreased from 5% to 4%, the price of the bond increased by 4.16%.

Interest Rate Sensitivity and Time to Maturity

6.9 Problem: Consider a 20-year coupon bond with 10% annual coupons and a $1000 face value. How much will the price of the bond change if its yield to maturity decreases from 5% to 4%? What is the percentage change in the price? How does this compare to the results you had for the five-year bond in Example 6.7?

Solution

Plan: We need to compute the price of the bond for each yield to maturity and then calculate the percentage change in the prices. The cash flows are $100 per year for 20 years and then the $1000 face value repaid at maturity. First, we need to discount these cash flows using a 5% discount rate to get the price the bond will sell for if the yield to maturity is 5%. Next, we need to discount these cash flows using a 4% discount rate to get the price the bond will sell for if the yield to maturity is 4%. Once we have these two prices, we can calculate the percentage change in the two prices.

Execute: We calculate the price of the bond with a 5% yield to maturity as:

$$P(\text{at a 5\% YTM}) = 100 \times \frac{1}{.05}\left(1 - \frac{1}{(1+.05)^{20}}\right) + \frac{1000}{(1+.05)^{20}}$$
$$= 1246.22 + 376.89$$
$$= 1623.11$$

We calculate the price of the bond with a 4% yield to maturity as:

$$P(\text{at a 4\% YTM}) = 100 \times \frac{1}{.04}\left(1 - \frac{1}{(1+.04)^{20}}\right) + \frac{1000}{(1+.04)^{20}}$$
$$= 1359.03 + 456.39$$
$$= 1815.42$$

The price of the bond increases from $1623.11 to $1815.42 if its yield to maturity decreases from 5% to 4%. This is a percentage change of:

$$\% \text{change} = \frac{1815.42 - 1623.11}{1623.11}$$
$$= \frac{192.31}{1623.11}$$
$$= 11.85\%$$

Evaluate: A lower yield to maturity resulted in a higher bond price. When the yield to maturity decreased from 5% to 4%, the price of the bond increased by 11.85%. The price of the 20-year bond in this problem increased by a larger percentage amount than the five-year bond in Example 6.7 did. This highlights the principle that longer-term bonds have greater interest rate sensitivity than shorter-term bonds.

Credit Spreads and Bond Prices

6.10 Problem: Your firm has a credit rating of A. You notice that the credit spread for 10-year maturity debt is 75 basis points (0.75%). Your firm's 10-year debt has a coupon rate of 6%, with interest paid semiannually. You see that new 10-year Treasury notes are being issued at par with a coupon rate of 4.75%. What should the price of your outstanding 10-year bonds be?

Solution

Plan: If the credit spread is 75 basis points, then the yield to maturity (YTM) on your debt should be the YTM on similar Treasuries plus 0.75%. The fact that new 10-year Treasuries are being issued at par with coupons of 4.75% means that with a coupon rate of 4.75%, these notes are selling for $100 per $100 face value. Thus, their YTM is 4.75% and your debt's YTM should be 4.75% + 0.75% = 5.5%. The cash flows on your bonds are $6 per year for every $100 face value, paid as $3.00 every six months. The six-month rate corresponding to a 5.5% yield is 5.5%/2 = 2.75%. You will use the formula:

$$P = CPN \times \frac{1}{y}\left(1 - \frac{1}{(1+y)^N}\right) + \frac{FV}{(1+y)^N}$$

Execute:

$$P = 3 \times \frac{1}{.0275}\left(1 - \frac{1}{(1+.0275)^{20}}\right) + \frac{100}{(1+.0275)^{20}}$$

$$= 45.68 + 58.13$$

$$= 103.81$$

Evaluate: Your bonds offer a higher coupon (6% vs. 4.75%) than Treasuries of the same maturity. Since your firm's debt has a higher probability of default, lenders demand a higher yield to maturity on your debt. If your debt paid 5.5% coupons it would sell at $100. Since your coupon rate is higher than 5.5%, your bonds will sell at a premium. At the price of $103.81, the yield to maturity on your bonds is 5.5%, which represents the 75 basis points above the Treasury yield to maturity of 4.75%.

Coupons and Interest Rate Sensitivity

6.11 Problem: Consider a five-year coupon bond with 6% annual coupons and a $1000 face value. How much will the price of the bond change if its yield to maturity decreases from 5% to 4%? What is the percentage change in the price? How does this change compare to the change that occurred to the price of the 5% coupon bond in Example 6.7 when the yield to maturity decreased by the same amount?

Solution

Plan: As in Example 6.7, we need to compute the price of the bond at 5% and 4% yield to maturities, and then compute the percentage change in price. The bond has five annual coupon payments of $60 remaining along with the repayment of par value at maturity.

Execute: We calculate the price of the bond with a 5% yield to maturity as:

$$P(\text{ata 5\% YTM}) = 60 \times \frac{1}{.05}\left(1 - \frac{1}{(1+.05)^5}\right) + \frac{1000}{(1+.05)^5}$$
$$= 259.77 + 783.53$$
$$= 1043.30$$

We calculate the price of the bond with a 4% yield to maturity as:

$$P(\text{ata 4\% YTM}) = 60 \times \frac{1}{.04}\left(1 - \frac{1}{(1+.04)^5}\right) + \frac{1000}{(1+.04)^5}$$
$$= 267.11 + 821.93$$
$$= 1089.04$$

The bond price increased from $1043.30 to $1089.04 when the yield to maturity dropped from 5% to 4%. In terms of a percentage change this is:

$$\% \text{ change in price} = \frac{1089.04 - 1043.30}{1043.30}$$
$$= 4.38\%$$

Evaluate: The bond with the smaller coupon payments is more sensitive to changes in interest rates. Because its coupons are smaller relative to its par value, a larger fraction of its cash flows are received later. As we learned in Example 6.8, later cash flows are affected more greatly by changes in interest rates, so compared to the 10% coupon bond, the effect of the interest change is greater on the cash flows of the 5% bond.

■ Questions and Problems

1. Consider a 10-year bond with a face value of $1000 that has a coupon rate of 8%, with semiannual payments.
   a. What is the coupon payment for this bond?
   b. Draw the cash flows for the bond on a timeline.

2. Suppose a 10-year, $1000 bond with a 6% coupon rate and semiannual coupons is trading at a price of $1163.51.
   a. What is the bond's yield to maturity (expressed as an APR with semiannual compounding)?
   b. If the bond's yield to maturity changes to 7% APR, what will the bond's price be?

3. Several major companies like Citigroup, Disney, and AT&T have issued Century Bonds. These bonds pay regular semiannual coupons, but do not mature until 100 years after they are issued. Some critics have stated that they are extremely risky because you cannot predict what will happen to the companies in 100 years. Assume that such bonds were just issued with a $1000 par value and an 8% semiannual coupon rate.
   a. If current market rates are 8%, what is the present value of the principal repayment at maturity?
   b. What is the total value today of the final 40 years (years 61–100) of payments, including coupons and principal?

4. Suppose that Ford has a B-rated bond with exactly 30 years until maturity, a face value of $1000, and a semiannual coupon rate of 6%. The yield to maturity on B-rated bonds today is 10%.
   a. What is the price of the bond today?
   b. Assuming the yield to maturity remains constant, what is the price of the bond immediately before and after it makes its next coupon payment?

5. The following table summarizes the yields to maturity on several one-year, zero-coupon bonds:

Bond	% Yield
Treasury	4.1
AA Corporate	4.8
BBB Corporate	6.2
CCC Corporate	10.5

   a. What is the value of a one-year, $1000 face value, zero-coupon corporate bond with a CCC rating?
   b. What is the credit spread on AA-rated corporate bonds?
   c. What is the credit spread on BBB-rated corporate bonds?

6. Lighthouse Entertainment is considering issuing a 20-year bond with a coupon rate of 6% (annual coupon payments) and a face value of $1000. In the past, the company has been able to receive a BB rating on its debt. Currently, the yield on BB-rated bonds is 5.9%. Lighthouse has recently had strong earnings and growth, so the company is hopeful that it will now be able to receive a BBB rating. Yields on BBB-rated bonds are currently 5.3%.
   a. What is the price of the bond if Lighthouse continues to receive a BB rating for the bond issue?
   b. What will the price be if Lighthouse is able to receive a BBB rating for its new issue?

■ Solutions to Questions and Problems

1. a. Each coupon payment will be $1000 × 0.08/2 = $40.
   b. The timeline for cash flows looks like:

Year	1		2		3		4		5		6		7		8		9		10	
Period	0	1	2	3	4	5	6	7	8	9	10	11	12	13	14	15	16	17	18	19	20
Cash Flow		40	40	40	40	40	40	40	40	40	40	40	40	40	40	40	40	40	40	40	40 + 1000

2. a.

$$P = CPN \times \frac{1}{y}\left(1 - \frac{1}{(1+y)^N}\right) + \frac{FV}{(1+y)^N}$$

$$1163.51 = 30 \times \frac{1}{y}\left(1 - \frac{1}{(1+y)^{20}}\right) + \frac{1000}{(1+y)^{20}} \Rightarrow y = 4$$

   b. If the YTM increases to 7%, then y in the equation above equals 3.5%, and the price will fall to $929.

3. a. $\dfrac{1000}{1.04^{200}} = \$0.39$

    b. $\dfrac{40\left[\dfrac{1}{0.04} - \dfrac{1}{0.04(1.04)^{80}}\right]}{(1.04)^{120}} + 0.39 = \dfrac{956.61}{110.66} = \$9.03$

4. a. $P = 30X\dfrac{1}{0.05}\left(1 - \dfrac{1}{(1.05)^{60}}\right) + \dfrac{1000}{1.05^{60}} = + = 567.88 + 53.54 = 5641.42$

    b. Before the next coupon payment, the price of the bond is:

    $P = 30X\dfrac{1}{0.05}\left(1 - \dfrac{1}{(1.05)^{59}}\right) + \dfrac{1000}{1.05^{59}} + 30 = 566.27 + 56.21 + 30 = 5652.48$

5. a. The price of this bond will be $P = 1000/1.105 = \$904.98$.
    b. The credit spread on AA-rated corporate bonds is $0.048 - 0.041 = 0.7\%$.
    c. The credit spread on BBB-rated corporate bonds is $0.062 - 0.041 = 2.1\%$.

6. a. The price of the BB rated bond with a 5.9% yield would be:

    $P = 60X\dfrac{1}{0.059}\left(1 - \dfrac{1}{(1.059)^{20}}\right) + \dfrac{1000}{1.059^{20}} = 693.82 + 317.75 = 1011.57$

    b. The price of a BBB rated bond with a 5.3% yield would be:

    $P = 60X\dfrac{1}{0.053}\left(1 - \dfrac{1}{(1.053)^{20}}\right) + \dfrac{1000}{1.053^{20}} = + = 729.07 + 355.99 = 1085.06$

■ Self-Test Questions

1. Callaway Enterprises issued a 6% coupon bond that has a bond with 10 years remaining to maturity. The yield to maturity on the bond is 5.3%. You know that
    a. this is a zero coupon bond.
    b. this bond will sell for a premium.
    c. this bond will sell for a discount.
    d. this bond has a negative risk premium.

2. Interest rates and bond prices
    a. always move in opposite directions.
    b. always move in the same direction.
    c. are uncorrelated.
    d. move in the same direction for zero-coupon bonds but in opposite directions for coupon bonds.

3. The _____ is a bond's cash price less an adjustment for accrued interest.
    a. Dirty price
    b. Clean price
    c. Invoice price
    d. Coupon price

4. As the time until the next coupon payment from a bond grows nearer,
   a. the price of the bond increases to reflect the increasing present value of that cash flow.
   b. the price of the bond decreases to reflect the decreasing present value of that cash flow.
   c. the price of the bond decreases to reflect the increasing present value of that cash flow.
   d. the clean price of the bond increases, the dirty price of the bond decreases, and the invoice price remains unchanged.

5. Which of the following is a TRUE statement?
   a. Investors pay more for bonds with credit risk than they would for an otherwise identical default-free bond.
   b. A higher yield to maturity implies that a bond's expected return is higher.
   c. The yield of bonds with credit risk will be higher than that of otherwise identical default-free bonds.
   d. The coupon rate on a bond is known as the "yield to maturity."

6. A 20-year, zero-coupon bond with a face value of $1000 is selling for $235.41. This bond's yield to maturity is:
   a. 4.2%
   b. 7.5%
   c. 9.4%
   d. 15.3%

7. If interest rates in the economy go up, which of the following bonds will respond the most?
   a. A five-year zero-coupon bond.
   b. A ten-year zero-coupon bond.
   c. A ten-year bond with a 4% coupon rate.
   d. An eight-year bond with a 4% coupon rate.

8. Consider a five-year, $10,000 bond with a 6% coupon rate and semiannual coupons. If its yield to maturity is 8% (expressed as an APR with semiannual compounding), what price will this bond be trading at?
   a. $6645
   b. $7782
   c. $8004
   d. $9189

9. Which of the following would be the best measure of the risk-free interest rate?
   a. The interest rate on U.S. Treasury bills.
   b. The interest rate on AAA corporate bonds.
   c. The yield to maturity on AAA corporate bonds.
   d. The expected yield on AAA corporate bonds.

10. Consider a 20-year, $1000 bond with an 8% coupon rate and semiannual coupons. If the bond is currently trading for $1231.15, what is the bond's yield to maturity (expressed as an APR with semiannual compounding)?
    a. 3%
    b. 4.5%
    c. 6%
    d. 7.5%

11. In which of the following situations would you be willing to pay a premium for a bond?
    a. It is a pure discount bond.
    b. It is a zero-coupon bond.
    c. Its coupon rate is greater than the current market interest rate on bonds with equivalent risk.
    d. Its coupon rate is less than the current market interest rate on bonds with equivalent risk.

12. The yield to maturity of a bond will increase as
    a. the risk of the bond increases.
    b. the price of the bond rises.
    c. market interest rates fall.
    d. the bond rating changes from BBB to A.

Answers to Self-Test Questions

1. b
2. a
3. b
4. a
5. c
6. b
7. b
8. d
9. a
10. c
11. c
12. a

■ Appendix A: Solving for the Yield to Maturity of a Bond Using a Financial Calculator

Problem: You are looking to purchase a three-year $1000 par, 5% annual coupon bond. Payments begin one year from now in November 2008. The relevant spot interest rates for these payments are given below. What is the yield to maturity of the bond?

Date	Yield
11/2008	4.39%
11/2009	4.84%
11/2010	5.20%

Solution

Plan: You must first calculate the price of the bond. The price of the bond is the present value of the cash flows you will receive discounted using the varying interest rates. Since the HP-10BII and the TI-BAII Plus Professional are unable to calculate the present value of a stream of cash flows with varying interest rates you will have to do this part by hand. Once you know the price of the bond you can then compute the yield to maturity using your financial calculator.

Execute: First, compute the price of the bond:

$$PV = \frac{50}{1.0439} + \frac{50}{(1.0484)^2} + \frac{1050}{(1.052)^3}$$
$$= \$47.90 + \$45.49 + \$901.87$$
$$= \$995.26$$

Now with the price of the bond in hand, you can compute the yield to maturity using your financial calculator.

	N	I/Y	PV	PMT	FV
Given:	3		−995.26	50	1000
Solve for:		5.17			

Evaluate: The price of the bond is the cash outflow you would need to make today in order to receive the cash flows promised in the bond contract in the future. If you spend $995.26 today to buy the bond, you will receive $50 a year for three years (an annuity) and a lump-sum payment of $1000 in three years. The IRR, or the interest rate that makes paying $995.26 exactly equivalent to receiving the promised cash flows in the future, is 5.17%.

■ Appendix B: The Yield Curve and the Law of One Price

It is possible to replicate the cash flows of a risk-free coupon bond using zero-coupon bonds. For example, a three-year, $1000 bond can be replicated with one-year, two-year, and three-year zero-coupon bonds. The Law of One Price states that the price of the portfolio of zero-coupon bonds must be the same as the price of the coupon bond. If the price of the coupon bond were lower, you could earn an arbitrage profit by buying the coupon bond and short selling the zero-coupon bonds.

The price of a risk-free coupon bond can also be found by discounting its cash flows using the risk-free zero-coupon yield using the following equation:

$$P = PV(\text{Bond Cash flows}) = \frac{CPN}{1+YTM_1} + \frac{CPN}{(1+YTM_x)^2} + \frac{CPN}{(1+YTM_3)^3} + \cdots + \frac{CPN+FV}{(1+YTM_N)^N}$$

where CPN is the bond coupon payment, YTM_n is the yield to maturity of a *zero-coupon* bond that matures at the same time as the nth coupon payment, and FV is the face value of the bond. Because we can determine the no-arbitrage price of a coupon bond by discounting its cash flows using the zero-coupon yields, the information in the zero-coupon yield curve is sufficient to price all other risk-free bonds.

Because a coupon bond provides cash flows at different points in time, the yield to maturity of a coupon bond is a weighted average of the yields of the zero-coupon bonds of equal and shorter maturities. The weights depend (in a complex way) on the magnitude of the cash flows each period. As the coupon increases, earlier cash flows become relatively more important than later cash flows in the calculation of the present value. The shape of the yield curve keys us in on trends with the yield to maturity:

1. If the yield curve is upward sloping, the resulting yield to maturity decreases with the coupon rate of the bond.

2. When the zero-coupon yield curve is downward sloping, the yield to maturity will increase with the coupon rate.

3. With a flat yield curve, all zero-coupon and coupon-paying bonds will have the same yield, independent of their maturities and coupon rates.

Chapter 7
Stock Valuation

■ Key Learning Objectives

- Describe the basics of common stock, preferred stock, and stock quotes
- Compare how trades are executed on the NYSE and NASDAQ
- Value a stock as the present value of its expected future dividends
- Understand the tradeoff between dividends and growth in stock valuation
- Appreciate the limitations of the valuing a stock based on expected dividends
- Value a stock as the present value of the company's total payout

■ Notation

Div_t	dividends paid in year t
EPS_t	earnings per share on date t
g	expected dividend growth rate
N	terminal date or forecast horizon
P_t	stock price at the end of year t
PV	present value
r_E	equity cost of capital

■ Chapter Synopsis

7.1 Stock Basics

Common stock is a share of ownership in a corporation which gives its owner rights to vote on the election of directors, mergers, or other major events. As owners of the company, shareholders have the right to share in the profits of the corporation through **dividends.** The shares also carry rights to vote to decide important matters, such as electing directors. If a company has **straight voting** each shareholder has as many votes for each director as shares held. With **cumulative voting** a shareholder's total vote allocation for all directors is equal to his or her number of shares multiplied by the number of open spots. Some companies issue **preferred stock,** which has preference over common stock in the payment of dividends and in liquidation, but carries no voting rights.

7.2 The Mechanics of Stock Trades

The NYSE has a physical trading location where **floor brokers** meet to negotiate the best execution prices for their clients. There is also a specialist for each stock on the NYSE who stands ready to buy at the quoted bid price and sell at the quoted ask price. NASDAQ is a computer network with no physical location. Stocks listed on NASDAQ have an average of 24 dealers making a market in the stock. These dealers maintain inventory in the stocks and post bid and ask quotes.

7.3 The Dividend-Discount Model

A stockholder generates cash flow from a stock by receiving dividends or from selling shares. An investor considering holding the stock for one year would be willing to pay:

$$P_0 = \frac{Div_1 + P_1}{1 + r_E}$$

Where Div_1 is the dividend paid in one year, P_1 is the stock price in one year, and r_E is the **equity cost of capital**, which is the expected rate of return available in the market on other investments with equivalent risk to the firm's shares. If the price was lower, it would be a positive NPV investment and investors would buy it, driving up the stock's price. If the price was greater than this amount, investors would sell and the price would fall.

Based on the one-year valuation equation, the equity cost of capital can be written as:

$$r_E = \frac{Div_1 + P_1}{P_0} - 1$$

$$= \frac{Div_1}{P_0} + \frac{P_1 - P_0}{P_0}$$

The stock's **dividend yield** is the percentage return the investor expects to earn from the dividend paid by the stock. The **capital gain rate** is the return the investor will earn based on the sale price minus the purchase price for the stock. The sum of the dividend yield and the capital gain rate is the total return of the stock.

All investors (with the same beliefs) will attach the same value to a stock, independent of their investment horizons because they can sell the stock at any date for the present value of the remaining dividends. Thus, how long they intend to hold the stock, and whether they collect their return in the form of dividends or capital gains, is irrelevant. Thus the value of a stock is:

$$P_0 = \frac{Div_1}{1 + r_E} + \frac{Div_2}{(1 + r_E)^2} + \frac{Div_3}{(1 + r_E)^3} + \cdots + \frac{Div_N}{(1 + r_E)^N} + \frac{P_N}{(1 + r_E)^N}$$

7.4 Estimating Dividends in the Dividend-Discount Model

The simplest forecast for the firm's future dividends is that they will grow at a constant rate, g, forever. Using this forecast, the expected dividends are a constant growth perpetuity, and the value of the dividend stream can be determined as:

$$P_0 = \frac{Div_1}{r_E - g}$$

This equation is known as the **constant dividend growth model.** This equation can be rewritten as:

$$r_E = \frac{Div_1}{P_0} + g$$

Written this way, the equation shows that the expected return on the stock investment equals the dividend yield plus the dividend growth rate. As we saw earlier, the expected return on the stock equals the dividend yield plus the capital gains yield. Therefore, with constant expected dividend growth, the growth rate of the dividends equals the growth rate of the share price.

The firm's stock price will increase if the current dividend level, D_1, increases or if the expected growth rate, g, increases. While a firm would like to increase both D_1 and g, the firm faces a trade-off: increase dividends or use the money to undertake investments that will lead to higher growth. Cutting the dividend to increase spending on investment will raise the stock price of the company, if, and only if, the new investments generate a return greater than their cost of capital.

7.5 Limitations of the Dividend-Discount Model

One major limitation of the dividend-discount model is its reliance on dividend forecasts given that a firm's future dividends carry a tremendous amount of uncertainty. A second major limitation is the lack of applicability to non dividend-paying stocks.

7.6 Share Repurchases and the Total Payout Model

In a **share repurchase** a company uses excess cash to buy back its own stock. The more cash a company uses to repurchase shares, the less cash it has to pay dividends. However, by repurchasing shares, the firm increases its earnings and dividends on a per-share basis because of the lower share count.

The **total payout model** discounts the total payouts that the firm makes to shareholders, which equals that total amount spent on both dividends and share repurchases, and then divides by the current number of shares outstanding to determine the share price. While this method is more reliable when the firm's future share repurchases can be forecasted, this is often difficult to do.

■ Selected Concepts and Key Terms

Common Stock

Ownership in a corporation is divided into shares of **stock.** These shares carry rights to share in the profits of the firm through future **dividend payments.** The stock of publicly traded companies is identified through a special abbreviation called a **ticker symbol.**

Capital Gain

The difference between the selling price of a share of stock and the price at which the investor purchased the stock is known as a **capital gain.** The **capital gain rate** is calculated as the capital gain divided by the purchase price of the stock.

Dividend Yield

The **dividend yield** of a stock is the dividend received divided by the purchase price of the stock.

Total Return

The **total return** of a stock is equal to its dividend yield plus its capital gain rate.

Equity Cost of Capital

The **equity cost of capital** is equal to the expected return of other securities available in the market with equivalent risk to the firm's equity.

Dividend-Discount Model

According to the **dividend-discount model,** the value of a firm's stock equals the present value of the future dividends it pays. All investors (with the same beliefs) will attach the same value to the stock, independent of their investment horizons because they can sell the stock at any date for the present value of the remaining dividends. Thus, how long they intend to hold the stock, and whether they collect their return in the form of dividends or capital gains, is irrelevant.

Constant Dividend Growth Model

The **constant dividend growth model** is an application of the present value of a perpetuity equation. When the dividend is expected to grow at a constant rate over time, the value of a firm's stock equals the dividend in one year divided by the difference in the equity cost of capital and the growth rate.

Dividend Payout Rate

The **dividend payout rate** is the fraction of a firm's earnings that it pays as dividends each year. The remaining earnings are retained to finance growth of the company; the fraction of the current earnings the firm retains is referred to as the **retention rate.**

Total Payout Model

The **total payout model** states that the value of a firm's stock equals the present value of the total payouts that the firm makes to shareholders. These payouts include both dividends and **share repurchases.**

■ Concept Check Questions and Answers

1. What is a share of stock and what are dividends?

   Common stock is a share of ownership in a corporation. Dividends are periodic payments, usually in the form of cash, which shareholders receive. Shareholders share in the profits of the corporation through dividend payments.

2. What are some key differences between preferred and common stock?

   Preferred stock has preference over common stock in the payment of dividends and in liquidation. Typically, common stocks carry the right to vote for the board of directors and in other important matters but preferred stock does not.

3. What is the role of a floor broker at the NYSE?

   The floor broker receives orders from investors to buy and sell stock and the broker negotiates in order to get the best execution price for the investors.

4. What is the role of a dealer at the NASDAQ?

   A dealer maintains inventory of a stock and posts a bid price at which the dealer is willing to buy the stock and an ask price at which the dealer is willing to sell the stock.

5. How do you calculate the total return of a stock?

   The total return of a stock is the sum of the dividend yield and the capital gain rate.

6. What discount rate do you use to discount the future cash flows of a stock?

   The equity cost of capital is used to discount the equity future cash flows. The equity cost of capital is the expected return of other investments available in the market that have the same risk as the firm's shares.

7. What are three ways that a firm can increase the amount of its future dividend per share?

   Because the dividend each year is the firm's earnings per share multiplied by its dividend payout ratio, the firm can increase its dividend in three ways: (1) by increasing its earnings (net income), (2) by increasing its dividend payout rate, or (3) by decreasing its shares outstanding.

8. Under what circumstances can a firm increase its share price by cutting its dividend and investing more?

   Cutting the firm's dividend to increase investment will raise the stock price if, and only if, the new investments have a positive NPV.

9. What are the main limitations of the dividend-discount model?

   Two major limitations of the dividend-discount model are its reliance on dividend forecasts given that a firm's future dividends carry a tremendous amount of uncertainty and the lack of applicability to non dividend-paying stocks.

10. What pieces of information are needed to forecast dividends?

    To forecast future dividends we need to forecast the firm's earnings, dividend payout rate, and the future share count.

11. How does the total payout model address part of the dividend discount model's limitations?

    The total payout model discounts the total payouts to shareholders, which includes both dividends and share repurchases and then divides by the current number of shares outstanding to determine share price.

12. How does the growth rate used in the total payout model differ from the growth rate used in the dividend-discount model?

    In the total payout model, we use the growth rate of earnings, rather than earnings per share when forecasting the growth of the firm's total payouts.

■ Examples with Step-by-Step Solutions

Stock Prices and Returns

7.1 **Problem:** You expect Hernandez Computer Peripherals to pay an annual dividend of $1.12 per share in the coming year and to trade for $42.90 per share at the end of the year. Investments with equivalent risk to Hernandez's stock have an expected return of 9%. What is the most you would pay today for a share of Hernandez's stock? What dividend yield and capital gain rate would you expect at this price?

Solution

Plan: We expect to receive a dividend of $1.12 and the future stock price of $42.90 a year from now. We will require a 9% return, similar to what we could earn on equivalent investments, on this investment. Therefore, we can use the following equation to determine the current price:

$$P_0 = \frac{\text{Div}_1 + P_1}{1 + r_E}$$

We will then be able to calculate the dividend yield as Div_1/P_0 and the capital gain rate as $(P_1 - P_0)/P_0$.

Execute: First, we calculate the maximum price we would be willing to pay today as:

$$P_0 = \frac{Div_1 + P_1}{1 + r_E}$$

$$= \frac{1.12 + 42.90}{1 + 0.09}$$

$$= \$40.39$$

Thus, the dividend yield is $1.12/40.39 = 2.8\%$ and the capital gain rate is $(\$42.90 - \$40.39)/\$40.39 = 6.2\%$.

Evaluate: At a price of $40.39, Hernandez's expected total return is $2.8\% + 6.2\% = 9\%$, which is equal to its equity cost of capital (the return being paid by investments with equivalent risk to Hernandez). This amount is the most we would be willing to pay for Hernandez's stock. If we paid more, our expected return would be less than 9% and we would rather invest elsewhere.

Valuing a Firm with Constant Dividend Growth

7.2 Problem: Wordsmith Books plans to pay $1.34 per share in dividends in the coming year. If its equity cost of capital is 11% and dividends are expected to grow by 3% a year in the future, estimate the value of Wordsmith's stock.

Solution

Plan: Because the dividends are expected to grow in perpetuity at a constant rate, we can use the following formula:

$$P_0 = \frac{Div_1}{r_E - g}$$

The next dividend (Div_1) is expected to be $1.34, the growth rate ($g$) is 3%, and the equity cost of capital (r_E) is 11%.

Execute:

$$P_0 = \frac{Div_1}{r_E - g}$$

$$= \frac{\$1.34}{0.11 - 0.03}$$

$$= \$16.75$$

Evaluate: You would be willing to pay more than 12 times the upcoming dividend of $1.34 to own Wordsmith stock because you are buying a claim to this year's dividend *and* to an infinite growing series of future dividends.

Cutting Dividends for Profitable Growth

7.3 Problem: McLeod Grocery expects to have earnings per share of $4 in the coming year. The firm has been paying out all of its earnings as a dividend rather than reinvesting these earnings and growing. With these expectations of no growth, McLeod's current share price is $50.

Suppose McLeod could cut its dividend payout rate from 100% to 50% for the foreseeable future and use the retained earnings to open new grocery stores. The return on its investment in these stores is expected to be 11%. If we assume that the risk of these new investments is the same as the risk of its existing investments, then the firm's equity cost of capital is unchanged. What effect would this new policy have on McLeod's stock price?

Solution

Plan: To figure out the effect of this policy on McLeod's stock price, we need to know several things. First, we need to compute its equity cost of capital. Next, we must determine McLeod's dividend and growth rate under the new policy.

Because we know that McLeod currently has a growth rate of 0 ($g = 0$), a dividend of $4, and a price of $50, we can use the following formula to solve for r_E:

$$P_0 = \frac{Div_1}{r_E - g}$$

If McLeod retains 50% of this year's dividend to fund the opening of new stores, the new dividend will simply be 50% of the old dividend of $4. The growth rate of the dividend will equal the retention rate multiplied by the return on new investment. Given this new dividend and growth rate, we can use the formula above to calculate P_0 given the new assumptions.

Execute: To find r_E:

$$P_0 = \frac{Div_1}{r_E - g} \Rightarrow \$50 = \frac{\$4}{r_E - 0}$$
$$\Rightarrow r_E = 0.08 = 8\%$$

Under the new policy the dividend next year will be $4 × 50% = $2.

The growth rate under the new policy will be 50% × 0.11 = 5.5%.

The new stock price would be:

$$P_0 = \frac{Div_1}{r_E - g}$$
$$= \frac{\$2}{0.08 - 0.055}$$
$$= \$80.00$$

Evaluate: McLeod's share price should rise from $50 to $80 if the company cuts its dividend in order to increase its investment and growth, implying that the investment has a positive NPV. By using its earnings to invest in projects that offer a rate of return (11%) greater than its equity cost of capital (8%), McLeod has created value for its shareholders.

Unprofitable Growth

7.4 **Problem:** Suppose that McLeod Grocery decides to cut its dividend payout rate to 50% to invest in new stores, as in Example 7.3. But now suppose that the return on these new investments is 6%, rather than the 11% assumed in Example 7.3. Given its expected earnings per share this year of $4 and its equity cost of capital of 8%, what will happen to McLeod's current share price in this case?

Solution

Plan: We will follow the steps in Example 7.3, except that in this case we assume a return on new investments of 6% when computing the new growth rate.

Execute: As we calculated in Example 7.3, McLeod's dividend will fall to $4 × 50% = $2. Its growth rate under the new policy will now be $g = 50\% \times 0.06 = 3\%$. The new share price is calculated as:

$$P_0 = \frac{Div_1}{r_E - g}$$
$$= \frac{\$2}{0.08 - 0.03}$$
$$= \$40.00$$

Evaluate: Even though McLeod will grow under the new policy, the new investments have a negative NPV. The company's share price will fall if it cuts its dividend to make new investments with a return of only 6%. By reinvesting its earnings in a project with a return of 6%, which is lower than its equity cost of capital of 8%, the company will reduce shareholder value.

Valuing a Firm with Different Growth Rates

7.5 **Problem:** Your broker is recommending a stock that is expected to pay its first dividend of $1.20 per share in exactly one year. The annual dividend is expected to be $1.44 the second year and $4.32 in the third year. In the fourth year, the dividend is expected to grow at 5% from then on. If you require a 20% return, how much would you pay for a share of the stock?

Solution

Plan: The value of the stock will be the present value of the expected future dividends. We know the expected dividends for the first three years: $D_1 = \$1.20$, $D_2 = \$1.44$, and $D_3 = \$4.32$. After Year 3, the dividend will grow at a rate of 5% a year, resulting in an expected dividend in Year 4 of 4.32(1.05) = $4.536. At the point that dividends begin growing at a constant 5% rate, we can use the constant dividend growth model to value all dividends after that point. Finally, we can pull everything together with the dividend-discount model.

Execute: Putting the dividends on a timeline will help us keep our work organized:

Year	0	1	2	3	4	5	6	...
Dividend		1.2	1.44	4.32	4.32(1.05)	$4.32(1.05)^2$	$4.32(1.05)^3$	...

Chapter 7 Stock Valuation 109

In Year 3, we will receive a dividend of $4.32 and the dividend will increase at a constant 5% rate after that. Therefore, the value at Year 2 of dividends for Year 3 and beyond is:

$$P_2 = \frac{Div_3}{r_E - g}$$
$$= \frac{\$4.32}{0.20 - 0.05}$$
$$= \$28.80$$

We can now apply the dividend-discount model:

$$P_0 = \frac{Div_1}{1+r_E} + \frac{Div_2}{(1+r_E)^2} + \frac{P_2}{(1+r_E)^2}$$
$$= \frac{\$1.20}{1.20} + \frac{\$1.44}{(1.20)^2} + \frac{\$28.80}{(1.20)^2}$$
$$= \$1.00 + \$1.00 + \$20$$
$$= \$22$$

Evaluate: The dividend-discount model is flexible enough to handle any forecasted pattern of dividends. Here the dividends are relatively low for the first two years and then jumped significantly in Year 3. Because the dividends are expected to settle into a constant growth rate at Year 3, we are able to use the constant growth rate model as a shortcut.

Valuation with Share Repurchases

7.6 **Problem:** Hamilton Enterprises has 230 million shares outstanding and expects earnings at the end of this year to be $900 million. Hamilton plans to pay out 40% of its earnings in total, paying 20% as a dividend and using 20% to repurchase shares. If Hamilton's earnings are expected to grow by 6% per year and these payout rates remain constant, determine Hamilton's share price. Assume an equity cost of capital of 12%.

Solution

Plan: We can compute the present value of Hamilton's future payouts as a constant growth perpetuity. We know that the equity cost of capital is 12% and the expected earnings growth rate is 6%. We need to know Hamilton's total payouts this year, which will be 40% of its total earnings. Since we are using Hamilton's total equity payouts, we will need to divide the total value by the number of shares outstanding (230 million) to obtain the price of a share of Hamilton stock.

Execute: Hamilton will have payouts this year of 40% × $900 million = $360 million. Using the constant growth perpetuity formula, we have:

$$\text{PV(Future Total Dividends and Repurchases)} = \frac{\$360 \text{ million}}{0.12 - 0.06} = \$6 \text{ billion}$$

To compute the share price, we divided the total value of Hamilton's equity ($6 billion) by the number of shares outstanding:

$$P_0 = \$6 \text{ billion}/230 \text{ million} = \$26.09 \text{ per share}$$

© 2012 Pearson Education, Inc. Publishing as Prentice Hall

Evaluate: Using the total payout method, we did not need to know the firm's split between dividends and share repurchases. To compare this method with the dividend-discount model, note that Hamilton will pay a dividend of 20% × $360 million/(230 million shares) = $0.31 per share, for a dividend yield of $0.31/$26.09 = 1.19%. We can calculate Hamilton's dividend growth rate as:

$$P_0 = \frac{Div_1}{r_E - g} \Rightarrow \$26.09 = \frac{\$0.31}{0.12 - g}$$

$$\Rightarrow g = 0.12 - \frac{0.31}{26.09} = 10.81\%$$

The 10.81% growth rate in dividends exceeds Hamilton's earnings growth rate of 6%; the dividend growth rate is larger than the earnings growth rate because Hamilton's number of shares outstanding will decline over time due to its share repurchases. Therefore, over time, there will be fewer and fewer shares to divide earnings amongst.

■ Questions and Problems

1. Ocean World's stock is priced at $25 per share. The firm is expected to pay an annual dividend of $0.50 per share in one year. Analysts are predicting a five-year growth rate in earnings of 8% per year. If the market expects Ocean World to keep its retention ratio (the fraction of earnings paid out as dividends) constant, and this growth rate continues in perpetuity, what is the market's required return for an investment in Ocean World's stock?

2. Woodchuck Cabinets will pay an annual dividend of $1.35 one year from now. Analysts expect this dividend to grow at 20% per year each year until five years from now. After Year 4, the growth will level off to 3% per year. According to the dividend discount model, what is the value of a share of Woodchuck's stock if the firm's required return is 8%?

3. Global Technology and Telecommunications (GTT) has a share price of $75. GTT is expected to pay a dividend of $1.20 a year from today. You expect GTT to increase its dividend by 5% per year in perpetuity.
    a. If GTT's equity cost of capital is 7%, what share price would you expect based on your estimate of the dividend growth rate?
    b. Given GTT's current share price and an equity cost of capital of 7%, what would you conclude about your assessment of GTT's future dividend growth?

4. Cartwright Industries expects to have earnings of $800 million at the end of this year. Cartwright's earnings are expected to grow by 5% per year. The company currently has 180 million shares outstanding. The equity cost of capital for the company is 11%.
    a. If Cartwright pays out 50% of its earnings in dividends, determine Cartwright's share price.
    b. If Cartwright pays out 50% of its earnings in total, 25% as a dividend and 25% as a share repurchase, determine Cartwright's share price.
    c. What can you conclude from your answers in part (a) and part (b)?

Solutions to Questions and Problems

1. The net present value of an investment in Ocean World is:

$$NPV = -25 + \frac{0.50}{r - 0.08} = 0$$

   Solving for r gives:

$$NPV = -25 + \frac{0.50}{r - 0.08} = 0 \Rightarrow r - 0.08 = \frac{0.50}{25}$$
$$\Rightarrow r = 0.02 + 0.08 = 0.10 = 10\%$$

   Thus, the implied market return is 10%.

2. The value of the first five dividend payments is:

$$PV_{1-5} = \frac{1.35}{(0.08 - 0.20)}\left(1 - \left(\frac{1.20}{1.08}\right)^5\right)$$
$$= (-11.25) \times (-0.6935)$$
$$= \$7.80$$

   The value at Year 5 of the rest of the dividend payments is:

$$PV_5 = \frac{1.35(1.20)^4 \times 1.02}{0.08 - 0.02}$$
$$= \$47.59$$

   Discounting this value to the present gives:

$$PV_0 = \frac{47.59}{(1.08)^5}$$
$$= \$32.39$$

   So the value of Woodchuck is:

$$P = \$7.82 + \$36.58$$
$$= \$44.40$$

3. a. $P = 1.20/(0.07 - 0.05) = \$60$.
   b. Based on the market price, your growth forecast may be too low. A growth rate consistent with the market price is $g = r_E -$ div yield $= 0.07 - 1.20/75 = 0.054 = 5.4\%$.

4. a. Cartwright's dividend at the end of this year will be (\$800 million × .50)/180 million shares or \$2.2222 a share. Thus, the share price is 2.22/(0.11 − 0.05) = \$37.04.
   b. Cartwright's total payout will be \$400 million. Thus the present value of the total future payouts is \$400 million /(.11 − .05) = \$6,667 million. The price per share is \$6,667million/180 million = \$37.04.
   c. The method in which Cartwright pays out its earnings to shareholders does not have an impact on the stock price. If the company pays out 50% of its earnings, whether all in dividends or in a combination of dividends and share repurchases, the stock price is \$37.04.

Self-Test Questions

1. According to the dividend-discount model, which of the following would cause a stock price to rise?
   a. An increase in the growth rate of the dividend.
   b. An increase in the equity cost of capital.
   c. A decrease in free cash flows.
   d. All of the above.

2. The total return of a stock is the
   a. dividend yield plus the capital gain rate.
   b. dividend yield minus the capital gain rate.
   c. dividend yield multiplied by the capital gain rate.
   d. dividend yield divided by the capital gain rate.

3. Seidel, Inc. is expected to pay a dividend of $1.53 next year. You expect Seidel to increase its dividend at a rate of 4% a year. If you require a 12% rate of return to invest in Seidel, what is the maximum price you would be willing to pay for the stock?
   a. $9.56
   b. $17.39
   c. $19.13
   d. $19.89

4. Which of the following would cause a firm's stock price to fall?
   a. The firm's dividend growth rate increases.
   b. The firm increases its retention rate and the cash is placed in investments that have a rate of return lower than the cost of capital.
   c. The firm decreases its dividend payout and the cash is placed in investments that have a rate of return higher than the cost of capital.
   d. The firm's cost of capital decreases.

5. A firm can increase its dividend by
   a. increasing its dividend payout rate.
   b. increasing its earnings (net income).
   c. decreasing its shares outstanding.
   d. All of the above.

6. Celestial Herbal Products is considering cutting its dividend in order to increase investment in new product lines. Cutting the dividend will
   a. decrease Celestial's stock price.
   b. increase Celestial's stock price.
   c. increase Celestial's stock price if, and only if, the new investments have a return greater than the cost of capital.
   d. have no impact in Celestial's stock price.

7. The equity cost of capital is
   a. calculated as the capital gain rate minus the dividend yield.
   b. the same for all U.S. companies according to the efficient markets hypothesis.
   c. higher for firms paying out relatively high dividends.
   d. the expected return of other investments available in the market that have the same risk as the firm's shares.

8. Luke owns 500 shares of KRDB stock. An election of five directors is taking place. If the company has straight voting then Luke
   a. has 500 votes for each position.
   b. has 2500 votes to use across the five director spots.
   c. has 100 votes for each position.
   d. has 500 votes to use across the five director spots.

9. Common stock carries
   a. the right to common dividends as well as rights to vote in the election of directors.
   b. the right to vote in the election of directors but not the right to dividends.
   c. the right to common dividends but not the right to vote in the election of directors.
   d. the right to vote on mergers and major events but not the right to vote in the election of directors.

10. The NYSE is _____, while the NASDAQ is _____.
    a. common stock market; preferred stock market
    b. based on the dividend valuation model; based on the total payout model
    c. a physical market where floor brokers negotiate for the best execution for investors; a computer network of dealers
    d. a physical market based on the total payout model; a computer network made up of floor brokers negotiating the best execution price for investors

11. The capital gain on a stock is
    a. the difference in the selling price and purchase price of the stock.
    b. the difference in the purchase price of the stock and the dividends.
    c. the difference in the selling price of the stock and the dividends.
    d. present value of the future expected stock dividends.

12. If a firm increases its dividend payout rate
    a. the firm's retention rate will also rise.
    b. the firm will have less cash available to put toward new investment.
    c. the number of shares outstanding will fall.
    d. the firm's stock price will always rise.

Answers to Self-Test Questions

1. a
2. a
3. c
4. b
5. d
6. c
7. d
8. a
9. a
10. a
11. c
12. b

■ Appendix: Using Excel to Build a Dividend-Discount Model

Problem: Advanced Pharmaceuticals had earnings per share of $1.75 this past year. The company just received FDA approval for a new arthritis medication and the company's earnings are expected to increase rapidly over the next few years due to increased sales. You estimate that the earnings per share will grow by 20% over the next two years and by 12% the following two years. After that, you think the growth in EPS will fall to a constant 4% growth rate. The company pays out 40% of its earnings in dividends. Develop a spreadsheet to determine the maximum price you would be willing to pay for this stock if you required a 13% rate of return.

Solution

Plan: The maximum price we will be willing to pay for a share of the stock is the present value of the future expected dividends. We estimate that the dividend growth rates will be:

Year	0	1	2	3	4	5	6	...
EPS Growth Rate		0.2	0.2	0.12	0.12	0.04	0.04	0.04

The EPS in Year 0 was $1.75, and the company pays 40% of earnings in dividends. First, we will need to calculate the expected future EPS. Second, we will need to calculate the dividends that will be paid out of those earnings. Third, we will discount all of the future expected cash flows (the dividends) using our required rate of return of 13%.

Execute: Expected EPS for each year is calculated in the spreadsheet below. We use the formula $EPS_i = EPS_{i-1}(1 + g_i)$; for example, the EPS for Year 2 is calculated by placing the formula "= C4 × (1 + D3)" in cell D4. Then we multiply the EPS by the dividend payout ratio to get the dividend. For example, the dividend for Year 2 is calculated by placing the formula "= D4 × D6" in cell D7.

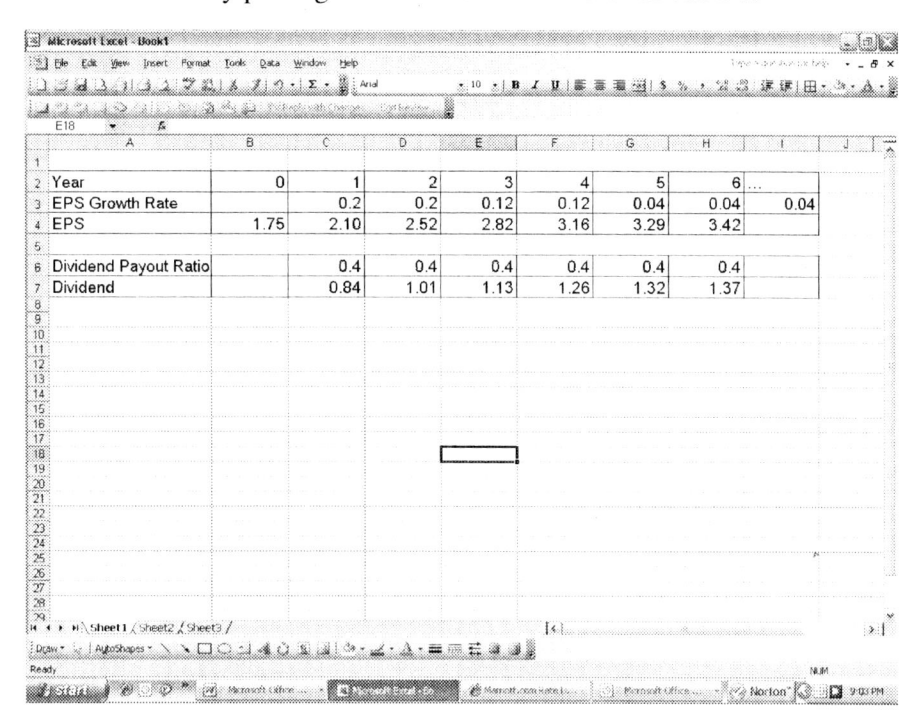

	B	C	D	E	F	G	H	I
Year	0	1	2	3	4	5	6	...
EPS Growth Rate		0.2	0.2	0.12	0.12	0.04	0.04	0.04
EPS	1.75	2.10	2.52	2.82	3.16	3.29	3.42	
Dividend Payout Ratio		0.4	0.4	0.4	0.4	0.4	0.4	
Dividend		0.84	1.01	1.13	1.26	1.32	1.37	

Now that we have the expected future dividends we can calculate the expected stock price at any point in time. We use the equity cost of capital as the discount rate. Remember that once the growth rate becomes a constant 4% the growing perpetuity formula can be used to determine the present value of all of the future dividends.

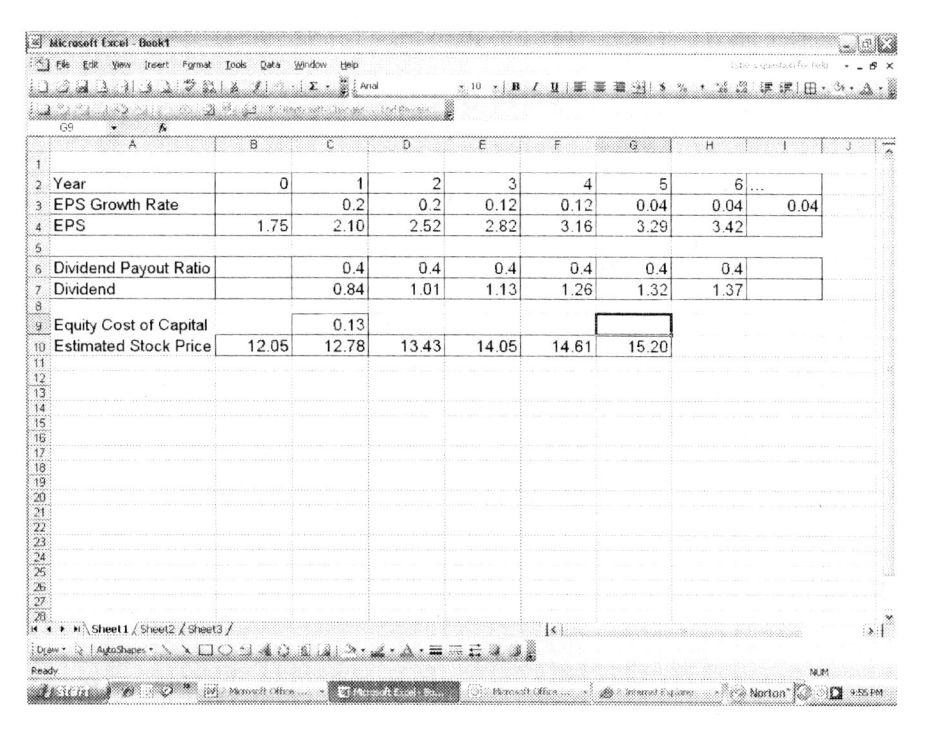

	B	C	D	E	F	G	H	I
Year	0	1	2	3	4	5	6	...
EPS Growth Rate		0.2	0.2	0.12	0.12	0.04	0.04	0.04
EPS	1.75	2.10	2.52	2.82	3.16	3.29	3.42	
Dividend Payout Ratio		0.4	0.4	0.4	0.4	0.4	0.4	
Dividend		0.84	1.01	1.13	1.26	1.32	1.37	
Equity Cost of Capital		0.13						
Estimated Stock Price	12.05	12.78	13.43	14.05	14.61	15.20		

Evaluate: The most we would be willing to pay for the stock today is $12.05. We are expecting to receive a dividend of $0.84 in one year and have a stock that is worth $12.78 in one year. Because we have set the problem up in a spreadsheet using formulas to make the calculations, we can easily see how the stock price will change as assumptions change. For example, let's see what happens if EPS is expected to grow by 20% for three years instead of only two; in the fourth year, EPS will grow at 12%, and after that, EPS will grow at a constant rate of 4%. Making this change in cell E3 will quickly change our spreadsheet:

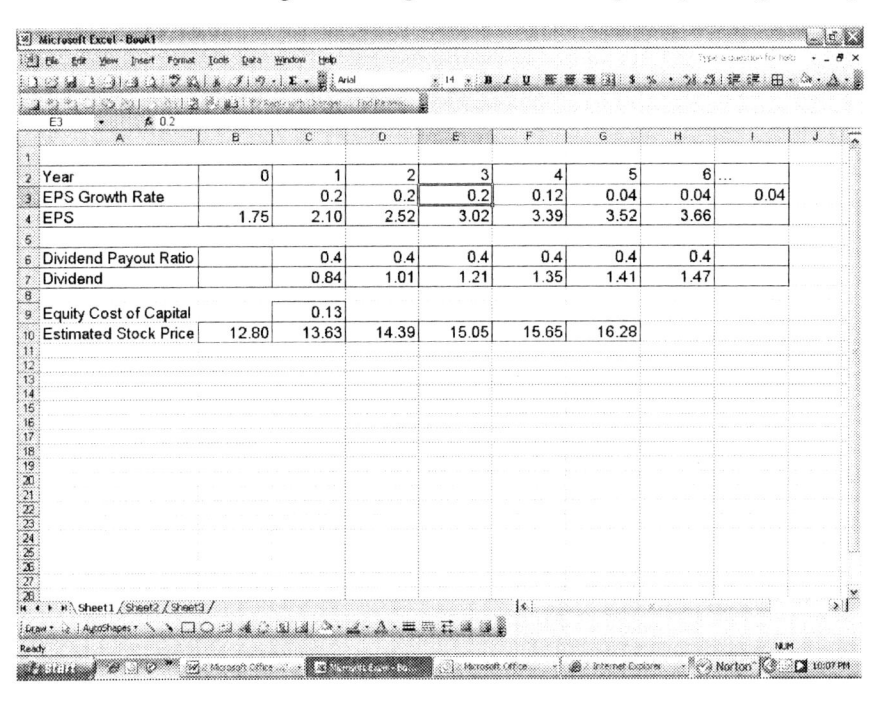

	A	B	C	D	E	F	G	H	I
2	Year	0	1	2	3	4	5	6	...
3	EPS Growth Rate		0.2	0.2	0.2	0.12	0.04	0.04	0.04
4	EPS	1.75	2.10	2.52	3.02	3.39	3.52	3.66	
5									
6	Dividend Payout Ratio		0.4	0.4	0.4	0.4	0.4	0.4	
7	Dividend		0.84	1.01	1.21	1.35	1.41	1.47	
8									
9	Equity Cost of Capital		0.13						
10	Estimated Stock Price	12.80	13.63	14.39	15.05	15.65	16.28		

Making one change in our spreadsheet results in a higher EPS calculation for Year 3 and beyond. This also causes the dividend for Year 3 and beyond to rise. As these cash flows increase, so does the estimated stock price for each year. Building a flexible spreadsheet like this allows us to see quickly how basic assumption changes will change our stock price estimate.

Chapter 8
Investment Decision Rules

■ Key Learning Objectives

- Calculate Net Present Value
- Use the NPV rule to make investment decisions
- Understand alternative decision rules and their drawbacks
- Choose between mutually exclusive alternatives
- Evaluate projects with different lives
- Rank projects when a company's resources are limited so that it cannot take all positive-NPV projects

■ Notation

CF_n	cash flow that arrives at date n
g	growth rate
IRR	internal rate of return
$MIRR$	modified internal rate of return
NPV	net present value
PV	present value
r	discount rate

■ Chapter Synopsis

8.1 The NPV Decision Rule

The **net present value (NPV)** of a project or investment is the difference between the present value of its benefits and the present value of its costs:

$$NPV = PV(\text{Benefits}) - PV(\text{Costs})$$

The NPV expresses the value of an investment decision as an amount of cash received today. If the NPV of a project is positive, the decision to take on the project increases the value of the firm and is a good decision. Projects with positive NPVs have benefits that exceed their costs. Projects with negative NPVs have costs that exceed their benefits. **The NPV decision rule** states:

When making an investment decision, take the alternative with the highest NPV. Choosing this alternative is equivalent to receiving its NPV in cash today.

8.2 Using the NPV Rule

When considering a stand-alone project, we should accept the project if its NPV is positive. Choosing a project with a positive NPV is equivalent to receiving its NPV in cash today. To calculate a project's NPV, we must consider the size and timing of the cash flows associated with the project. For example, if we have a project that will cost us $4.5 million today and will generate positive cash flows of $2 million dollars each year for the next three years, the timeline for this project looks like:

Period	0	1	2	3
Cash Flow	−4.5	2	2	2

The NPV of this project is:

$$\text{NPV} = -4.5 + \frac{2}{(1+r)^1} + \frac{2}{(1+r)^2} + \frac{2}{(1+r)^3}$$

The NPV is telling us the present value of the benefits net of the costs of the project. All cash flows must be put into present values, so that all costs and benefits can be compared. We would use the cost of capital for the project as the "r" in the equation above.

An **NPV profile** graphs the project's NPV over a range of discount rates, allowing us to see what the NPV of the project is for a variety of values for cost of capital. When the discount rate used equals the project's (IRR), then the NPV will equal zero. When a discount rate lower than the IRR is used, the NPV will be positive.

8.3 Alternative Decision Rules

Even though the NPV rule is the most accurate and reliable rule, in practice a wide variety of rules are applied, often in tandem with the NPV rule. The simplest investment rule is the **payback investment rule.** The payback investment rule is based on the idea that an opportunity that pays back its initial investment quickly is a good idea. To apply the payback rule, first calculate the amount of time it takes to pay back the initial investment, called the **payback period.** If this payback period is less than a prespecified length of time, accept the project. The payback rule is not a reliable method of determining if a project will increase the value of the firm since it does not consider the timing of a project's cash flows, the cash flows that occur after the payback period, or the cost of capital.

The **IRR investment rule** states that you should accept an investment opportunity if the IRR exceeds the opportunity cost of capital. The IRR rule will give the same answer as the NPV rule in many, but not all, applications. The IRR rule may fail to provide the correct decision:

- When the initial cash flow is positive and all later cash flows are negative; the IRR rule will provide the opposite decision that the NPV rule provides in this case.
- When there is no required investment for a project, because IRR does not exist.
- When a project has multiple IRRs. Multiple IRRs can occur when the sign of the project's cash flows changes more than once.

While these are limitations of the usefulness of the IRR rule, the IRR itself is a useful tool. Not only does the IRR measure the sensitivity of the NPV to estimation error in the cost of capital, it also measures the average return of the investment.

Modified Internal Rate of Return

To overcome the potential problem of multiple IRRs for the cash flows from a project, various ways of modifying the cash flows before computing the IRR are sometimes used. All of these modifications have the common feature that they group the cash flows so that there is only one negative cash flow. With only one negative cash flow, there is only one sign change for the cash flows as a whole and hence only one IRR. This new IRR, computed as the discount rate that sets the NPV of the modified cash flows of the project equal to zero, is called the **modified internal rate of return (MIRR).**

There is no set way to modify project cash flows to produce an MIRR. Three possible approaches that solve the multiple IRR problem are:

- Discount all of the negative cash flows to Time 0 and move all of the positive cash flows to the end of the final project.
- Discount all of the negative cash flows to Time 0 and leave the positive cash flows alone.
- Leave the initial cash flow alone and compound all of the remaining cash flows to the final period of the project.

There is considerable debate about whether MIRR is truly better than IRR. Most of the argument centers on whether it is advisable to modify the cash flows of the project. The IRR is truly an internal rate of return based solely on the actual cash flows of the project. However, the IRR implicitly assumes that all cash flows generated by the project are reinvested at the project's IRR rather than at the firm's cost of capital until the project ends. For a project with a high IRR, this may be an unrealistic assumption. Further, there may be more than one IRR, which complicates its use. The MIRR avoids these problems, but is based on a set of cash flows modified through the use of a chosen discount and compounding rate. Thus, it is not really an internal rate of return and is no longer based solely on the actual cash flows of the project. Finally, as we will see in the next section, MIRR still does not solve some of the other problems associated with using IRR when choosing among projects.

8.4 Choosing Between Projects

Sometimes a firm must choose among **mutually exclusive projects,** in which only one of two or more projects being considered may be selected. In this case, the NPV rule advises picking the project with the highest NPV and provides the best answer.

8.5 Evaluating Projects with Different Lives

Capital budgeting decisions become more complicated when we are comparing two investment possibilities that last for different time periods. Suppose, for example, you are considering two different companies to provide phone service. Company A will provide phone service based on a three-year contract that requires you to pay $500,000 upfront and $100,000 a year. Company B requires a five-year contract that requires you to pay only $300,000 upfront but obligates you to pay $150,000 a year for five years. To compare these alternatives, we can compute the **Equivalent Annual Annuity** for each project, which is the level annual cash flow with the same present value as the cash flows of the alternative. In other words, we would find the annuity that would give the same NPV as the alternative so that we could get a measure of the yearly cost of the contract. When considering these types of projects, however, we must also consider the **required life** (whether we will need the service for the length of the longer contract) and what the **replacement cost** will be at the end of the life of the shorter contract.

8.6 Choosing among Projects When Resources Are Limited

In some situations, different investment opportunities demand different amounts of a particular resource. If there is a fixed supply of the resource so that you cannot undertake all possible opportunities, simply picking the highest-NPV opportunity might not lead to the best decision. The **profitability index** can be used to identify the optimal combination of projects to undertake in such situations. We calculate a project's profitability index as:

$$\text{Profitability Index} = \frac{\text{Value Created}}{\text{Resource Consumed}} = \frac{\text{NPV}}{\text{Resource Consumed}}$$

We rank the projects, starting with the project with the highest profitability index. While this procedure generally leads to the most valuable combination of projects, it can break down in certain instances, such as when multiple constraints apply. The only guaranteed way to find the best combination of projects is to search through all of them.

8.7 Putting It All Together

The decision rules we have discussed in this chapter are summarized in the table below. While alternative decision rules may sometimes (or even often) agree with the NPV decision rule, only the NPV decision rule is always correct. The NPV rule is the only rule that provides you with a measure that is directly tied to your goal of maximizing shareholder wealth.

Summary of Decision Rules

NPV		
	Definition	• The difference between the present value of an investment's benefits and the present value of its costs
	Rule	• Take any investment opportunity where the NPV is not negative; turn down any opportunity where it is negative
	Advantages	• Corresponds directly to the impact of the project on the firm's value
		• Direct application of the Valuation Principle
	Disadvantages	• Relies on an accurate estimate of the discount rate
		• Can be time consuming to compute
IRR		
	Definition	• The interest rate that sets the net present value of the cash flows equal to zero; the average return of the investment
	Rule	• Take any investment opportunity where IRR exceeds the opportunity cost of capital; turn down any opportunity whose IRR is less than the opportunity cost of capital
	Advantages	• Related to the NPV rule and usually yields the same (correct) decision
	Disadvantages	• Hard to compute
		• Multiple IRRs lead to ambiguity
		• Cannot be used to choose among projects

Payback Period	*Continued*
Definition	• The amount of time it takes to pay back the initial investment
Rule	• If the payback period is less than a prespecified length of time—usually a few years—accept the project; otherwise, turn it down
Advantages	• Simple to compute • Favors liquidity
Disadvantages	• No guidance as to correct payback cutoff • Ignores cash flows after the cutoff completely
Profitability Index	
Definition	• NPV/Resource Consumed
Rule	• Rank projects according to their PI based on the constrained resource and move down the list accepting value-creating projects until the resource is exhausted
Advantages	• Uses the NPV to measure the benefit • Allows projects to be ranked on value-created per unit of constraint
Disadvantages	• Breaks down when there is more than one constraint • Requires careful attention to make sure the constrained resource is completely utilized

■ Selected Concepts and Key Terms

Net Present Value (NPV) Investment Rule

The **net present value (NPV)** of a project is PV(Benefits) − PV(Costs). The **net present value rule** states that managers should select all projects that have a positive net present value (NPV), where NPV is the difference between the present value of an investment's benefits and the present value of its costs. A project's NPV represents its value in terms of cash today. Choosing this alternative is equivalent to receiving its NPV in cash today, so positive NPV projects should be accepted.

NPV Profile

An **NPV profile** graphs a project's NPV over a range of discount rates, showing what the NPV of the project is for a variety of values for cost of capital.

Payback Investment Rule

To use the **payback investment rule,** you calculate the amount of time it takes to pay back the initial investment; this time period is known as the **payback period.** If the payback period is less than a prespecified length of time, the rule says to accept the project. The payback rule is not a reliable method of determining if a project will increase the value of the firm.

Internal Rate of Return (IRR) Investment Rule

The **internal rate of return (IRR) investment rule** states that an investment opportunity should be taken if the IRR exceeds the opportunity cost of capital. The **internal rate of return (IRR)** is the rate of return that makes the net present value of a stream of cash flows equal to zero. The IRR investment rule will give the same answer as the NPV rule in many, but not all, situations. For example, with an abnormal series of cash flows, multiple IRRs can exist, and the IRR rule cannot be used. Project cash flows can be modified and a **modified IRR** calculated.

Mutually Exclusive Projects

When only one of two or more projects being considered can be selected, the projects are referred to as **mutually exclusive projects.** When considering mutually exclusive projects, the NPV rule provides the best answer. Pick the project with the highest NPV.

Profitability Index

A project's **profitability index** is the project's NPV divided by the amount of resources (such as capital) consumed. When there is a limited resource, projects should be selected in order of profitability index ranking starting with the project with the highest index and moving down the ranking until the resource is used.

■ Concept Check Questions and Answers

1. What is the NPV decision rule? How is it related to the Valuation Principle?

    The NPV decision rule states that when choosing among alternatives, we should take the alternative with the highest NPV. Choosing this alternative is equivalent to receiving its NPV in cash today.

2. Why doesn't the NPV decision rule depend on the investor's preferences?

    Regardless of our preferences for cash today versus cash in the future, we should always maximize the NPV first. We can then borrow or lend to shift cash flows through time and find our most preferred pattern of cash flows.

3. Explain the NPV rule for stand-alone projects.

    The NPV is the difference between the present value of the benefits of a project and the present value of the costs of the project. If the NPV is positive, the project should be accepted. Accepting this project is the same as receiving the NPV in cash today.

4. How can you interpret the difference between the cost of capital and the IRR?

    The difference between the cost of capital and a project's IRR is a measure of the sensitivity of the NPV to an estimation error in the cost of capital.

5. How do you apply the payback rule?

    To apply the payback rule you calculate the length of time it takes to recover your initial cash outflow. This tells you how long it is before the project breaks even, but it ignores the time value of money.

6. Under what conditions will the IRR rule lead to the same decision as the NPV rule?

    The IRR rule will lead to the same decision as the NPV rule in most cases. The IRR rule may fail to lead to the same decision when mutually exclusive projects are considered, the cash flows of a project change signs more than once, or when the project has an initial cash inflow followed by cash outflows.

7. What is the most reliable way to choose between mutually exclusive projects?

   The NPV rule is the most reliable way to choose between mutually exclusive projects.

8. For mutually exclusive projects, explain why picking one project over another because it has a larger IRR can lead to mistakes.

   For mutually exclusive projects, one project may have a much higher IRR than another project but be of a much smaller scale. If this is the case, less value may be added for the shareholders by taking the project that has the higher IRR.

9. Explain why choosing the option with the highest NPV is not always correct when the options have different lives.

   Suppose you are considering two projects that have an initial cash outflow and a yearly expense associated with them. If the project with the higher NPV lasts for a shorter period of time, the per year cost may actually be higher for that project if we are going to continue the project beyond the life of the shorter alternative.

10. What issues should you keep in mind when choosing among projects with different lives?

    You must consider the time period for which you will actually need the project and you need to consider the replacement cost at the end of the project's life.

11. Explain why picking the project with the highest NPV might not be optimal when you evaluate mutually exclusive projects with different resource requirements.

    Choosing the project with the highest NPV might not lead to the greatest amount of value creation for the firm when you are considering mutually exclusive projects with different resource constraints. One project may have a high NPV but use up so much of the constrained resource that two projects with a combined NPV that is higher than the chosen project cannot be done.

12. What does the profitability index tell you?

    The profitability index allows us to determine the amount of value that is created relative to the constrained resources that are being used.

■ Examples with Step-by-Step Solutions

The NPV Is Equivalent to Cash Today

8.1 **Problem:** Your brother offers to pay you $3200 in one year if you give him $3000 today. If you can earn 5% per year on money in your savings account, what is the NPV of this offer? Show that its NPV represents cash in your pocket.

   Solution

   Plan: You are giving up $3000 today to get $3200 in one year. Placing this information on a timeline give us cash flows of:

Today	In One Year
+$3000	−$3200

The discount rate for calculating the present value of the money received in one year is 5%. You need to compare the present value of the benefit ($3200 in one year) to the cost ($3000 today) to compute the NPV.

Execute: NPV = – 3000 + 3200/1.05 = – 3000 + 3047.62 = 47.62

Evaluate: To receive $3200 from your bank in one year, you would have to place $3047.62 in the bank today if your savings account earns 5% interest. If instead, you take $3000 and give it to your brother today you can have $3200 in one year. This leaves $47.62 in your pocket today.

Using the Payback Rule

8.2 **Problem:** Microsoft is considering moving 1000 help desk call center employees from Seattle to Bombay. The total after-tax cost of a Seattle worker is $50,000 per year and the total after-tax cost of a Bombay worker is $30,000 per year. The move would require paying an upfront severance package worth $40,000 after taxes per former Seattle employee. Assume for this analysis that the cost savings would last forever. Microsoft's projects require a three-year payback period. Would this project be accepted using the payback rule?

Solution

Plan: In order to implement the payback rule, we need to know whether the sum of the inflows from the project will exceed the initial investment before the end of three years. The project has inflows of $20 million per year and an initial investment of $40 million.

Execute: The sum of the cash flows from Year 1 and Year 2 is $20 × 2 = $40 million, which covers the initial investment of $40 million. The payback period for this project is two years. The company will accept projects that have a payback period of three years or less; Microsoft will accept the project.

Evaluate: While simple to compute, the payback rule requires us to use an arbitrary cutoff period in summing the cash flows. Further, the payback rule does not discount future cash flows. Instead it simply sums the cash flows and compares them to a cash outflow in the present. In this case, the payback period gives the same answer as does the NPV rule, but this will not always be the case.

NPV and Mutually Exclusive Projects

8.3 **Problem:** You just inherited a piece of property with a bowling alley on it. The building is old and is in need of some repairs. A local investor has offered to pay you $300,000 for the land. You are considering whether you should sell the property, do some minor repairs and keep the bowling alley open, or if you should make some major investments in the property and run a very nice bowling alley. If you keep the property you assume that you would run it indefinitely, eventually leaving the business to your heirs. After analyzing the alternatives, you have come up with the following projections:

	Cash Flow in Period 0	Cash Flow in Period 1	Growth Rate	Cost of Capital
Sell the property	300,000			
Minor repairs	–90,000	25,000	1.50%	11%
Major renovation	–250,000	30,000	5%	12.50%

Which option should you choose?

Solution

Plan: Since you can only do one project (you only have one piece of land), these are mutually exclusive projects. In order to decide which project is most valuable, you need to rank them by NPV. Each of these projects (except for selling the land) has cash flows that can be valued as a growing perpetuity. The present value of the inflows is $CF_1/(r - g)$. The NPV of each investment will be:

$$\frac{CF_1}{r-g} - \text{Initial Investment}$$

Execute: The NPVs are:

Sell the property: NPV = $300,000

Minor repairs: NPV $= \dfrac{25{,}000}{0.11 - 0.015} - 90{,}000 = 263{,}158 - 90{,}000 = \$173{,}158$

Major renovation: NPV $= \dfrac{30{,}000}{0.125 - 0.05} - 250{,}000 = 400{,}000 - 250{,}000 = \$150{,}000$

Selling the property has the highest NPV, so that choice should be taken.

Evaluate: All of the alternatives have positive NPVs, but you can only take one of them. Therefore, you should choose the one that creates the most value.

Computing the Cross-Over Point

8.4 Problem: You want to try your hand at an entrepreneurial opportunity for the remaining time you are in college. You are considering leasing a concession stand in the local park to operate on weekends. There are two concession stands currently available for lease: an ice cream stand and a popcorn stand. You will need to pay $25,000 today for a three year lease on the ice cream stand. You estimate that your cash inflows would be $12,000 a year for the next three years if you operate the ice cream stand. A three year lease on the popcorn stand costs $15,000 today. You estimate that you will make $8000 a year for the next three years if you operate the popcorn stand. Calculate the cross-over point for the two investment opportunities.

Solution

Plan: The cross-over point is the discount rate that makes the NPV of the two alternatives equal. We can find the discount rate by setting the equations for the NPV of each project equal to each other and solving for the discount rate.

Execute: Setting the difference of the NPV of the two options equal to 0:

$$\text{NPV(ice cream)} - \text{NPV(popcorn)} = 0$$

$$\left[\frac{12{,}000}{1+r} + \frac{12{,}000}{(1+r)^2} + \frac{12{,}000}{(1+r)^3} - 25{,}000\right] - \left[\frac{8000}{1+r} + \frac{8000}{(1+r)^2} + \frac{8000}{(1+r)^3} - 15{,}000\right] = 0$$

$$\left[\frac{4000}{1+r} + \frac{4000}{(1+r)^2} + \frac{4000}{(1+r)^3} - 10{,}000\right] = 0$$

Solving for the cross-over point is just like solving for the IRR. So, we will need to use trial and error, a financial calculator, or a spreadsheet to solve for r:

	N	I/Y	PV	PMT	FV
Given:	3		−10,000	4000	0
Solve for:		9.7			

Excel Formula: = RATE(NPER,PMT,PV,FV) = RATE(3,4000, − 10,000,0)

The cross-over occurs at a discount rate of 9.7%.

Evaluate: The ice cream stand has a higher initial investment, but it also has a higher annual cash inflow than does the popcorn stand. The cross-over rate tells us the discount rate that would make us indifferent between choosing the ice cream stand and the popcorn stand. At a 9.7% discount rate, the ice cream stand and the popcorn stand have the same NPV ($5000). Just as the NPV of a project tells us the value impact of taking the project; the difference of the NPVs of two alternatives tells us the *incremental* impact of choosing one project over another. The cross-over point is the discount rate at which we would be indifferent between the two projects because the incremental value of choosing one over the other would be zero.

Computing an Equivalent Annual Annuity

8.5 Problem: The Kline Co. is considering two different companies to provide phone service. Company A will provide phone service based on a three-year contract that requires Kline to pay $500,000 upfront and $100,000 a year. Company B requires a five-year contract that requires Kline to pay only $300,000 upfront but obligates Kline to pay $150,000 a year for five years. Assume a discount rate of 9%. Calculate an equivalent annual annuity for each option. Which option should Kline choose?

Solution

Plan: To calculate the equivalent annual annuity for each option, we must first compute the NPV for Option A and the NPV for Option B using a 9% discount rate. Once, we know the NPV for Option A, we compute an equivalent three-year annuity. Using the NPV for Option B, we will compute an equivalent five-year annuity. Then, we will be able to compare the annual cost of the two options.

Execute: First, we calculate the NPV of each option:

$$\text{NPV(Option A)} = -500{,}000 - 100{,}000\left(\frac{1}{0.09} - \frac{1}{0.09(1.09)^3}\right)$$
$$= -500{,}000 - 100{,}000(11.11 - 8.58)$$
$$= -753{,}000$$

$$\text{NPV(Option B)} = -300{,}000 - 150{,}000\left(\frac{1}{0.09} - \frac{1}{0.09(1.09)^5}\right)$$
$$= -300{,}000 - 150{,}000(11.11 - 7.22)$$
$$= -883{,}500$$

Next, we calculate the equivalent annual annuity for each option:

$$\text{Cash Flow(Option A)} = \frac{PV}{\left(\dfrac{1}{0.09} - \dfrac{1}{0.09(1.09)^3}\right)}$$

$$= \frac{-753,000}{\left(\dfrac{1}{0.09} - \dfrac{1}{0.09(1.09)^3}\right)}$$

$$= -297,628$$

$$\text{Cash Flow(Option B)} = \frac{PV}{\left(\dfrac{1}{0.09} - \dfrac{1}{0.09(1.09)^5}\right)}$$

$$= \frac{-883,500}{\left(\dfrac{1}{0.09} - \dfrac{1}{0.09(1.09)^5}\right)}$$

$$= -227,121$$

The annual cost of Option B is less than the annual cost of Option A. So, Kline should go with Option B.

Evaluate: When considering only NPV, Option A has a less negative NPV. However, choosing Option A provides Kline with phone service for only three years; the company will have to incur additional costs to have phone service after three years. Option B provides phone service for a lower annual cost than does Option A. When making a final decision, Kline must also consider what the replacement cost will be in three years if Option A is chosen. If technological improvements cause phone service contracts to decrease in price significantly over the next few years, Option A could prove to be the better option.

Profitability Index with a Constraint

8.6 **Problem:** Alamo Properties, Inc. (API) has purchased 100 acres in suburban San Antonio. They are considering the following development options:

Project	NPV in Millions	Acres Used
Housing Development A	$30	100
Housing Development B	24.5	70
Drug Store	3	3
Strip Mall	3.5	7
Medical Complex	8	20

All five projects have a positive NPV; however, API only has 100 acres of land to use. Which project(s) should API choose?

Solution

Plan: The goal is to maximize the total NPV we can create with 100 acres (at most). We need to calculate the profitability index for each project. Since acreage is API's limited resource, we will use "acres used" in the denominator:

$$\text{Profitability Index} = \frac{\text{NPV}}{\text{Resource Consumed}}$$

$$= \frac{\text{NPV}}{\text{Acres Used}}$$

Once we have the profitability index for each project, we can sort them based on the index.

Execute:

Project	NPV in Millions	Acres Used	Profitability Index
Housing Development A	$30	100	0.30
Housing Development B	24.5	70	0.35
Drug Store	3	3	1.00
Strip Mall	3.5	7	0.50
Medical Complex	8	20	0.40

We now assign the resource to the projects in descending order according to the profitability index.

Project	NPV in Millions	Acres Used	Profitability Index	Cumulative Acreage Used
Drug Store	3	3	1.00	3
Strip Mall	3.5	7	0.50	10
Medical Complex	8	20	0.40	30
Housing Development B	24.5	70	0.35	100
Housing Development A	$30	100	0.30	200

The final column shows the cumulative use of the resource as each project is taken on until the resource is used up. To maximize NPV within the constraint of 100 acres, API should choose the drug store, strip mall, medical complex, and housing development B.

Evaluate: By ranking projects in terms of their NPV per acre, we find the most value we can create, given the 100-acre constraint. There is no other combination of projects that will create more value without using more than the 100 acres API has available.

■ Questions and Problems

1. You own a gold mining company and are considering opening a new mine. The mine is expected to generate $10 million for the next 21 years. After 21 years, the gold is expected to be depleted but the site can be sold for an expected $20 million. If the cost of capital is 8%, what is the most you should invest to open the mining operation at Time 0?

2. Microsoft is considering moving 1000 help desk call center employees from Seattle to Bombay. The total after-tax cost of a Seattle worker is $50,000 per year and the total after-tax cost of a Bombay worker is $30,000 per year. The move would require paying an upfront severance package worth $40,000 after taxes per former Seattle employee. Assume for this analysis that the cost savings would last forever and that Microsoft's cost of capital is 20%. Should this project be accepted based on the NPV rule?

3. Consider Microsoft's project in Problem 2. What is the IRR of the project? Using the IRR rule, would this project be accepted?

4. You are considering opening a new hotel. The hotel will cost $150 million upfront and will be built immediately. It is expected to produce profits of $20 million every year forever. Calculate the NPV of this investment opportunity if your cost of capital is 10%. Should you make the investment? Calculate the IRR and use it to determine the maximum deviation allowable in the cost of capital estimate to leave the decision unchanged.

5. The Professional Golf Association (PGA) is considering developing a new PGA-branded golf ball. Development will take three years at a cost of $250,000 per year. Once in production, the ball is expected to make $250,000 per year for five years at which time new technology will make it obsolete. The cost of capital is 10%. Calculate the NPV of this investment opportunity. Should the PGA make the investment?

6. You are considering making a movie. The movie is expected to cost $100 million upfront and take a year to make. After that, it is expected to make $85 million in the first year it is released and $5 million for the following 20 years. What is the payback period of this investment? If you require a payback period of two years, will you make the movie? Does the NPV rule agree with the payback rule if the cost of capital is 10%?

7. Your corporation has $1 million to spend on capital investments this year and is evaluating four investments. The following table summarizes the NPV and cost of these investments.

Investment	NPV	Cost
1	$400,000	$400,000
2	$300,000	$200,000
3	$650,000	$400,000
4	$150,000	$600,000

Which project(s) should you take?

■ Solutions to Questions and Problems

1. Using X as the initial investment:

$$\text{NPV} = X + \frac{10}{0.08}\left(1 - \frac{1}{1.08^{21}}\right) + \frac{20}{1.08^{21}}$$
$$= X + 100 + 4 \Rightarrow X = \$-104 \text{ million}$$

Thus, the most you should invest is $104 million.

2. The Time 0 cost is $40,000 × 1000 = $40 million. This is the severance package that must be paid. The annual savings is $50,000 × 1000 = $50 million and the new annual cost is $30,000 × 1000 = $30 million. Thus, the annual net incremental cash flow is $20 million.

Period	0	1	2	3	...
Cash Flow	−40	20	20	20	20

The cash flows after Time Period 0 are a perpetuity. We will calculate the NPV by subtracting the initial cost in Time 0 from the present value of the perpetuity. We will use the cost of capital of 20% as the discount rate.

$$NPV = PV(\text{cash inflow}) - PV(\text{cash outflow})$$
$$= \frac{20,000,000}{0.2} - 40,000,000$$
$$= \$60 \text{ million}$$

The NPV of this project is $60 million, so it should be accepted.

3. $NPV = 0 \Rightarrow \dfrac{20,000,000}{r} - 40,000,000 = 0$

$\Rightarrow IRR = \dfrac{20,000,000}{40,000,000} = 0.50 = 50\%$

The IRR of 50% exceeds 20%, so the rule says to accept the project.

4. $NPV = -150 + \dfrac{20}{0.10} = -150 + 200 = \$50$ million, so you should accept the project.

The IRR can be found by setting the NPV = 0:

$$NPV = -150 + \frac{20}{IRR} = 0 \Rightarrow IRR = \frac{20}{150} 13.3\%$$

So, the cost of capital can be underestimated by 3.3% without changing the decision.

5. $NPV = \dfrac{-250,000}{0.10}\left(1 - \dfrac{1}{(1.10)^3}\right) + \left(\dfrac{1}{(1.10)^3}\right)\dfrac{250,000}{0.10}\left(1 - \dfrac{1}{(1.10)^5}\right)$

$= -621,713 + 712,019$

$= 90,306 > 0$

NPV > 0, so the company should take the project.

6. It will take four years to pay back the initial investment $(-100 + 85 + 5 + 5 + 5 = 0)$ so the payback period is four years. Using the payback period rule, you will not make the movie.

$$NPV = -100 + \frac{85}{1.10^2} + \frac{5}{0.10}\left(1 - \frac{1}{1.10^{20}}\right)\frac{1}{(1+r)^2}$$
$$= -100 + 70.2 + 35.2$$
$$= \$5.4 \text{ million} > 0$$

So, the NPV does not agree with the payback rule in this case.

7. The profitability index for each investment is:

Investment	NPV	Cost	Profitability Index
1	$400,000	$400,000	1
2	$300,000	$200,000	1.5
3	$650,000	$400,000	1.625
4	$150,000	$600,000	0.25

Pick investments 1, 2, and 3.

■ Self-Test Questions

1. When the discount rate used in a capital budgeting problem is equal to the IRR
   a. the NPV is positive.
   b. the NPV is zero.
   c. the NPV is negative.
   d. the payback period is negative.

2. Which of the following decision rules is always correct because it is directly tied to the goal of maximizing shareholder wealth?
   a. IRR rule
   b. MIRR rule
   c. Payback period rule
   d. NPV rule

3. Your company is considering upgrading its assembly line and has estimated that this upgrade has an NPV of $350,000. Which of the following is the best way to interpret the NPV of this project?
   a. Upgrading the assembly line is equivalent to receiving $350,000 today.
   b. This assembly line should be upgraded so long as the upgrade costs less than $350,000.
   c. Taking the money that would be spent on the assembly line upgrade and investing it at the project's IRR would result in a value of $350,000 at the end of the project.
   d. After the payback period, this project generates cash flows worth $350,000.

4. Software Design, Inc. is considering a number of capital budgeting projects. However, the company is currently constrained by the number of programmers that it has. The company has 20 programmers on its staff and will not be able to hire any new programmers in the near future. Which of the following methods should the company use to choose which projects to accept?
   a. Rank the projects based on payback period and choose the projects with the shortest payback period.
   b. Rank the projects based on IRR and choose the projects with the highest IRR.
   c. Rank the projects based on NPV and choose the projects with the highest NPV.
   d. Rank the projects based on the profitability index and choose the projects with the highest profitability index.

5. Gulf Coast Refiners (GCR) is considering opening a new refinery that will cost the company $5 million. The refinery will generate positive cash flows over the next few years, but will become obsolete in five years. At that time, GCR will need to close the plant and pay to have toxic waste cleaned up from the site. Because the sign of the cash flows of this capital budgeting problem changes more than once,
   a. GCR should use the IRR rule instead of the NPV rule to determine whether the project should be done.
   b. following the IRR rule may not be reliable because of the possibility of multiple IRRs.
   c. the payback period is the most reliable decision tool in this situation.
   d. the project should only be accepted if the MIRR exceeds the IRR.

6. Your company has just been offered a contract worth $500,000 per year for five years. However to take the contract, you will need to purchase some new equipment. If the discount rate for this project is 9%, what is the most you can pay for the equipment and still have a positive NPV for this project?
   a. $225,000
   b. $324,966
   c. $1,944,826
   d. $3,553,911

7. Travis Telecommunications is investing in a new communications network that will cost the company $6 million today. The network will increase cash flows by $1.5 million each year for the next five years when the system will become obsolete. What is the IRR of this project?
   a. 7.9%
   b. 9.3%
   c. 10.7%
   d. 12.6%

8. Your company is considering a contract to provide food services at the upcoming World's Fair. It will cost your company $2 million in setup costs in the year before the World's Fair. The year of the fair, your company expects to generate cash flows of $4.5 million. The following year, your company will have to pay $1 million to dismantle the project. To evaluate this project, your colleagues suggest that the $1 million dismantling cost be discounted to Time Period 0 using the company's cost of capital to prevent any problems that may occur in an IRR calculation due to the cash flow signs changing twice for this project. Your colleague is suggesting that
   a. an MIRR be calculated.
   b. the payback rule be implemented.
   c. a profitability index be calculated.
   d. a constrained NPV be calculated.

9. The owners of Central City Strip Mall are deciding what types of businesses to place in the 20,000 square feet of empty retail space. One of the businesses they are considering is a 700-square foot ice cream shop; they estimate the NPV of the ice cream shop is $400,000. Another project they are considering is a 2800-square foot drug store; they estimate the NPV of the drug store is $950,000. Which of the following can you conclude from this information?
   a. The owners should choose the drug store over the ice cream shop because it has a higher NPV.
   b. The owners would need to know the IRR of the two projects to compare the projects.
   c. The ice cream shop's profitability index is greater than the drug store's profitability index.
   d. The drug store's profitability index is greater than the ice cream store's profitability index.

10. Clementine Clothing is considering a project that has an IRR of 15%. The company's cost of capital for the project is 12%. Which of the following is a TRUE statement?
    a. Clementine should not undertake the project since the cost of capital is less than the IRR.
    b. If Clementine is deciding between this project and another mutually exclusive project that has an IRR of 14%, you know that Clementine should choose the project with an IRR of 15%.
    c. This project will have a negative NPV.
    d. The IRR of 15% measures the sensitivity of the project's NPV in case the firm has made an error in estimating the cost of capital.

11. An NPV profile is
    a. a graph of project's NPV over a range of different discount rates and is useful when there is uncertainty regarding a project's cost of capital.
    b. a chart of a project's NPV at different points in time and is useful when evaluating projects with different lives.
    c. an estimate of a project's IRR using the trial-and-error approach.
    d. a chart of the relationship between the NPV of a firm's projects and the value created for the firm.

12. Carlisle Car Company is considering a project that has an NPV of $250,000. This NPV can best be interpreted as
    a. the value of the project's benefits today when the present value of the costs are not considered.
    b. adding $250,000 value to the company today.
    c. the project's benefits in today's dollars outweigh the future benefits by $250,000.
    d. adding $250,000 value to the company at the end of the life of the project.

Answers to Self-Test Questions

1. b
2. d
3. a
4. d
5. b
6. c
7. a
8. a
9. c
10. d
11. a
12. b

Chapter 9
Fundamentals of Capital Budgeting

■ Key Learning Objectives

- Identify the types of cash flows needed in the capital budgeting process
- Forecast incremental earnings in a pro forma earnings statement for a project
- Convert forecasted earnings to free cash flows and compute a project's NPV
- Recognize common pitfalls that arise in identifying a project's incremental free cash flows
- Assess the sensitivity of a project's NPV to changes in your assumptions
- Identify the most common options available to managers in projects and understand why these options can be valuable

■ Notation

$CapEx$	capital expenditures
$EBIT$	earnings before interest and taxes
FCF_t	free cash flow in year t
IRR	internal rate of return
NPV	net present value
NWC_t	net working capital in year t
PV	present value
r	projected cost of capital

■ Chapter Synopsis

9.1 The Capital Budgeting Process

A **capital budget** lists all of the projects that a firm plans to undertake during future years. The **capital budgeting** process is the selection of the projects that should be included in the capital budget. To determine the NPV of a project, we need to estimate the project's cash flows. We generally begin this process by determining the **incremental earnings** of a project; the incremental earnings forecast tells us how the decision will affect the firm's reported profits from an accounting perspective. The incremental earnings forecast is then used to estimate the cash flows of the project.

9.2 Forecasting Incremental Earnings

First, we need to generate revenue and cost estimates and forecast expected incremental income statements for the project being considered. For example, in the decision about whether to upgrade the manufacturing plant in this chapter, the following incremental earnings were forecasted:

Year	0	1	2	3	4	5
Incremental Revenues		500	500	500	500	500
Incremental Costs	–50	–150	–150	–150	–150	–150
Depreciation		–204	–204	–204	–204	–204
EBIT	–50	146	146	146	146	146
Taxes (at 40%)	20	–58.4	–58.4	–58.4	–58.4	–58.4
Incremental Earnings	–30	87.6	87.6	87.6	87.6	87.6

The table above is called a **pro forma** statement because it is based on hypothetical assumptions rather than actual data. Let's look a little more closely at how these earnings are developed.

Operating Expenses versus Capital Expenditures

The $50,000 spent on redesigning the plant is an operating expense in Year 0. However, investments in plant, property, and equipment (the $1,020,000 spent to buy, ship, and install the machine in our example) are not directly listed as expenses when calculating earnings. Instead, the firm deducts a fraction of the cost of these items each year as depreciation. The simplest depreciation method is **straight-line depreciation,** in which the asset's cost is divided equally over its life. Assuming that the equipment has a 5-year depreciable life and that we use the straight-line method, we would expense $1,020,000/5 = $204,000 per year for five years. In other words, the upfront cash outflow of $1,020,000 to purchase and set up the machine is not recognized as an expense in Year 0; instead, it appears as depreciation expenses in Years 1 through 5.

Incremental Revenue and Cost Estimates

Our next step is to estimate the ongoing revenues and costs for the project. All our revenue and cost estimates should be *incremental,* meaning that we only account for additional sales and costs generated by the project. In our plant upgrade example, additional capacity will allow us to generate incremental revenues of $500,000 per year for 5 years. The increased production is also associated with incremental costs of $150,000 per year.

Taxes

The final expense we must account for is corporate taxes. We use the firm's **marginal corporate tax rate,** which is the tax rate it will pay on an *incremental* dollar of pretax income.

What about Interest Expenses?

When evaluating a capital budgeting decision, interest expense is generally not included in the income statement. The effects of using debt financing, such as incurring interest expense, is accounted for in the appropriate discount rate used to evaluate this project, the weighted average cost of capital (which we will discuss later in the text). Thus, the net income computed in the spreadsheet above is referred to as the **unlevered net income** of the project, to indicate that it does not include any interest expenses associated with debt.

9.3 Determining Incremental Free Cash Flow

While earnings are an accounting measure of the firm's performance, they do not represent real profits. To evaluate a capital budgeting decision, we must determine its consequences for the firm's available cash. The incremental effect of a project on the firm's available cash is the project's incremental **free cash flow.** Free cash flow can be calculated as:

$$\text{Free Cash Flow} = (\text{Revenue} - \text{Cost} - \text{Depreciation}) \times (1 - \text{Tax Rate})$$
$$+ \text{Depreciation} - \text{Cap Expen} - \text{Change in NWC}$$

- Since depreciation is not a cash expense (it is a method used for accounting and tax purposes to allocate the original purchase cost of the asset over its life) it should be added back to unlevered net income. Depreciation does have an effect on FCF—it reduces taxes by Depreciation X(T), which is known as the **depreciation tax shield.**
- **Capital expenditures** are cash payments made to acquire fixed assets.
- **Net working capital (NWC)** is the difference between current assets and current liabilities. The main components of net working capital are cash, inventory, accounts receivable, and accounts payable. Net working capital reflects a short-term investment that ties up cash flow that could be used elsewhere. Thus, whenever net working capital increases, reflecting additional investment in working capital, it represents a reduction in cash flow that year. Only changes in net working capital impact cash flows.

Calculating the NPV

We forecast incremental free cash flows so that we will have the necessary inputs to calculate the project's NPV. To compute a project's NPV, we must discount its free cash flow at the appropriate cost of capital. The cost of capital for a project is the expected return that investors could earn on their best alternative investment with similar risk and maturity. Using r to represent the cost of capital, the present value of the free cash flow in year t (or FCF_t) is:

$$PV(FCF_t) = \frac{FCF_t}{(1+r)^t}$$
$$= FCF_t \times \underbrace{\frac{1}{(1+r)^t}}_{t\text{-year discount factor}}$$

9.4 Other Effects on Incremental Free Cash Flows

When computing the incremental free cash flows of an investment decision, we should include all changes between the firm's free cash flows with the project versus without the project. These include opportunities forgone due to the project and effects of the project on other parts of the firm. For example, if a project uses a resource that the company already owns, the **opportunity cost** of using the resource should be included as an incremental cost of the project. Firms must also be sure to consider any **project externalities,** which are indirect effects of the project that may increase or decrease the profits of other activities of the firm. For example, **cannibalization** can occur when the sales of a new product displace sales of an existing product.

Because **sunk costs** must be paid regardless of the decision whether or not to proceed with a project, they are not incremental costs and should not be included in the cash flow analysis. **Fixed overhead expenses** that are not directly attributable to a single business activity and **past research** and **developmental expenses** are typical sunk costs a firm may face.

Although the cash flows of projects will be spread throughout the year, for simplicity, we typically treat the cash flows as if they occur at annual intervals. When greater accuracy is required, a firm can forecast free cash flows on a shorter-term basis.

Because depreciation contributes positively to the firm's cash flow through the depreciation tax shield, firms want to use the most accelerated method of depreciation that is allowable for tax purposes. Using **MACRS depreciation,** the firm will accelerate and increase the present value of its tax savings. The **liquidation** or **salvage value** of assets must also be considered. When the assets are no longer needed they may have resale value; if the firm will incur a cost to remove and dispose of the asset, the asset will have a negative liquidation value. Taxes that must be paid on any capital gain that is received when an asset is sold for more than its book value must also be considered. Another tax consideration is any **tax loss carryforwards** or **carrybacks.**

9.5 Analyzing the Project

When evaluating a capital budgeting project, financial managers should make the decision that maximizes NPV. The cash flows and the cost of capital used in this process are estimates. **Sensitivity analysis** shows how the NPV varies when changing one variable. **Scenario analysis** considers the effect on the NPV of changing multiple project variables together. To see how far a variable can be changed until the project's NPV is 0, a **breakeven analysis** can be performed.

9.6 Real Options in Capital Budgeting

If a project has a **real option,** the company has the right, but not the obligation, to take particular business actions. Because the company is not obligated to take the action, it will only do it if it increases the NPV of the project. In particular, because real options allow a decision maker to choose the most attractive alternative after new information has been learned, the presence of real options adds value to an investment opportunity. For example, the **option to delay commitment** (the option to time the investment) is almost always present. A project may also have an **option to expand,** which is the option to start a project and expand only if it is successful. An **abandonment option** is the option to walk away. Abandonment options can add value to a project because a firm can drop a project if it turns out to be unsuccessful. All these options point to the same conclusion: *if you can build greater flexibility into your project, you will increase the NPV of the project.*

■ Selected Concepts and Key Terms

Capital Budgeting

The **capital budget** lists all of the projects that a firm plans to undertake during the next period. The process of analyzing investment opportunities and deciding which ones to accept is referred to as **capital budgeting.** We use the NPV rule to evaluate capital budgeting decisions, making decisions that maximize NPV. We accept projects with a positive NPV.

Incremental Earnings

The **incremental earnings** of a project include all incremental revenues and costs associated with the project. Interest expense is generally not included as a cost of the project; it is reflected in the discount rate used to evaluate the project. When financing-related expenses are excluded in the calculation of earnings, we determine the project's **unlevered net income.**

Incremental Free Cash Flow

We compute **incremental free cash flow** from incremental earnings by eliminating all noncash expenses and including all capital investment. The basic calculation for free cash flow is:

$$\text{Free Cash Flow} = (\text{Revenue} - \text{Cost} - \text{Depreciation}) \times (1 - \text{Tax Rate})$$
$$+ \text{Depreciation} - \text{Cap Expen} - \text{Change in NWC}$$

Net working capital is defined as Cash + Inventory + Receivables − Payables; an increase in net working capital is a cash outflow.

Opportunity Cost

An **opportunity cost** is the cost of using an existing asset. The value an existing asset has in another opportunity should be used as a cost of using that asset in a project being considered.

Project Externalities

Project externalities are cash flows that occur when a project affects other areas of the company's business. These externalities must be considered when deciding whether to accept a project.

Sunk Cost

A **sunk cost** is an unrecoverable cost that has already been incurred. Sunk costs should not be used in making a decision about a project.

Depreciation

Depreciation expenses affect free cash flow only through the **depreciation tax shield.** The depreciation tax shield is the savings that result from the ability to deduct depreciation and equals the depreciation expense × marginal tax rate.

The firm should use the most accelerated depreciation schedule possible. With **straight-line depreciation,** an asset's cost is divided equally over its life. **Modified Accelerated Cost Recovery System (MACRS) depreciation** is the most accelerated depreciation method allowed by the Internal Revenue Service. Assets are categorized according to their asset class and a corresponding MACRS depreciation table assigns a fraction of the purchase price that the firm can depreciate each year.

Trade Credit

Trade credit is the difference between accounts receivable and accounts payable; it is the net amount of the firm's capital that is used as a result of credit transactions.

The discount rate for a project is its **cost of capital:** The expected return of securities with comparable risk and horizon.

Cannibalization

The term **cannibalization** is used when sales of a new product displace sales of an existing product.

Sensitivity Analysis

Sensitivity analysis breaks the NPV calculation into its component assumptions and shows how the NPV varies as the underlying assumptions change. In this way, sensitivity analysis allows us to explore the impact of estimate errors for the project.

Scenario Analysis

Scenario analysis considers the effect on NPV of changing multiple project parameters simultaneously.

Real Options

Real options are options to take a business action, often after gathering more information. The presence of real options in a project increases the project's NPV. A project may have an **abandonment option** which would be an option to end the project sooner, an **option to expand** which would allow the project to become bigger than originally planned, or an **option to delay** which would allow the decision about the project to be made at a later date.

Break-Even Analysis

Break-even analysis computes the level of a parameter that makes the project's NPV equal zero.

■ Concept Check Questions and Answers

1. What is capital budgeting, and what is its goal?

   Capital budgeting is the process of selecting projects that the firm plans to undertake during future years. The goal of capital budgeting is to choose projects that will add value for the shareholders.

2. Why is computing a project's effect on the firm's earnings insufficient for capital budgeting?

   Earnings are not equivalent to cash flows. In order to evaluate a project, we must consider both the size and the timing of cash flows.

3. How are operating expenses and capital expenditures treated differently when calculating incremental earnings?

   Operating expenses are considered an expense in the year that they occur. The cost of a capital expenditure is spread out over the life of the asset in the form of a depreciation expense.

4. Why do we focus only on *incremental* revenues and costs, rather than all revenues and costs of the firm?

   In capital budgeting, we want to determine how a particular project impacts the firm. Therefore, we want to focus on the changes in revenues and the changes in costs that will occur if the project is accepted.

5. If depreciation expense is not a cash flow, why do we have to subtract it and add it back? Why not just ignore it?

   Although depreciation is not a cash outflow, it is considered an expense when calculating taxable income. Therefore, there is a depreciation tax shield that impacts the earnings of a project.

6. Why does an increase in net working capital represent a cash outflow?

   Net working capital reflects a short-term investment that ties up cash flow that could be used elsewhere. Thus, whenever net working capital increases it represents a reduction in cash flow that year.

7. Should we include sunk costs in the cash flows of a project? Why or why not?

   No, we should not include sunk costs in the cash flows of a project because sunk costs must be paid regardless of the decision to proceed or not with the project. Sunk costs are not incremental with respect to the current decision.

8. Explain why it is advantageous for a firm to use the most accelerated depreciation schedule possible for tax purposes.

   Because depreciation contributes positively to the firm's cash flow through the depreciation tax shield, it is in the firm's best interest to use the most accelerated method of depreciation that is allowable for tax purposes. By doing so, the firm will accelerate its tax savings and increase its present value.

9. What is sensitivity analysis?

   Sensitivity analysis breaks the NPV calculation into its component assumptions, and shows how the NPV varies as the underlying assumptions change. In this way, sensitivity analysis allows us to explore the impact of estimate errors for the project.

10. How does scenario analysis differ from sensitivity analysis?

    Sensitivity analysis considers one parameter at a time. Scenario analysis considers the effect on NPV of changing multiple project parameters simultaneously.

11. What are real options?

    Real options are options to take a business action, often after gathering more information.

12. Why do real options increase the NPV of the project?

    The presence of real options in a project increases the project's NPV. Because real options allow a decision maker to choose the most attractive alternative after new information has been learned, the presence of real options adds value to an investment opportunity. Because the decision maker has the option, but not the obligation, to take the action, he or she will choose to take the action only if it increases NPV.

■ Examples with Step-by-Step Solutions

Incremental Earnings

9.1 **Problem:** Your firm owns a Volkswagen dealership, and you are considering entering into a 5-year agreement to sell Audi A4s also. The cars would cost $26,000, and you believe that you can sell 50 Audis per year at an average price of $30,000. You would have to hire two new salespeople that you would pay $30,000 per year each plus 5% of the revenue they each generate. Audi would require that you invest $200,000 (depreciable straight line over 5 years) in Audi-related signs, equipment, and furniture to place in your dealership. After 5 years, the unneeded equipment would have a market value of $50,000. Your firm requires a 12% return on all new investments, and the tax rate is 40%.

Calculate the incremental earnings of this project.

Solution

Plan: We need four items to calculate incremental earnings: (1) incremental revenues, (2) incremental costs, (3) depreciation, and (4) the marginal tax rate:

Incremental Revenues are additional units sold × price = 50 × $30,000 = $1,500,000.

Incremental Costs are:

$$\begin{aligned} \text{Cost of goods sold} &= \text{additional units sold} \times \text{production costs} \\ &= 50 \times \$26,000 \\ &= \$1,300,000 \end{aligned}$$

$$\begin{aligned} \text{Selling, General and Administrative} &= \text{Salary} + \text{Commission} \\ &= 60,000 + 75,000. \end{aligned}$$

Depreciation is Depreciable Base/Depreciable Life = $200,000/5 = $40,000

Marginal Tax Rate: 40%

Execute:

	Year 0	Years 1–5
Revenues		1,500,000
Costs of Goods Sold		–1,300,000
Gross Profit		200,000
Selling, General and Admin		
Salary		–60,000
Commission		–75,000
Depreciation		–40,000
EBIT		25,000
Income Tax at 40%		–10,000
Incremental Earnings		15,000

Evaluate: The cost of the equipment does not affect earnings in the year it is purchased, but does so through the depreciation expense in the following 5 years.

Taxing Losses for Projects in Profitable Companies

9.2 **Problem:** Sierra Shoes expects to earn pretax income of $30 million next year on its existing operations. The company is considering expanding into a new product line and producing hiking boots. The high initial costs and advertising expenses the company would incur next year to launch this line of hiking boots would lead to an estimated operating loss of $4 million for the hiking boot line next year. If Sierra Shoes pays a 30% tax rate on its pretax income, what will it owe in taxes next year if it does not enter into the hiking boot business? What will it owe if it does enter into the new line of business?

Solution

Plan: We can calculate the taxes if the company does not enter the hiking boot business by multiplying the company's tax rate of 30% by the expected pretax income of $30 million. We can calculate Sierra's taxes if it does enter into the new line of business by combining the pre-hiking boot pretax income ($30 million) and the operating loss from the boot line ($4 million) and multiplying the amount by the tax rate of 30%.

Execute: Without the new product line, Sierra will owe $30 million × 0.30 = $9 million in taxes. With the new product line, Sierra will owe ($30 million - $4 million) × 0.30 = $26 million × 0.30 = $7.8 million in taxes.

Evaluate: Launching the new product line will reduce Sierra's taxes by $9 million − $7.8 million = $1.2 million next year.

Determining Incremental Free Cash Flows

9.3 **Problem:** In Example 9.1, we calculated the incremental earnings for the Audi project. Using the information from that example, calculate incremental free cash flows for the project.

Solution

Plan: We know the incremental earnings for each year from Example 9.1. To calculate the incremental free cash flow in this example, we need to add back depreciation and subtract capital expenditures from incremental earnings for each year. We need to recognize the $200,000 cash outflow associated with the equipment purchase in Year 0 and add back the $40,000 depreciation expenses from Years 1 to 5 as they are not actually cash outflows.

At the end of Year 5, the equipment can be sold for $50,000 resulting in an after-tax cash flow = sale price − tax rate × (sale price − book value) = $50,000 − 0.40($50,000 − 0) = $30,000.

Execute:

	Year 0	Years 1–4	Year 5
Revenues		1,500,000	1,500,000
Costs of Goods Sold		−1,300,000	−1,300,000
Gross Profit		200,000	200,000
Selling, General and Admin		60,000	60,000
Salary		75,000	75,000
Commission			
Depreciation		−40,000	−40,000
EBIT		25,000	25,000
Income Tax at 40%		−10,000	−10,000
Incremental Earnings		15,000	15,000
Add Back Depreciation		40,000	40,000
Subtract Purchase of Equipment	200,000	0	30,000
Incremental Free Cash Flows	−200,000	55,000	85,000

Evaluate: The Audi project has no impact on earnings in Year 0. However, the firm would have $200,000 in cash leaving the company at the time for equipment. For Years 1–5, the cash inflow is higher than the incremental earnings reported.

Incorporating Changes in Net Working Capital

9.4 Problem: In Examples 9.1 and 9.3, we calculated incremental earnings and free cash flows for the Audi project. Suppose that you find out that you will also be required to invest in 20 cars to keep in inventory over the life of the project. This inventory requirement will impact your investment in working capital. Assuming that after 5 years you can recover this investment in working capital, how does the requirement of keeping 20 cars in inventory impact the project's free cash flow?

Solution

Plan: An increase in net working capital represents an investment that reduces the cash available to the company and so reduces free cash flow. The Year 0 investment in working capital is 20 cars at $26,000 or $520,000. Because you must keep 20 cars in inventory over the life of the project, there are no net working capital changes for Years 1 to 4. At the end of the project, the investment in working capital can be recovered, resulting in a decrease in working capital of $520,000.

Execute:

The cash flow effect of the net working capital each year would be:

Year	0	1	2	3	4	5
Net Working Capital	520,000	520,000	520,000	520,000	520,000	0
Change in NWC	−520,000	0	0	0	0	+520,000
Cash Flow Effect	−520,000	0	0	0	0	+520,000

The incremental free cash flows would then be:

	Year 0	Years 1–4	Year 5
Revenues		1,500,000	1,500,000
Costs of Goods Sold		−1,300,000	−1,300,000
Gross Profit		200,000	200,000
Selling, General and Admin		60,000	60,000
Salary		75,000	75,000
Commission			
Depreciation		−40,000	−40,000
EBIT		25,000	25,000
Income Tax at 40%		−10,000	−10,000
Incremental Earnings		15,000	15,000
Add Back Depreciation		40,000	40,000
Subtract Purchase of Equipment	200,000		30,000
Subtract Changes in NWC	520,000		−520,000
Incremental Free Cash Flows	−720,000	55,000	605,000

Evaluate: The Audi project has no impact on earnings in Year 0. However, the firm would have $200,000 in cash leaving the company for equipment and $520,000 in cash leaving the company for working capital in Year 0. Thus, the cash outflow in Year 0 is −$720,000. For Years 1 to 5, the cash inflow is higher than the incremental earnings reported.

Calculating a Project's NPV

9.5 Problem: Given the information provided in Examples 9.1, 9.3, and 9.4, the Volkswagen dealership wants to know if it should accept the Audi project.

Solution

Plan: From Example 9.4, the incremental free cash flows for the Audi project are:

	Year 0	1	2	3	4	5
Incremental Free Cash Flows	−720,000	55,000	55,000	55,000	55,000	605,000

To compute the NPV, we sum the present values of all of the cash flows, noting that the Year 0 cash outflow is already a present value. We will use the firm's required rate of return on new investments of 12% to discount the cash flows.

Execute:

$$NPV = -720,000 + \frac{55,000}{(1.12)} + \frac{55,000}{(1.12)^2} + \frac{55,000}{(1.12)^3}$$
$$+ \frac{55,000}{(1.12)^4} + \frac{605,000}{(1.12)^5}$$
$$= -\$209,653 < 0$$

Evaluate: Based on our estimates, the NPV of the Audi project is −$209,653. While the dealership's upfront cost is $720,000, the present value of the additional free cash flow that the company will receive from the project is only $510,347. Thus, taking the Audi project would be equivalent to losing $209,653 of the shareholder's value.

Computing Accelerated Depreciation

9.6 Problem: Nationwide Trucking has purchased a truck for $90,000. What depreciation deduction would be allowed using the MACRS method, assuming the truck is designated to have a 5-year recovery period.

Solution

Plan: The table below provides the percentage of the cost that can be depreciated each year. Under MACRS, we take the percentage in the table for each year and multiply it by the original purchase price of the equipment to calculate the depreciation for that year.

Depreciation Rate for Recovery Period

Year	3 Years	5 Years	7 Years	10 Years	15 Years	20 Years
1	33.33	20.00	14.29	10.00	5.00	3.750
2	44.45	32.00	24.49	18.00	9.50	7.219
3	14.81	19.20	17.49	14.40	8.55	6.677
4	7.41	11.52	12.49	11.52	7.70	6.177
5		11.52	8.93	9.22	6.93	5.713
6		5.76	8.92	7.37	6.23	5.285
7			8.93	6.55	5.90	4.888
8			4.46	6.55	5.90	4.522
9				6.56	5.91	4.462
10				6.55	5.90	4.461
11				3.28	5.91	4.462
12					5.90	4.461

Execute: The MACRS schedule (including Year 0) gives us depreciation amounts of:

Year	0	1	2	3	4	5
Dep rate	20.00%	32.00%	19.20%	11.52%	11.52%	5.76%
Dep amount	18,000	28,800	17,280	10,368	10,368	5,184

Evaluate: Compared to straight-line depreciation, the MACRS method allows for larger depreciation deductions earlier in the asset's life, which increases the present value of the depreciation tax shield. The total depreciation over the life of the asset (18,000 + 28,800 + 17.280 + 10,368 + 10,368 + 5184) equals the initial price of the truck (90,000).

Computing After-Tax Cash Flows for an Asset Sale

9.7 **Problem:** Suppose that Nationwide Trucking from Example 9.6, purchased the $90,000 truck 3 years ago and has been depreciating the truck according to the 5-year MACRS schedule. The company has decided to sell the truck. If Nationwide can sell the truck for $20,000, what is the after-tax cash flow that the company can expect from selling the equipment? Assume that Nationwide's marginal tax rate is 40%.

Solution

Plan: The after-tax cash flow will equal: Selling Price − Marginal Tax Rate × (Capital Gain). We know that the selling price is $20,000 and that the marginal tax rate is 40%; therefore, we must calculate the capital gain. The capital gain equals the selling price minus the book value of the truck. Because the book value of the truck equals the original purchase price (which is $90,000) minus the accumulated depreciation, we need to calculate the accumulated depreciation for the truck.

Thus, we need to follow these steps:
a. Determine the accumulated depreciation.
b. Determine the book value as purchase price minus accumulated depreciation.
c. Determine the capital gain as the sale price less the book value.
d. Compute the tax owed on the capital gain and subtract it from the sale price.

Execute: In Example 9.6, the first 3 years of the 5-year MACRS schedule (including Year 0) gave us depreciation amounts of:

Year	0	1	2	3
Dep rate	20.00%	32.00%	19.20%	11.52%
Dep amount	18,000	28,800	17,280	10,368

So, the accumulated depreciation is 18,000 + 28,800 + 17,280 + 10,368 = 74,448. The remaining book value is $90,000 − $74,448 = $15,552. The capital gain is then $20,000 − $15,552 = $4448 and the tax owed is 0.40 × $4448 = $1779.

Nationwide's after-tax cash flow is then found as $20,000 − $1779 = $18,221.

Evaluate: Because Nationwide is only taxed on the capital gain portion of the sale price, figuring the after-tax cash flow is not as simple as subtracting the tax rate multiplied by the sales price. Instead, we must determine the portion of the sales price that represents a gain and compute the tax from there. The same procedure holds for selling equipment at a loss relative to book value—the loss creates a deduction for taxable income elsewhere in the company.

Replacing an Existing Asset

9.8 Problem: Castillo Delivery Service is trying to decide whether to replace three of its delivery trucks. The old delivery trucks are fully depreciated, but Castillo could sell them for $4000 each. The three new trucks would cost $25,000 each. However, these new trucks are much more efficient and would reduce Castillo's costs by $19,000 per year. The new trucks would be depreciated over a 5-year life using MACRS. Castillo's marginal tax rate is 40%. How will this decision impact cash flows over the next 5 years?

Solution

Plan: Castillo will receive no incremental revenues if it purchases the new delivery trucks; however, the company will have incremental costs of −$19,000 per year. We will need to use the MACRS 5-year depreciation schedule to calculate depreciation on the new trucks; the depreciable basis for the trucks will be $75,000.

Year	0	1	2	3	4	5
Dep rate	20.00%	32.00%	19.20%	11.52%	11.52%	5.76%
Dep amount	15,000	24,000	14,400	8640	8640	4320

We will also need to consider the tax consequences of selling the old trucks:

$$\text{Capital gain on salvage} = \text{selling price} - \text{book value}$$
$$= \$12,000 - \$0$$
$$= \$12,000$$
$$\text{Cash flow from salvage value} = \$12,000 - (0.40)(12,000)$$
$$= \$7200$$

The incremental free cash flow in each year will equal the incremental earnings plus depreciation minus equipment purchases plus salvage cash flow.

Execute:

	Year 0	Year 1	Year 2	Year 3	Year 4	Year 5
Incr. Revenues						
Incr. Costs of Goods Sold		–19,000	–19,000	–19,000	–19,000	–19,000
Incr. Gross Profit		19,000	19,000	19,000	19,000	19,000
Depreciation	–15,000	–24,000	–14,400	–8640	–8640	–4320
EBIT	–15,000	–5000	4600	10,360	10,360	14,680
Income Tax at 40%	–6000	–2000	1840	4144	4144	5872
Incremental Earnings	–9000	–3000	2760	6216	6216	8808
Add Back Depreciation	15,000	24,000	14,400	8640	8640	4320
Purchase of Equipment	–75,000					
Salvage Cash Flow	7200					
Incremental Free Cash Flows	–61,800	21,000	17,160	14,856	14,856	13,128

Evaluate: Even though the decision has no impact on revenues, it still matters for cash flows because it reduces costs. Further, both selling the old machine and buying the new machine involve cash flows with tax implications.

■ Questions and Problems

1. Your large, highly profitable golf course management firm owns 200 acres in Surprise, Arizona, that is surrounded by a housing development and is zoned exclusively for a golf course. The nondepreciable land has increased in value over the years since you bought it from $10 million to $35 million and someone has offered to buy it for this price. Your original plan was to develop the land over the next 3 years by spending $20 million per year in pretax development costs. You would also have to spend $30 million in capital equipment today, and this would be depreciated straight-line over 3 years. Based on the performance of the other courses you own, you expect annual revenue for the course to be $40 million when it opens 3 years from today and that all operational costs (excluding tax and depreciation) will amount to 50% of revenue. From then on, you expect that the free cash flow the course generates will grow by 3% forever. Your tax rate is 40%. Assuming that your discount rate is 15%, should you sell the land?

2. You are considering the purchase of 1000 Coke machines in the greater Chicago area. The machines cost $2500 each and are depreciable straight-line over 5 years. Sales are expected to be 3000 bottles per machine in the first year at a selling price of $1 per bottle. Sales revenue is expected to be constant every year thereafter. The cost of each bottle is $0.30. Operating expenses include stocking and maintenance and are expected to amount to $1000 per year per machine. You would have to stock each machine with 200 bottles at the beginning of the project. After 5 years you plan to sell the machines for $1000 each and recover any investment in working capital. The tax rate is 40%. The firm uses all equity financing, and stockholders require a 15% return. Determine whether the project is a good idea.

3. Polar Bear Ice is upgrading its ice-making equipment that will allow it to produce 50% more ice in the same amount of time. The company currently sells 200,000 bags of ice per year at a price of $1 per bag. If the company increases it sales by 50% next year, what will the incremental revenues be next year from the upgrade?

4. TexMex Café operates a restaurant in the central Dallas area. The company is considering opening another restaurant in the northern Dallas area. The company already owns the land where they would locate the second restaurant. The company has just spent $7500 on market research to estimate the extent of customer demand for the food at the new location. How would each of the following factor into the capital budgeting process?
   a. The original purchase price of the land where the restaurant will be located.
   b. The $7500 spent on market research to evaluate customer demand.
   c. Construction costs of the new restaurant.
   d. The loss of sales at the existing restaurant location, if customers who previously drove across town to eat there become diners at the new location instead.
   e. Interest expense on the debt borrowed to pay for the construction costs.
   f. TexMex Café's advertising expenses.

5. Andersen Appliances currently has $900,000 in annual sales. Cost of goods sold for the company is 70% of sales. Andersen receives trade credit from its suppliers and payables are 12% of cost of goods sold. Andersen also extends credit to its customers and receivables account for 15% of annual sales. Andersen is expecting its sales to grow by 5% a year over the next 4 years. The company assumes that it will not have any incremental cash needs or inventory requirements related to this increase level of sales. How will this growth impact the company's net working capital free cash flow?

6. Burger Barn plans to open a second location this year. The company expects high start-up costs associated with this new location; in fact, the company expects that the new location will generate an operating loss of $60,000. The company expects to earn pretax income of $140,000 from the operations of its existing location. If Burger Barn pays a 40% tax rate on its pretax income, what will it owe in taxes next year without the new location? What will it owe with the new location?

■ Solutions to Questions and Problems

1. The project's NPV will indicate whether the project is worth more than the value of just selling the land, so it should be calculated.

   Determine the income statements from Years 1 through 4 for the project along with the operating cash flows.

	Years 1–3	Year 4
Revenue	0	40,000,000
Cost of Goods Sold + SG & A	20,000,000	20,000,000
EBITDA	–20,000,000	20,000,000
Depreciation	10,000,000	0
EBIT	–30,000,000	20,000,000
–Tax @ 40%	–12,000,000	8,000,000
Net Income	–18,000,000	12,000,000
+Depreciation	10,000,000	0
Operating Cash Flow	–8,000,000	12,000,000

Depreciation = $30,000,000/3 = $10,000,000 for Years 1–3 and $0 after Year 3.

Calculate the free cash flows for Years 0–4:

	Year 0	Years 1–3	Year 4
Operating Cash Flow		−8,000,000	12,000,000
−Capital Expenditures	30,000,000	0	0
−Increases in Working Capital	0	0	0
Free Cash Flow	−30,000,000	−8,000,000	12,000,000

Calculate the NPV.

$$\text{NPV} = -30 + \frac{-8}{1.15} + \frac{-8}{1.15^2} + \frac{-8}{1.15^3} + \frac{\left(\frac{12}{0.15-0.03}\right)}{1.15^3}$$

$$= \$17.5 \text{ million}$$

You would generate 35 − (35 − 10) 0.4 = $25 million > $17.5 million by selling the land, so you should sell.

2. If the NPV is above zero, the project is acceptable given the forecasts. Begin by determining the income statements from Years 1 through 5 for the project. (In this case, each year will be the same.)

	Years 1–5
Revenue	3,000,000
Cost of Goods Sold	900,000
Gross Profit	2,100,000
Selling, General & Admin Expenses	1,000,000
EBITDA	1,100,000
Depreciation	500,000
EBIT	600,000
−Tax @ 40%	240,000
Net Income	360,000
+Depreciation	500,000
Operating Cash Flow	860,000

The free cash flows for Years 0 through 5 are:

	Year 0	Years 1–4	Year 5
Operating Cash Flow		860,000	860,000
−Capital Expenditures	2,500,000	0	−600,000
−Increases in Working Capital	60,000	0	−60,000
Free Cash Flow	−2,560,000	860,000	1,520,000

(Note that the –$600,000 capital expenditure in Year 5 is the after-tax salvage value and is calculated as $1,000,000 × (1 − 0.4). The working capital is 200 bottles × 0.30 × 1000 machines.)

Now, the NPV can be calculated:

$$\text{NPV} = -2,560,000 + 860,000 \left(\frac{1}{0.15} - \frac{1}{0.15(1.15)^4} \right) + \frac{1,520,000}{1.15^5}$$

$$= 650,990 > 0$$

Since the NPV is positive, the project should be accepted.

3. Polar Bear will sell 300,000 bags of ice next year, which is an increase of 100,000 bags. If each bag sells for $1, the incremental revenue will be $100,000.

4. a. The original purchase price of the land is irrelevant going forward. The opportunity cost of the land is important to the decision-making process. TexMex Café should consider what other opportunities it has (selling the land, etc.) and factor this into its decision.
   b. The $7500 spent on market research is a sunk cost and is irrelevant to the decision-making process going forward.
   c. The construction costs would be a capital expenditure (cash outflow) at the time they occur; these costs would be depreciated over time when calculating incremental earnings.
   d. If the existing restaurant loses customers to the new location, then these customers should not be considered as incremental revenue at the new location.
   e. The interest expense is part of the cost of financing and is reflected in the discount rate.
   f. Any advertising expense that TexMex would incur with its existing restaurant should not be considered in the decision of whether or not to open a second location. Only additional (incremental) advertising should be considered.

5. To calculate the sales level for each year, we use the formula:

$$\text{Sales}_i = \$900,000 \times (1.05)^i$$

To calculate the COGS, we use the formula:

$$\text{COGS}_i = \text{Sales}_i \times 0.70$$

For Years 1 through 4, sales and COGS are projected to be:

	Year 0	Year 1	Year 2	Year 3	Year 4
Sales	900,000	945,000	992,250	1,041,863	1,093,956
COGS	630,000	661,500	694,575	729,304	765,769

Next, we will calculate receivables as 15% of sales and payables as 12% of COGS:

	Year 0	Year 1	Year 2	Year 3	Year 4
Sales	900,000	945,000	992,250	1,041,863	1,093,956
COGS	630,000	661,500	694,575	729,304	765,769
Receivables	135,000	141,750	148,838	156,279	164,093
Payables	75,600	79,380	83,349	87,516	91,892

The net working capital associated with the growth in sales can now be calculated:

Year	0	1	2	3	4
Net Working Capital Forecast					
1 Cash Requirements	0	0	0	0	0
2 Inventory	0	0	0	0	0
3 Receivables (15% of Sales)	135,000	141,750	148,838	156,279	164,093
4 Payables (12% of COGS)	75,600	79,380	83,349	87,516	91,892
5 Net Working Capital	59,400	62,370	65,489	68,763	72,201

Net working capital will be increasing each year. An increase in net working capital is a cash outflow.

6. Without the new location, Burger Barn will owe $140,000 × 0.40 = $56,000 in corporate taxes next year. With the new location, the company's pretax income next year will be $140,000 − $60,000 = $80,000; with the new location the company will owe $80,000 × 0.40 = $32,000 in corporate taxes. Thus, launching the new product reduces Burger Barn's taxes next year by $56,000 − $32,000 = $24,000. Because the losses on the new location reduce Burger Barn's taxable income dollar for dollar, it is the same as if the new location had a tax bill of a negative $24,000.

■ Self-Test Questions

1. We only want to consider incremental earnings in the capital budgeting process. Incremental earnings are the
    a. additional sales and costs associated with the project.
    b. externalities generated from the project.
    c. capital expenditures minus the salvage values of the assets.
    d. opportunity cost of the asset being used multiplied by the marginal tax rate.

2. An increase in net working capital
    a. occurs when accounts payable increases.
    b. occurs when the marginal tax rate increases.
    c. is a cash outflow.
    d. arises when MACRS depreciation is used instead of straight-line depreciation.

3. To compute a project's NPV,
    a. discount its incremental earnings at the appropriate cost of capital.
    b. discount its free cash flow at the appropriate cost of capital.
    c. subtract its incremental earnings from its free cash flow.
    d. subtract the present value of incremental earnings from the free cash flow that occurs in the first year of the project.

Chapter 9 Fundamentals of Capital Budgeting   153

4. Tricia's Treasures, a gift shop in Tulsa wants to begin selling Schwarzwald Christmas ornaments. Tricia will need to initially stock 300 of the ornaments and expects to sell 1000 of these ornaments each year. Tricia will pay $2 each for these ornaments and sell them for $5 each. Which of the following is a TRUE statement?
   a. Because Tricia will stock the ornaments in inventory, she will have a capital expenditure of $600 the first year that will need to be depreciated over the life of the project.
   b. Because Tricia will stock the ornaments in inventory, she will have a capital expenditure of $1500 the first year that will need to be depreciated over the life of the project.
   c. Because Tricia will stock the ornaments in inventory, she will have an increase in net working capital of $600 at the beginning of the project.
   d. Tricia will have a cash outflow of $1500 in the first year, but no change in net working capital.

5. Tricia (from Question 4) is currently spending $2000 a month in overhead expenses (electric bill, etc.). When evaluating if she should sell the Schwarzwald ornaments, Tricia should
   a. include a portion of the $2000 as selling, general, and administrative expenses in her incremental earnings estimate.
   b. include a portion of the $24,000 yearly overhead expense in her depreciable base each year.
   c. include an overhead cost of $2 an ornament in her analysis.
   d. ignore the $24,000 a year in overhead expenses because they are not incremental to her decision.

6. Tricia (from Question 4) currently sells 3000 Navidad Christmas ornaments each year. If she expands her selection to include Schwarzwald ornaments, she estimates that 10% of her customers who were buying Navidad ornaments will now buy Schwarzwald ornaments. This is known as
   a. canabilization and should be factored into the capital budgeting analysis.
   b. a real option to abandon and should be factored into the capital budgeting analysis.
   c. a real option to expand and should be factored into the capital budgeting analysis.
   d. a real option to expand and should not be included in the capital budgeting analysis.

7. Snoopy's Submarine Sandwich Shop just signed a 5-year lease for 1000 square feet of space in the Outback Strip Center. Snoopy's will pay $750 a month for this lease. The contract states that Snoopy may also lease the adjacent 500 square feet of space at any time during the contract for $400 a month. Thus, Snoopy has
   a. a real option to expand.
   b. a real option to abandon.
   c. an opportunity cost of $400 a month.
   d. a sunk cost of $400 a month.

8. An east coast chain, Sea Harbor Restaurants, just paid $25,000 to a market research firm to analyze the feasibility of the restaurant expanding to several west coast locations. The $25,000
   a. is a capital expenditure to be depreciated over the life of the project.
   b. represents an increase in net working capital.
   c. represents a decrease in net working capital.
   d. is a sunk cost and should not be considered in evaluating the project at this point.

9. Toyota is considering building an additional U.S. plant to produce trucks. In considering this project, the interest expense associated with borrowing money to build the plant is
   a. considered a general and administrative expense.
   b. considered a depreciable capital expenditure.
   c. subtracted from incremental earnings when calculating free cash flows.
   d. captured in the cost of capital used to discount future cash flows.

10. Sunshine Consulting purchased $10,000 of computer equipment 6 years ago. The equipment has been fully depreciated. Sunshine can sell the equipment for $1500 and purchase all new computer equipment for $9000. Sunshine is in the 30% tax bracket. Which of the following is a TRUE statement?
    a. If Sunshine sells the computer equipment, it will have a capital gain of $1500 and will have to pay $450 in taxes on that gain.
    b. If Sunshine sells the computer equipment, it will have a capital gain of $7500 and will have to pay $2250 in taxes on that gain.
    c. If Sunshine sells the computer equipment and buys the new computer equipment, it will have a cash outflow of $7500 and will reduce its tax bill by $2250.
    d. Since the old computer equipment is fully depreciated, there is no impact to Sunshine for selling the equipment.

11. Which of the following would result in an increase in net working capital?
    a. An increase in accounts payable
    b. A decrease in accounts receivable
    c. An increase in inventory
    d. All of the above would result in an increase in net working capital

12. Which of the following is the most accurate statement regarding depreciation?
    a. It is in a firm's best interest to use the most accelerated method of depreciation allowable for tax purposes because depreciation contributes positively to the firm's cash flow through the depreciation tax shield.
    b. The depreciation method a firm chooses is irrelevant because depreciation is not an actual cash flow; it is simply an accounting reporting technique.
    c. It is in a firm's best interest to use straight-line depreciation rather than an accelerated method because a firm would always prefer to spend money later in time rather than sooner.
    d. A firm's choice of depreciation method impacts the company's operating income but not its taxable income or tax liability because depreciation is not an actual cash outflow.

Answers to Self-Test Questions

1. a
2. c
3. b
4. c
5. d
6. a
7. a

8. d

9. d

10. a

11. c

12. a

■ Appendix: Using Excel for Capital Budgeting

Problem: 3com is considering producing a new hand-held, wireless Internet device. Management spent $2 million last year on test marketing and has developed a forecast. Total cash costs (COGS, SG & A, etc.) of the device will be $25 each and they will sell them for $100 each. They expect to produce and sell 50,000 of the devices each year for the next 5 years. They would have to construct a manufacturing plant immediately, which would cost $7 million and be depreciated over 10 years using straight-line depreciation. They would have to invest $2 million in inventory beginning today, and this amount would not change over the life of the project. In 5 years, they will quit, dispose of the plant for $1 million, and recover working capital. The tax rate is 35%, the firm uses stock financing, and stockholders require a 12% return. Should 3com accept the project? How sensitive is the result to the sales forecast of 50,000 units per year?

Solution

Plan: We will use Excel to build a pro forma statement and perform sensitivity analysis. We will begin by putting our assumptions in Excel. Our basic assumptions are:

Assumptions	
Units Sold	50,000
Sale Price ($/unit)	100
Cost ($/unit)	25
NWC ($ thousands)	2,000,000
Depreciation	700,000
Tax Rate	35%
Cost of Capital	12%

Note that the $2 million spent last year on test marketing is a sunk cost and will not factor into any decisions going forward. We will create a spreadsheet to calculate incremental free cash flows by having the formulas reference the cells containing our assumptions. This way, the assumptions can be changed easily to perform sensitivity analysis. Once we have the free cash flows, we will be able to calculate the NPV to determine whether the company should go forward with the project.

Execute: The assumptions are placed in the shaded rectangle portion of the spreadsheet. Then formulas are used with these cell references to generate net income. For example, "B2 × B3" is placed in cell c12 to calculate sales.

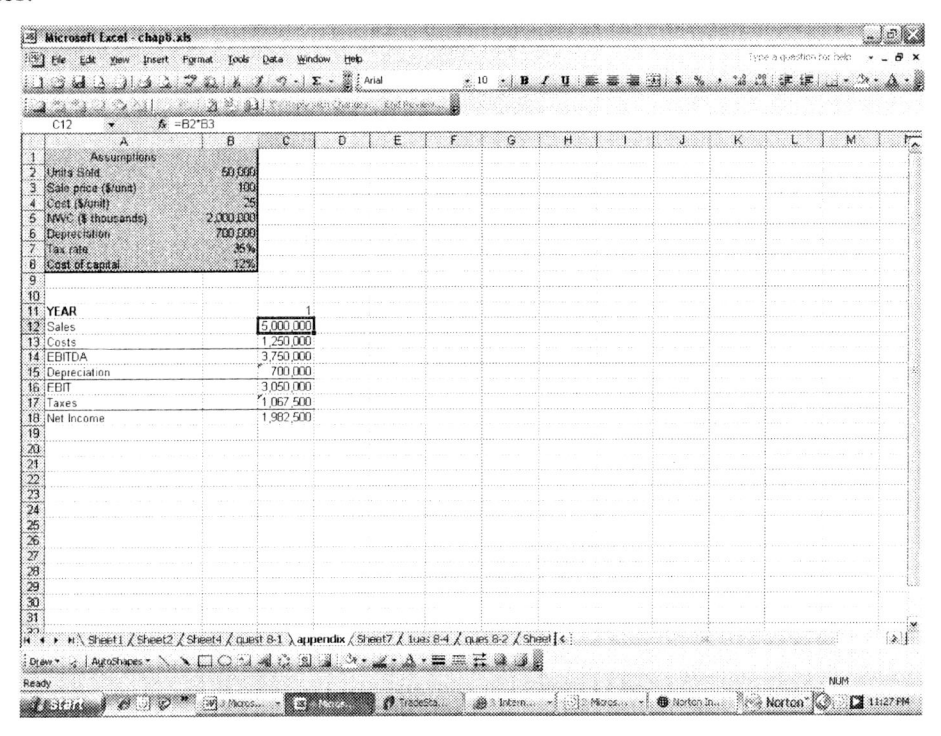

Once we calculate incremental earnings, we can calculate free cash flow. This is shown in the spreadsheet below. Remember, using cell references when setting up the spreadsheet will allow us to change assumptions and quickly see the results.

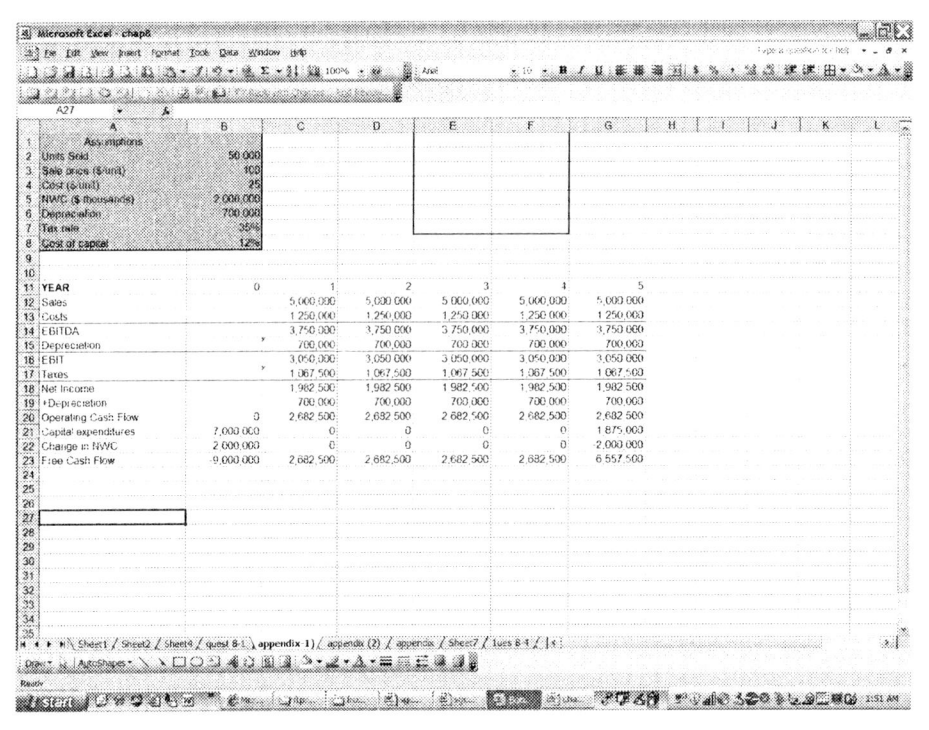

To see if the company should do the project, we need to calculate the NPV. We can do this using the NPV function in Excel. However, we must keep in mind the quirk in the Excel NPV calculation. Excel does not consider the initial cash outflow that occurs in Year 0; therefore, we must subtract that amount when calculating NPV. We will use the company's cost of capital when discounting the cash flows. We will place the cell reference for the cost of capital into the NPV equation.

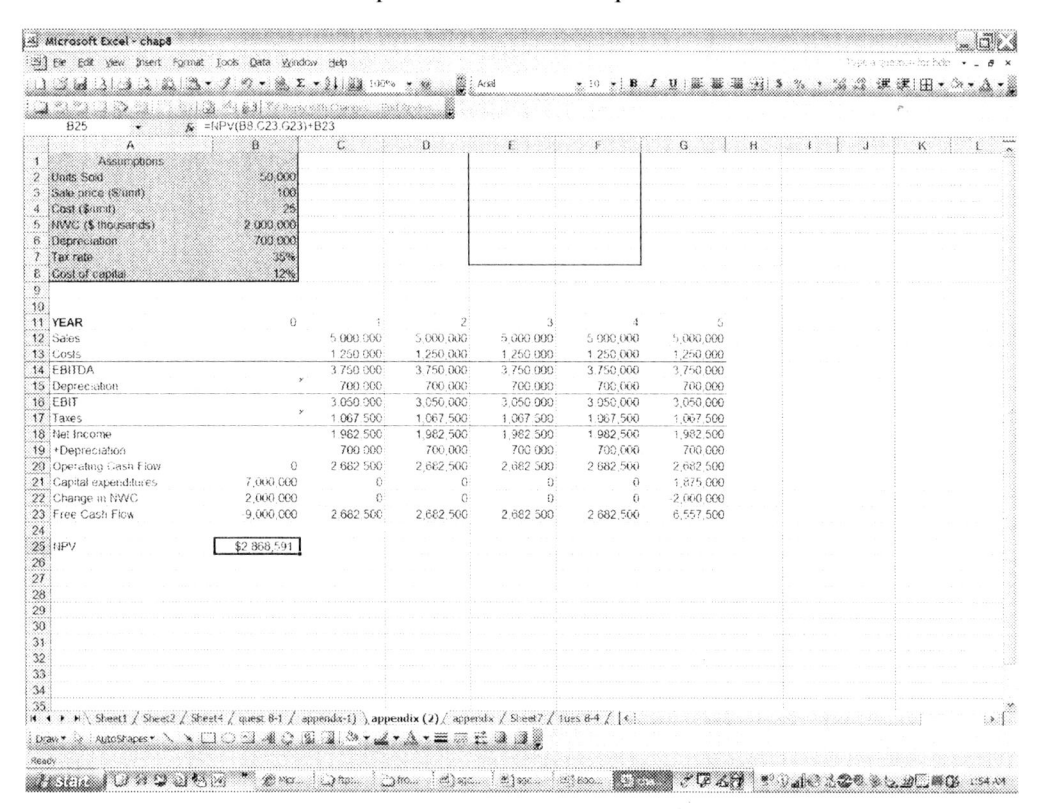

In the screen shot above, we can see that the NPV of this project, given the original assumptions, is a positive $2.7 million; this indicates we should accept the project. Of course, this NPV figure is based upon 3com's projections. Let's consider how sensitive this outcome is to the company's assumption that they will sell 50,000 units.

We can use Excel's Data Table tool to construct an NPV profile. Recall that a Data Table shows how the outcome of a formula (such as the NPV of 3com's project) changes when we change one of the cells in the spreadsheet. To set up the Data Table, we first create a cell that simply repeats the NPV; we do that in this example by setting cell F1 equal to B25 to create a new NPV column. Next, we create the column that will contain different assumptions regarding the number of units sold. This column must be directly to the left of the NPV cell (F1). Finally, we select the units sold and NPV columns and select "Table" from the "Data" menu. As the screen shot below shows, the Table Input Box will appear. Because our Units Sold assumptions are in a column, we enter "B2" into the column input cell in our spreadsheet. (Cell B2 contains the base case Units Sold assumption.) Once we do this and hit enter, Excel will create the sensitivity table shown in the screen shot below.

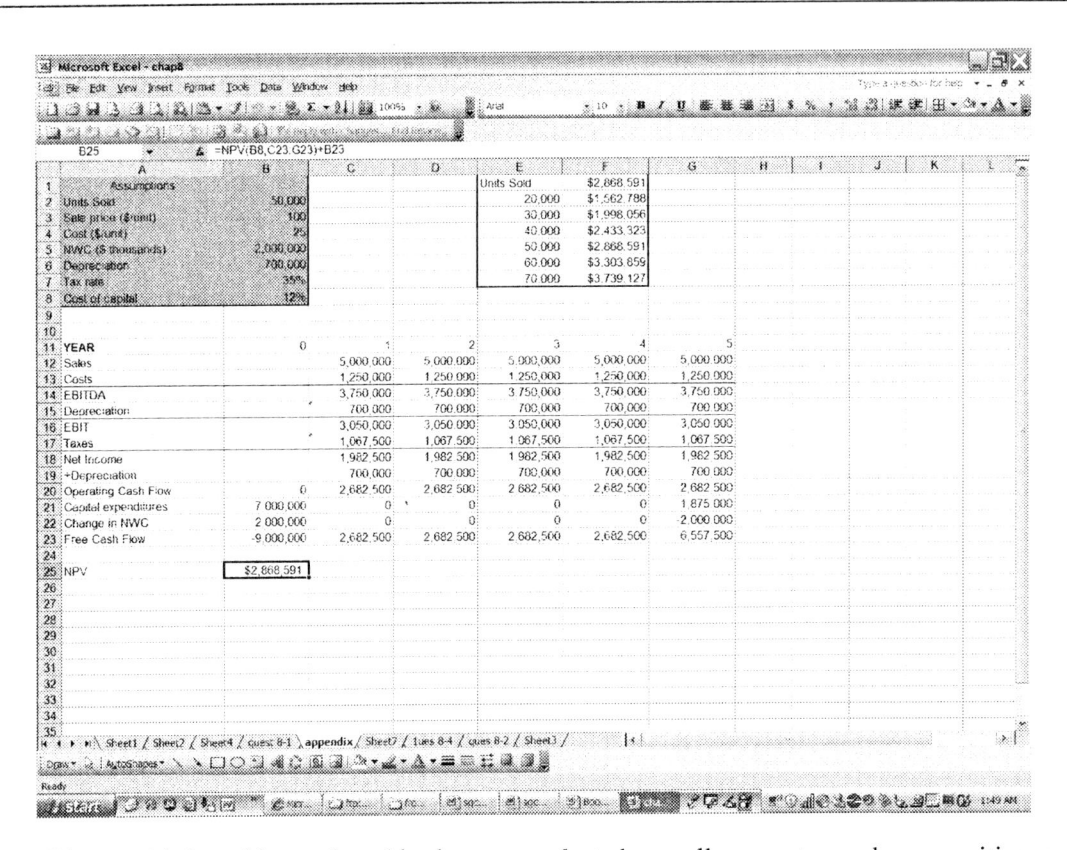

Evaluate: The sensitivity table produced in the screen shot above allows us to see how sensitive our decision to accept this project is to the initial assumption of 50,000 units being sold. As we can see in the table, even if the units sold falls far below the company's initial estimate, the NPV for this project is still positive. This same type of sensitivity analysis could be done for other variables, such as the selling price or the cost of goods sold.

Chapter 10
Stock Valuation: A Second Look

■ Key Learning Objectives

- Value a stock as the present value of the company's free cash flows
- Value a stock by applying common multiples based on the values of comparable firms
- Understand how information is incorporated into stock prices through competition in efficient markets
- Describe some of the behavioral biases that influence the way individual investors trade

■ Notation

Div_t	stock price at the end of year t
$EBIT$	earnings before interest and taxes
$EBITDA$	earnings before interest, taxes, depreciation, and amortization
EPS_t	earnings per share on date t
FCF_t	free cash flow on date t
g	expected dividend growth
g_{FCF}	expected free cash flow growth rate
N	terminal date or forecast horizon
P_t	stock price at the end of year t
PV	present value
r_E	equity cost of capital
r_{WACC}	weighted average cost of capital
V_t	enterprise value on date t

■ Chapter Synopsis

10.1 The Discounted Free Cash Flow Model

The **discounted free cash flow model** determines a firm's **enterprise value,** which is the value of the firm to all investors, including both equity and debt holders. Enterprise value is defined as:

$$\text{Enterprise Value} = \text{Market Value of Equity} + \text{Debt} - \text{Cash}$$

A firm's enterprise value can be estimated as the present value of the free cash flows that the firm has available to pay all investors. FCF is usually calculated as:

$$\text{Free Cash Flow} = \text{EBIT} \times (1 - \text{Tax Rate}) + \text{Depreciation}$$
$$- \text{Capital Expenditures} - \text{Increase in NWC}$$

Enterprise value, V_0, can thus be expressed as:

$$V_0 = \frac{FCF_1}{1+r_{wacc}} + \frac{FCF_2}{(1+r_{wacc})^2} + \cdots + \frac{FCF_N}{(1+r_{wacc})^N} + \frac{V_N}{(1+r_{wacc})^N}$$

Where V_N (the terminal value) is often estimated as a growing perpetuity, $\frac{FCF_N(1+g)}{(r_{wacc}-g)}$.

10.2 Valuation Based on Comparable Firms

Stocks can also be valued by using a **valuation multiple,** which is a ratio of the value to some measure of the firm's scale. The most common valuation multiple is the price-earnings ratio, which is equal to a firm's stock price divided by its earnings per share. If earnings over the prior 12 months are used in this calculation, we are calculating a **trailing P/E. A forward P/E** ratio calculation is based upon the expected earnings over the coming 12 months.

Many other valuation multiples are possible. Valuation multiples based on the firm's enterprise value are very common. For firms with substantial tangible assets, the ratio of price to book value of equity per share is sometimes used. Some multiples are specific to an industry; for example, in the cable TV industry it is useful to consider the multiple of enterprise value to the number of subscribers.

If comparable firms were identical, the multiple used was always proportionately related to value, and comparable firms were always valued correctly, the comparable multiples approach would be accurate and reliable. However, this is not generally the case. Most importantly, firms are not identical and the usefulness of a valuation multiple depends on the nature of the differences between firms and the sensitivity of the multiples to these differences. The differences in multiples for a sample of firms generally reflect differences in expected future growth rates and risk.

Furthermore, the comparable firm multiples approach does not take into account the important differences among firms. The fact that a firm has an exceptional management team, has developed an efficient manufacturing process, or has just secured a patent on a new technology is ignored when a valuation multiple is used. Discounted cash flow methods have the advantage that they allow specific information about the firm's cost of capital or future growth to be incorporated. Thus, because the true driver of value for any firm is its ability to generate cash flows for its investors, the discounted cash flow methods have the potential to be more accurate than the use of valuation multiples.

10.3 Information, Competition, and Stock Prices

For a publicly traded firm, the stock price is a reflection of the information from a multitude of investors about the value of the firm. Therefore, a valuation model can be applied to learn something about the firm's expected future cash flows or cost of capital. Only if you happen to have superior information that other investors lack regarding the firm's cash flows and cost of capital would it make sense to second-guess the stock price.

The idea that competition among investors works to eliminate all positive-NPV trading opportunities is referred to as the **efficient markets hypothesis.** It implies that securities will be fairly priced given all information that is available to investors. There are two types of information:

- **Public, easy to interpret information.** Competition between investors should cause stock prices to react nearly instantaneously to information that is available to all investors, such as news reports, financial statements, and corporate press releases. A few investors might be able to trade a small quantity of shares before the price fully adjusts. Most investors, however, will find that the stock price already reflects the new information before they are able to trade on it. It is generally believed that the efficient markets hypothesis holds very well with respect to this type of information.

- **Private, difficult to interpret information.** When private (nonpublic or difficult to determine) information is known by a single or small number of investors, it may be profitable to trade on the information. In this case, the efficient markets hypothesis does not hold. However, as these informed traders begin to trade, they will tend to move prices, so over time, prices will begin to reflect their information as well. If the profit opportunities from having this type of information are large, other individuals will attempt to gain the expertise and devote the resources needed to acquire it. As more individuals become better informed, competition to exploit this information will increase. Thus, in the long run, we should expect that the degree of inefficiency in the markets will be limited by the costs of obtaining the information.

If stocks are fairly valued as the efficient markets hypothesis suggests, then the value of a firm is determined by the cash flows that it can pay to its investors. Therefore managers should:

- Focus on NPV and free cash flow and make investments that increase the NPV of the firm.
- Avoid accounting illusions. The NPV of a firm's FCFs, not the accounting consequences of a decision, determines the value of the firm, so accounting measures should not drive decision making.
- Use financial transactions to finance valuable investments. Since buying or selling a security is a zero-NPV transaction, it is not a source of value for the firm. Financial policy should therefore be driven by the firm's real investment needs.

10.4 Individual Biases and Trading

The **overconfidence hypothesis** states that individual investors mistakenly believe that they can pick winners and losers better than investment professional; this overconfidence results in the investors trading too much. The **disposition effect** is the tendency of investors to hold on to stocks that have lost value and sell stocks than have risen in value since the time of purchase. The behavior of individual investors appears to be influenced by news stories and events, their moods, and their own personal experiences. The behavioral biases can lead to lower returns and harm investors.

■ Selected Concepts and Key Terms

Total Payout Model

The **total payout model** states that the value of a firm's stock equals the present value of the total payouts that the firm makes to shareholders. These payouts include both dividends and **share repurchases.**

Discounted Free Cash Flow Model

The **discounted free cash flow model** is a method for estimating a firm's enterprise value by discounting its future free cash flows.

Weighted Average Cost of Capital (WACC)

The **weighted average cost of capital (WACC)** is the cost of capital that reflects the risk of the overall business, which is the combined risk of the firm's equity and debt.

Method of Comparables

The **method of comparables** is a method of estimating the value of a firm based on the value of other comparable firms which are expected to generate similar cash flows in the future and have the same level of risk. A **valuation multiple** is a ratio of value to another variable. One commonly used ratio is the price-earnings (P/E) ratio. If **trailing earnings** (earnings from the past 12 months) are used in the calculation, a **trailing P/E** is calculated. A **forward P/E** is calculated using the earnings expected over the next 12 months, known as **forward earnings.**

Efficient Markets Hypothesis

The **efficient markets hypothesis** is the idea that competition among investors works to eliminate all positive-NPV trading opportunities. It implies that securities will be fairly priced given all information that is available to investors.

Individual Biases

According to the **overconfidence hypothesis,** individual investors mistakenly think that they can outperform professional investors and, thus, trade too frequently. The **disposition effect** refers to the tendency of investors to sell winners and keep losers, lowering their return.

■ Concept Check Questions and Answers

1. How does the growth rate used in the total payout model differ from the growth rate used in the dividend-discount model?

   In the total payout model, we use the growth rate of earnings, rather than earnings per share when forecasting the growth of the firm's total payouts.

2. Why do we ignore interest payments on the firm's debt in the discounted free cash flow model?

   We ignore interest payments on the firm's debt in the discounted free cash flow model because the financing costs are captured in the discount rate.

3. What are some common valuation multiples?

   Valuation multiples commonly used to value stocks include the price-earnings ratio, the ratio of enterprise value to EBIT, the ratio of enterprise value to EBITDA, the ratio of enterprise value to free cash flow, the ratio of enterprise value to sales, and the ratio of price to book value.

4. What implicit assumptions are made when valuing a firm using multiples based on comparable firms?

   Using valuation multiples based on comparable firms assumes that comparable firms have the same risk and future growth as the firm being valued.

5. State the efficient markets hypothesis.

   The efficient markets hypothesis states that competition eliminates all positive-NPV trades, which is equivalent to stating that securities with equivalent risk have the same expected rate of return.

6. What are the implications of the efficient market hypothesis for corporate managers?

   In an efficient market, to raise the stock price, corporate managers should (1) focus on NPV and free cash flow from the firm's investments, (2) avoid accounting illusion, and (3) use financial transactions to support investments.

7. What are several systematic behavioral biases that individual investor fall prey to?

   Individual investors display overconfidence in their trading ability which leads to overtrading. Individual investors tend to sell winners too soon and hold losers too long, known as the disposition effect. Also, individual investors are influenced by their mood, their past experiences, news reports, and events.

8. Why would excessive trading lead to lower realized returns?

   If a trader has no above average ability but trades excessively, the trader will experience high costs of trading due to commissions and bid-ask spreads. These high trading costs will lead to lower returns.

Examples with Step-by-Step Solutions

Valuing a Company using Free Cash Flow

10.1 Problem: Norris Communication Equipment Co. had sales of $540 million in 2010. The company has been experiencing a strong growth period, and you expect the company's sales to grow at a rate of 11% in 2011 and 8% in 2012. After that, you expect the company's long-run growth rate to be 4%. Historically, Norris's EBIT has been 12% of sales, and you expect that ratio to remain constant going forward. As the company grows, you expect increases in net working capital requirements to be 15% of any increase in sales. You also expect capital expenditures to equal depreciation expenses each year. Norris has a tax rate of 30% and a weighted average cost of capital of 9%. If Norris begins 2011 with $32 million in cash, $832 million in debt, 100 million shares outstanding, what is your estimate of the value of a share of Norris's stock at the beginning of 2011?

Solution

Plan: We need to build a pro forma statement for Norris so that we can estimate the firm's future free cash flow. We will also need to calculate a continuation value for Norris at the end of our explicit projects. Because we expect Norris to grow at a constant rate after 3 years, we can use Eq. (10.6) to compute a terminal enterprise value. The present value of the free cash flows for 2011 and 2012, and the terminal value will be the total enterprise value for Norris. Using that value, we can subtract the debt, add the cash, and divide by the number of shares outstanding to compute the price per share.

Execute: The spreadsheet below presents a simplified pro forma for Norris based on the information we have:

Year	2010	2011	2012	2013
FCF Forecast ($ million)				
Sales	540.000	599.400	647.352	673.246
Growth Rate		11%	8%	4%
EBIT (12% of sales)		71.928	77.68224	80.78953
Less Income Tax (30%)		21.578	23.305	24.237
Plus: Depreciation		—	—	—
Less Capital Expenditures		—	—	—
Less Increases in NWC		8.910	7.193	3.884
Free Cash Flow		41.440	47.185	52.669

Because capital expenditures are expected to equal depreciation, we can set both to zero rather than explicitly forecast them.

Given our assumption of a constant long-run growth rate of 4% in free cash flows after 2013 and a weighted average cost of capital of 9%, we can compute a terminal enterprise value of

$$V_{2013} = \left(\frac{1+g_{FCF}}{r_{wacc} - g_{FCF}}\right) \times FCF_{2013} = \left(\frac{1.04}{0.09-0.04}\right) \times 52.669 = \$1096 \text{ million}$$

Norris's current enterprise value is the present value of its free cash flows plus the firm's terminal value:

$$V_0 = \frac{41.440}{1.09} + \frac{47.185}{1.09^2} + \frac{52.669}{1.09^3} + \frac{1096}{1.09^3} = \$964.7 \text{ million}$$

We can now estimate the value of a share of Norris's stock:

$$P_0 = \frac{964.7 + 32 - 832}{100} = \$1.647$$

Evaluation: The Valuation Principle tells us that the present value of all future cash flows generated by Norris plus the value of the cash held by the firm today must be equal to the total value of all the claims on those cash flows and cash. Because Norris has $832 million in debt claims, the remaining $164.7 million must be equity claims. Because there are 100 million shares outstanding, this results in a claim of $1.647 for each share outstanding.

Sensitivity Analysis for Stock Valuation

10.2 **Problem:** In Example 10.1, Norris's EBIT was assumed to be 12% of sales. If Norris's operating expenses increase and its EBIT falls to 11% of sales, how would the estimate of the stock's value change?

Solution

Plan: In this scenario, EBIT will decrease by 1% of sales compared to Example 10.1. Given this information, we can compute the effect on the free cash flow for each year. Once we have the new free cash flows, we repeat the approach used in Example 10.1 to arrive at a new stock price.

Execute: Due to the rising expenses, in each year EBIT will be lower than it was in Example 10.1. Following the same procedure as in Example 10.1, we calculate free cash flow for 2011, 2012, and 2013 using the chart below:

Year	2010	2011	2012	2013
FCF Forecast ($ million)				
Sales	540.000	599.400	647.352	673.246
Growth Rate		11%	8%	4%
EBIT (11% of sales)		65.934	71.20872	74.05707
Less Income Tax (30%)		19.780	21.363	22.217
Plus: Depreciation		—	—	—
Less Capital Expenditures		—	—	—
Less Increases in NWC		8.910	7.193	3.884
Free Cash Flow		37.244	42.653	47.956

Now we estimate the terminal value as:

$$V_{2013} = \left(\frac{1 + g_{FCF}}{r_{wacc} - g_{FCF}}\right) \times FCF_{2013} = \left(\frac{1.04}{0.09 - 0.04}\right) \times 47.956 = \$997.48 \text{ million}$$

The firm's enterprise value is now:

$$V_0 = \frac{37.244}{1.09} + \frac{42.653}{1.09^2} + \frac{47.956}{1.09^3} + \frac{997.48}{1.09^3} = \$877.34 \text{ million}$$

This new estimate for the value of the stock is:

$$P_0 = \frac{877.34 + 32 - 832}{100} = \$0.7734$$

Evaluate: The estimation of the value of Norris's stock price is extremely sensitive to changes in the estimation of operating expenses. A small change in this assumption, led to a drop of over 50% in the estimation of the stock price.

Valuation Using the Price-Earnings Ratio

10.3 Problem: Toronto Textiles has earnings per share of $2.65. The average P/E of comparable textile companies is 19.8. Estimate the value of Toronto's stock using the P/E as a valuation multiple.

Solution

Plan: We estimate a share price for Toronto Textiles by multiplying its EPS by the P/E of comparable firms:

EPS × P/E = Earnings per Share × (Price per Share/Earnings per Share) = Price per Share

Execute:

$$P_0 = \$2.65 \times 19.8 = \$52.47$$

Evaluate: If Toronto has a P/E multiple similar to the comparable textile companies, the stock's price would be 19.8 times earnings or $52.47. Valuation multiples are simple to use; however, we are relying on a very strong assumption about the similarity of the comparable firms to Toronto. It is important to consider whether this assumption is likely to be reasonable.

Growth Prospects and the Price-Earnings Ratio

10.4 Problem: Century Meds and Bio Medical are both companies in the pharmaceutical industry. Century Meds has a stock price of $45.25 and a forward earnings per share of $3.60. Bio Medical has a stock price of $118.50 and a forward earnings per share of $4.90. Calculate their forward P/E ratios and explain the difference.

Solution

Plan: We can calculate their P/E ratios by dividing each company's price per share by its forward earnings per share. The difference we find is most likely due to different growth expectations.

Execute: The forward P/E for Century Meds = $45.25/$3.60 = 12.57. The forward P/E for Bio Medical = $118.50/$4.90 = 24.18.

Evaluate: Although both companies are in the pharmaceutical industry, Bio Medical has a much higher forward P/E ratio. Investors in Bio Medical are willing to pay over 24 times the expected earnings for this coming year because they are also buying the expected future earnings of the company. The market is expecting these earnings to grow at a higher rate for Bio Medical than it is for Century Meds.

Valuation Using the Enterprise Value Multiple

10.5 Problem: Fresh Express, Inc. is a wholesale produce company and has EBITDA of $750,000. The company has cash of $70,000 and debt of $123,000. The EV/EBITDA ratio for the wholesale produce industry as a whole is 7.2. The company has 2 million shares outstanding. Estimate Fresh Express's enterprise value using the enterprise value multiple. What is the corresponding estimate of its stock price?

Solution

Plan: We can estimate Fresh Express's enterprise value using its EBITDA and the average EV/EBITDA ratio for the industry. To estimate the stock price we will first need to calculate the equity value by subtracting the debt from the enterprise value and adding in the company's cash. This equity value will then be divided by the number of shares outstanding (2 million).

Execute: To estimate Fresh Express's enterprise value we multiply $750,000 by 7.2, which gives us $5.4 million. We calculate the equity value as $5,400,000 − $123,000 + $70,000 = $5,347,000. Thus, the corresponding stock price estimate is $5.347 million/2 million = $2.67.

Evaluate: If we assume that Fresh Express should be valued similarly to the rest of the industry, then $5.347 million is a reasonable estimate of its enterprise value and $2.67 is a reasonable estimate of its stock price. This, however, relies upon the assumption that Fresh Express's expected free cash flow growth is captured by the average industry valuation. If this assumption is wrong, then our valuation will be incorrect.

Using the Information in Market Prices

10.6 **Problem:** Renew Flooring is expected to pay a dividend of $2.20 one year from today. Its equity cost of capital is 12%, and you expect its dividends to grow at a rate of approximately 3% a year. You see that Renew's stock is currently trading at $27.50 a share. Given this stock price, how would you update your beliefs about its dividend growth rate?

Solution

Plan: We will apply the constant dividend growth model to estimate the growth rate the market expects. The formula for the constant dividend growth model is:

$$P_0 = \frac{D_1}{r_E - g}$$

We will use $2.20 for D_1, 12% for r_E, and $27.50 for P_0. We will solve for g.

Execute:

$$P_0 = \frac{D_1}{r_E - g} = \$27.50 = \frac{\$2.20}{0.12 - g} \Rightarrow g = 0.12 - \frac{2.20}{27.50} = 0.04 = 4\%$$

Evaluate: Given the market price of $27.50, the average investor is expecting a 4% dividend growth rate for this stock. Unless you have very strong reasons to trust your own estimate, you will want to increase your 3% growth rate estimate. If you think that your 3% growth rate estimate is indeed better than the market's estimate, you would be willing to pay only $2.20/(0.12 − 0.03) = $24.44 for this stock. Because the price you are willing to pay is below the current market price, you would not purchase this stock.

Stock Price Reactions to Public Information

10.7 **Problem:** SA Aeronautics just announced that it won a 5-year defense contract. The company expects its free cash flow to increase by $30 million for each of the next 5 years because of this contract. SA Aeronautics has 20 million shares outstanding, no debt, and an equity cost of capital of 9%. If this news came as a complete surprise to investors, what should happen to SA's stock price upon the announcement?

Solution

Plan: We will use the discounted free cash flow method to determine how this will impact SA Aeronautics' stock price. The impact of the contract on SA's enterprise value is the gain of a 5-year annuity of $30 million. We can compute the effect today as the present value of that annuity, using the equity cost of capital of 9% as the discount rate.

Execute: Using the annuity formula, the increase in expected free cash flow will increase SA's enterprise value by:

$$\$30 \text{ million} \times \frac{1}{0.09}\left(1 - \frac{1}{1.09^5}\right) = \$116.69 \text{ million}$$

The enterprise value will increase by $116.69 million. Because there are 20 million shares outstanding, this is an increase of $116.69 million/20 million shares = $5.83 per share.

Evaluate: This is good news about the company being publicly released. Because the effect on the firm's expected free cash flow is clear, we would expect the stock price to rise by $5.83 per share as soon as the information is released.

■ Questions and Problems

1. Trendsetters, Inc. had an EPS of $1.08 last year and a book value of equity of $6 per share. The company is currently trading at $16 per share. Firms in the clothing retail industry have an average price-to-earnings ratio of 22 and an average market-to-book ratio of 2.3. Is this stock overvalued based on:
   a. The industry-average P/E multiple?
   b. The industry-average price-to-book multiple?

2. Kelley and Kelley Pharmaceuticals just announced that it is pulling one of its major drugs off of the market because of health concerns that have arisen with several patients taking the drug. The company expects its free cash flow to be $10 million lower than expected for each of the next 10 years because of this drug withdrawal. Kelley and Kelley has 30 million shares outstanding, no debt, and an equity cost of capital of 11%. If this news came as a complete surprise to investors, what will happen to Kelley and Kelley Pharmaceuticals' stock price upon the announcement?

3. NetApps is a developer of iPhone and iPad applications. In 2010, the company had sales of $610,000. The company has experienced phenomenal growth over the past 3 years and expects strong growth to occur for the next several years. NetApps is expecting sales to grow at a rate of 25% in 2011, 35% in 2012, and 30% in 2013. After that, the company's long-run expected growth rate is 6%. You expect the company's EBIT to be 40% of sales going forward. You expect the company's capital expenditures to equal depreciation expenses each year. As NetApps expands, you expect increases in net working capital to be 12% of any increase in sales.
   a. Calculate the free cash flow for NetApps for 2011–2014, assuming that the company pays 30%.
   b. Assume that NetApps has a weighted average cost of capital of 8%. If the company has a 6% growth in free cash flows after 2014, compute the terminal enterprise value for NetApps in 2014.
   c. Calculate the current enterprise value for NetApps given your answers to part (a) and part (b).
   d. Estimate the value of a share of NetApps stock if the company begins 2001 with $12,000 in cash, $300,000 in debt, and 1 million shares of stock outstanding.

4. In Problem 3 above, we assumed that the company's tax rate was 30%. Suppose that overall tax rates fall and that NetApps will pay only a 25% tax rate.
   a. How will this lower the tax rate impact on the company's free cash flow for 2011–2014 and its terminal enterprise value in 2014?
   b. Estimate the value of a share of NetApps stock if the company begins 2001 with $12,000 in cash, $300,000 in debt, and 1 million shares of stock outstanding.
   c. How did the assumption about the tax rate impact the estimate of the stock price for NetApps?

5. Going back to NetApps in Problem 3 (assuming a 30% tax rate), what would happen to your estimate of NetApps stock price if the company decided it needed to keep more cash if its increases in net working capital were 15% of any increase in sales rather than only 12%?

6. Concord Jetliner Supply, Inc. (CJS) is currently selling for $3.20 a share. The company's EBITDA is $1.2 million. CJS has cash of $128,000 and debt of $650,000. The average EV/EBITDA ratio for the industry that CJS is in is 7.8. CJS has 5 million shares outstanding. Is the stock overvalued based on the enterprise value multiple?

7. Logan, a stock analyst, says that the most he is willing to pay for LOL stock is $13.00 a share and that he would expect to receive a 12% rate of return on the stock. You see that the stock just paid a dividend of $1.00 a share. What must Logan be expecting the growth rate in dividends to be if he is willing to pay $13.00 for this stock?

■ Solutions to Questions and Problems

1. a. $\dfrac{P}{EPS} \times EPS = 22 \times 1.08 = \$23.76 > 16$; so, based on a comparable price-to-earnings ratio valuation, Trendsetters is undervalued.

   b. $\dfrac{P}{\text{Book Value per Share}} \times \text{Book Value per Share} = 6 \times 2.3 = \$13.80 < \$16$; so, based on a comparable market-to-book ratio valuation, Trendsetters is overvalued.

2. Kelley and Kelley's enterprise value will decrease by:

$$\$10 \text{ million} \times \dfrac{1}{0.11}\left(1 - \dfrac{1}{1.11^{10}}\right) = \$58.89 \text{ million}$$

The stock price will fall by $58.89 million/30 million = $1.96 a share.

3. a.

Year	2010	2011	2012	2013	2014
FCF Forecast ($ million)					
Sales	610,000	762,500	1,029,375	1,338,188	1,418,479
Growth Rate		0.25	0.35	0.30	0.06
EBIT (40% of sales)		305,000	411,750	535,275	567,392
Less Income Tax (30%)		91,500	123,525	160,583	170,217
Plus: Depreciation		—	—	—	—
Less Capital Expenditures		—	—	—	—
Less Increases in NWC		18,300	32,025	37,058	9635
Free Cash Flow		195,200	256,200	337,635	387,539

Chapter 10   Stock Valuation: A Second Look   169

b. $V_{2014} = \left(\dfrac{1+0.06}{0.08-0.06}\right) \times 387,539 = \dfrac{1.06}{0.02} \times 387,539 = 20,539,567$

c. $V_0 = \dfrac{195,200}{1.08} + \dfrac{256,200}{1.08^2} + \dfrac{337,635}{1.08^3} + \dfrac{387,539}{1.08^4} + \dfrac{20,539,567}{1.08^4} = \$16,050,464$

d. $P_0 = \dfrac{16,050,464 + 12,000 - 300,000}{1,000,000} = \$15.76$

4. a.

Year	2010	2011	2012	2013	2014
FCF Forecast ($ million)					
Sales	610,000	762,500	1,029,375	1,338,188	1,418,479
Growth Rate		0.25	0.35	0.30	0.06
EBIT (40% of sales)		305,000	411,750	535,275	567,392
Less Income Tax (25%)		76,250	102,938	133,819	141,848
Plus: Depreciation		—	—	—	—
Less Capital Expenditures		—	—	—	—
Less Increases in NWC		18,300	32,025	37,058	9,635
Free Cash Flow		210,450	276,788	364,399	415,909

The terminal enterprise value is: $V_{2014} = \left(\dfrac{1+0.06}{0.08-0.06}\right) \times 415,909 = \dfrac{1.06}{0.02} \times 415,909 = \$22,043,177$

b. The current enterprise value is: $V_0 = \dfrac{210,450}{1.08} + \dfrac{276,788}{1.08^2} + \dfrac{364,399}{1.08^3} + \dfrac{415,909}{1.08^4} + \dfrac{22,043,177}{1.08^4} = \$17,229,533$

Therefore, we estimate the stock price as: $P_0 = \dfrac{17,229,533 + 12,000 - 300,000}{1,000,000} = \$17.54$

c. Lowering the estimated tax rate increased the value of the stock. A drop in the assumed tax rate from 30% to 25% resulted in a price increase of $1.78, or over 11%.

5.

Year	2010	2011	2012	2013	2014
FCF Forecast ($ million)					
Sales	610,000	762,500	1,029,375	1,338,188	1,418,479
Growth Rate		0.25	0.35	0.30	0.06
EBIT (40% of sales)		305,000	411,750	535,275	567,392
Less Income Tax (30%)		91,500	123,525	160,583	170,217
Plus: Depreciation		—	—	—	—
Less Capital Expenditures		—	—	—	—
Less Increases in NWC		22,875	40,031	46,322	12,044
Free Cash Flow		190,625	248,194	328,371	385,130

The terminal enterprise value is: $V_{2014} = \left(\dfrac{1+0.06}{0.08-0.06}\right) \times 385,130 = \dfrac{1.06}{0.02} \times 385,130 = \$20,411,890$

The current enterprise value is:

$$V_0 = \frac{190{,}625}{1.08} + \frac{248{,}194}{1.08^2} + \frac{328{,}371}{1.08^3} + \frac{385{,}130}{1.08^4} + \frac{20{,}411{,}890}{1.08^4} = \$15{,}936{,}393$$

Therefore, we estimate the stock price as: $P_0 = \dfrac{15{,}936{,}393 + 12{,}000 - 300{,}000}{1{,}000{,}000} = \$13.65$

6. CJS's enterprise value can be estimated as $1.2 million × 7.8 = $9.36 million. The equity value is $9,360,000 + $128,000 − $650,000 = $8,890,000. The corresponding stock price estimate is $8.89 million/5 million = $1.78. Thus, CJS's stock price of $3.20 a share is greater than what the enterprise value multiple would suggest it should be. Market participants must believe that CJS's expected free cash flow growth is not captured by the average industry valuation. Market participants must expect CJS's growth to be higher than the industry average, or they would conclude that CJS is overvalued.

7. $P_0 = D_1/(r_e - g) = (D_0 + D_0^* g)/r_e - g$

$$13.00 = (1 + 1 * g)/(0.12 - g)$$
$$1.56 - 13g = 1 + g$$
$$0.56 = 14g$$
$$g = 0.04 = 4\%$$

■ Self-Test Questions

1. Claudia is a financial analyst who estimates what the earnings for Microsoft will be over the next 12 months and then divides the current stock price by her estimation of future earnings. Claudia is calculating a
   a. trailing P/E ratio.
   b. forward P/E ratio.
   c. discounted enterprise value.
   d. terminal value.

2. A firm's enterprise value is
   a. calculated as the market value of stock + the value of debt − excess cash.
   b. the value of the enterprise after debt holders have been paid.
   c. the present value of the future dividends paid by the company.
   d. the price of a share of stock multiplied by the number of shares outstanding.

3. In an efficient market, corporate managers should
   a. focus on NPV and free cash flow from the firm's investments to increase stock price.
   b. focus on accounting techniques and methods to maximize net income and increase stock price.
   c. focus on its dividend policy.
   d. not attempt to increase the stock price because it is already at an efficient level.

4. According to the efficient markets hypothesis
   a. competition competes away any positive NPV investments.
   b. all firms will have the same required rate of return, despite the level of risk within the company.
   c. new information is not important in determining a stock's price.
   d. All of the above.

5. The equity cost of capital is
   a. calculated as the capital gain rate minus the dividend yield.
   b. the same for all U.S. companies according to the efficient markets hypothesis.
   c. higher for firms paying out relatively high dividends.
   d. the expected return of other investments available in the market that have the same risk as the firm's shares.

6. Caroline bought six stocks in January. By May, three of the six stocks had increased in price; the three remaining stocks decreased in price. Caroline sold the three winning stocks to lock in her gains and is waiting for the three losing stocks to recover before she sells them. Caroline's behavior is an example of the
   a. overconfidence hypothesis.
   b. disposition effect.
   c. mood dominance effect.
   d. economic environment hypothesis.

7. A firm's enterprise value can be estimated as
   a. the present value of all of the future dividends that the firm will pay to its shareholders.
   b. the future value of all of the net income that the firm will earn over the estimated life of the firm.
   c. the present value of all of the net income plus dividends the firm will earn over the estimated life of the firm.
   d. the present value of the free cash flows that the firm has available to pay all investors.

8. The efficient markets hypothesis implies
   a. that stocks will be fairly priced given all information that is available to investors.
   b. that information is not an important determinant of stock prices.
   c. firms, rather than investors, set stock prices.
   d. that stock prices will be equivalent to the future value of dividends rather than the present value of dividends.

9. When the discounted free cash flow model is used to determine firm value, interest payments are ignored because
   a. they are difficult to predict and lead to inaccurate estimations.
   b. interest payments are an optional expense of the business.
   c. the cost of borrowing is captured in the discount rate.
   d. investors are not concerned about interest payments because of the tax advantage of paying interest.

10. According to the total payout model
    a. the value of a firm's stock equals the present value of both dividends the firm pays and share repurchases by the firm.
    b. the value of a firm's stock equals the present value of only the dividends the firm pays.
    c. the value of a firm's stock equals the present value of only the share repurchases made by the firm.
    d. the value of a firm's stock is unrelated to the firm's dividends or share repurchases.

11. Which of the following is a TRUE statement?
    a. The more difficult and costly it is for investors to attain information, the less efficient a market will be.
    b. A market is efficient if valuation multiples are used and inefficient if a total payout method is used.
    c. An increase in the expected growth rate in a company's dividends should result in a lower current stock price for the company.
    d. The discounted free cash flow model results in biased estimates of firm value because it ignores interest payments.

12. A publicly traded firm's financial statements would be an example of
    a. private, easy to interpret information.
    b. public information.
    c. private, difficult to interpret information.
    d. inefficient information.

Answers to Self-Test Questions

1. b
2. a
3. a
4. a
5. d
6. b
7. d
8. a
9. c
10. a
11. a
12. b

Chapter 11
Risk and Return in Capital Markets

■ Key Learning Objectives

- Identify which types of securities have historically had the highest returns and which have been the most volatile
- Compute the average return and volatility of returns from a set of historical asset prices
- Understand the tradeoff between risk and return for large portfolios versus individual stocks
- Describe the difference between common and independent risk
- Explain how portfolios diversify away independent risk, leaving common risk as the only risk requiring a risk premium

■ Notation

Div_t	dividend paid on date t
P_t	price on date t
R_t	realized or total return of a security from date $t-1$ to t
$\bar{R}$	average return
$SD(R)$	standard deviation of return R
$Var(R)$	variance of return R

■ Chapter Synopsis

11.1 A First Look at Risk and Return

Historically, there has been a large difference in the returns and variability from investing in different types of investments. Figure 11.1 in your textbook shows the value of $100 invested at the end of 1925 in different assets at the end of 2009.

11.2 Historical Risks and Returns of Stocks

The **realized return** is the sum of the dividend yield and the capital gain rate of return over a time period. If you assume that all dividends are immediately reinvested and used to purchase additional shares of the same security, and the stock pays dividends at the end of each quarter, then the total annual return is:

$$1 + R_{annual} = (1 + R_1)(1 + R_2)(1 + R_3)(1 + R_4)$$

The **average annual return** of an investment during some historical period is simply the average of the realized returns for each year. That is, if R_t is the realized return of a security in each year t, then the average annual return for Years 1 through T is:

$$\bar{R} = \frac{1}{T}(R_1 + R_2 + \cdots + R_T)$$

Variance indicates the tendency of the historical returns to be different from their average and how far away from the average they tend to be. We calculate the variance using the equation:

$$\text{Var}(R) = \frac{1}{T-1}((R_1 - \bar{R})^2 + (R_2 - \bar{R})^2 + \cdots + (R_T - \bar{R})^2)$$

The **standard deviation,** which we will call the volatility, is the square root of the variance:

$$\text{SD}(R) = \sqrt{\text{Var}(R)}$$

The standard deviation plays an important role in describing a **normal distribution,** which is a symmetric probability distribution that is completely described by its average and standard deviation. Importantly, about two-thirds of all possible outcomes fall within one standard deviation above or below the average and about 95% of all possible outcomes fall within two standard deviations above and below the average.

Summary of Risk and Return Definitions and Formulas

Concept	Definition	Formula
Realized Returns	Total return earned over a particular period of time	$R_{t+1} = \dfrac{\text{Div}_{t+1} + P_{t+1} - P_t}{P_t}$
Average Annual Return	Average of realized returns for each year	$\bar{R} = \dfrac{1}{T}(R_1 + R_2 + \cdots + R_T)$
Variance of Returns	A measure of the variability of returns	$\text{Var}(R) = \dfrac{1}{T-1}((R_1 - \bar{R})^2 + (R_2 - \bar{R})^2 + \cdots + (R_T - \bar{R})^2)$
Standard Deviation or Volatility of Returns	The square root of the variance (which puts it in the same units as the average—namely "%")	$\text{SD}(R) = \sqrt{\text{Var}(R)}$
95% Prediction Interval	The range of returns within which we are 95% confident that next period's return will lie	$\bar{R} \pm 2 \times \text{SD}(R)$

11.3 The Historical Tradeoff between Risk and Return

Historically, the average return for small stocks has been higher than for other investment categories, such as the S&P 500, corporate bonds, or Treasury bills. However, the historical volatility, measured by standard deviation, of the small stock returns has also been higher than for the other asset classes. There is a positive relation between risk (as measured by standard deviation) and average return for portfolios of assets.

Although there is a relationship between risk and return for portfolios, there is no clear relationship between volatility and returns for individual stocks. When we consider individual stocks, we find:
- There is a relationship between size and risk—larger stocks have lower volatility overall.
- Even the largest stocks are typically more volatile than a portfolio of large stocks, like the S&P 500.
- All individual stocks have lower returns and/or higher risk than do large portfolios.

Thus, while volatility (standard deviation) seems to be a reasonable measure of risk when evaluating a large portfolio, the volatility of an individual security does not explain the size of its average return.

11.4 Common Versus Independent Risk

There are two kinds of risk:

- **Independent risk** is the risk that is uncorrelated and independent for all risky assets. For example, if theft insurance policy risks are independent, the number of claims is predictable for a large insurance company in a given period and, thus, the number of claims expected is not very risky.
- **Common risk** is the risk that affects the value of all risky assets. For example, common risk cannot be eliminated for a large portfolio of earthquake insurance policies in the same geographic region, and so the number of claims expected is very risky, even for a large insurance company.

The averaging out of independent risks in a large portfolio is called **diversification**. Because common risk affects all risky assets, it cannot be eliminated in a diversified portfolio.

11.5 Diversification in Stock Portfolios

Over any given time period, the risk of holding a stock is that the dividends plus the final stock price will be higher or lower than expected, which makes the realized return risky. Stock prices and dividends fluctuate due to two types of news:

1. *Company or industry-specific news:* This is good or bad news about a company (or industry) itself. For example, a firm might announce that it has been successful in gaining market share within its industry. This type of risk is unrelated across stocks and is referred to as **unsystematic risk.** When we combine many stocks in a large portfolio, unsystematic risk will be diversified away.

2. *Market-wide news:* This is news that affects the economy as a whole and therefore affects all stocks. For instance, the Federal Reserve might announce that it will lower interest rates to boost the economy. This type of risk is known as **systematic risk.** Because systematic risk affects all firms it cannot be diversified away.

Diversification eliminates idiosyncratic risk but does not eliminate systematic risk. Because investors can eliminate idiosyncratic risk, they should not require a risk premium for bearing it. Because investors cannot eliminate systematic risk, they must be compensated for taking it on. Therefore, it is a security's systematic risk that determines the risk premium investors require to hold it.

■ Selected Concepts and Key Terms

Stock Returns

The **realized return** is the sum of the dividend yield and the capital gain rate of return over a time period. If all dividends are immediately reinvested and used to purchase additional shares of the same security, and the stock pays dividends at the end of each quarter, then the **total annual return** is:

$$1 + R_{annual} = (1 + R_1)(1 + R_2)(1 + R_3)(1 + R_4)$$

The average annual return of an investment is simply the average of the realized returns for each year.

Risk of Stocks

Variance measures the tendency of the historical returns to be different from their average and how far away from the average they tend to be. Variance is calculated as:

$$\text{Var}(R) = \frac{1}{T-1}((R_1 - \bar{R})^2 + (R_2 - \bar{R})^2 + \cdots + (R_T - \bar{R})^2)$$

The **standard deviation,** or the volatility, is the square root of the variance:

$$\text{SD}(R) = \sqrt{\text{Var}(R)}$$

A **normal distribution** is a symmetric probability distribution that is completely described by its average and standard deviation. The **95% prediction interval** falls within two standard deviations above and below the average.

Common Risk

Common risk is the risk that is perfectly correlated across investments. This risk affects all risky assets and cannot be eliminated through diversification.

Independent Risk

Risk that is uncorrelated across investments is **independent risk.** Independent risk can be eliminated in a diversified portfolio.

Diversification

Diversification is the averaging out of independent risks in a large portfolio.

Systematic Risk

The risk that market-wide news and events will affect the value of all assets simultaneously is known as **systematic risk.** This risk is also called undiversifiable risk or market risk.

Unsystematic Risk

Unsystematic risk is the risk arising that a firm-specific event will impact the value of an asset. Investors can diversify and eliminate unsystematic risk.

■ Concept Check Questions and Answers

1. Historically, which types of investments have had the highest average returns and which have been the most volatile from year to year? Is there a relation?

    On average, stocks have had higher returns than bonds, with small company stocks having higher returns than large company stocks. Stocks have also had more volatile returns, with small company stock returns being the most volatile. There is a relationship that the investments with the greatest (least) amount of volatility have the greatest (least) average return.

2. Why do investors demand a higher return when investing in riskier securities?

   Investors do not like risk. If two securities have the same expected return and different levels of risk, investors will choose the security with the lower level of risk. The only way to entice investors to purchase the more risky security is for it to have a higher expected return.

3. For what purpose do we use the average and standard deviation of historical stock returns?

   The average and the standard deviation describe the distribution of returns for a normal distribution. The average tells us what the return tends to be, and the standard deviation tells us how far away from the average the return in any particular year is likely to be.

4. How does the standard deviation of historical returns affect our prediction in predicting the next period's return?

   The larger the standard deviation, the farther away from the average the next period's return might be. About 95% of the time, the return will be within ±2 standard deviations of the average.

5. What is the relation between risk and return for large portfolios? How are individual stocks different?

   There is a positive relation between risk (as measured by standard deviation) and average return for large portfolios of assets. There is no clear relationship between volatility and returns for individual stocks.

6. Do portfolios or the stocks in the portfolios tend to have the lower volatility?

   Portfolios tend to have lower volatility than the individual stocks in the portfolio have.

7. What is the difference between common and independent risk?

   Common risk is the risk that is perfectly correlated across investments. This risk affects all risky assets and cannot be eliminated through diversification. Independent risk is uncorrelated across investments and can be eliminated in a diversified portfolio.

8. How does diversification help with independent risk?

   Because independent risk is uncorrelated across investments, when one investment is impacted negatively by an event, other investments are not impacted. Therefore, only one investment in the portfolio decreases in value.

9. Why is the risk of a portfolio usually less than the average risk of the stocks in the portfolio?

   By holding a number of stocks in a portfolio, the investor is diversifying away unsystematic risk.

10. Does systematic or unsystematic risk require a risk premium? Why?

    Only systematic risk requires a risk premium. Investors can eliminate unsystematic risk through diversification; therefore, they receive no return premium for unsystematic risk.

Examples with Step-by-Step Solutions

Realized Return

11.1 **Problem:** You bought McDonald's stock on February 1, 2008, for $54.22 a share. The company paid a dividend of $0.375 a share on February 28. On February 29, you sold the stock for $54.11 a share. What was your realized return from holding McDonald's stock?

Solution

Plan: We know the purchase price ($54.22), the selling price ($54.11), and the dividend ($0.375). To calculate the realized return, we will use the equation:

$$R_{t+1} = \frac{Div_{t+1} + P_{t+1} - P_t}{P_t}$$

Execute: The return from February 1, 2008 until February 29, 2008 is equal to:

$$R_{t+1} = \frac{Div_{t+1} + P_{t+1} - P_t}{P_t}$$

$$= \frac{0.375 + 54.11 - 54.22}{54.22}$$

$$= 0.004887$$

$$= 0.4887\%$$

Evaluate: The realized return on McDonald's stock was 0.4887%. This can be broken down into the dividend yield and the capital gain yield:

$$Div\ Yield = \frac{Div_{t+1}}{P_t}$$

$$= \frac{0.375}{54.22}$$

$$= 0.6916\%$$

$$Capital\ Gain\ Yield = \frac{P_{t+1} - P_t}{P_t}$$

$$= \frac{54.11 - 54.22}{54.22}$$

$$= -0.2029\%$$

These returns include both the capital gain (or in this case a capital loss) and the return generated from receiving dividends. Both dividends and capital gains contribute to the total realized return.

Compounding Realized Returns

11.2 **Problem:** The stock prices and dividends for General Electric (GE) from June 16, 2005 through June 15, 2006 are shown below:

Date	Price	Dividend
6/16/05	30.44	
9/15/05	30.22	0.22
12/15/05	31.34	0.22
3/15/06	33.45	0.25
6/15/06	32.22	0.25

What was the annual return on GE in this period?

Solution

Plan: We need to analyze the cash flows from holding GE stock for each quarter. First, we must calculate the quarterly return for each of the 3-month time periods. To do this, we will use the equation:

$$R_{t+1} = \frac{Div_{t+1} + P_{t+1} - P_t}{P_t}$$

We will then compound the returns for all of the periods using the equation:

$$R_{annual} = (1+R_{Q1})(1+R_{Q2})(1+R_{Q3})(1+R_{Q4}) - 1$$

Execute: The realized returns for each quarter are:

$$R_1 = \frac{0.22 + 30.22 - 30.44}{30.44} = 0$$

$$R_2 = \frac{0.22 + 31.34 - 30.22}{30.22} = 0.0443$$

$$R_3 = \frac{0.25 + 33.45 - 31.34}{31.34} = 0.0753$$

$$R_4 = \frac{0.25 + 32.22 - 33.45}{33.45} = -0.0293$$

We then determine the 1-year return by compounding:

$$R_{annual} = (1+0)(1+0.0443)(1+0.0753)(1+(-0.0293)) - 1$$
$$= 1.09 - 1$$
$$= 9\%$$

Evaluate: If you bought GE stock on June 16, 2005 and sold it on June 15, 2006, your annual return would have been 9%. We can see that returns are risky. The return for the first 3-month period was zero and the return in the final 3-month period was negative. The majority of the gain occurred during the third period.

Computing Historical Volatility

11.3 **Problem:** You are considering investing in Yahoo!, which has never paid dividends and had the following end of year stock prices (adjusted for splits) for the 1996–2005 time period.

Date	Stock Price
12/31/1996	0.71
12/31/1997	4.33
12/31/1998	29.62
12/31/1999	108.17
12/31/2000	15.03
12/31/2001	8.87
12/31/2002	8.18
12/31/2003	22.51
12/31/2004	37.68
12/31/2005	39.18

Using this data, what is the standard deviation of Yahoo!'s historical returns for the time period 1996–2005?

Solution

Plan: First, we will need to calculate the return for each year using the equation:

$$R_{t+1} = \frac{Div_{t+1} + P_{t+1} - P_t}{P_t}$$

Second, we will compute the average return over this time period using the equation:

$$\bar{R} = \frac{1}{T}(R_1 + R_2 + \cdots + R_T)$$

Third, we will be able to calculate the variance using the equation:

$$Var(R) = \frac{1}{T-1}((R_1 - \bar{R})^2 + (R_2 - \bar{R})^2 + \cdots + (R_T - \bar{R})^2)$$

The standard deviation is calculated as the square root of the variance.

Execute: The realized return for each time period is shown in the table below:

Date	Stock Price	Realized Return
12/31/1996	0.71	
12/31/1997	4.33	509.86%
12/31/1998	29.62	584.06%
12/31/1999	108.17	265.19%
12/31/2000	15.03	−86.11%
12/31/2001	8.87	−40.98%
12/31/2002	8.18	−7.78%
12/31/2003	22.51	175.18%
12/31/2004	37.68	67.39%
12/31/2005	39.18	3.98%

The average annual return is:

$$\bar{R} = \frac{1}{9}(5.0986 + 5.8406 + 2.6519 - 0.8611 - 0.4098 - 0.0778$$
$$+ 1.7518 + .6739 + 0.0398)$$
$$= 163.42\%$$

Now, we calculate the variance as:

$$\text{Var}(R) = \left(\frac{1}{9-1}\right)\{(5.0986 - 1.6342)^2 + (5.8406 - 1.6342)^2$$
$$+ (2.6519 - 1.6342)^2 + (-0.8611 - 1.6342)^2 + (-0.4098 - 1.6342)^2$$
$$+ (-0.778 - 1.6342)^2 + (1.7518 - 1.6342)^2$$
$$+ (0.6739 - 1.6342)^2 + (0.0398 - 1.6342)^2\}$$
$$= 5.94313$$

The standard deviation of the returns is simply the square root of the variance:

$$\text{SD}(R) = 2.438$$
$$= 243.8\%$$

Evaluate: The average annual return for Yahoo! over the time period was extremely high at 163.42%; however, investing in Yahoo! stock was also risky; the standard deviation of returns was 243.8%. The return in any particular year was likely to be far away from the average return.

Prediction Intervals

11.4 Problem: In Example 11.3 we found the average return for Yahoo! from 1996–2005 to be 163.42% with a standard deviation of 243.8%. What is a 95% prediction interval for 2006's return?

Solution

Plan: We use the equation $\bar{R} \pm 2 \times \text{SD}(R)$ to compute the prediction interval.

Execute:

$$\bar{R} \pm 2 \times \text{SD}(R) = 163.42\% \pm 2 \times 243.8\%$$
$$= 163.42\% - 2 \times 243.8\% \text{ to } 163.42\% + 2 \times 243.8\%$$
$$= -324.18\% \text{ to } 651.02\%$$

Evaluate: Even though the average return from 1996–2005 was 163.42%, the return for Yahoo! was volatile. Based on the historical returns, if we want to be 95% confident of 2006's return, we can say that it will lie between −324% and 651%. Of course, since the lowest a stock price can go is to zero, the lowest the actual return could be is −100%.

Diversification

11.5 **Problem:** Professor Browne has 50 students in his class. He is going to demonstrate a simple gambling game in his class. Each student has a six-sided die. Each student will roll the die; if the die lands on an even number, Professor Browne will pay the student $1; if the die lands on an odd number, the student will pay Professor Browne $1. How is Professor Browne's risk different if he plays this game one time with each of his 50 students than if he played the game one time with one student and a bet of $50 (instead of $1)?

Solution

Plan: The risk of losing on one roll of the die is independent of the risk of losing the next one. Each time, there is a 50% chance the die will land on an odd number and Professor Browne will lose. We can compute the expected outcome of any flip as a weighted average by weighting the possible winnings (+$1) by 50% and the possible losses (−$1) by 50%. We can then compute the probability of losing all $50 under either scenario.

Execute: If Professor Browne plays the game 50 times, he should lose 50% of the time and win 50% of the time. Therefore, his expected outcome is $25 \times (+\$1) + 25 \times (-\$1) = \$0$. He should break even. On average, Professor Browne would expect to lose on 50% of the die rolls. The chance that he will lose to all 50 students is 0.50^{50}, which is extremely small. While it is *possible* for Professor Browne to lose all 50 die rolls the probability that this will occur is extremely small.

If instead, Professor Brown makes a single $50 bet on the roll of a single die, he has a 50% chance of winning $50 and a 50% chance of losing $50. Under this scenario, his expected outcome is $0.5 \times (+\$50) + 0.5 \times (-\$50) = \$0$. While the expected outcome is the same as playing all 50 students, betting a dollar on each die roll, there is a 50% chance Professor Browne will lose all $50 when he bets on the single die roll. So, his risk is far greater if he makes a single $50 bet than if he makes 50 one-dollar bets.

Evaluate: In each case, Professor Browne puts $50 at risk, but by spreading out that risk across 50 different bets, he has diversified much of his risk away, compared to placing a single bet of $50.

■ Questions and Problems

1. You bought a stock 1 year ago for $43 per share and sold it today for $45 per share. It paid a $1.20 per share dividend today.
   a. What was your realized return?
   b. How much of the return came from dividend yield and how much came from capital gain?

2. You have just purchased a share of stock for $30. The company is expected to pay a dividend of $1.00 per share in exactly 1 year. If you want to earn a 12% return on your investment, what price do you need to be able to expect to sell the share for immediately after it pays the dividend?

3. Which of the following risks of a stock are likely to be firm-specific, diversifiable risks, and which are likely to be systematic risks? Which risks will affect the risk premium that investors will demand?
   a. One of the firm's largest factories may be destroyed by fire.
   b. Interest rates may rise in the economy.
   c. The housing market may crash, leading to negative economic growth for several years.
   d. The firm's major drug may be found to cause cancer and may be removed from the market.

4. The returns for Richard's Sporting Goods for the past 6 years are:

1	2	3	4	5	6
6.20%	−3.50%	−2.10%	19.20%	3.00%	17.40%

  a. What is the average annual return?
  b. What is the variance of the stock's returns?
  c. What is the standard deviation of the stock's returns?
  d. What is a 95% prediction interval for the following year's return?

5. You are playing a simple betting game with your friend. Your friend will roll a die. If the die lands on 1 or 2, you win. If the die lands on 3, 4, 5, or 6, your friend wins. If you and your friend play five times, what is the probability you will lose all five games?

6. You purchased a share of SuperQuotient stock (SQ) for $25 on December 31, 2006. The following chart shows the price for SQ at the end of the next 4 years. This company did not pay any dividends over the 2006–2010 time period.

Dec 31, 2007	Dec 31, 2008	Dec 31, 2009	Dec 31, 2010
$29.50	$27.00	$32.25	$27.50

  a. Calculate the arithmetic average return over this period.
  b. Calculate the geometric average return over this period.
  c. Why do these numbers differ?

■ Solutions to Questions and Problems

1. a. $R_t = (45 - 43 + 1.20)/43 = 7.44\%$.

   b. The dividend yield is $1.2/43 = 2.79\%$ and the capital gains yield is $2/43 = 4.65\%$.

2. $R_{expected} = 0.12 = (P - 30 + 1)/30 \Rightarrow P = \$32.60$; if you sell the stock for $32.60 in 1 year, you will have a 12% realized return.

3. a. Firm-specific risk that is diversifiable.
   b. Systematic risk because interest rates impact all firms; this is nondiversifiable and will affect the risk premium that investors demand.
   c. Systematic risk because the health of the economy impacts all firms; this is nondiversifiable and will affect the risk premium that investors demand.
   d. Firm-specific risk that is diversifiable.

4.

Year	Realized Return	Average Return	(Rel Ret – Avg. Ret)^2
1	0.0620	0.0670	0.0000
2	–0.0350	0.0670	0.0104
3	–0.0210	0.0670	0.0077
4	0.1920	0.0670	0.0156
5	0.0300	0.0670	0.0014
6	0.1740	0.0670	0.0114
Avg. Ret	0.0670	**Variance**	0.00932
		Std. Dev	9.654%

a. The average annual return is 6.7%.
b. The variance is 0.00932.
c. The standard deviation is 0.09654 or 9.654%.
d. The 95% prediction interval is 6.7% ± 2 × 9.654%, which is from –12.6 to 26.

5. Your chance of losing on one roll of the die is 4/6 or 2/3. The probability of losing five consecutive rolls is (2/3)^5 = 13.17%.

6. a. To calculate the arithmetic average return, calculate the return for each year and find the mean:

Date	Price	Return
Dec 2006	$25.00	
Dec 2007	$29.50	0.180
Dec 2008	$27.00	–0.085
Dec 2009	$32.25	0.194
Dec 2010	$27.50	–0.147
Average		3.55%

b. The geometric average return is 25(1 + R)^4 = 27.50 or R = 2.41%.
c. The arithmetic average, or mean, return was 3.55%, but the geometric average return was only 2.41%. This difference is due to the fact that the returns were volatile. The stock fell by 8.5% during 2008. The stock would have to increase by **more** than 8.5% the following year in order to get back to the $29.50 price at which it ended in 2007.

■ Self-Test Questions

1. Your great grandparents placed $1 in an investment in 1925. Which of the following securities would have given them the highest average annual return over the past eight decades?
   a. Small stocks
   b. Large stocks
   c. U.S. Treasury bills
   d. Corporate bonds

2. The _____ indicates the tendency of historical returns to be different from their average and how far away from the average they tend to be.
   a. expected return
   b. variance
   c. unsystematic risk
   d. systematic risk

3. The normal distribution is a symmetrical distribution that is described by its
   a. systematic risk and unsystematic risk.
   b. variance and standard deviation.
   c. compounded return and realized return.
   d. mean and standard deviation.

4. Which of the following is a TRUE statement?
   a. Larger stocks tend to have more volatility than smaller stocks.
   b. Although there is a clear relationship between risk and return for individual stocks, there is no relationship between volatility and returns for portfolios of stocks.
   c. Individual stocks have lower returns and/or higher risk than do large portfolios.
   d. Purchasers of stocks face systematic risk, while holders of stock portfolios face unsystematic risk.

5. Which of the following would be the best example of systematic risk?
   a. A Kroger's warehouse burns to the ground.
   b. *E-coli* bacteria is found in a meat processing plant that supplies McDonald's with beef, contaminating the beef throughout the McDonald's distribution system.
   c. The Federal Reserve tightens the money supply to fight inflation, which causes interest rates to rise.
   d. A computer system failure causes disruption in order processing for Amazon.

6. Over the past 20 years, the average annual return for ShortStop Baseball Gear has been 9% and the standard deviation has been 4%. Given this information,
   a. you know that the variance is 2%.
   b. 95% prediction interval is from 1% to 17%.
   c. You know that the stock has more systematic risk than unsystematic risk.
   d. The expected return for the following year is 13%.

7. Which of the following is the best description of systematic risk?
   a. Risk that is diversifiable within a portfolio, but not with a single stock.
   b. The risk that an event will occur that will affect the value of all assets simultaneously.
   c. Risk that is eliminated in a large stock portfolio.
   d. The risk that occurs 95% of the time.

8. You purchased Hobo Hats stock last year for $60 a share. Today, you received a $2 a share dividend and immediately sold the stock for $63. Your realized return on the stock was
   a. 3.33%
   b. 6.67%
   c. 7.94%
   d. 8.33%

9. You are considering two securities. Security A has an historical average annual return of 7% and a standard deviation of 3%. Security B has an historical average annual return of 7% and a standard deviation of 9%. From this information you can conclude that
   a. 95% of the time, the returns of the two securities will be equal.
   b. 95% of the time, the return of Security B will exceed the return of Security A.
   c. Security A is more risky than Security B.
   d. Security B is more risky than Security A.

10. The stock prices and annual realized returns for the years 2002 through 2005 are given in the chart below. The average annual return over this period is _____ and the standard deviation of returns is _____.

Date	Stock Price	Realized Return
12/31/2001	8.87	
12/31/2002	8.18	−7.78%
12/31/2003	12.54	53.30%
12/31/2004	11.99	−4.39%
12/31/2005	15.27	27.36%

   a. 17.12% and 28.85%
   b. 28.85% and 17.12%
   c. 0.725% and 172.5%
   d. 1.725% and 28.85%

11. You are going to throw a fair coin four times. What is the probability of the coin landing on heads each of the four times?
   a. 50%
   b. $0.5^4 = 6.25\%$
   c. $0.4^5 = 1.02\%$
   d. $0.5\% + 0.5\% + 0.5\% + 0.5\% = 2\%$

12. Trudy paid $30 for a share of stock on December 31, 2008. The stock fell in value to $25 a share on December 31, 2009. Which of the following is a true statement?
   a. The stock price fell by 16.67% in 2009, so it will have to rise by 16.67% in 2010 for the price to return to $30 a share.
   b. The stock price fell by 16.67% in 2009, so it will have to rise by more than 16.67% in 2010 for the price to return to $30 a share.
   c. If the price returns to $30 a share in 2010, both the arithmetic and the geometric average return will be 0%.
   d. If the price returns to $30 a share in 2010, both the arithmetic and the geometric average return will be positive.

Answers to Self-Test Questions

1. a
2. b
3. d
4. c
5. c
6. b
7. b
8. d
9. d
10. a
11. b
12. b

Chapter 12
Systematic Risk and the Equity Risk Premium

■ Key Learning Objectives

- Calculate the expected return and volatility (standard deviation) of a portfolio
- Understand the relation between systematic risk and the market portfolio
- Measure systematic risk
- Use the Capital Asset Pricing Model (CAPM) to compute the cost of equity capital for a stock

■ Notation

β_i	the beta of security i with respect to the market portfolio
$Corr(R_i, R_j)$	correlation between the returns of security i and security j
$E[R_i]$	expected return of security i
$E[R_{Mkt}]$	expected return of the market portfolio
$E[R_P]$	expected return of a portfolio
R_i	return of security i
R_P	return of portfolio P
$SD(R_i)$	standard deviation (volatility) of the return of security I
$Var(R_i)$	Variance of the return of security I
w_i	fraction of the portfolio invested in security i (its relative *weight* in the portfolio)

■ Chapter Synopsis

12.1 The Expected Return of a Portfolio

We can describe a portfolio by its **portfolio weights**, which is the fraction of the total investment in the portfolio held in each individual investment in the portfolio:

$$w_i = \frac{\text{Value of investment } i}{\text{Total value of portfolio}}$$

These portfolio weights must add up to 100% (that is, $w_1 + w_2 + \ldots + w_N = 100\%$).

The **return on a portfolio,** R_P, is the weighted average of the returns on the investments in the portfolio, where the weights correspond to portfolio weights:

$$R_P = w_1 R_1 + w_2 R_2 + \ldots + w_n R_n$$

If we know the expected returns of the individual securities, we can compute the **expected return of a portfolio,** which is simply the weighted average of the expected returns of the investments within it, using the portfolio weights:

$$E[R_P] = w_1 E[R_1] + w_2 E[R_2] + \ldots + w_n E[R_n]$$

Summary of Portfolio Concepts and Equations

Term	Concept	Equation
Portfolio Weight	The relative investment in your portfolio.	$w_i = \dfrac{\text{Value of investment } i}{\text{Total value of portfolio}}$
Portfolio Return	The total return earned on your portfolio, accounting for the returns of all of the securities in the portfolio and their weights.	$R_P = w_1 R_1 + w_2 R_2 + \ldots + w_n R_n$
Portfolio Expected Return	The return you can expect to earn on your portfolio, given the expected returns of the securities in that portfolio and the relative amount you have invested in each.	$E[R_P] = w_1 E[R_1] + w_2 E[R_2] + \ldots + w_n E[R_n]$

12.2 The Volatility of a Portfolio

The **volatility of a portfolio,** measured as standard deviation, is the total risk of the portfolio. The standard deviation of the portfolio is generally less than the weighted average of the standard deviations of the portfolio's components. *By combining stocks into a portfolio, we reduce risk through diversification.* Because the stocks do not move identically, some of the risk is averaged out in a portfolio. *The amount of risk that is eliminated in a portfolio depends upon the degree to which the stocks face common risks and move together.*

To find the risk of a portfolio we need to know the degree to which the stocks' returns move together. **Correlation** is a measure, ranging from −1 to +1, of the degree to which returns share common risk. The closer the correlation is to +1, the more the returns tend to move together as a result of common risk. When the correlation equals 0, the returns are uncorrelated, meaning the return of the assets move independently. The closer the correlation is to −1, the more the returns tend to move in opposite directions.

Stock returns tend to move together if they are affected similarly by economic events. Thus, stocks in the same industry tend to have more highly correlated returns than stocks in different industries. For example, we would expect two retail companies, such as Walmart and Target, to have a higher correlation than two companies in different industries, such as Walmart and ExxonMobil.

Once we know the standard deviation of two securities, the weights of the securities, and the correlation between the two securities, we can compute the variance of a portfolio of the two securities. The formula for the variance of a two-stock portfolio is:

$$\text{Var}(R_P) = \underbrace{w_1^2 SD(R_1)^2}_{\text{Accounting for the risk of stock 1}} + \underbrace{w_2^2 SD(R_2)^2}_{\text{Accounting for the risk of stock 2}} + \underbrace{2 w_1 w_2 \text{Corr}(R_1, R_2) SD(R_1) SD(R_2)}_{\text{Adjustment for how much the two stocks move together}}$$

Looking at this equation we make several important observations:
- There are three important determinants of the overall variance of a portfolio: the risk of stock 1, the risk of stock 2, and the correlation between the two stocks.
- The more the stocks move together, the more volatile the portfolio will be.
- Unless the stocks have a perfect positive correlation of +1, the risk of the portfolio will be lower than the weighted average volatility of the individual stocks.

We can gain additional benefits of diversification by holding more than two stocks in our portfolio. As we add more stocks to our portfolio, the diversifiable firm-specific risk for each stock matters less and less. Volatility declines as the number of stocks in the portfolio grows. Even for a very large portfolio, however, we cannot eliminate all of the risk—the systematic risk remains.

12.3 Measuring Systematic Risk

The only risk that is related to return is systematic risk; therefore, we need a way to measure the systematic risk of an investment opportunity. So far we have established:

1. The amount of a stock's risk that is diversified away depends on the portfolio that you put it in.

2. If you build a large enough portfolio, you can diversify away all unsystematic risk, but you will be left with systematic risk.

The **market portfolio** is the portfolio of all risky investments, held in proportion to their value. The investment in each security is proportional to its **market capitalization,** which is the total market value of its outstanding shares:

$$\text{Market Value of a Firm} = (\text{Number of Shares Outstanding}) \times (\text{Price per Share})$$

In the market portfolio, stocks are held in proportion to their market capitalization (value), so we say that the portfolio is **value-weighted.** We use the market portfolio to measure systematic risk.

Instead of building a market portfolio that contains all possible investments, in practice we use a **market proxy**—a portfolio whose return should track the underlying, unobservable market portfolio. The most common proxy portfolios are *market indexes,* which are broadly used to represent the performance of the stock market. A **market index** reports the value of a particular portfolio of securities. The Dow Jones Industrial Average, or DJIA, consists of a portfolio of 30 large stocks, and is the most familiar stock index in the United States. The **S&P 500** provides a better representation of the entire U.S. stock market; it is a value-weighted portfolio of 500 of the largest U.S. stocks.

If a stock's returns are highly correlated with the market portfolio's returns, then that stock is highly sensitive to systematic risk. If a stock's returns are not very correlated with the market's returns, then it has little systematic risk—when systematic events happen, they are not strongly reflected in its returns. We compare a stock's historical returns to the market's historical returns to determine a stock's **beta,** a measure of the sensitivity of an investment to the fluctuations of the market portfolio. Using **excess returns** (the difference between the security's return and the risk-free rate), we say that:

> *For each 1% change in the market portfolio's excess return, the investment's excess return is expected to change by beta (β) percent due to risks that it has in common with the market.*

The beta of the overall market portfolio is 1; therefore, a stock with a beta of 1 has the average exposure to systematic risk. Securities that tend to move more than the market, have higher betas, while those that move less than the market have lower betas.

12.4 Putting It All Together: The Capital Asset Pricing Model

The expected return on any investment should come from two components:

1. A baseline risk-free rate of return that we would demand to compensate for inflation and the time value of money, even if there were no risk of losing our money.

2. A risk premium that varies with the amount of systematic risk in the investment.

   Therefore, Expected Return = Risk-Free Rate + Risk Premium for Systematic Risk

Because beta is our measure of systematic risk, the expected return for an investment can be calculated as:

Expected Return for investment i = Risk-Free Rate + $\beta_i \times$ Risk Premium per unit of systematic risk (per unit of β).

The risk premium per unit of systematic risk is the historical average excess return on the market portfolio, known as the **market** or **equity risk premium.** Using the market risk premium in the equation above, we have:

$$E[R_i] = r_f + \underbrace{\beta_i \, (E[R_{Mkt}] - r_f)}_{\text{Risk Premium for Security } i}$$

This equation for the expected return of any investment is the **Capital Asset Pricing Model (CAPM).** In words, the CAPM simply says that the return we should expect on any investment is equal to the risk-free rate of return plus a risk premium proportional to the amount of systematic risk in the investment. The expected return calculated using the CAPM is also called the investment's required return because investors will only invest in this security if they expect to earn at least this return.

When we plot the beta of securities and the expected return of those securities, we can derive the **security market line (SML).** The SML is a straight line drawn through the risk-free investment (which has a beta of zero) and the market (which has a beta of one). According to the CAPM, all stocks should lie on the SML. Thus we the expected return for each security will be a function of its beta.

Because the security market line applies to all securities, we can apply it to portfolios as well. The market portfolio, as well as any other portfolio, lies on the SML. Therefore, the expected return of a portfolio should correspond to the portfolio's beta.

We calculate the beta of a portfolio made up of securities, each with weight w_i as follows:

$$\beta_P = w_1 \beta_1 + w_2 \beta_2 + \ldots + w_n \beta_n$$

That is, the beta of a portfolio is the weighted average beta of the securities in the portfolio.

The CAPM is a powerful tool widely used to estimate the expected return on stocks and on investments within companies. To summarize the model and its use:

- Investors require a risk premium proportional to the amount of *systematic* risk they are bearing.
- We can measure the systematic risk of an investment by its β. For each 1% change in the market portfolio's excess return, the investment's excess return is expected to change by β percent due to risks that it has in common with the market.
- The most common way to estimate a stock's beta is to regress its historical excess returns on the market's historical excess returns. The stock's beta is the slope of the line that best explains the relation between the market's excess return and the stock's excess return.
- The CAPM says that we can compute the expected, or required, return for any investment using the following equation: $E[R_i] = r_f + \beta_i (E[R_{Mkt}] - r_f)$, which when graphed is called the *Security Market Line*.

■ Selected Concepts and Key Terms

Expected Return on a Portfolio

The **expected return of a portfolio** is the weighted average of the expected returns of the investments within it. The weights used in the calculation are the **portfolio weights,** a portfolio weight is the fraction of an investor's money invested in a particular asset. The portfolio weights must add up to one. In an **equally weighted portfolio,** an investor has the same amount of money invested in each asset in the portfolio.

Correlation

Correlation measures the comovement of returns of two securities. The correlation is always between –1 and +1. A correlation of –1 means that the two securities are perfectly negatively correlated, and a correlation of +1 means that the two securities are perfectly positively correlated. The correlation represents the fraction of the volatility due to risk that is common to the two securities.

Volatility of a Portfolio

The **volatility of a portfolio** depends on the standard deviation of the individual securities in the portfolio and the correlation of the securities within the portfolio. The lower the correlation between two stocks in a portfolio, the lower the portfolio variance. Diversification eliminates independent, firm-specific risks, and the volatility of a large portfolio results from the common systematic risk among the stocks in the portfolio.

Market Portfolio

In theory, the **market portfolio** is a **value-weighted** index of all risky investments. In a value-weighted index, each security is held in proportion to its **market capitalization.** In practice, we often use a stock **market index,** such as the S&P 500, as a **market proxy** to represent the market.

Beta

Beta (β) measures the sensitivity of a security's return to the return of the overall market. It measures the expected percent change in the **excess return** of a security for a 1% change in the excess return of the market portfolio. The excess return is the return on a security above the return on a risk-free investment.

Capital Asset Pricing Model (CAPM)

According to the **Capital Asset Pricing Model (CAPM)**, the risk premium of a stock is equal to the **market risk premium** multiplied by the beta of the security. The market risk premium is defined as the average stock market return minus the risk-free rate. The **security market line (SML)** is a straight line drawn through the risk-free investment (which has a beta of 0) and the market (which has a beta of 1). All stocks should lie on the SML, and the **required return** that investors have for an individual stock will be a function of the stock's beta.

■ Concept Check Questions and Answers

1. What do the weights in a portfolio tell us?

   Portfolio weights tell us the fraction of the total investment in the portfolio held in each individual security.

2. How is the expected return of a portfolio related to the expected returns of the stocks in the portfolio?

   The expected return of a portfolio is the weighted average of the expected returns of the individual stocks in the portfolio.

3. What determines how much risk will be eliminated by combining stocks in a portfolio?

   The amount of risk that will be eliminated by combining stocks in a portfolio depends on the correlation between the two stocks. The higher the correlation between the two stocks, the more the two stocks move together, and the less the risk will be lowered by combining the two stocks.

4. When do stocks have more or less correlation?

   Stocks that are in the same industry and stocks that are impacted by the same economic conditions are more correlated. For example, two airline companies would be more correlated than an airline company and a pharmaceutical company would be.

5. What is the market portfolio?

   The market portfolio is the portfolio of all risky investments, held in proportion to their market capitalization.

6. What does beta (β) tell us?

   Beta measures the sensitivity of an investment to the fluctuations of the market portfolio. Beta tells us how much an investment's excess return is expected to change for each 1% change in the market portfolio's excess return.

7. What does the CAPM say about the required return of a security?

   The CAPM model says that the required return of a security equals the risk-free rate plus a percentage of the market risk premium, where the percentage of the market risk premium is based on beta, or the security's systematic risk.

8. What is the Security Market Line?

   The Security Market Line (SML) is the line that goes through the risk-free investment (with a beta of 0) and the market (with a beta of 1). It shows the linear relation between the expected return and systematic risk, as measured by beta.

Examples with Step-by-Step Solutions

Calculating Portfolio Returns

12.1 Problem: Suppose you have $10,000 to invest. You purchase 100 shares of Cambridge stock at $30 a share and 100 shares of Woodridge stock at $70 a share. If Cambridge stock increases to $40 a share and Woodridge stock increases to $80 a share, what is your return on your portfolio? If you do not buy or sell any shares after the price change what are the new portfolio weights?

Solution

Plan: To calculate the return on your portfolio, you need to compute its value using the new prices and compare it to the original $100,000 investment. Alternatively, you could compute the return on each stock individually and multiply those returns by their original weights in the portfolio. To determine the new portfolio weights, simply divide the value of your holding in each particular stock by the value of your portfolio.

Execute: Your portfolio is now worth: $40 per share × 100 shares of Cambridge + $80 per share × 100 shares of Woodridge = $12,000. This is a 20% gain in the value of the portfolio. Alternatively, Cambridge increased by 33.33% and Woodridge increased by 14.29%. This would be a portfolio gain of 0.30 × 33.33% + 0.70 × 14.29% = 9.99% + 10.00% = 20%.

The new weight for Cambridge is $40,000/$120,000 = 33.33%.

The new weight for Woodridge is $80,000/$120,000 = 66.67%

Evaluate: Cambridge stock increased by $10 a share and Woodridge stock increased by $10 share. However, because Cambridge was a lower priced stock, the $10 gain represented a larger percentage change. The lower percentage gain for Cambridge stock led to it being more heavily weighted in the portfolio than it was previously. Remember that the portfolio weights must sum to 100%. Therefore, if Cambridge's weight increases, Woodridge's weight must decrease.

Portfolio Expected Return

12.2 Problem: Suppose you invest $2000 in Delta Airlines (DAL) and $8000 in Walmart (WMT). You expect a return of 15% on DAL and 8% on WMT. What is the expected return for your portfolio?

Solution

Plan: You have a total of $10,000 invested. DAL's expected return is 15% and its weight is 0.20. WMT's expected return is 8% and its weight is 0.80. To calculate the portfolio's expected return, we will calculate the weighted average of the expected returns.

Execute:

The expected return on your portfolio is:

$E(R_p) = w_{DAL} \times E(R_{DAL}) + w_{WMT} \times E(R_{WMT}) = 0.20 \times 15\% + 0.80 \times 8\% = 3\% + 6.4\% = 9.4\%$

Evaluate:

The importance each stock plays in the expected return of the overall portfolio is determined by the relative amount of money you have invested in it. Most (75%) of your money is invested in Tyco, so the overall expected return of the portfolio is much closer to Tyco's expected return than it is to Ford's.

Computing the Volatility of a Two-Stock Portfolio

12.3 Problem: Using the data below, what is the volatility (standard deviation) of a two-security portfolio with equal amounts invested in Dell and Target? What is the standard deviation of a two-stock portfolio with equal amounts invested in Dell and HP-Compaq?

Stock	Standard Deviation	Correlation with Dell
Dell	50%	1
Target	30%	0.37
HPCompaq	41%	0.52

Solution

Plan: We will use the following equation to calculate the variance for each portfolio:

$$Var(R_P) = w_1^2 SD(R_1)^2 + w_2^2 SD(R_2)^2 + 2w_1 w_2 Corr(R_1, R_2) SD(R_1) SD(R_2)$$

After computing the portfolio's variance, we take the square root of the variance to get the portfolio's standard deviation.

Execute: For Dell and Target the portfolio's variance is:

$$Var(R_P) = 0.5^2(0.5)^2 + 0.5^2(0.3)^2 + 2(0.5)(0.5)(0.37)(0.5)(0.3) = 0.0625 + 0.0225 + 0.02775 = 0.11275$$

The standard deviation of the Dell and Target portfolio is:

$$SD(R_P) = \sqrt{Var(R_P)} = \sqrt{0.11275} = 0.3358 = 33.58\%$$

For the portfolio of Dell and HP-Compaq, the variance is:

$$Var(R_P) = 0.5^2(0.5)^2 + 0.5^2(0.41)^2 + 2(0.5)(0.5)(0.52)(0.5)(0.41)$$
$$= 0.0625 + 0.04203 + 0.0533 = 0.15783$$

The standard deviation of the Dell and HPCompaq portfolio is:

$$SD(R_P) = \sqrt{Var(R_P)} = \sqrt{0.15783} = 0.3973 = 39.73\%$$

Evaluate: The weights, standard deviations, and correlation of the two stocks are needed to compute the variance and then standard deviation of the portfolio. Here we computed the standard deviation of the portfolio of Dell and Target to be 33.58% and of Dell and HP-Compaq to be 39.73%. The Dell and Target portfolios have a lower standard deviation than do the Dell and HP-Compaq portfolios because Target has a much lower standard deviation than HP-Compaq and because the correlation between Dell and Target is much lower than the correlation between Dell and HP-Compaq.

Total Risk versus Systematic Risk

12.4 Problem: Suppose that in the coming year, you expect Lowe's to have a standard deviation of 39% and a beta of 0.80. You also expect Home Depot to have a standard deviation of 32% and a beta of 1.40. Which stock carries more total risk? Which has more systematic risk?

Solution

Plan: We will use standard deviation as the measure of total risk and beta as the measure of systematic risk.

Chapter 12 Systematic Risk and the Equity Risk Premium   197

Execute: Lowe's standard deviation of 39% is higher than Home Depot's standard deviation of 32%; therefore, Lowe's has more total risk. Home Depot has a much higher beta than does Lowe's; therefore, Home Depot has more systematic risk.

Evaluate: Lowe's has high total risk, but a lot of the risk is diversifiable; in fact, with a beta less than 1, Lowe's has below average systematic risk.

Computing the Expected Return for a Stock

12.5 Problem: Suppose the risk-free return is 4% and the average return on the S&P 500 has been 12%. If Lowe's has a beta of 0.8, according to the CAPM, what is the expected rate of return for Lowe's?

Solution

Plan: We can use the following equation to calculate the expected return:

$$E[R_i] = r_f + \beta_i (E[R_{Mkt}] - r_f)$$

We are given the risk-free rate as 4% and the company's beta of 0.8. We were not given the market risk premium, but we can calculate it as the difference between the average market return and the risk-free return. We will use the S&P 500 return as a proxy for the market return.

Execute: First, we need to compute the market risk premium. The market risk premium is the difference between the market rate of return and the risk-free rate of return or 12% − 4% = 8%. Now, using the formula we have:

$$E[R_i] = r_f + \beta_i (E[R_{Mkt}] - r_f)$$
$$= 0.04 + 0.8(0.12 - 0.4)$$
$$= 0.04 + 0.8(0.08)$$
$$= 0.04 + 0.064$$
$$= 0.104 = 10.4\%$$

Evaluate: Investors could earn 4% investing in the risk-free security. Investors will require a premium of 6.4% over the risk-free rate of 4% in order to invest in Lowe's. This 6.4% premium compensates the investors for the systematic risk of Lowe's stock. This leads to a total expected return of 10.4%. You will notice that this is less than the S&P 500 return of 12%. Because Lowe's has less systematic risk than the average stock, its return would be expected to be less than the average.

The Expected Return of a Portfolio

12.6 Problem: Suppose Lowe's has a beta of 0.8 and that Motorola has a beta of 1.2. If the risk-free interest rate is 4%, and the market risk premium is 8%, what is the expected return of an equally weighted portfolio of Lowe's and Motorola, according to the CAPM?

Solution

Plan: We have the following information:

$r_f = 4\%$, $E[R_{Mkt}] - r_f = 8\%$

LOW: $\beta_{LOW} = 0.8$, $w_{LOW} = 0.50$
MOT: $\beta_{MOT} = 1.4$, $w_{MOT} = 0.50$

© 2012 Pearson Education, Inc. Publishing as Prentice Hall

We can compute the expected return of the portfolio in two ways. First, we can use the SML, which is $E[R_i] = r_f + \beta_i(E[R_{Mkt}] - r_f)$, to compute the expected return of each stock. Then, we will compute the expected return for the portfolio as the weighted average of the stock returns. Second, we could compute the beta of the portfolio as $\beta_P = w_1\beta_1 + w_2\beta_2 + ... + w_n\beta_n$. Then we can calculate the portfolio's expected return using the SML.

Execute: Using the first approach, we compute the expected return for LOW and MOT:

Expected return for LOW:
$$E[R_i] = r_f + \beta_i(E[R_{Mkt}] - r_f) = 0.04 + 0.8(0.12 - 0.4) = 0.04 + 0.8(0.08) = 0.04 + 0.064 = 0.104 = 10.4\%$$

Expected return for MOT:
$$E[R_i] = r_f + \beta_i(E[R_{Mkt}] - r_f) = 0.04 + 1.2(0.12 - 0.4) = 0.04 + 1.2(0.08) = 0.04 + 0.096 = 0.136 = 13.6\%$$

Then the expected return of the equally weighted portfolio P is:
$$E[R_P] = 0.5(10.4\%) + 0.5(13.6\%) = 12\%$$

Alternatively, we can compute the beta of the portfolio:
$$\beta_P = w_{LOW}\beta_{LOW} + w_{MOT}\beta_{MOT} = 0.5(0.8) + 0.5(1.2) = 0.4 + 0.6 = 1.0$$

Now, we can find the portfolio's expected return from the SML:
$$E[R_P] = 4\% + 1.0(8\%) = 12\%$$

Evaluate: The CAPM is an effective tool for analyzing securities and portfolios of those securities. You can compute the expected return of each security using its beta and then compute the weighted average of those expected returns to determine the portfolio expected return. Or, you can compute the weighted average of the securities' betas to get the portfolio beta and then compute the expected return of the portfolio using the CAPM. Either way, you will get the same answer.

■ Questions and Problems

1. Hall Enterprises has an expected return of 14% and Graham Industries has an expected return of 19%. If you put 60% of your portfolio in Hall and 40% in Graham, what is the expected return of your portfolio?

2. You just inherited $100,000 and have decided to invest it in three stocks: $45,000 of the money in Alexander (currently $90 a share), $30,000 in Bloomfield (currently $100 a share), and $25,000 in Chandler (currently $20 a share).
   a. If Alexander goes up to $120 a share, Bloomfield goes up to $110 a share, and Chandler falls to $18 a share, what will be the new value of your portfolio?
   b. If the price changes in part (a) occur, what return will your portfolio have earned?
   c. If you do not buy or sell shares after the price change, what are your new portfolio weights?

3. Using the data in the following table, estimate the average return and volatility for each stock.

Year	Realized Returns Stock A	Stock B
1998	−10%	15%
1999	15%	30%
2000	5%	−10%
2001	5%	−3%
2002	−2%	−8%
2003	9%	25%

4. Consider stocks A and B from Problem 3. Assume that the correlation of A and B is 0.35, calculate the volatility (standard deviation) of a portfolio that is 60% invested in stock A and 40% invested in stock B.

5. Given $100,000 to invest, construct a value-weighted portfolio of the four stocks listed below.

Stock	Price/Share ($)	Number of Shares Outstanding (millions)
Davidson	15	1
Embassy	22	3
Fieldhouse	40	30
Greenhouse	10	5

6. Suppose Hamilton stock has a beta of 1.6, whereas Indigo stock has a beta of 1.2. If the risk-free interest rate is 3% and the expected return of the market portfolio is 10%, according to the CAPM:
   a. What is the expected return of Hamilton stock?
   b. What is the expected return of Indigo stock?
   c. What is the beta of a portfolio that consists of 65% Hamilton stock and 35% Boeing stock?
   d. What is the expected return of a portfolio that consists of 80% Hamilton stock and 20% Boeing stock?

Solutions to Questions and Problems

1. The expected return is 0.60(14%) + 0.40(19%) = 8.4% + 7.6% = 16.0%.

2. a. Alexander: 500 shares × $120 = $60,000
      Bloomfield: 300 shares × $110 = $33,000
      Chandler: 1250 shares × $18 = $22,500
   b. The value of the portfolio increased (115,500 − 100,000)/100,000 = 15.5%.
   c. Alexander's weight = 60,000/115,000 = 51.95%, Bloomfield's weight = 33,000/115,500 = 28.57%, Chandler's weight = 22.500/115,500 = 19.48%.

3. Stock A: average return = 6.4% and standard deviation = 6.2%

   Stock B: average return = 15% and standard deviation = 17.8%

4. Variance of the portfolio = $(0.6^2)(0.062^2) + (0.4^2)(0.178^2) + 2(0.6)(0.4)(0.35)(0.062)(0.178) = 0.0014 + 0.0051 + 0.0019 = 0.0084$; the standard deviation is $0.0084^{1/2} = 0.0917 = 9.17\%$.

5.

Stock	Price/Share ($)	Number of Shares Outstanding (millions)	Market Capitalization	Weight	Amount to Invest
Davidson	15	1	15	0.0112697	$ 1126.97
Embassy	22	3	66	0.0495868	$ 4954.68
Fieldhouse	40	30	1200	0.9015778	$ 90,157.78
Greenhouse	10	5	50	0.0375657	$ 3756.57
			1331	1	$100,000.00

6. a. Expected return for Hamilton: $0.03 + 1.6(0.10 - 0.03) = 14.2\%$
    b. Expected return for Indigo: $0.03 + 1.2(0.10 - 0.03) = 11.4\%$
    c. $Beta_{port} = (0.65)(1.6) + (0.35)(1.2) = 1.04 + 0.42 = 1.46$
    d. $Beta_{port} = (.80)(1.6) + (0.20)(1.2) = 1.28 + 0.24 = 1.52$

■ Self-Test Questions

1. The expected return of a portfolio is
   a. equal to the portfolio's beta multiplied by the risk-free rate.
   b. equal to the portfolio's beta multiplied by the market risk premium.
   c. is calculated as the weighted average of the expected returns of the securities in the portfolio.
   d. greater than the return of any individual security in the portfolio.

2. We measure a stock's systematic risk using
   a. the variance of the stock's returns.
   b. the standard deviation of the stock's returns.
   c. the stock's beta.
   d. the stock's total return divided by the stock's unsystematic risk.

3. If a stock's returns are highly correlated with the market portfolio's returns
   a. then that stock is highly sensitive to systematic risk.
   b. then that stock is highly sensitive to unsystematic risk.
   c. then that stock's average historical return will exceed its standard deviation.
   d. then the stock's beta will be 0.

4. Dash Enterprises has a beta of 1.3. The best interpretation of this is
   a. if the excess market return falls by 1%, Dash's excess return is expected to fall by 1.3%.
   b. Dash's return, on average, will be 1.3 times as large as the market's return.
   c. if the risk-free rate is 3% and the market risk premium is 8%, then Dash's expected return is 12.3%.
   d. Dash's standard deviation of historical returns is 1.3 times larger than its variance of historical returns.

5. You are going to form a portfolio of two stocks, Walmart and Starbucks. Which of the following will be a factor in determining the overall variance of your portfolio?
   a. The risk of Walmart stock.
   b. The risk of Starbucks stock.
   c. The correlation between Walmart and Starbucks stocks.
   d. All of the above.

6. According to the Capital Asset Pricing Model:
   a. All stocks should lie on the Security Market Line.
   b. Investors are only rewarded for taking on unsystematic risk.
   c. The best estimate of the expected return for a stock which has a beta of 0, is the average market return.
   d. The market risk premium equals the difference in the average return of a stock with a beta of 1 and the average return of a stock with a beta of 0.

7. Naomi has formed a two-stock portfolio. Which of the following is a TRUE statement about her portfolio?
   a. The risk of the portfolio will be the weighted average of the risk of the two stocks.
   b. If the stocks have a correlation of 0, Naomi faces no systematic risk.
   c. If the stocks have a correlation of 1, Naomi faces no unsystematic risk.
   d. Unless the stocks have a perfect positive correlation of +1, the risk of the portfolio will be lower than the weighted average volatility of the individual stocks.

8. Cavalier Corp. has a beta of 0.9. If the risk-free return is 3% and the average return on the S&P 500 is 11%, then the best estimate of the required rate of return for Cavalier is:
   a. 7.2%
   b. 10.2%
   c. 12.9%
   d. 15.2%

9. Which of the following pairs of stock would you expect to have the highest correlation?
   a. McDonalds and Walmart
   b. Walmart and Apple
   c. Delta Airlines and ExxonMobil
   d. Delta Airlines and American Airlines

10. Which of the following is a conclusion of the Capital Asset Pricing Model?
    a. Investors require a risk premium proportional to the amount of systematic risk they are bearing.
    b. In perfectly competitive markets, no risk premium will exist.
    c. Investors are only compensated for unsystematic risk because systematic risk is fully expected.
    d. Because markets are competitive, there are no benefits of diversification to the investor.

11. By combining stocks into a portfolio, we reduce risk through diversification. The amount of risk that is eliminated in a portfolio depends upon the
    a. expected returns of each of the individual stocks.
    b. expected return of the portfolio relative to the risk-free rate.
    c. amount of risk each stock has relative to the risk-free rate.
    d. degree to which the stocks face common risks and move together.

12. The expected return for an individual security would equal
    a. the risk-free rate plus a risk premium for systematic risk.
    b. the risk premium for systematic risk minus the risk-free rate.
    c. the risk premium for systematic risk multiplied by the risk-free rate.
    d. the risk-free rate divided by the risk premium for systematic risk.

Answers to Self-Test Questions

1. c
2. c
3. a
4. a
5. d
6. a
7. d
8. b
9. d
10. a
11. d
12. a

■ Using Excel

Calculating the Correlation between Two Sets of Returns Using Excel

1. **Problem:** Calculate the correlation between Apple stock (AAPL) and AT&T (T) using the monthly returns for the two stocks in the table below:

Date	AT&T	Apple
2/1/2005	0.0127	0.1667
3/1/2005	−0.0154	−0.0711
4/1/2005	0.0181	−0.1346
5/2/2005	−0.0177	0.1026
6/1/2005	0.0156	−0.0742
7/1/2005	0.0437	0.1587
8/1/2005	−0.0152	0.0994
9/1/2005	−0.0047	0.1433
10/3/2005	0.0089	0.0742
11/1/2005	0.0442	0.1776
12/1/2005	−0.0169	0.0600
1/3/2006	0.0739	0.0504
2/1/2006	0.0633	−0.0930
3/1/2006	−0.0199	−0.0842
4/3/2006	−0.0186	0.1223
5/1/2006	−0.0058	−0.1509
6/1/2006	0.0702	−0.0418
7/3/2006	0.0885	0.1867
8/1/2006	0.0378	−0.0016
9/1/2006	0.0460	0.1346
10/2/2006	0.0627	0.0533
11/1/2006	−0.0099	0.1305
12/1/2006	0.0543	−0.0744
1/3/2007	0.0636	0.0105
2/1/2007	−0.0220	−0.0131
3/1/2007	0.0714	0.0981
4/2/2007	−0.0090	0.0742
5/1/2007	0.0675	0.2143
6/1/2007	0.0038	0.0070
7/2/2007	−0.0480	0.0796
8/1/2007	0.0181	0.0510
9/4/2007	0.0612	0.1082
10/1/2007	−0.0039	0.2377
11/1/2007	−0.0857	−0.0407
12/3/2007	0.0879	0.0870

Solution

Plan: We calculate the correlation by comparing the returns of the two stocks to each other. We will use Excel to do this. Under the "Tools" tab, we will choose "Data Analysis" and then choose "Correlation".

Execute: All of the data is placed in an Excel spreadsheet as shown in the screen shot below. From the "Tools" menu, we choose "Data Analysis". Once we choose "Correlation" a popup box appears as shown in the screen shot. All we need to put is the input range where the monthly returns for our individual stocks appear. Next, we choose "OK".

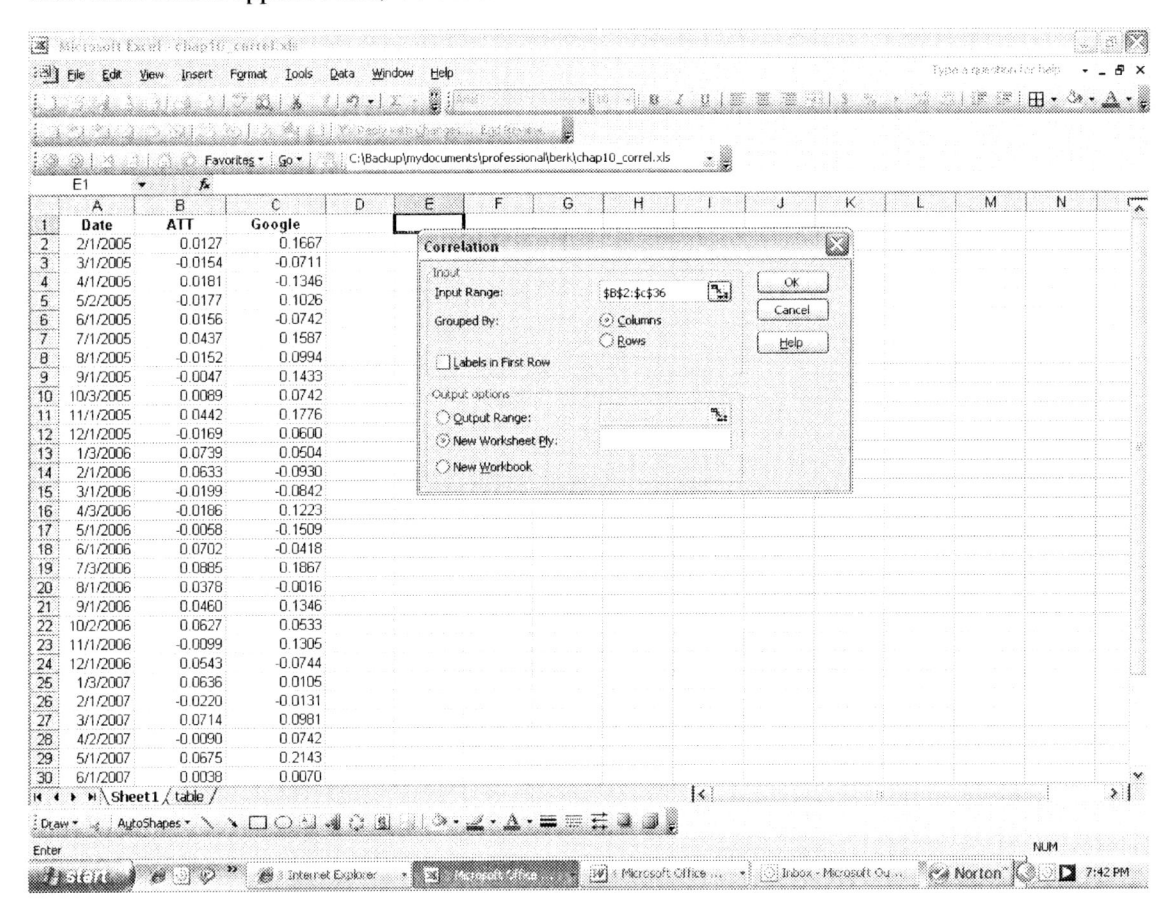

A box like the one below will appear on a new sheet in the Excel workbook:

	Column 1	Column 2
Column 1	1	
Column 2	0.162223	1

We are interested in the correlation between Column 1 and Column 2. (Column 1 has the monthly returns for AT&T, and Column 2 has the monthly returns for Google.) We can see that the returns for the two stocks have a positive correlation of 0.1622.

Chapter 12 Systematic Risk and the Equity Risk Premium

Evaluate: To calculate correlation we need returns for two stocks. Monthly stock data can be downloaded from Yahoo!Finance into Excel and the monthly returns calculated from that data. In this example, we considered the monthly returns of AT&T and Apple. We found a correlation of 0.1622 for these two stocks. A correlation of 0 would mean that the two stocks do not move together at all, and a correlation of 1 would mean that the two stocks move together perfectly. Thus, AT&T and Apple tended to move together during the 2005–2007 time period, but the correlation was not strong. Therefore, the risk of a portfolio that combines these two stocks will be lower than the weighted average volatility of the individual stocks.

Using Excel to Calculate a Stock's Beta

2. **Problem:** Using the 2005–2007 time period, calculate the beta for AT&T.

   Solution

   Plan: To calculate AT&T's beta, we will need to have historical returns for AT&T and for the market. We will use the S&P 500 as the market proxy. We can use an online source, such as Yahoo! Finance to import monthly historical data into Excel. We will then use the data analysis tool "regression" to calculate the beta.

   Execute: First, we import the historical returns for AT&T and the S&P 500 into an Excel spreadsheet. Then we use the "Tools" pull-down menu to access the data analysis tool. We will choose "Regression". A pop-up box like the one in the screen shot below appears. For the "Y Range" we want to make sure we put the column containing the stock returns, and we want to make sure that the information regarding the S&P 500 stock returns is used for the "X Range."

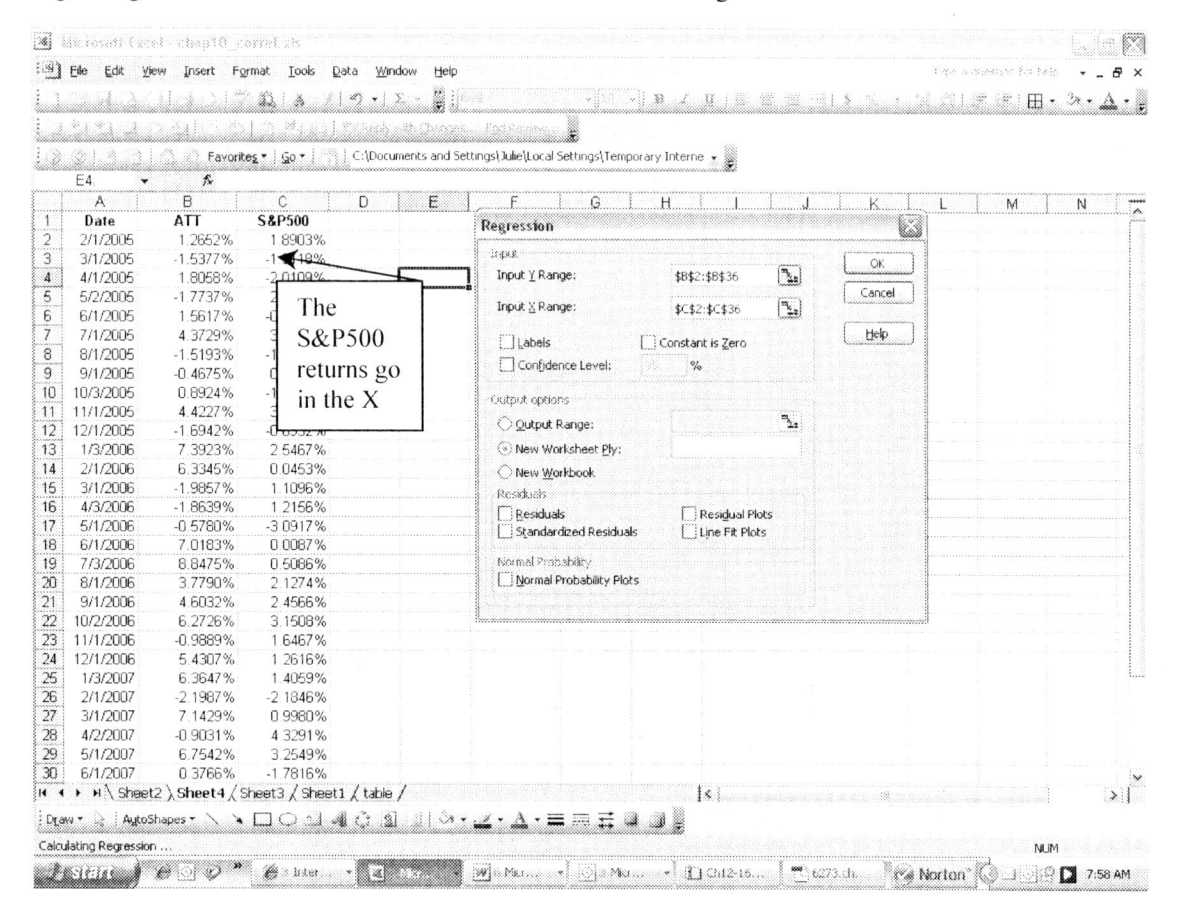

Once we press "OK" in the popup box, Excel will place the output from the regression analysis in a separate sheet in the workbook. This output is shown in the screen shot below. We look at the coefficient value for "X Variable 1" to find AT&T's beta. For the time period we are considering, AT&T's beta is 0.9212.

Evaluate: We used the regression function in Excel to calculate AT&T's beta. We want to see how sensitive AT&T stock is to overall movements in the market. Therefore, the S&P 500 is the X Variable and AT&T is the Y Variable in our model.

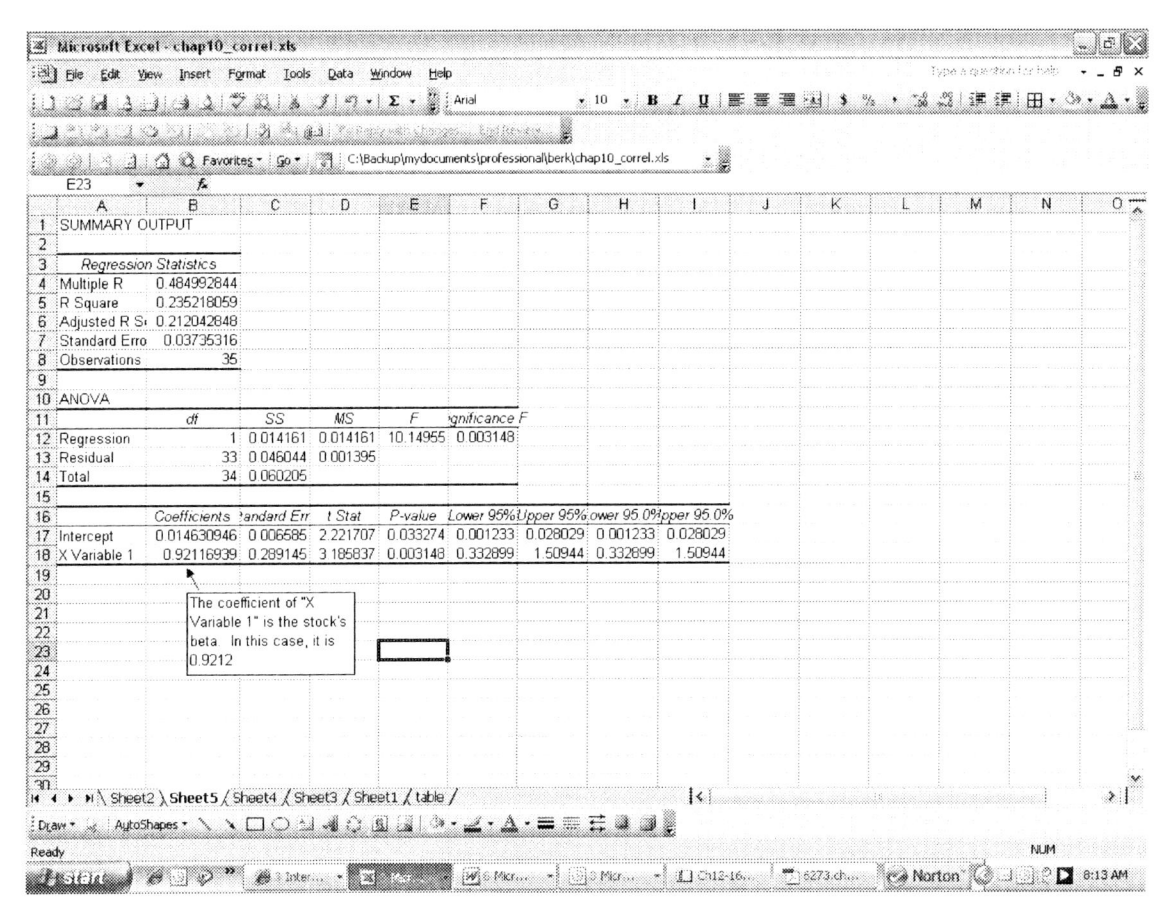

Appendix: Alternative Models of Systematic Risk

Using only the S&P 500, or some other simple proxy for the true market portfolio, leads to consistent pricing errors from the CAPM. Therefore, researchers have added new portfolios to the CAPM pricing equation in an attempt to construct a better proxy for the true market portfolio. So long as the market portfolio can be constructed from a collection of portfolios, the collection itself can be used to measure risk. Thus, we can use a collection of portfolios to capture the components of systematic risk, referred to as **risk factors.** A **multifactor model** uses more than one portfolio to capture risk. Each portfolio can be thought of as either the risk factor itself or a portfolio of stocks correlated with an unobservable risk factor. The model is also referred to as the **Arbitrage Pricing Theory (APT).**

Professors Eugene Fama, Kenneth French, and Mark Carhart developed a multifactor model that is based on four portfolios. The first portfolio is one that is constructed by buying small firms and selling large firms. This portfolio is widely known as the small-minus-big (SMB) portfolio. The second portfolio buys high book-to-market firms and sells low book-to-market firms and we call it the high-minus-low (HML) portfolio. The third portfolio buys stocks that have recently done extremely well and sells those that have done extremely poorly; it is called the prior 1-year momentum (PR1YR) portfolio. The fourth portfolio is the stock market (Mkt).

Using this collection of four portfolios, the expected return of security i is given by

$$E[R_i] = r_f + \beta_i^{Mkt}(E[R_{Mkt}] - r_f) + \beta_i^{SMB} E[R_{SMB}] + \beta_i^{HML} E[R_{HML}] + \beta_i^{PR1YR} E[R_{PR1YR}]$$

where $\beta_i^{Mkt}, \beta_i^{SMB}, \beta_i^{HML}$, and β_i^{PR1YR} are the factor betas of stock i and measure the sensitivity of the stock to each portfolio. The average monthly returns for each of the four portfolios in the FFC are given in 0.

Table 12.1 FFC Portfolio Average Monthly Returns (1926–2005)

	Average Monthly Return (%)
Mkt-r_f	0.64
SMB	0.17
HML	0.53
PR1YR	0.76

(*Source*: Professor Kenneth French's personal Web site.)

Using the FFC Factor Specification to Calculate the Cost of Capital

Problem: You want to compute an estimate for the required rate of return for Jurassic Unlimited using the FFC factor specification model. You have regressed the monthly excess returns (the realized return each month minus the risk-free rate) of Jurassic's stock on the return of each of the four-factor portfolios. You determine that the factor betas for Jurassic are:

$$\beta^{Mkt} = 0.93$$
$$\beta^{SMB} = 1.21$$
$$\beta^{HML} = 0.86$$
$$\beta^{PR1YR} = 1.09$$

You know that historically the average monthly returns for each of the portfolios are:

	Average Monthly Return (%)
Mkt-r_f	0.64
SMB	0.17
HML	0.53
PR1YR	0.76

The current risk-free monthly rate is 3%/12% = 0.25%. Determine the cost of capital by using the FFC factor specification.

Solution

Plan: First, we gather the information that we have:

	Average Monthly Return (%)	Jurassic's β with factor
Mkt-r_f	0.64	0.93
SMB	0.17	1.21
HML	0.53	0.86
PR1YR	0.76	1.09

We also know that the monthly risk-free rate is 0.25%.

We will put this information into the equation:

$$E[R_i] = r_f + \beta_i^{Mkt}(E[R_{Mkt}] - r_f) + \beta_i^{SMB}E[R_{SMB}] + \beta_i^{HML}E[R_{HML}] + \beta_i^{PR1YR}E[R_{PR1YR}]$$

This equation will give the monthly expected return for investing in Jurassic Unlimited. We can then multiply by 12 to get the annual expected return, represented as an APR.

Execute: The monthly expected return of investing in Jurassic is:

$$E[R_i] = r_f + \beta_i^{Mkt}(E[R_{Mkt}] - r_f) + \beta_i^{SMB}E[R_{SMB}] + \beta_i^{HML}E[R_{HML}] + \beta_i^{PR1YR}E[R_{PR1YR}]$$

$$= 0.25 + 0.93(0.64) + 1.21(0.17) + 0.86(0.53) + 1.09(0.76)$$

$$= 0.25 + 0.5952 + 0.206 + 0.456 + 0.828$$

$$= 2.335$$

The annual expected return is 2.335% × 12 = 28.02%.

Evaluate: By gathering all of the inputs and applying the FFC specification, in the same way we would apply the CAPM, we can calculate this alternative estimate of the cost of capital for a company. According to this approach, we would conclude that the annual expected rate of return for the stock is approximately 28%.

Chapter 13
The Cost of Capital

■ Key Learning Objectives

- Understand the drivers of the firm's overall cost of capital
- Measure the costs of debt, preferred stock, and common stock
- Compute a firm's overall, or weighted average, cost of capital
- Apply the weighted average cost of capital to value projects
- Adjust the cost of capital for the risk associated with the project
- Account for the direct costs of raising external capital

■ Notation

$D\%$	fraction of the firm financed with debt
Div_1	dividend due in one year
Div_{pfd}	dividend on preferred stock
$E\%$	fraction of the firm financed with equity
FCF_t	incremental free cash flow in year t
g	expected growth rate for dividends
$P\%$	fraction of the firm financed with preferred stock
P_E	price of common stock
P_{pfd}	price of preferred stock
r_D	required return (cost of capital) for debt
r_E	required return (cost of capital) of levered equity
r_{pfd}	required return (cost of capital) for preferred stock
r_{wacc}	weighted average cost of capital
T_C	marginal corporate tax rate
V_0^L	initial levered value

■ Chapter Synopsis

13.1 A First Look at the Weighted Average Cost of Capital

A firm's sources of financing, which usually consist of debt and equity, represent its **capital.** The relative proportions of debt, equity, and other securities that a firm has outstanding constitute its **capital structure.** Financial managers take into account each component of the firm's capital structure when determining the firm's overall cost of capital. The **weighted average cost of capital (WACC)** is the average of a firm's equity and debt cost of capital, weighted by the fractions of the firm's value that correspond to equity and debt, respectively. The market values of debt and equity must be used to determine the proportions. A **market-value balance sheet** lists assets, debt, and equity at their market values, rather than their book values.

The **unlevered firm** does not issue any debt; when some of a firm's financing comes from debt, the firm is **levered.** Therefore, we refer to the relative amount of debt on the balance sheet as the firm's **leverage.**

If a firm is unlevered, we can estimate the firm's cost of capital by estimating the firm's equity cost of capital using the Capital Asset Pricing Model (CAPM). If the firm has debt, then the pretax cost of capital is calculated as:

> Weighted Average Cost of Capital (Pretax) = r_{wacc} = (Fraction of Firm Value Financed by Equity)(Equity Cost of Capital) + (Fraction of Firm Value Financed by Debt)(Debt Cost of Capital)

13.2 The Firm's Costs of Debt and Equity Capital

A firm's cost of debt is the interest rate it would have to pay to refinance its existing debt. Because the yield to maturity on the company's bonds represents the yield investors demand to purchase the firm's bonds, it is the firm's current cost of debt. Because interest paid on debt is a tax-deductible expense, the return paid to the debt holders is not the same as the cost to the firm. The **effective cost of debt** is a firm's net cost of interest after accounting for the interest tax deduction. The effective cost of debt, or effective after-tax borrowing rate equals $r_D(1 - T_C)$.

Some firms raise capital by issuing preferred stock. Generally, holders of preferred stock receive a fixed dividend which must be paid before any dividends can be paid to common shareholders. If the preferred dividend is known and fixed, we can estimate its cost of capital as:

$$r_E = \frac{Div_1}{P_0} + g$$

A firm cannot directly observe its cost of common stock. Two major methods for estimating the cost of common stock are using the CAPM and using the constant dividend growth model. Using the CAPM the cost of equity is estimated as:

> Cost of Equity = Risk-Free Rate + Equity Beta × Market Risk Premium

Using the constant dividend growth model, the cost of equity is estimated as:

$$\text{Cost of Equity} = \frac{Div_1}{P_E} + g$$

13.3 A Second Look at the Weighted Average Cost of Capital

The weights used when calculating the firm's overall WACC are the percentage of firm value financed by equity, preferred stock, and debt. They are represented by $E\%$, $P\%$, and $D\%$, respectively. The WACC equation is:

$$r_{wacc} = r_E E\% + r_{pfd} P\% + (1 - T_C) r_D D\%$$

The WACCs vary widely across industries and companies. A particular company's WACC is driven by the risk of the company's line of business and its leverage.

When calculating the weights for the WACC, many financial managers use **net debt,** which is the total debt outstanding minus any cash balances. When using this approach, the weights in the WACC become (Market value of equity/Enterprise value) and (Net debt/Enterprise value).

Using the CAPM to estimate the equity cost of capital requires a measure of the risk-free interest rate and the market risk premium. The majority of financial analysts use the yields of long-term U.S. Treasury bonds to determine the risk-free rate. Many financial managers currently estimate the market risk premium to be around 5%.

13.4 Using the WACC to Value a Project

When the market risk of a project is similar to the average market risk of the firm's investments, then the project's cost of capital is equal to the firm's WACC. An investment's **levered value** is the value of an investment, including the benefit of the interest tax deduction, given the firm's leverage policy. The **WACC method** is the process of discount future incremental free cash flows using the firm's WACC; this method produces the levered value of a project.

It is important to be aware of the underlying assumptions we make when using the WACC as the discount rate in capital budgeting. First, we assume that the market risk for the project is equivalent to the average market risk of the firm's investments. Second, we assume that the firm maintains a constant **debt-equity ratio**. Third, we assume that the main effect of leverage on valuation follows from the interest tax deduction and that any other factors (such as possible financial distress) are not significant at the chosen debt level.

13.5 Project-Based Costs of Capital

When the risk or the leverage of a specific project differs from the average investment made by the firm, a cost of capital for the project must be calculated. A multidivisional firm might benchmark the WACC for its own divisions off of competing companies that focus on a single line of business.

13.6 When Raising External Capital Is Costly

Issuing new equity or bonds carries a number of costs, including Securities & Exchange Commission filing and registering costs and the fees charged by investment bankers to place the securities. We can adjust the costs of equity and debt capital in the WACC to incorporate these issuing costs. Or, a better method is to treat the issuing costs as cash outflows necessary to the project and incorporate this as a negative cash flow in the NPV analysis.

■ Selected Concepts and Key Terms

Capital

A firm's debt and equity represent its **capital.** The firm's capital structure is its relative proportions of debt, equity, and other securities that it has outstanding. The relative proportions of debt, equity, and other securities that a firm has outstanding constitute its **capital structure.** The firm's **weighted average cost of capital (WACC)** is the average of a firm's equity and debt costs of capital, weighted by the fractions of the firm's value that correspond to equity and debt, respectively.

Market-Value Balance Sheet

A market-value balance sheet is similar to an accounting balance sheet, but all values are current market values rather than historical costs.

Unlevered

An **unlevered** firm had no outstanding debt.

Levered

A **levered** firm has debt outstanding. **Leverage** refers to the relative amount of debt on a firm's balance sheet.

Effective Cost of Debt

A firm's net cost of interest on its debt after accounting for the interest tax deduction is the **effective cost of debt.**

Levered Value

The value of an investment, including the benefit of the interest tax deduction, given the firm's leverage policy is known as the **levered value.**

WACC Method

The **WACC method** is the process of discounting future incremental free cash flows using the firm's WACC. This method produces the levered value of a project.

Debt-Equity Ratio

The **debt-equity ratio** is a ratio of the market value of debt to the market value of equity.

■ Concept Check Questions and Answers

1. Why does a firm's capital have a cost?

    To attract potential investors, the firm must offer them an expected return equal to what they could expect to earn elsewhere for assuming the same level of risk. This return is the cost a company bears to obtain capital from its investors.

2. Why do we use market value weights in the weighted average cost of capital?

    Market value weights are used because equity and debt holders assess the firm based on the market value of its assets rather than the book value of its assets.

3. How can you measure a firm's cost of debt?

    A firm's cost of debt can be measured by the yield to maturity on the firm's existing debt because it is the return that current purchasers of the debt would earn if they held the debt to maturity.

4. What are the major tradeoffs of using the CAPM versus the CDGM to estimate the cost of equity?

    To use the CAPM, we need to know the equity beta, the risk-free rate, and the market risk premium; we must assume that the estimated beta and market risk premium are accurate and the CAPM is a correct model. The CDGM requires that we know the current stock price, the expected dividend for next year, and the future dividend growth rate. CDGM can only be used if we assume that the future dividend growth rate is constant.

5. Why do different companies have different WACCs?

    The WACC of companies will differ depending on the risk of the line of business of the companies and the amount of leverage the companies have.

6. **What are the tradeoffs in estimating the market risk premium?**

   To estimate the market risk premium, we rely on historical data. It takes many years of historical data to estimate reliably the market risk premium. However, older data may have little relevance to how investors view market risk today.

7. **What are the main assumptions you make when you use the WACC method?**

   The main underlying assumptions of the WACC method are that the market risk of the project is equivalent to the average market risk of the firm's investments, the firm's debt-equity ratio remains constant, and the main effect of leverage on valuation follows from the interest tax deduction.

8. **What inputs do you need to be ready to apply the WACC method?**

   To apply the WACC method, you need to determine the incremental free cash flow of the investment and the weighted average cost of capital. You use this information to compute the value of the investment, including the tax benefit of leverage, by discounting the incremental free cash flow of the investment using the WACC.

9. **When evaluating a project in a new line of business, which assumptions about the WACC method are most likely to be violated?**

   Specific projects often differ from the average investment made by the firm, violating the assumption that the project's risk is equivalent to the average risk of the firm's investments. Projects may also vary in terms of the amount of leverage they will support and the assumption that the debt-equity ratio will remain constant does not hold.

10. **How can you estimate the WACC to be used in a new line of business?**

    You can estimate the WACC to be used in a new line of business by benchmarking off of companies that compete in the new line of business and are focused in that single line of business.

11. **What types of additional costs does a firm incur when accessing external capital?**

    Costs of issuing external capital include Securities & Exchange Commission filing and registration fees and fees paid to investment bankers.

12. **What is the best way to incorporate these additional costs into capital budgeting?**

    The best way to incorporate these additional costs is to consider the issuing costs as cash outflows and incorporate the costs as negative cash flows in the NPV process.

■ Examples with Step-by-Step Solutions

Calculating the Weights in the WACC

13.1 **Problem:** Apple Cider Corp. has debt outstanding that has a market value of $20 billion. The book value of the company's stock is $23 billion, and the market value of the company's stock is $30 billion. What are the weights that should be used in calculating Apple Cider's WACC?

Solution

Plan: The weights are the fractions of the company financed with debt and financed with equity. These weights should be based on market values because the cost of capital is based on investors' current assessment of the value of the firm, not their assessment of accounting-based book values. As a consequence, we can ignore the book value of equity.

Execute: Given its $20 billion in debt and $30 billion in equity, the total value of the firm is $50 billion. The weight for debt is $20 billion/$50 billion = 40%. The weight for equity is $30 billion/$50 billion = 60%.

Evaluate: When calculating its overall cost of capital, Apple Cider will use a weighted average of the cost of its debt capital and the cost of its equity capital, giving a weight of 40% to its cost of debt and a weight of 60% to its cost of equity.

Effective Cost of Debt

13.2 **Problem:** The yield to maturity on Maine Lobster Co.'s debt is 8.4%. If the company's marginal tax rate is 30%, what is its effective cost of debt?

Solution

Plan: The company's effective cost of debt will equal $r_D(1 - T_C)$. We know that r_D is 8.4% and that T_C is 30%.

Execute: Maine Lobster Co.'s effective cost of debt is $0.084(1 - 0.30) = 5.88\%$.

Evaluate: For every $100 it borrows, the company pays its bondholders $8.40 in interest every year. Every dollar in interest it pays saves Maine Lobster $0.30 in taxes. Because it can deduct the $8.40 in interest from its income for every $100 it borrows, the interest tax deduction reduces the firm's tax payment to the government by 0.30($8.40) = $2.52. Thus, the company's net cost of debt is the $8.40 it pays in interest minus the $2.52 in tax savings, which is $5.88 per $100 or 5.88%.

Estimating the Cost of Equity

13.3 **Problem:** The equity beta for Lakeside Boats is 1.3. The company just issued a dividend of $2.25 a share and you expect the company's dividend to increase at a constant rate of 3% a year. The stock of Lakeside Boats is currently trading at $32 a share. The yield on 10-year U.S. Treasury bonds is 4% and you estimate the market risk premium to be 5%. Estimate the cost of equity for Lakeside Boats in two ways.

Solution

Plan: The two ways to estimate the company's cost of equity are to use the CAPM and the CDGM. The CAPM says that the cost of equity can be calculated as:

$$\text{Cost of Equity} = \text{Risk-Free Rate} + \text{Equity Beta} \times \text{Market Risk Premium}$$

We can use the 10-year Treasury bond rate of 4% as an estimate of the risk-free rate. We are given an equity beta of 1.3 and a risk premium of 5% in the problem.

Using the CDGM, we estimate the cost of equity as:

$$\text{Cost of Equity} = \frac{\text{Div}_1}{P_E} + g$$

Execute: Using CAPM, we estimate the cost of equity as:

$$\text{Cost of Equity} = 0.04 + 1.3(0.05) = 0.105 = 10.5\%$$

Using CDGM, we estimate the cost of equity as:

$$\text{Cost of Equity} = \frac{2.25(1.03)}{32.00} + 0.03 = 0.0924 = 9.24\%$$

Evaluate: According to the CAPM, the cost of equity capital is 10.5%; the CDGM produces a result of 9.24%. Because of the different assumptions we make when using each method, it is highly unlikely that the two methods will produce the exact same answer.

Computing the WACC

13.4 Problem: Jakob's Coffeehouse has a yield to maturity on its debt of 7% and an expected return on its equity of 12%. Jakob's capital structure is 30% debt and 70% equity. If the company's tax rate is 30%, what is its WACC?

Solution

Plan: We can calculate the WACC using the equation:

$$r_{wacc} = r_E E\% + r_{pfd} P\% + (1 - T_C) r_D D\%$$

Since Jakob has no preferred stock in its capital structure, the weight for the preferred stock will be zero.

Execute:

$$r_{wacc} = 0.7(12\%) + (1 - 0.3)(0.3)(7\%) = 8.4\% + 1.47\% = 9.87\%$$

Evaluate: Jakob's Coffeehouse needs to earn at least a 9.87% return on its investment in current and new shops to satisfy both its debt and equity holders.

The WACC Method

13.5 Problem: Jakob's Coffeehouse (from Example 13.4) is considering introducing a sandwich menu at its coffeehouses. The company will incur marketing costs and the costs of equipping its locations with the necessary equipment to offer the sandwich menu. Jakob's estimates that the total costs of introducing the sandwich menu will be $7 million. The firm expects first-year incremental free cash flows from the sandwich line to be $1 million and to grow at 2% per year thereafter. Should Jakob's Coffeehouse go ahead with the project?

Solution

Plan: We can use the WACC method to value the sandwich expansion and then subtract the upfront cost of $7 million. We will need Jakob's Coffeehouse's WACC, which we estimated in Example 13.4 as 9.87%.

Execute: The cash flows for the expansion project are a growing perpetuity. Applying the growing perpetuity formula with the WACC method, we have:

$$V_0^L = FCF_0 + \frac{FCF_1}{r_{wacc} - g}$$

$$= -7m + \frac{1m}{0.0987 - 0.02}$$

$$= \$5.706 \text{ m}$$

Evaluate: The sandwich expansion has a positive NPV because it is expected to generate a return on the $7 million investment that is far in excess of Jakob's Coffeehouse's WACC of 9.87%. Taking on this positive NPV project will add value to the firm.

A Project in a New Line of Business

13.6 **Problem:** Bordertown Seasonings produces a number of seasonings and canned sauces. The company is considering capitalizing on its success and brand recognition by expanding into the frozen foods market. Bordertown's WACC is 9.6%. Because the frozen foods market would be a new line of business for Bordertown with different characteristics, the systematic risk of the frozen food line would likely be different from the systematic risk of the company's current business. A major producer in the frozen food industry is Fresh Meals Fast (FMF). FMF has no debt and a beta of 1.2. The risk-free rate is 3% and the market risk premium is 6%. What is a reasonable estimate for the cost of capital for Bordertown's new frozen food business?

Solution

Plan: Using FMF's beta of 1.2, the risk-free interest rate of 3%, and the 6% market risk premium, we can use the CAPM to estimate the cost of equity capital for FMF. Because FMF has no debt, its cost of equity is the same as its cost of capital for its assets.

Execute: Using the CAPM we have

FMF's Cost of Equity = Risk-Free Rate + FMF's Equity Beta × Market Risk Premium
$$= 3\% + 1.2 \times 6\% = 10.2\%$$

Because FMF has no debt, its WACC is equivalent to its cost of equity.

Evaluate: Bordertown should use a cost of capital of 10.2% for evaluating the frozen food line business opportunity. This is higher than the 9.6% WACC for Bordertown's existing business due to different risks that are associated with the new line of business. If Bordertown failed to use the higher 10.2% in evaluating the new opportunity, the new project's NPV would be overstated. This could cause Bordertown to accept a project that truly had a negative NPV.

Evaluating an Acquisition with Costly External Financing

13.7 **Problem:** Moonbeam Coffee is considering acquiring Jakob's Coffeehouse (from Example 13.4). Moonbeam plans to offer $50 million as the purchase price for Jakob's, and it will need to issue additional debt and equity to finance such a large acquisition. You estimate that the issuance costs will be $750,000 and will be paid as soon as the transaction closes. You estimate that the incremental free cash flows from the acquisition will be $5 million in the first year and will grow at a rate of 2% thereafter. What is the NPV of the proposed acquisition?

Solution

Plan: The correct cost of capital for this acquisition is Jakob's cost of capital, which we estimated as 9.87% in Example 13.4. We can value the incremental free cash flows as a growing perpetuity. The NPV of the transaction, including the costly external financing, is the present value of this growing perpetuity net of both the purchase cost and the transaction costs of using external financing.

Execute:

$$\text{NPV} = -\$50,000,000 - \$750,000 + (\$5,000,000)/(0.0987 - 0.02)$$
$$= \$12.78 \text{ million}$$

Chapter 13 The Cost of Capital 217

Evaluate: It is not necessary to adjust the WACC for the issuance costs of debt and equity. Instead, we can subtract the issuance costs from the NPV of the acquisition. Because the NPV remains positive when the costs of this external financing are considered, the project is a positive NPV project for Moonbeam and will add value to the company.

■ Questions and Problems

1. RB Corp. has common equity with a book value of $200 million. The company has debt outstanding with a market value of $500 million. The company's stock is currently trading for $50 a share and the company has 5 million shares outstanding. What weights should RB use in its WACC?

2. RB Corp.'s outstanding debt has a coupon rate of 7% and a yield to maturity of 6%. The company is in the 35% tax bracket. What is the firm's effective cost of debt?

3. RB Corp. is expected to pay a dividend of $2.50 a share next year, and the dividend is expected to grow at a rate of 3% per year thereafter. The company's equity beta is 0.9, and its stock is currently trading at $50 a share. The yield on the 10-year Treasury note is 4.5% and the market risk premium is 5%. Estimate the company's cost of equity using (a) CAPM and (b) CDGM.

4. Using the information from the previous three problems, what is RB's WACC?

5. RB Corp. is considering investing in a project that will cost $50 million this year and generate a positive free cash flow of $80 million in 3 years. Should the company invest in this project?

6. RB Corp. realizes that it would need to raise external finance to undertake the project in Question 5. The company would incur $5 million in issuance costs. How should RB account for these costs in evaluating the project? Should the company go ahead with the project?

7. Sun Flower Seeds is a major seller of vegetable and flower seeds used by home gardeners. The company is considering expanding into a new line of business—gardening tools. The company's current WACC of capital is 8.9%. Sun Flower has estimated that its major competitor in the gardening tool line, Green Thumb Tools, has a WACC of 8.1%. What should Sun Flower consider as it determines what WACC to use to evaluate the new line of business?

■ Solutions to Questions and Problems

1. The market value of the firm's equity is $250 million. The weight for the firm's equity is 250 m/750 m = 0.333 and the weight for the firm's debt is 500 m/750 m = 0.666.

2. Effective cost of debt = 0.06(1 − .035) = 3.9%.

3. a. Using the CAPM the cost of equity equals 0.045 + 0.9(0.05) = 9%.
   b. Using the CDGM the cost of equity equals ($2.50/50) + 0.03 = 8%.

4. The two methods of estimating the cost of equity resulted in two different answers. If we use the CAPM estimation, the WACC = 0.333 × 9% + 0.666 × 3.9% = 2.997% + 2.597% = 5.594%. If we use the CDGM estimation, the WACC = 0.333 × 8% + .666 × 3.9% = 2.664% + 2.597% = 5.261%.

© 2012 Pearson Education, Inc. Publishing as Prentice Hall

5. We need to calculate the NPV of the project using the WACC as the discount rate. Using the WACC of 5.594%, the NPV of the project is calculated as:

$$NPV = -50\,m + \frac{80\,m}{(1.05594)^3}$$
$$= -50\,m + 67.947\,m$$
$$= 17.947\,m$$

Because the NPV is positive, accepting the project adds value for the company. Note that if we used the WACC of 5.261%, we would still have a positive NPV because we would be using an even lower discount rate.

6. RB can consider the $5 million in issuance costs as a cash outflow today. This would decrease the NPV of the project to $12.947 million. Because the NPV is still positive, the firm should still undertake the project.

7. Sun Flower Seeds should use its 8.9% WACC to evaluate new projects only if the new project has a market risk similar to that of the rest of the firm. If the new line faces different market risks, then Sun Flower will want to use a WACC that reflects the particular risks of the new line. If Green Thumb's only line of business is garden tools, Green Thumb's WACC may be relevant for Sun Flower Seeds. However, Sun Flower will need to consider how the financial leverage differs between the two companies.

■ Self-Test Questions

1. The capital structure of Athletic Clothing Corp. is 70% equity and 30% debt. We would say that this company
   a. is unlevered.
   b. levered.
   c. has more leverage than Sports Gear, Inc., which has a capital structure of 40% equity and 60% debt.
   d. pays out all free cash flows generated by its assets to its equity holders.

2. Corona Publishing has debt outstanding with a market value of $10 million. The company's common stock has a book value of $20 million and a market value of $30 million. What weight for equity should Corona use in its WACC calculation?
   a. 25%
   b. 50%
   c. 66%
   d. 75%

3. Which of the following should be used as the firm's cost of debt?
   a. The coupon rate on existing debt outstanding.
   b. The U.S. Treasury bill rate plus the coupon rate on existing debt outstanding.
   c. The coupon rate on existing debt outstanding minus the U.S. Treasury Bill rate.
   d. The yield to maturity on the existing debt outstanding.

4. The effective cost of debt is
   a. the return paid to the debt holders.
   b. more than the return paid to the debt holders because of the tax consequences of the interest paid on debt.
   c. less than the return paid to the debt holders because of the tax deductibility of the interest expense.
   d. is equal to the firm's beta multiplied by the return paid to the debt holders.

5. To use the CAPM to estimate the cost of equity, you need to know
   a. the equity beta.
   b. the risk-free rate.
   c. the market risk premium.
   d. All of the above.

6. Which of the following do you NOT need to know to use the CDGM to estimate the cost of equity?
   a. Current stock price.
   b. Risk-free rate.
   c. Expected dividend next year.
   d. Future dividend growth rate.

7. The stock of Canadian Ski Wear is currently trading at $45 a share and the equity beta of the company is estimated to be 1.3. The company is expected to pay a dividend of $1.50 a share next year, and this dividend is expected to grow at a rate of 4% a year. The rate on the 10-year U.S. Treasury bond is 4% and you estimate the market risk premium to be 5%. Using the CAPM, what is the company's cost of equity?
   a. 5.6%
   b. 7.3%
   c. 10.5%
   d. 12.9%

8. Using the information in Question 7 for Canadian Ski Wear, what is the company's cost of equity using the CDGM?
   a. 5.6%
   b. 7.3%
   c. 10.5%
   d. 12.9%

9. Net debt equals
   a. total debt outstanding minus the value of the firm's assets.
   b. total debt outstanding minus the value of the company's equity.
   c. total debt outstanding minus any interest payments due.
   d. total debt outstanding minus any cash balances.

10. When we use the WACC as the discount rate in capital budgeting, we are assuming
    a. that the market risk of the project is equivalent to the average risk of the firm's investments.
    b. that the firm maintains a constant debt-equity ratio.
    c. that the main effect of leverage on valuation is the interest tax deduction and any other factors, such as financial distress, are not significant.
    d. All of the above.

11. The debt issued by Coastal Construction has a coupon rate of 5% and a yield-to-maturity of 6.2%. The company is in the 25% tax bracket. Coastal Construction's effective cost of debt is:
    a. 3.75%
    b. 4.65%
    c. 8.40%
    d. 9.00%

12. The value of an investment, including the benefit of the interest tax deduction, given the firm's use of debt is known as the
    a. levered value.
    b. debt/equity ratio.
    c. unlevered beta.
    d. incremental free cash flow.

Answers to Self-Test Questions

1. b
2. d
3. d
4. c
5. d
6. b
7. c
8. b
9. d
10. d
11. b
12. a

Chapter 14
Raising Equity Capital

■ Key Learning Objectives

- Contrast the different ways to raise equity capital for a private company
- Understand the process of taking a company public
- Gain insight into puzzles associated with initial public offerings
- Explain how to raise additional equity capital once the company is public

■ Chapter Synopsis

14.1 Equity Financing for Private Companies

A private company can raise outside equity capital from several potential sources:

- **Angel investors** are individual investors—frequently friends or acquaintances of the entrepreneur—who buy equity in small private firms. Because their capital investment is often relatively large, they typically receive a sizeable equity share in the business and have substantial influence in the business decisions of the firm.
- **Venture capital firms** are limited partnerships formed to invest in the private equity of young firms. Institutional investors, such as pension funds, are typically the limited partners. Most general partners charge an annual management fee of 2% of the fund's committed capital plus 20% of any positive return they generate.
- **Institutional investors,** such as pension funds, insurance companies, endowments, and foundations, may invest directly in private firms, or they may invest indirectly by becoming limited partners in venture capital firms.
- **Corporate investors** are corporations that invest in private companies—they are often referred to as **corporate partners, strategic partners,** or **strategic investors.**

When a company sells equity to outside investors for the first time, it typically issues **convertible preferred stock.** This gives investors all of the future benefits of common stock if things go well, and if the company runs into financial difficulties, the preferred stockholders have a senior claim on the assets of the firm.

Firms generally raise capital in different rounds. The **pre-money valuation** is the value of the shares outstanding prior to a new funding round at the price in the funding round. The **post-money value** is the value of the whole firm (old plus new shares) at the funding round price.

The method equity investors use to realize a return from their initial equity investment is called an **exit strategy.** There are two general types of exit strategies: an acquisition by another firm or a public equity offering.

14.2 Taking Your Firm Public: The Initial Public Offering

The process of selling stock to the public for the first time is called an **initial public offering (IPO).** Going public has advantages and disadvantages. The main advantages of going public are improved liquidity for the equity investors and better access to capital, both from the IPO proceeds and in subsequent equity offerings. A disadvantage of going public is that the equity holders of the corporation become more widely dispersed. This undermines investors' ability to monitor the company's management and thus represents a loss of control. Furthermore, once a company goes public, it must satisfy all of the increasingly stringent requirements of public companies. Organizations such as the Securities & Exchange Commission (SEC), the securities exchanges, and Congress (through the Sarbanes-Oxley Act of 2002) have adopted new standards that require more thorough financial disclosure, greater accountability, and more stringent requirements for the board of directors. Compliance with the new standards is costly and time-consuming for public companies.

After deciding to go public, managers of the company work with an **underwriter,** which is an investment banking firm that manages the offering and designs its structure. The shares that are sold in the IPO may be either new shares that raise capital, known as a **primary offering,** or existing shares that are sold by current shareholders, known as a **secondary offering.**

The **lead underwriter** is the primary investment banking firm responsible for managing the IPO along with a group of other underwriters, collectively called the **syndicate,** to help market and sell the issue. Underwriters are responsible for marketing and pricing the IPO, as well as helping the firm with all of the necessary filings.

Issuers must file a **registration statement** that provides financial and other information about the company to investors prior to an IPO. A **preliminary prospectus,** or **red herring,** is part of the registration statement that circulates to investors before the stock is offered. After the company satisfies the SEC's disclosure requirements, the SEC approves the stock for sale to the general public. The company then prepares the **final prospectus** which contains all the details of the IPO, including the number of shares offered and the offer price.

The underwriters work closely with the issuing company to determine a price range that they believe provides a reasonable valuation for the firm. The underwriters also attempt to determine what the market thinks of the valuation during a **road show,** in which senior management and the lead underwriters travel around the country explaining the deal to their largest customers. At the end of the road show, customers provide nonbinding indications of their demand. The underwriters then study the total demand and adjust the price until it is unlikely that the issue will fail. This process is called **book building.**

Usually, the underwriter and the issuing firm agree to a **firm commitment** IPO; with this arrangement, the underwriter guarantees that it will sell all of the stock at the offer price. If the entire issue does not sell out, the underwriter must take the loss.

Once the IPO process is complete, the company's shares trade publicly on an exchange. Usually, the pre-existing shareholders are subject to a 180-day **lockup** in which they cannot sell their shares for 180 days after the IPO.

14.3 IPO Puzzles

There are four puzzling IPO characteristics:

1. On average, IPOs appear to be underpriced: The price at the end of trading on the first day is often substantially higher than the IPO price.

2. The number of issues is highly cyclical. When times are good, the market is flooded with new issues; when times are bad, the number of issues dries up.

3. The costs of the IPO are very high, and it is unclear why firms willingly incur such high costs.

4. The long-run performance of a newly public company (3 to 5 years from the date of issue) is poor. That is, on average, a 3- to 5-year buy-and-hold strategy appears to be a bad investment.

14.4 Raising Additional Capital: The Seasoned Equity Offering

A firm's need for outside capital rarely ends at the IPO. A **seasoned equity offering (SEO)** is the process in which a public firm issues new shares. An SEO involves many of the same procedures as an IPO. The main difference is that the price setting process is not necessary because a market price for the stock already exists.

Two kinds of seasoned equity offerings exist: a cash offer and a rights offer. In a cash offer, the firm offers the new shares to investors at large. In a rights offer, the firm offers the new shares only to existing shareholders.

■ Selected Concepts and Key Terms

Angel Investors

Angel investors are individuals, frequently friends or acquaintances of the entrepreneur, who buy equity in small private firms. Because their capital investment is often relatively large, they typically receive a sizeable equity share in the business and have substantial influence in the business decisions of the firm.

Convertible Preferred Stock

Convertible preferred stock gives investors all of the future benefits of common stock if things go well, but if the company runs into financial difficulties, these investors have a senior claim on the assets of the firm.

Corporate Investor

Corporate investors are corporations that invest in private companies. Often they are referred to as **corporate partners, strategic partners,** and **strategic investors.**

Pre-Money and Post-Money Valuation

The **pre-money valuation** is the value of the shares outstanding prior to a new funding round using the price in the funding round. The **post-money valuation** is the value of the entire firm, including both the old shares and the new shares, using the funding round price.

Venture Capitalists

Venture capitalists provide equity capital to private firms. A **venture capital firm** is a limited partnership formed to invest in the private equity of young firms.

Exit Strategy

An **exit strategy** is the method by which equity investors realize a return from their initial equity investment.

Initial Public Offering (IPO)

An **initial public offering (IPO)** is the first time a company sells its stock to the public. The shares that are sold in the IPO may be either new shares that raise capital, known as a **primary offering,** or existing shares that are sold by current shareholders, known as a **secondary offering.**

In a **firm commitment** IPO, the underwriter guarantees the sell of all of the issued shares at the IPO price. An **auction IPO** is a rarely used method in which investors place bids in an auction process which sets the highest price such that the number of bids at or above that price equals the number of offered shares. All winning bidders pay this price, even if their bid was higher. In another rarely used method, the **best-efforts offer,** the underwriter does not guarantee that the stock will be sold, but instead tries to sell the stock for the best possible price.

Underwriter

An **underwriter** is an investment bank that manages the IPO process and helps the company sell its stock. A group of underwriters, called a **syndicate,** may be formed to help sell the stock. Within the syndicate, the **lead underwriter** is responsible for managing the IPO.

Initial Public Offering Process

The SEC requires that a company file a **registration statement** prior to an IPO. Included in this registration statement is a **preliminary prospectus** or **red herring**. After SEC approval, the firm files a **final prospectus.**

Road Show and Book Building

Underwriters attempt to determine what the market thinks of the valuation of an IPO during a **road show,** in which senior management and the lead underwriters travel around the country explaining the deal to their largest customers. **Book building** is the process in which customers provide nonbinding indications of their demand. The underwriters then add up the total demand and adjust the price until it is virtually certain that the issue will succeed.

Lockup

A **lockup** is an agreement that forbids pre-IPO shareholders from selling their shares for a period, generally 180 days, after an IPO.

Over-Allotment Provision

An **over-allotment provision,** or **greenshoe provision,** is an option which allows an underwriter to issue additional stock, amounting to 15% of the original offer size, at the IPO offer price.

Seasoned Equity Offering (SEO)

A **seasoned equity offering (SEO)** is the process in which a public firm issues new shares. In a **cash offer** the firm offers new shares to investors in exchange for cash. In a **rights offer** the firm offers new shares only to existing shareholders.

Tombstone

Historically, intermediaries would advertise the sale of stock by taking out advertisements in newspapers called **tombstones.**

■ Concept Check Questions and Answers

1. What are the main sources of funding for private companies to raise outside equity capital?

    Private companies can raise outside equity capital from angel investors, venture capital firms, institutional investors, and corporate investors.

2. What is a venture capital firm?

    A venture capital firm is a limited partnership that specializes in raising money to invest in the private equity of young firms.

3. What services does the underwriter provide in a traditional IPO?

    An underwriter is an investment banking firm that manages the offering and designs its structure. The underwriter markets the IPO, helps the company with all the necessary filings, and actively participates in determining the offer price. Often the underwriter will also commit to making a market in the stock by matching buyers and sellers after this issue to guarantee liquidity.

4. Explain the mechanics of an auction IPO.

    In an auction IPO, the company that goes public lets the market determine the price by auctioning off the company. Investors place bids over a set period of time. An auction IPO sorts the bids from high to low and sells the stock at the highest price that will sell all of the offered shares. All winning bidders pay this price, even if they initially bid something higher.

5. List and discuss four characteristics about IPOs that are puzzling.

    First, on average IPOs appear to be underpriced; the price at the end of trading on the first day is often substantially higher than the IPO price. Second, the number of issues is highly cyclical; when times are good, there are many new issues, when times are bad, the number of issues dries up. Third, the costs of the IPO are very high and it is unclear why firms are willing to incur such high costs. Fourth, the long-run performance of a newly public company is poor; on average, a 3- to 5-year buy-and-hold strategy appears to be a bad investment.

6. For each of the characteristics, identify its relevance to financial managers.

    Because IPOs are underpriced, the firm is not raising as much capital as it would if the stock price were higher. Issuance of new stock is highly cyclical, meaning that when the stock market is weak firms either forego raising capital or choose other alternatives. Because IPO costs are high, the amount of capital that the firm actually gets to use is low relative to the amount investors have paid. The poor long-run performance of newly public companies raises the question of what the situation was that caused these companies to need to raise capital in the first place.

7. **What is the difference between a cash offer and a rights offer for a seasoned equity offering?**

   In a cash offer, a firm offers the new shares to investors at large. In a rights offer, a firm offers the new shares only to existing shareholders.

8. **What is the typical stock price reaction to an SEO?**

   Researchers have found that the stock price reaction to an SEO is negative on average. Often the value destroyed by the price decline can be a significant fraction of the new money raised.

■ Examples with Step-by-Step Solutions

Funding and Ownership

14.1 **Problem:** You initially funded your start-up company by contributing $25,000 for 250,000 shares of stock. Since then, you have sold an additional 500,000 shares to angel investors. You are now considering raising even more capital from a venture capital limited partnership (VC). This VC would invest $4.5 million and would receive 750,000 newly issued shares. What is the post-money valuation? What percentage will you own? What is the value of your shares? What percentage of the firm will the VC end up owning?

Solution

Plan: After this funding round, there will be a total of 1,500,000 shares outstanding:

Your shares	250,000
Angel investors' shares	500,000
Newly issued shares	750,000
Total	1,500,000

The VC would be paying $4,500,000/750,000 = $6 per share. The post-money valuation will be the total number of shares multiplied by the price per share paid by the VC. The percentage of the firm owned by the VC is the VC's shares divided by the total number of shares. Your percentage will be your shares divided by the total shares and the value of your shares will be the number of shares you own multiplied by the price the VC paid.

Execute: There are 1,500,000 shares and the VC paid $6 per share. Therefore, the post-money valuation would be 1,500,000($6) = $9 million.

Because the VC is buying 750,000 shares, and there will be 1,500,000 total shares outstanding after the funding round, the VC will end up owning 750,000/1,500,000 = 50% of the firm.

You will own 250,000/1,500,000 = 16.67% of the firm, and the post-money valuation of your shares is 250,000 × $6 = $1,500,000.

Evaluate: Funding your firm with new equity capital, be it from an angel or venture capitalist, involves a tradeoff—you must give up part of the ownership of the firm in return for the money you need to grow. If you can negotiate a higher price per share, you will be giving up a small percentage of your firm for a given amount of capital.

Valuing an IPO Using Comparables

14.2 Problem: Vogtlin Pharmaceuticals is a private company that distributes over-the-counter medicines to drug stores. During the most recent fiscal year, Vogtlin had revenues of $475 million and earnings of $25 million. Vogtlin has filed a registration statement with the SEC for its IPO. The investment bankers would like to estimate the value of the company using comparable companies. They have assembled the following information based on data for other companies in the same industry that have recently gone public. In each case, the ratios are based on the IPO price:

Company	Price/Earnings	Price/Revenues
Ochre, Inc.	20.2X	1.3X
Devonshire Drugs	18.6X	0.9X
Consumer Medical Supply	25.3X	0.8X
American Pharmaceutical Supplies	21.3X	1.2X
Average	21.35X	1.05X

After the IPO, Vogtlin will have 25 million shares outstanding. Estimate the IPO price for the company using the price/earnings ratio and the price/revenues ratio.

Solution

Plan: To compute the IPO price based on the P/E ratio, we will first take the average P/E ratio from the comparison group and multiply it by Vogtlin's total earnings. This will give us a total value of equity for Vogtlin. To get the per share IPO price, we need to divide the total equity value by the number of shares outstanding after the IPO, which will be 25 million shares. We will then follow this same approach for using the average price-to-revenues ratio.

Execute: The average P/E ratio for recent deals is 21.35. Given earnings of $25 million, the total market value of Vogtlin's stock will be ($25 million)(21.35) = $533.75 million. With 25 million shares outstanding, the price per share should be $533.75 million/25 million = $21.35.

Similarly, if Vogtlin's IPO price implies a price/revenues ratio equal to the recent average of 1.05, then using its revenues of $475 million, the total market value of Vogtlin will be ($475 million)(1.05) = $498.75 million, or $498.75 million/25 million = $19.95 per share.

Evaluate: Using multiples for valuation will produce a range of estimates. Based on these estimates, the underwriters will probably establish an initial price range for Vogtlin stock of $19 to $22 per share to take on the road show.

Auction IPO Pricing

14.3 Problem: Your firm is ready to issue stock in an initial public offering. You will issue 4 million shares using an auction IPO. After the deadline for submitting bids, the following bids were received:

Price	Number of Shares
12.00	200,000.00
11.50	300,000.00
11.00	500,000.00
10.50	1,500,000.00
10.00	2,000,000.00
9.50	3,000,000.00
9.00	4,500,000.00

What will the offer price of the shares be?

Solution

Plan: We must determine the cumulative demand schedule. Then, we pick the highest price that will allow us to sell the full issue (4 million shares).

Execute: Converting the table of bids into a table of cumulative demand produces:

Price	Number of Shares	Cumulative Demand
12.00	200,000.00	200,000.00
11.50	300,000.00	500,000.00
11.00	500,000.00	1,000,000.00
10.50	1,500,000.00	2,500,000.00
10.00	2,000,000.00	4,500,000.00
9.50	3,000,000.00	7,500,000.00
9.00	4,500,000.00	12,000,000.00

The offer price is the highest price such that the number of bids at or above that price equals the number of offered shares. Thus, the offer price will be $10.00.

Evaluate: All auction participants who bid prices higher than $10 will receive the number of shares they bid. Bidders were willing to buy 2.5 million shares at a price greater than $10 a share. Since you are issuing 4 million shares, there are 1.5 million shares to be allocated to the group willing to pay $10 a share. Because there were bids for 2 million shares at $10, the shares will have to be rationed among this group. Shares will be awarded on a pro rata basis to bidders who bid $10.

Raising Money with Rights Offers

14.4 Problem: Pringle Construction has 100 million shares outstanding, and the shares are trading at $15 per share. The company needs to raise $250 million and has announced a rights issue. Each existing shareholder is sent one right for every share he or she owns. Pringle is deciding whether it should require five rights to purchase one share at $10 per share or eight rights to purchase two shares at $7 per share. Which approach will raise more money for Pringle?

Solution

Plan: In order to know how much money will be raised, we need to compute how many total shares would be purchased if everyone exercises his or her rights. Then we can multiply it by the price per share to calculate the total amount raised.

Execute: There are 100 million shares, each with one right attached. In the first case, five rights will be needed to purchase a new share, so 100 million/5 = 20 million new shares will be purchased. At a price of $10 per share, that would raise $10 × 20 million = $200 million.

In the second case, for every eight rights, two new shares can be purchased, so there will be 2 × (100 million/8) = 25 million new shares. At a price of $7 per share, that would be $7 × 25 million = $175 million.

Evaluate: If all of the shareholders exercise their rights, the first option of five rights to purchase a new share will raise the most money for Pringle.

In the first case, the value of the firm after the issue is $1.7 billion. There would be 120 million shares outstanding. This leads to a value per share of $1.7 billion/120 million = $14.17. This price exceeds the issue price of $10 per share, so the shareholders will exercise their rights.

In the second case, the number of shares outstanding will increase to 125 million. The value of the firm after the issue will be $1.675 billion, resulting in a per share price of $13.40 a share. The share price of $13.40 exceeds the issue price of $7 per share, so the shareholders will exercise their rights.

■ Questions and Problems

1. Moonbeam Coffee has 800 million shares outstanding at $40 per share. The company wants to raise $2 billion and is considering using a rights offering.
   a. If the offering requires 10 rights to purchase one share at $25 per share, how much will the company raise? What is the value per share after the rights issue?
   b. If the offering requires eight rights to purchase one share at $20 per share, how much will Moonbeam raise? What is the value per share after the rights issue?

2. Colonial Construction plans to offer 4 million shares at $10 each with Morgan Merrill serving as the lead underwriter.
   a. If the underwriter's spread is the standard 7%, how much will the firm raise?
   b. If the first day's closing price is $12.44, how much is the issue underpriced?

3. You founded a new alternative energy development firm last year, investing $1 million and receiving 1 million shares of stock. To expand, you need to raise additional capital. You have found a venture capitalist who is interested in investing. The venture capitalist is willing to invest $10 million in exchange for 25% ownership of the company.
   a. How many shares must the venture capitalist receive in order to end up with 25% of the company?
   b. What is the post-money valuation?
   c. What is the value of your shares?

4. Your company is conducting an auction IPO of 1 million shares. The following bids were received:

Price	Number of Shares
$5.75	10,000
$5.50	40,000
$5.25	350,000
$5.00	600,000
$4.75	1,000,000
$4.50	1,500,000

How much money will the offering raise?

5. You are a mutual fund manager considering an IPO for a firm that produces hydroelectric energy that is expected to be priced at $12 per share. Last year, the firm had sales of $100 million and earnings of $5 million. You have identified the following information for the two closest competitors, Gulf Electric and Columbia Power:

Company	Price/Earnings	Price/Sales
Gulf Electric	26.2	2.2
Columbia Power	32.5	2.8

After the IPO, the issuing firm will have 10 million shares outstanding. Based on the comparable firm multiples, is the IPO an attractive investment?

6. Andy tells you that he has the opportunity to purchase shares in Colonial Corp.'s upcoming IPO. He has heard mixed stories about how profitable purchasing shares in an IPO usually is. Use your knowledge of the IPO puzzles to explain to Andy what usually happens to the value of the shares purchased in an IPO the first day the shares are offered and then within 3 to 5 years of the IPO.

■ Solutions to Questions and Problems

1. a. If investors exercise their rights, 800 million/10 = 80 million shares will be purchased at $25, raising $2 billion. The value of the firm after the issue is 800 million × $40 + $2 billion = $34 billion. The value per share after the issue is $34 billion/880 million = $38.64.

   b. If investors exercise their rights, 800 million/8 = 100 million shares will be purchased, raising $2 billion. The value of the firm after the issue is 800 million × $40 + $2 billion = $34 billion. The value per share after the issue is $34 billion/900 million = $37.78.

2. a. The spread is the difference between the underwriter's purchase price and the offer price. In this case, it equals 0.07 × $10 per share = $0.70 per share. Thus, the firm would raise $9.30 × 4 million = $37.2 million.

   b. The underpricing equals ($12.44 − $10)/$10 = 24.4%.

3. a. The venture capitalist will receive 333,333.33 shares.

   b. The post-money value is the value of the whole firm (old plus new shares) at the fund round price. Since the venture capitalist is contributing $10 million for 25% of the corporation's equity, the post-money valuation is 4 × $10 million = $40 million.

   c. You own 75% of the equity, which is worth $30 million.

4. The cumulative demand schedule is:

Price	Number of Shares	Cumulative Shares
$5.75	10,000	10,000
$5.50	40,000	50,000
$5.25	350,000	400,000
$5.00	600,000	1,000,000
$4.75	1,000,000	2,000,000
$4.50	1,500,000	3,500,000

The offer price is the highest price such that the number of bids at or above that price equals the number of offered shares. All winning bidders pay this price, even if their bid was higher. The winning price will be $5 and you will raise $5 million before any fees.

5. The average P/E multiple for the comparable firms is 29.4, giving a total equity value of 5,000,000 × 29.4 = $147,000,000 and a value per share of $147,000,000/10,000,000 = $14.70.

    The average P/S multiple for the comparable firms is 2.5, giving a total equity value of 100,000,000 × 2.5 = $250,000,000 and a value per share of $250,000,000/10,000,000 = $25.00.

    Based on the comparable firm multiples, the price of $10 looks attractive.

6. IPO stocks appear to be, on average, initially underpriced. Many of these stocks see a substantial increase in their price on the first day they are traded. Therefore, those who initially purchased the shares often earn a high 1-day return. Evidence suggests, however, that these stocks do not make good long-term investments. These stocks generally perform poorly over a 3- to 5-year time period. Thus, a buy-and-hold strategy over a 3- to 5-year time frame is generally unsuccessful.

■ Self-Test Questions

1. When a firm raises capital, the _____ refers to the value of the shares outstanding prior to a new funding round and the _____ is the value of the whole firm (old plus new shares) at the funding round price.
    a. inside value; underwritten value
    b. cash value; rights value
    c. underwritten value; rights value
    d. pre-money valuation; post-money valuation

2. "Book building" refers to:
    a. A company using a number of underwriters, venture capitalists, and angel investors to finance an IPO.
    b. The process in which investors place binding bids in an auction process which sets the price of shares at the highest price possible for all shares to be purchased.
    c. The process in which customers provide nonbinding indications of their demand early in the IPO process.
    d. A method of raising seasoned equity in which the firm offers new shares only to existing shareholders.

3. A(n) _____ is the process by which a public firm issues new shares.
    a. auction IPO
    b. seasoned equity offering
    c. syndicate offering
    d. post-money valuation

4. A rights offer is:
    a. A seasoned equity offering in which the firm offers new shares only to existing shareholders.
    b. The right to purchase a security at the underwriter's purchase price.
    c. Is an exit strategy that involves the acquisition by another firm.
    d. An option which allows an underwriter to issue 15% more shares in an IPO.

5. Which of the following is a common IPO characteristic that financial economists find puzzling?
   a. On average, IPOs appear to be overpriced.
   b. The price at the end of trading on the first day is often substantially less than the IPO price.
   c. The costs of an IPO are very low.
   d. On average, the long-run performance of a newly public company is poor.

6. In an auction IPO
   a. all winning bidders pay the same price.
   b. all winning bidders pay the price they bid.
   c. all winning bidders pay the average bid price.
   d. only the bidders who bid exactly the winning price are awarded any shares of the stock.

7. An advantage of going public is:
   a. Improved liquidity for the equity investors.
   b. That the company must meet SEC reporting requirements, making the company more efficient.
   c. Increased financial disclosure, greater accountability, and more stringent requirements for the board of directors.
   d. Investor's increased ability to monitor the company's management due to the dispersion of ownership.

8. Jerome Lloyd's eight grandchildren each owned equal shares of the company he started, the Lloyd Company, which produces lawn and garden tools. In order to raise money for expansion, the company recently went through an IPO. As the pre-IPO shareholders, the Lloyd grandchildren are not allowed to sell their shares for 180 days after the IPO. This is known as a
   a. lockup provision.
   b. book building provision.
   c. red herring.
   d. rights offer.

9. Which of the following is a TRUE statement?
   a. While the SEC requires companies to meet disclosure requirements once they are publicly traded, the SEC does not require any disclosure of companies during the IPO process.
   b. Once a company receives SEC approval to sell stock to the general public, the company prepares a final prospectus that details the IPO, including the number of shares offered.
   c. Many firms want to go public because raising money through an IPO is usually very inexpensive compared to other ways a company might raise funds because of the very low underwriting spread.
   d. On average, a 4-year buy-and-hold strategy of newly public companies has been a good investment with above average returns.

10. Which of the following statements is consistent with the fact that there is a negative reaction to an SEO issuance?
    a. A firm that is concerned about the interest of its existing stockholders will tend to issue only stock that is undervalued.
    b. A firm that is concerned about the interest of its existing stockholders will tend to issue only stock that is overvalued.
    c. On average, a firm's stock price increases by 5% when the company announces an SEO.
    d. On average, a firm will only issue additional shares of stock if the stock is undervalued by at least 7%, so that the firm can recoup the issuance costs.

11. Aaron has developed and patented donut-making equipment that allows bakeries to automate making fresh donuts in a much smaller space than was previously needed. Aaron needed $1.2 million to start the production of this new equipment. His brother-in-law invested $600,000 and now owns 50% of the stock in the business. Aaron's brother-in-law would be known as
    a. a secondary investor.
    b. a seasoned investor.
    c. an angel investor.
    d. a strategic investor.

12. A(n) _____ designs the structure of an IPO, markets the IPO, and assists with the necessary filings for an IPO.
    a. underwriter
    b. angel investor
    c. seasoned investor
    d. convertible stockholder

Answers to Self-Test Questions

1. d
2. c
3. b
4. a
5. d
6. a
7. a
8. a
9. b
10. b
11. c
12. a

Chapter 15
Debt Financing

■ Key Learning Objectives

- Identify different types of debt financing available to a firm
- Understand limits within bond contracts that protect the interests of bondholders
- Describe the various options available to firms for the early repayment of debt

■ Notation

PV	present value
YTC	yield to call on a callable bond
YTM	yield to maturity on a bond

■ Chapter Synopsis

15.1 Corporate Debt

Corporate debt can be public debt, which trades in a public market, or **private debt,** which is negotiated directly with a bank or a small group of investors. An advantage of issuing private debt is that it avoids the cost and delay of registration with the SEC. However, because it is not publicly traded, it is illiquid.

A **bank loan** is a **term loan** that lasts for a specific length of time. When a single loan is funded by a group of banks, it is called a **syndicated bank loan. A revolving line of credit** is a credit commitment for a specific time period up to some limit, which a company can access as needed.

A **private placement** is another type of private debt. A **private placement** is a bond issue that does not trade on a public market but is sold to a small group of investors. Because it is not publicly traded it does not need to be registered with the SEC and can be tailored to a particular situation.

In order to issue public bonds, a prospectus must be produced that describes the details of the offering and includes an **indenture,** a formal contract between the bond issuer and a trust company. The trust company represents the bondholders and makes sure that the terms of the indenture are enforced.

While corporate bonds generally make semiannual coupon payments, corporations sometimes issue zero-coupon bonds as well. Most corporate bonds have maturities of 30 years or less, although in the past there have been original maturities of up to 999 years. A bond's face value, typically $1000, does not always correspond to the actual cash raised because of underwriting fees and the possibility that the bond may be issued at a discount to face value. If a coupon bond is issued at a discount, it is called an **original issue discount (OID) bond.**

Four types of corporate debt are typically issued: **notes, debentures, mortgage bonds,** and **asset-backed bonds.** These types of debt fall into two categories: **unsecured** and **secured debt.** Debentures and notes are unsecured debt, and, in the event of bankruptcy, the holders have a claim to only the assets of the firm that are not already pledged as collateral on the other debt. Notes typically have shorter maturities (less than 10 years) than debentures. Asset-backed bonds and mortgage bonds are secured debt, meaning specific assets are pledged as collateral that bondholders have a direct claim to in the event of bankruptcy. Mortgage bonds are secured by real property, whereas asset-backed bonds can be secured by any kind of asset. Although the word "bond" is commonly used to mean any kind of debt security, technically a corporate bond must be secured.

A bondholder's priority in claiming assets in the event of default is known as the bond's **seniority.** Most debenture issues contain clauses restricting the company from issuing new debt with equal or higher priority than existing debt. When a firm conducts a subsequent debenture issue that has a lower priority than its outstanding debt, the new debt is known as a **subordinated debenture.**

International bonds are classified into four broadly defined categories:

- **Domestic bonds** are bonds issued by a local entity and traded in a local market, but purchased by foreigners. They are denominated in the local currency.
- **Foreign bonds** are bonds issued by a foreign company in a local market and are intended for local investors. They are also denominated in the local currency. Foreign bonds in the United States are known as **Yankee bonds.** In Japan, they are called **Samurai bonds;** in the United Kingdom, they are known as **Bulldogs.**
- **Eurobonds** are international bonds that are not denominated in the local currency of the country in which they are issued.
- **Global bonds** combine the features of domestic, foreign, and Eurobonds, and are offered for sale in several different markets simultaneously.

15.2 Bond Covenants

Covenants are restrictive clauses in a bond contract that limit the issuer from taking actions that may undercut its ability to repay the bonds. For example, covenants may restrict the ability of management to pay dividends or they may limit the level of further indebtedness or specify that the issuer must maintain a minimum amount of working capital. If the issuer fails to live up to any covenant, the bond goes into default.

By including more covenants, users can reduce their cost of borrowing. If there are stronger covenants in the bond contract, the issuer is less likely to default on the bond; as a result, investors will require a lower interest rate to buy the bond.

15.3 Repayment Provisions

While an issuer can always retire one of its bonds early by repurchasing the bond in the open market, **callable** bonds give the issuer of the bond the right to retire all outstanding bonds on (or after) a specific **call date** for the **call price,** generally set at or above the bond's face value. If the call provision offers a cheaper way to retire the bonds, the issuer can forgo the option of purchasing the bonds in the open market and call the bonds instead.

Before the call date, investors anticipate the optimal strategy that the issuer will follow, and the bond price reflects this strategy. When market yields are high relative to the bond coupon, investors anticipate that the likelihood that the firm will exercise the call is low and the bond price is similar to an otherwise identical noncallable bond. When market yields are low relative to the bond coupon, investors anticipate that it is likely that the firm will call the bond; so, the bond's price is close to the price of a noncallable bond that matures on the call date. The **yield to call** (YTC) is the annual yield of a callable bond assuming that the bond is called at the earliest opportunity.

Some bonds are repaid through a **sinking fund** in which the issuer makes regular payments into a fund that is used to repurchase bonds. Bonds selling at a discount are repurchased in the open market; if a bond is trading at a premium, the bonds are repurchased at par in a lottery.

Convertible bonds give bondholders the right to convert the bond into stock at any time up to the maturity date of the bond. Thus, a convertible bond can be thought of as a regular bond plus a warrant (a call option written by the company on new stock it will have to issue if the warrant is exercised), so a convertible bond is worth more than an otherwise identical straight bond.

At maturity, the strike price, or **conversion price,** of the embedded warrant in a convertible bond is equal to the face value of the bond divided by the **conversion ratio** which equals the number of shares of common stock each bond owned can be converted into. If the stock does not pay a dividend, the holder of a convertible bond should wait until maturity before deciding whether to convert. When convertible bonds are also callable, if the issuer calls them, the holder can choose to convert rather than let the bonds be called. When the bonds are called, the holder faces exactly the same decision as he or she would on the maturity date of the bonds: he or she will choose to convert if the stock price exceeds the conversion price and let the bonds be called otherwise.

■ Selected Concepts and Key Terms

Private Debt

Private debt is negotiated directly with a bank or small group of investors and is not publicly traded. A **term loan** is a bank loan that lasts for a particular length of time. A **revolving line of credit** is a credit commitment for a specific time period up to some limit, which a company can use as needed. A **private placement** is a bond issue that is sold to a small group of investors rather than trading on a public market.

Secured Debt

With **secured debt,** specific assets are pledged as collateral that bondholders have a direct claim to in the event of bankruptcy. **Asset-backed bonds** are secured by specific assets. In the event of default, the bondholders have a right to seize the assets that serve as collateral. **Mortgage bonds** are secured by real property.

Unsecured Debt

With **unsecured debt,** in the event of bankruptcy, bondholders have a claim to only the assets of the firm that are not already pledged as collateral on other debt. **Notes** are unsecured debt with maturities typically of less than 10 years while **debentures** are unsecured debt with maturities of 10 years or longer.

International Bonds

International bonds are classified into four broadly defined categories: **domestic bonds** that trade in foreign markets, **foreign bonds** that are issued in a local market by a foreign entity, **Eurobonds** that are not denominated in the local currency of the country in which they are issued, and **global bonds** that trade in several markets simultaneously. **Bulldogs** are bonds issued by a foreign company in the United Kingdom, which are intended for local investors and denominated in pounds. **Yankee bonds** are foreign bonds issued in the United States, intended for U.S. investors and denominated in dollars. **Samurai bonds** are foreign bonds issued in Japan.

Indenture

An **indenture** is the formal contract between the bond issuer and a trust company. The trust company represents the bondholders and makes sure that the terms of the indenture are enforced.

Original Issue Discount (OID) Bonds

A bond that is issued at a discount to its face value is called an **original issue discount (OID) bond.**

Seniority

Seniority is a bondholder's priority in claiming assets in the event of default.

Sinking Fund

The issuer of a bond may make regular payments into a **sinking fund** administered by a trustee over the life of the bond that is used to repurchase bonds.

Subordinated Debenture

A **subordinated debenture** is a debenture issue that has lower priority than other outstanding debentures.

Syndicated Bank Loan

A **syndicated bank loan** is issued by a group of banks in which one lead bank typically takes a small percentage of the loan and syndicates the rest to other banks.

Covenants

Covenants are restrictive clauses in a bond contract that limit the issuer from taking actions that may weaken its ability to repay the bonds.

Callable Bonds

Callable bonds give the issuer of the bond the right (but not the obligation) to retire all outstanding bonds on (or after) a specific **call date** for the **call price,** generally set at or above the bond's face value. The **yield to call (YTC)** is calculated as the annual yield of a callable bond assuming that the bond is called at the earliest opportunity.

Convertible Bonds

Convertible bonds give bondholders the right to convert the bond into stock at any time up to the maturity date for the bond. At maturity, the strike price, or **conversion price,** of the embedded warrant in a convertible bond is equal to the face value of the bond divided by the **conversion ratio** which specifies the number of shares of common stock each bond owned can be converted into.

Straight Bond

A **straight bond** is a noncallable, nonconvertible bond.

Leveraged Buyout (LBO)

In a **leveraged buyout (LBO),** a group of private investors purchases all the equity of a public corporation.

Tranches

A debt issue can be divided into different groups that are called **tranches.**

Concept Check Questions and Answers

1. List four types of corporate public debt that are typically issued.

   Four types of corporate debt that are typically issued are notes, debentures, mortgage bonds, and asset-backed bonds.

2. What are the four categories of international bonds?

   Domestic bonds are bonds that are issued by a local entity and traded in a local market, but purchased by foreigners. Foreign bonds are bonds issued by a foreign company in a local market and are intended for local investors. Eurobonds are international bonds that are not denominated in the local currency of the country in which they are issued. Global bonds combine the features of domestic, foreign, and Eurobonds, and are offered for sale in several different markets simultaneously.

3. What happens if an issuer fails to live up to a bond covenant?

   If the issuer fails to live up to any covenant, the bond goes into default. That event may lead the firm into bankruptcy.

4. Why can bond covenants reduce a firm's borrowing cost?

   The stronger the covenants in the bond contract, the less likely the issuer will default on the bond, and so the lower the interest rate investors will require to buy the bond. That is, by including more covenants, issuers can reduce their costs of borrowing.

5. Do callable bonds have a higher or lower yield than otherwise identical bonds without a call feature? Why?

   The issuer will exercise the call option only when the market rates are lower than the bond's coupon rate. Therefore, the holder of a callable bond faces reinvestment risk precisely when it hurts. This makes the callable bonds relatively less attractive to the bondholder than the identical noncallable bonds. Consequently, callable bonds will trade at a lower price and therefore have a higher yield than otherwise identical bonds without a call feature.

6. What is a sinking fund?

   A sinking fund provision requires a company to make regular payments into a sinking fund administered by a trustee over the life of the bond. These payments are then used to repurchase bonds.

Examples with Step-by-Step Solutions

Calculating Yield to Maturity and Yield to Call

15.1 **Problem:** Thurman Enterprises has just issued 20-year, $1000 face value, 6% semiannual coupon bonds that are callable at 105% of par. The bond can be called in 1 year or any time thereafter on a coupon payment date. The bonds are trading at 95% of par. What is the bond's yield to maturity (YTM) and yield to call (YTC)?

Solution

Plan: The timeline of the promised payments for this bond (if it is not called) is:

Period	0	1	2	...	40
Cash Flow	−950	$30	$30	$30	$1030

The YTM for the bond will be the discount rate that makes the price of $950 exactly equal to the present value of the future cash flows.

If Thurman calls the bond at the first available opportunity, it will call the bond at Year 1. The timeline for the cash flows in this instance will be:

Period	0	1	2
Cash Flow	–950	$30	$30 + $1050

To solve for the YTC, we use these cash flows and proceed, as in Chapter 6, to solve for the discount rate that sets the price equal to the discounted cash flows.

Execute: For the YTM, we have:

$$\$950 = \frac{30}{YTM}\left(1 - \frac{1}{(1+YTM)^{40}}\right) + \frac{1000}{(1+YTM)^{40}} \Rightarrow YTM = 3.2\%$$

Because semiannual coupon payments are made, and we receive $30 every 6 months, the 3.2% from the equation above is a semiannual amount. We must multiply this number by 2 to get an annual interest rate. Thus, the YTM for this bond is 6.4%. We could also do this calculation using a financial calculator. To do so, we would need to enter the following:

	N	I/Y	PV	PMT	FV
Given:	40		–950	30	1,000
Solve for:		3.2			

We need to remember to multiply the 3.2 by 2 to get a YTM of 6.4%.

If the bond is called at its first call date, the YTC is calculated as:

$$\$950 = \frac{30}{YTC}\left(1 - \frac{1}{(1+YTC)^{2}}\right) + \frac{1050}{(1+YTC)^{2}} \Rightarrow YTC = 8.2\%$$

Again, with semiannual payments, we must multiply the 8.2% by 2 to get a YTC of 16.4%. To do this calculation with a financial calculator we would use the following keystrokes:

	N	I/Y	PV	PMT	FV
Given:	2		–950	30	1050
Solve for:		8.2			

We need to remember to multiply the 8.2 by 2 to get a YTC of 16.4%.

Evaluate: In this situation, the YTC is higher than the YTM. To call the bond, Thurman must pay 105% of par. While you forego receiving the coupon payments for the next 19 years if the company calls the bond, receiving the $1050 in a year leads to a higher rate of return. So, we would not expect Thurman to call the bonds.

Chapter 15 Debt Financing

■ Questions and Problems

1. Medina and Co. has just issued a callable 20-year, 8% coupon bond with annual coupon payments. The bond can be called at par in 1 year or anytime thereafter on a coupon payment date. It has a price of $102.
   a. What is the bond's yield to maturity?
   b. What is its yield to call?

2. Kim Enterprises has just issued a callable (at par) 5-year, 6% coupon bond with semiannual coupon payments. The bond can be called at par in 2 years or any time thereafter on a coupon payment date. It has a price of $97.
   a. What is the bond's yield to maturity?
   b. What is its yield to call?

3. You own a convertible bond with a face value of $1000 and a conversion ratio of 25. If the stock is trading at $37 at the maturity date, should you covert the bond into stock?

4. There are two bonds that Evan is considering purchasing. Other than the fact that one is a convertible bond, the two bonds are identical. Evan notices that the convertible bond has a lower yield than the otherwise identical bond without the option to convert. Explain to Evan why this is the case.

■ Solutions to Questions and Problems

1. a. YTM = 7.799%

	N	I/Y	PV	PMT	FV
Given:	20		−102	8	100
Solve for:		7.799			

   b. YTC = 5.882%

	N	I/Y	PV	PMT	FV
Given:	1		−102	8	100
Solve for:		5.882			

2. a. YTM = 3.358% × 2 = 6.716%

	N	I/Y	PV	PMT	FV
Given:	10		−97	3	100
Solve for:		3.358			

   b. YTC = 3.823% × 2 = 7.646%

	N	I/Y	PV	PMT	FV
Given:	4		−97	3	100
Solve for:		3.823			

3. The conversion ratio is 25, so the bond can be converted into 25 shares of stock. The value of 25 shares of stock is $37 × 25 = $925. Since the conversion value of the bond is less than $1000, you should not convert the bond into stock.

4. A convertible bond has a lower yield than an otherwise identical bond without the option to convert because it has an embedded warrant. If the stock price of a firm were subsequently to rise so that the bondholders choose to convert, the current shareholders will have to sell an equity stake in their firm for below market value. The lower interest rate is compensation for the possibility that this event will occur.

■ Self-Test Questions

1. Siemens Construction has made an arrangement with First State Bank, which allows it to borrow up to $250,000 any time it needs to over the next 12 months. This arrangement is an example of
   a. a line of credit.
   b. a syndicated bank loan.
   c. an original issue discount.
   d. a debenture.

2. Which of the following is an example of unsecured corporate debt?
   a. A syndicated loan
   b. Mortgage bonds
   c. Asset-backed bonds
   d. Debentures

3. Covenants are
   a. restrictive clauses in a bond contract that protect equity holders.
   b. restrictive clauses in a bond contract that protect debt holders.
   c. a type of secured debt.
   d. an asset-backed security.

4. Callable bonds
   a. are paid through a trustee who repurchases bonds over the life of the bond issue.
   b. generally sell for a higher price than noncallable bonds because of the protection the call feature gives to investors.
   c. give the bondholder an option to convert each bond owned into a fixed number of shares of common stock.
   d. allow issuers the right (but not the obligation) to retire all outstanding bonds prior to maturity.

5. Convertible debt
   a. carries a higher interest rate than comparable nonconvertible debt.
   b. carries a lower interest rate than comparable nonconvertible debt.
   c. allows stockholders to exchange their shares for bonds.
   d. gives the bond issuer the right to convert a callable bond to a noncallable bond before the maturity date.

6. Landon Industrial has issued a callable bond with a 6% coupon interest rate. Which of the following statements is TRUE?
   a. Landon will call the bonds if the market interest rate falls below 6%.
   b. Landon will call the bonds if the market interest rate rises above 6%.
   c. Rising interest rates make it more likely that Landon will call the bond.
   d. If the market yield is 8%, the bond will sell at a premium and the likelihood of a call is high.

7. In the event of bankruptcy,
   a. convertible bondholders are paid before straight bondholders.
   b. senior debt is paid in full before subordinated debt is paid.
   c. callable debt is paid before noncallable debt is paid.
   d. equity holders are paid before subordinated debt is paid.

8. An advantage of private debt is that
   a. it is much more liquid than public debt.
   b. it avoids the cost and delay of registration with the SEC.
   c. the company does not have to report this debt on its financial statements.
   d. it is callable, while public debt is not.

9. Brandies Textiles just issued a callable (at par) 10-year, 6% coupon bond with annual payments. The bond can be called at par in 3 years or any time thereafter on a coupon payment date. It has a price of $1030 and a face value of $1000. What is the bond's yield to call?
   a. 2.9%
   b. 4.9%
   c. 6.0%
   d. 9.0%

10. In a leveraged buyout,
    a. a private company becomes public through the use of debt securities.
    b. a public company becomes private.
    c. a public company issues additional debt that has a convertibility clause.
    d. a public company issues subordinated debt to establish a sinking fund.

11. Which of the following would be an example of a foreign bond?
    a. A bond issued by a German company in the United States, denominated in dollars, and intended for U.S. investors.
    b. A bond issued by a Japanese company in yen but sold to U.S. investors.
    c. A bond issued by a Greek company, denominated in Euros, and intended for Greek investors.
    d. A bond issued by a Greek company, denominated in yen, and intended for U.S. investors.

12. In 2000, Washington Enterprises issued bonds. In 2005, the company issued additional bonds which had a lower priority than the outstanding 2000 debentures. The 2000 debentures are said to have _____, and the 2005 debentures are called _____.
    a. call ability; covenant debentures
    b. seniority; subordinated debentures
    c. convertibility; covenant bond
    d. security; unsecured debt

Answers to Self-Test Questions

1. a
2. d
3. b
4. d
5. b
6. a
7. b
8. b
9. b
10. b
11. a
12. b

Chapter 16
Capital Structure

■ Key Learning Objectives

- Examine how capital structures vary across industries and companies
- Understand why investment decisions, rather than financing decisions, fundamentally determine the value and cost of capital of the firm
- Describe how leverage increases the risk of the firm's equity
- Demonstrate how debt can affect a firm's value through taxes and bankruptcy costs
- Show how the optimal mix of debt and equity trades off the costs (including financial distress costs) and benefits (including the tax advantage) of debt
- Analyze how debt can alter the incentives of managers to choose different projects and can be used as a signal to investors
- Weigh the many costs and benefits to debt that a manager must balance when deciding how to finance the firm's investments

■ Notation

D	market value of debt
E	market value of levered equity
EPS	earnings per share
NPV	net present value
PV	present value
r_D	expected return (cost of capital) of debt
r_E	expected return (cost of capital) of levered equity
r_U	expected return (cost of capital) of unlevered equity
r_{wacc}	weighted average cost of capital
T_C	marginal corporate tax rate
V^L	value of the firm with leverage
V^U	value of the unlevered firm

■ Chapter Synopsis

16.1 Capital Structure Choices

A firm's capital structure refers to the debt, equity, and other securities used to finance its fixed assets. Equity and debt are the securities most commonly used. A firm's **debt-to-value ratio**, $D/(E + D)$, is the fraction of the firm's total value that corresponds to debt.

16.2 Capital Structure in Perfect Capital Markets

When considering the types of securities to use to fund a new investment, a financial manager considers whether the different choices will affect the value of the firm. Let's consider the impact of these choices in a **perfect capital market**. A perfect capital market is a simple environment in which:

1. Investors and firms can trade the same set of securities at competitive market prices equal to the present value of their future cash flows.

2. There are no taxes, transaction costs, or issuance costs associated with security trading.

3. A firm's financing decisions do not change the cash flows generated by its investments, nor do they reveal new information about them.

If a firm uses no debt, it has no financial leverage, and the equity in the firm is called **unlevered equity.** Equity in a firm that also has debt outstanding is called **levered equity.** In an important paper, Modigliani and Miller (MM) argued that with perfect capital markets, the total value of a firm should not depend on its capital structure. They proved their results by arguing that, in perfect capital markets, the total cash flow paid out to all of a firm's security holders is equal to the total cash flow generated by the firm's assets. Therefore, by the Law of One Price, the firm's securities and its assets must have the same total market value. Thus, so long as the firm's choice of securities does not change the cash flows generated by its assets, the capital structure decision will not change the total value of the firm or the amount of capital it can raise. This observation leads to:

> **MM Proposition I:** In a perfect capital market, the total value of a firm is equal to the market value of the total cash flows generated by its assets and is not affected by its choice of capital structure.

Even if investors prefer an alternative capital structure to the one chosen by the firm, MM demonstrated that the firm's capital structure is still irrelevant because investors can borrow or lend on their own and achieve the same result. For example, an investor who would like more leverage can add leverage to his or her own portfolio. When investors use leverage in their own portfolios to adjust the leverage choice made by the firm, we say that they are using homemade **leverage.** As long as investors can borrow or lend at the same interest rate as the firm, homemade leverage is a perfect substitute for the use of leverage by the firm.

Modigliani and Miller showed that a firm's financing choice does not affect its value. But how can we reconcile this conclusion with the fact that the cost of capital differs for debt and equity? By holding a portfolio of the firm's equity and debt, you can replicate the cash flows from holding unlevered equity. Because the return of a portfolio is equal to the weighted average of the returns of the securities in it, this equality implies the following relationship between the returns of levered equity (R_E), debt (R_d), and unlevered equity (R_U):

$$\frac{E}{E+D} R_E + \frac{D}{E+D} R_D = R_U$$

If we solve this equation for R_E, we obtain the following expression for the return of levered equity:

$$R_E = \underbrace{R_U}_{\text{Return due to risk without leverage}} + \underbrace{\frac{D}{E}(R_U - R_D)}_{\text{Return due to additional risk created by leverage}}$$

This equation shows that the levered equity return equals the unlevered return plus an additional effect due to leverage. This leads to higher returns on levered equity when the firm performs well, but causes a lower return when the firm does poorly. The amount of additional risk depends on the amount of leverage, measured by the firm's market value debt-equity ratio, D/E. This observation leads to Modigliani and Miller's second proposition:

> **MM Proposition II:** The cost of capital of levered equity is equal to the cost of capital of unlevered equity plus a premium that is proportional to the market value debt-equity ratio.

The cost of capital of the firm's assets should equal the return that is available on other investments with similar risk. The weighted average of the firm's equity and debt cost of capital is the firm's **weighted average cost of capital (WACC).**

For an unlevered firm (one with no debt), the WACC is equal to the unlevered equity cost of capital. As the firm borrows money, it is using some of the lower cost debt in place of the higher cost equity; at the same time, the equity cost of capital rises because of the increased risk to the shareholder. The net effect of adding the leverage is that the WACC is unchanged. As more and more leverage is used, the debt becomes more risky because there is an increasing chance the firm will default; therefore, as the amount of debt increases, the debt cost of capital rises. In the extreme, the firm that uses 100% debt, the debt would be as risky as the assets themselves, given a risk level and return level equal to unlevered equity. In other words, as more leverage is used, the debt cost of capital and the equity cost of capital both rise, but more weight is put on the lower-cost debt, causing the WACC to remain constant.

16.3 Debt and Taxes

Modigliani and Miller explicitly assumed the absence of taxes in deriving their famous result. Let's look at the impact that taxes have. Interest on debt is tax deductible, creating a tax advantage to debt financing. The WACC with taxes is calculated as:

$$r_{WACC} = \frac{E}{E+D} r_E + \frac{D}{E+D} r_D (1 - T_C)$$

Corporate taxes lower the effective cost of debt financing, which translates into a reduction in the weighted average cost of capital. We can arrange the equation above to highlight this tax shield as:

$$r_{WACC} = \underbrace{\frac{E}{E+D} r_E + \frac{D}{E+D} r_D}_{\text{Pretax WACC}} - \underbrace{\frac{D}{E+D} r_D T_C}_{\substack{\text{Reduction due} \\ \text{to interest tax shield}}}$$

The reduction in the WACC increases with the amount of debt financing. The higher the firm's leverage, the more the firm exploits the tax advantage of debt, and the lower its WACC. The fact that corporations can deduct the interest they pay from their taxable income reduces the taxes they pay and thereby increases their earnings. In doing so, the interest tax deduction increases the value of the corporation.

The gain to investors from the tax deductibility of interest payments is referred to as the **interest tax shield** and can be calculated as:

$$\text{Interest Tax Shield} = \text{Corporate Tax Rate} \times \text{Interest Payments}$$

The interest tax shield provides a corporate tax benefit each year. The benefit of leverage for the value of the firm depends on the present value of the stream of future interest tax shields the firm will receive.

Because the cash flows of the levered firm are equal to the sum of the cash flows from the unlevered firm plus the interest tax shield, the same must be true for the present values of these cash flows. Letting V^L and V^U represent the value of the firm with and without leverage, respectively, we have the following change to MM Proposition I in the presence of taxes:

> The total value of the levered firm exceeds the value of the firm without leverage due to the present value of the tax savings from debt:

$$V^L = V^U + \text{PV(Interest Tax Shield)}$$

16.4 The Costs of Bankruptcy and Financial Distress

Although increasing debt can increase the value of the firm, firms do not shift to nearly 100% debt. With more debt, there is a greater chance that the firm will be unable to make its required interest payments and will default on its debt obligations. A firm that has trouble meeting its debt obligations is said to be in financial distress. There are both **direct costs** (such as fees paid to legal and accounting experts, consultants, appraisers, and auctioneers) and **indirect costs** (such as loss of customers and suppliers) to bankruptcy.

16.5 Optimal Capital Structure: The Tradeoff Theory

Tradeoff theory weighs the benefits of debt that result from shielding cash flows from taxes against the costs of financial distress associated with leverage. According to this theory, the total value of a levered firm equals the value of the firm without leverage plus the present value of the tax savings from debt, less the present value of financial distress costs:

$$V^L = V^U + \text{PV(Interest Tax Shield)} - \text{PV(Financial Distress Costs)}$$

This equation shows that leverage has costs as well as benefits. Firms have an incentive to increase leverage to exploit the tax benefits of debt. But with too much debt, they are more likely to risk default and incur financial distress costs. Calculating the precise present value of financial distress costs is very difficult if not impossible. Two key qualitative factors determine the present value of financial distress costs: (1) the probability of financial distress and (2) the magnitude of the costs after a firm is in distress.

What is a company's optimal amount of leverage given taxes and the costs of financial distress? We know that when a company has low levels of debt, the risk of default remains low and the main effect of an increase in leverage is an increase in the interest tax shield. If there were no costs of financial distress, the value would continue to increase until the interest on debt is larger than the firm's earnings before interest and taxes and the tax shield is exhausted. At some point, however, the tax savings that result from increasing leverage are just offset by the increased probability of incurring the costs of financial distress. For firms that have higher costs of financial distress, this point will be reached sooner; therefore, firms with higher costs of financial distress will have a lower optimal level of leverage than firms with lower costs of financial distress.

Tradeoff theory offers two important facts regarding leverage:

1. The presence of financial distress costs can explain why firms choose debt levels that are too low to exploit the interest tax shield.

2. Differences in the magnitude of financial distress costs and the volatility of cash flows can explain the differences in the use of leverage across industries.

16.6 Additional Consequences of Leverage: Agency Costs and Information

Leverage can alter managers' incentives and change their investment decisions. **Agency costs** are costs that arise when there are conflicts of interest between stakeholders.

In most large corporations the managers own a small fraction of the shares. Although the shareholders do have the power to fire managers through the board of directors, they rarely do so. This separation of ownership and control creates the possibility of **management entrenchment;** facing little threat of being fired and replaced, managers are free to run the firm in their own best interests. As a result, managers may make decisions that benefit themselves at investors' expense.

When a firm has leverage, a conflict of interest exists if investment decisions have different consequences for the value of equity and the value of debt. Such a conflict is most likely to occur when the risk of financial distress is high. In some circumstances, managers may take actions that benefit shareholders but harm the firm's creditors and lower the total value of the firm. This incentive leads to an **overinvestment problem.** Shareholders have an incentive to invest in risky negative-NPV projects; if the project fails, nothing is lost because the company was going to fail anyway. If, however, the project does succeed, the owners retain the business. Anticipating this behavior, security holders will pay less for the firm initially. This cost is likely to be highest for firms that can easily increase the risk of their investments.

On the other hand, when default is very likely, then undertaking even a good project before default will mostly or entirely benefit bondholders when they take the firm from shareholders in bankruptcy. Thus, when a firm faces financial distress, it may choose not to finance new, positive-NPV projects. In this case, there is an **underinvestment problem.**

The firm should increase its leverage up until the point that the benefits of increased leverage are exactly equal to the costs of the increase in leverage. Including the costs and benefits of the incentives that arise when the firm has leverage, we can calculate the value of the leveraged firm as:

$$V^L = V^U + PV(\text{Interest Tax Shield}) - PV(\text{Financial Distress Costs})$$
$$- PV(\text{Agency Costs of Debt}) + PV(\text{Agency Benefits of Debt})$$

Another market imperfection is related to the role of information. **Asymmetric information** exists when managers' information about the firm and its future cash flows is superior to that of external investors. A firm may commit to large future debt payments to convince the stock market that it has great projects; the use of leverage as a way to signal good information to investors is known as the **signaling theory of debt.** When managers believe that the stock is overvalued, they may attempt to engage in market timing by selling new shares. If this is the case, the firm's capital structure may deviate above or below the optimal level described by the tradeoff theory depending on management's view of the share price relative to its true value.

Asymmetric information also occurs when a seller has more information than a buyer does. When it is hard for the buyer to determine the true quality of the item being purchased, the buyer is skeptical that the seller is selling a product that is below average quality; if not, why would the seller, who knows the quality of the item, be willing to sell it at an average price? This leads to **adverse selection**—when the quality is hard to judge, the average quality of goods being offered for sale will be below average. The adverse selection problem has implications for capital structure. Managers do not want to sell equity if they have to underprice it to find buyers.

Thus, managers who perceive the firm's equity is underpriced will have a preference to fund investments using retained earnings, or debt, rather than equity. The idea that managers will prefer to use retained earnings first, and will issue new equity only as a last resort, is often referred to as the **pecking order hypothesis.**

16.7 Capital Structure: Putting It All Together

The optimal capital structure depends on market imperfections, such as taxes, financial distress costs, agency costs, and asymmetric information. Financial managers should remember to:

1. *Make use of the interest tax shield if your firm has consistent taxable income.* The interest tax shield allows firms to repay investors and avoid the corporate tax.

2. *Balance the tax benefits of debt against the costs of financial distress when determining how much of the firm's income to shield from taxes with leverage.* While the risk of default is not itself a problem, financial distress may lead to other consequences that reduce the value of the firm.

3. *Consider short-term debt for external financing when agency costs are significant.* Too much debt can motivate managers and equity holders to take excessive risks or underinvest in a firm. When free cash flows are high, too little leverage may encourage wasteful spending.

4. *Increase leverage to signal managers' confidence in the firm's ability to meet its debt obligations.* Investors understand that bankruptcy is costly for managers.

5. *Be mindful that investors know you have an incentive to issue securities that you know are overpriced.* Thus when an issue is announced, investors will lower their valuation of that security. This effect is most pronounced for equity issues, because the value of equity is most sensitive to the manager's private information.

6. *Rely first on retained earnings, then debt, and finally equity.* This pecking order of financing alternatives will be most important when managers are likely to have a great deal of private information regarding the value of the firm.

7. *Do not change the firm's capital structure unless it departs significantly from the optimal level.* Actively changing a firm's capital structure (for example, by selling or repurchasing shares or bonds) entails transactions costs. Most changes to a firm's debt-equity ratio are likely to occur passively, as the market value of the firm's equity fluctuates with changes in the firm's stock price.

■ Selected Concepts and Key Terms

Homemade Leverage

When investors use leverage in their own portfolios to adjust the leverage choice made by the firm, they are creating **homemade leverage.**

Levered Equity

The equity in a firm that has debt outstanding is known as **levered equity.**

Unlevered Equity

Equity in a firm that has no debt outstanding is called **unlevered equity.**

Perfect Capital Markets

Perfect capital markets are said to exist when the following criteria are met:

1. Investors and firms can trade the same set of securities at competitive market prices equal to the present value of their future cash flows.

2. There are no taxes, transaction costs, or issuance costs associated with security trading.

3. A firm's financing decisions do not change the cash flows generated by its investments, nor do they reveal new information about them.

Debt-to-Value Ratio

The **debt-to-value ratio** measure the firm's leverage. It is the fraction of the firm's total value that corresponds to debt.

Financial Distress

When a firm has trouble meeting its debt obligations we say the firm is in **financial distress.**

Interest Tax Shield

The **interest tax shield** is the gain to investors from the tax deductibility of interest payments. It is the additional amount that a firm would have paid in taxes if it did not have leverage and is calculated as the corporate tax rate multiplied by the firm's interest payments.

Tradeoff Theory

Tradeoff theory weighs the benefits of debt that result from shielding cash flows from taxes against the costs of financial distress associated with leverage. The total value of a levered firm equals the value of the firm without leverage plus the present value of the tax savings from debt, less the present value of financial distress costs.

Adverse Selection

This lemons principle—that when quality is hard to judge, the average quality of goods being offered for sale will be below average—is referred to as **adverse selection.**

Agency Costs

Agency costs are costs that arise when there are conflicts of interest between stakeholders.

Asymmetric Information

Asymmetric information can occur when managers' information about the firm and its future cash flows is superior to that of outside investors. This asymmetric information may motivate managers to alter a firm's capital structure.

Dilution

Dilution refers to the idea that if the firm issues new shares, the cash flows generated by the firm must be divided among a larger number of shares, thereby reducing the value of each individual share.

Management Entrenchment

Management entrenchment can occur when there is a separation of ownership and control; managers feel little threat of being fired and replaced and are free to run the firm in their own best interests, which is not necessarily in the investors' best interests.

Overinvestment Problem

When a company is in financial distress, an **overinvestment problem** can occur because shareholders have an incentive to invest in risky negative-NPV projects.

Pecking Order Hypothesis

The idea that managers will prefer to use retained earnings first, and will issue new equity only as a last resort, is known as the **pecking order hypothesis.**

Signaling Theory of Debt

The **signaling theory of debt** is the idea that the additional use of leverage is a credible signal of managers' confidence that they are investing in projects with positive NPV; they are only willing to take on these projects if they think there is a strong likelihood that debt holders will be paid.

Under-Investment Problem

The **under-investment problem** refers to the notion that when default is very likely, the firm will choose not to finance new, positive NPV projects because the projects will mostly or entirely benefit bondholders when they take the firm from shareholders in bankruptcy.

■ Concept Check Questions and Answers

1. What constitutes a firm's capital structure?

    A firm's capital structure is the relative amounts of debt, equity, and other securities it has outstanding.

2. What are some factors a manger must consider when making a financing decision?

    A manager must consider the future amounts promised to security holders in exchange for the cash raised today, whether the securities will trade at a fair price in the market, the tax consequences, transactions costs, and changes in future investment opportunities when making financing decisions.

3. How does leverage affect the risk and cost of equity for the firm?

    As more leverage is used, equity becomes more risky and the cost of equity increases.

4. In a perfect capital market, can you lower the firm's WACC by relying more on debt capital?

    No, in perfect capital markets the advantage of using additional lower cost debt capital is exactly offset by the increased riskiness and cost of equity.

5. How does the interest tax deduction affect firm value?

    The interest tax deduction creates an interest tax shield due to the tax savings. The value of the firm increases by the present value of the interest tax shield.

6. How does the firm's WACC change with leverage?

   The firm's WACC declines as the firm increases its reliance on debt financing and the benefit of the interest tax deduction grows.

7. What are the direct costs of bankruptcy?

   The direct costs of bankruptcy include the hiring of outside professionals, such as legal and accounting experts, consultants, appraisers, auctioneers, and others with experience selling distressed assets.

8. Why are the indirect costs of financial distress likely to be more important than the direct costs of bankruptcy?

   The indirect costs are difficult to measure accurately but are often much larger than the direct costs of bankruptcy. The firm can face these costs even if it is not yet in financial distress if there is a significant possibility of bankruptcy in the future. Some examples of indirect costs are loss of customers, loss of suppliers, increased labor costs, and the fire sale of assets.

9. According to the tradeoff theory, how should a financial manager determine the right capital structure for a firm?

   Increasing leverage increases the interest tax shield but also increases the possibility of financial distress. The firm should increase its leverage up to the point at which the tax savings that result from increasing leverage are just offset by the increased probability of incurring the costs of financial distress.

10. Why would managers in one industry choose different capital structures than those in another industry?

    The costs and the likelihood of financial distress vary by industry. Companies that have tangible assets that can easily be liquidated have lower costs of financial distress than a firm that lacks tangible assets. Also, companies with more stable cash flows have a lower probability of financial distress than companies with very volatile cash flows.

11. How can too much debt lead to excessive risk taking?

    When a company is near financial distress, shareholders have an incentive to invest in risky, negative-NPV projects. If the project fails, the shareholders are no worse off because the firm was headed for default anyway. If the project succeeds, the shareholders avoid default and retain ownership of the company.

12. What is the "pecking order" hypothesis?

    The pecking order hypothesis states that to avoid "lemons cost" managers will fund investments using retained earnings, followed by debt, and will only choose to issue equity as a last resort.

Examples with Step-by-Step Solutions

The Risk and Return of Levered Equity

16.1 **Problem:** Your hometown is the host city for the upcoming World's Fair. One-year licenses are available to entrepreneurs who want to operate a food kiosk on the grounds for 1 year. You will need to make an upfront investment of $40,000 to begin the business. After covering your operating expenses, you estimate you will generate a cash flow of $65,000 at the end of the year. The current risk-free interest rate is 4%. Your profits will be somewhat risky and sensitive to the success of the World's Fair; therefore, an 8% risk premium is appropriate, for a total discount rate of 12%.

Suppose you borrow $10,000 when financing your kiosk. According to Modigliani and Miller, what should the value of the equity be? What is the expected return?

Solution

Plan: The value of the firm's total cash flows is $65,000/1.12 = $58,036. This value is the same whether you use 100% equity financing or a combination of debt and equity financing. If you finance the kiosk only with equity, you would be able to raise $58,036 by selling stock. If you borrow $10,000, your firm's equity will be worth $48,036. To determine its expected return, we will have to compute the cash flows to equity under the two scenarios. The cash flows to equity are the cash flows of the firm, net of the cash flows to debt (repayment of principal plus interest).

Execute: If you use only equity, the shareholders are willing to pay $58,036 for the stock today and receive cash flows of $65,000 in 1 year, for a return of 12%.

If you sell $10,000 in debt, the firm will owe debt holders $10,000 × 1.04 = $10,400 in 1 year. Thus, the equity holders will receive $65,000 − $10,400 = $54,600, for a return of $54,600/$48,036 − 1 = 13.66%.

Evaluate: While the total value of the firm is unchanged, the firm's equity is more risky with debt than it would be without debt. Therefore, the cost of equity financing rises as debt is used.

Computing the Equity Cost of Capital

16.2 **Problem:** Suppose you borrow $10,000 to finance the kiosk from Example 16.1. What will your firm's equity cost of capital be?

Solution

Plan: Because your firm's assets have a market value of $58,036, by MM Proposition I the equity will have a market value of $58,036 − $10,000 = $48,036. To calculate the cost of equity, we can use the equation:

$$r_E = r_U + \frac{D}{E}(r_U - r_D)$$

We know the unlevered cost of equity is 12%. We also know that since the debt is risk-free (the cash flows of the firm will always be enough to repay the debt), r_D is 4%.

Execute:

$$r_E = 12\% + \frac{10,000}{48,036}(12\% - 4\%)$$
$$= 12\% + 0.2082(8\%)$$
$$= 13.66\%$$

Evaluate: This result matches the expected return calculated in Example 16.1 where we also assumed a debt of $10,000. The equity cost of capital should be the expected return of the equity holders.

Computing the Interest Tax Shield

16.3 Problem: Shown below is the income statement for Park Supplies, Inc. Given its marginal corporate tax rate of 35%, what is the amount of the interest tax shield for Park in years 2006 through 2009?

Park Income Statement ($ thousands)	2006	2007	2008	2009
Total sales	$3959	$4386	$4566	$4890
Cost of sales	−2359	−2630	−2998	−3249
Selling, general, and administrative expense	−290	−299	−313	−314
Depreciation	−21	−24	−26	−29
Operating Income	$1289	$1433	$1229	$1298
Other income	7	8	10	12
EBIT	$1296	$1441	$1239	$1310
Interest expense	−60	−80	−90	−110
Income before Tax	$1236	$1361	$1149	$1200
Taxes (35%)	−432.6	−476.4	−402.2	−420.0
Net Income	$803.4	$884.7	$746.9	$780.0

Solution

Plan: The interest tax shield is the tax rate of 35% multiplied by the interest payments in each year.

Execute:

($ thousands)	2006	2007	2008	2009
Interest expense	−60	−80	−90	−110
Interest tax shield (35% × interest expense)	21	28	31.5	38.5

Evaluate: By using debt, Park is able to reduce its taxable income. This reduction in taxable income leads to a decrease in taxes of $119,000 over the 2006–2009 time period. This means that the total cash flows available to all investors (debt holders and equity holders) is $119,000 higher over this 4-year time period than it would have been without the tax shield.

Valuing the Interest Tax Shield

16.4 Problem: Suppose Green Thumb Gardening borrows $2.5 million by issuing 20-year bonds. Green Thumb's cost of debt is 7%, so it will need to pay $175,000 in interest each year for the next 20 years, and then repay the principal of $2.5 million in Year 20. Green Thumb's marginal tax rate will remain 30% throughout this period. By how much does the interest tax shield increase the value of Green Thumb?

Solution

Plan: The interest tax shield will last for 20 years, so we need to value it as a 20-year annuity. Because the tax savings are as risky as the debt that creates them, we can discount them at Green Thumb's cost of debt: 7%.

Execute: The interest tax shield each year is 30% × $175,000 = $52,500. Valued as a 20-year annuity at 7%, we have:

$$\text{PV(Interest Tax Shield)} = \$52,500 \times \frac{1}{0.07}\left(1 - \frac{1}{1.07^{20}}\right)$$
$$= \$556,185.75$$

Alternatively, the present value of the interest tax shield can be found using a financial calculator:

	N	I/Y	PV	PMT	FV
Given:	20	7		−52,500	0
Solve for:			556,185.75		

The final repayment of principal in Year 20 is not deductible, so it does not contribute to the tax shield.

Evaluate: We know that in perfect capital markets, financing transactions have an NPV of zero—the interest and principal repayment have exactly a present value of the amount of the bonds: $2.5 million. However, the interest tax deductibility makes this a positive-NPV transaction for the firm. Because the government effectively subsidizes the payment of interest, issuing these bonds has an NPV of $556,185.75.

The Pecking Order of Financing Alternatives

16.5 **Problem:** La Cantera Mining needs to raise $20 million for a new investment project. If the firm issues 1-year debt, it may have to pay an interest rate of 8%, although La Cantera's managers believe that 7% would be a fair rate given the level of risk. However, if the firm issues equity, they believe the equity may be underpriced by 4%. What is the cost to current shareholders of financing the project out of retained earnings, debt, and equity?

Solution

Plan: We can evaluate the financing alternatives by comparing what the firm would have to pay to get the financing versus what its managers believe it should pay if the market had the same information as they do.

Execute: If the firm spends $20 million out of retained earnings, rather than paying that money out to shareholders as a dividend, the cost to shareholders is $20 million.

Using debt costs the firm $20 × (1.08) = $21.6 million in 1 year, which has a present value based on management's view of the firm's risk of $21.6 million ÷ (1.07) = $20.187 million.

If equity is underpriced by 4%, then to raise $20 million the firm will need to issue shares that are actually worth $20 million/0.96 = $20.8333 million. Thus, the cost of financing the project with equity will be $20.8333 million.

Evaluate: Comparing the three options, retained earnings is the cheapest source of funds, followed by debt, and finally by issuing new equity.

■ Questions and Problems

1. A firm expects free cash flow of $10 million each year. Its unlevered cost of capital is 10%. The firm also has outstanding debt of $35 million, and it expects to maintain this level of debt permanently. There are no corporate taxes or other market imperfections.
   a. What is the firm's value without leverage?
   b. What is the firm's value with the $35 million of debt? How much is the equity worth in this case?

2. An unlevered firm has 50 million shares outstanding and a stock price of $20. The firm plans to announce unexpectedly that it will issue $500 million in 10% coupon rate debt financing and use the proceeds to repurchase shares. The debt level is expected to remain at this level. There are no corporate taxes or other market imperfections.
   a. What is the firm's market value before the announcement?
   b. What is the market value of the firm after the debt is issued, but before the shares are repurchased?
   c. What is the share price just before the share repurchase? How many shares will be repurchased at this price?

3. Katie's Kitchen is currently an all-equity firm with an expected return of 14%. It is considering borrowing money to repurchase existing shares.
   a. Suppose Katie's borrows to the point that its debt-equity ratio is 0.75. With this amount of debt, the debt cost of capital is 6%. What will the expected return of equity be after this transaction?
   b. Suppose instead that Katie's borrows to the point that its debt-equity ratio is 1.25. With this amount of debt, the company's debt will be much riskier. As a result, the debt cost of capital will be 9%. What will the expected return of equity be in this case?
   c. A senior manager argues that it is in the best interest of the shareholders to choose the capital structure that leads to the highest expected return for the stock. How would you respond to this argument?

4. Tulsa Technology and Equipment (TTE) has $20 million in permanent debt outstanding. The firm will pay interest only on this debt. TTE's marginal tax rate is expected to be 30% for the foreseeable future.
   a. Suppose TTE pays interest of 8% per year on its debt. What is its annual interest tax shield?
   b. What is the present value of the interest tax shield, assuming its risk is the same as the loan?

5. Gulf Coast Enterprises is a firm whose only asset is a vacant lot in New Orleans. (There was an office building on the lot before Hurricane Katrina.) The company's only liability is debt of $10 million due in 1 year. If left vacant, the land will be worth $12 million in 1 year. Alternatively, the firm can develop the land at an upfront cost of $18 million. The developed land will be worth $36 million in 1 year. Suppose the risk-free interest rate is 10%, assume all cash flows are risk-free, and assume there are no taxes.
   a. If the firm chooses not to develop the land, what is the value of the firm's equity today? What is the value of the debt today?
   b. What is the NPV of developing the land?
   c. Suppose the firm raises $18 million from equity holders to develop the land. If the firm develops the land, what is the value of the firm's equity today? What is the value of the firm's debt today?
   d. Given your answer to part (c), would equity holders be willing to provide the $18 million needed to develop the land?

6. Medina Apple Co. forecasts net income this coming year as shown below:

EBIT	$8,000,000
Interest expense	0
Income before tax	8,000,000
Taxes	2,800,000
Net income	$5,200,000

Approximately $800,000 of Medina's earnings will be needed to make new, positive-NPV investments. Unfortunately, Medina's managers are expected to waste 10% of its net income on needless perks, pet projects, and other expenditures that do not contribute to the firm. All remaining income will be distributed to shareholders.

a. What are the two benefits of debt financing for Medina?
b. By how much would each $1 of interest expense reduce Medina's distributions to shareholders?

■ Solutions to Questions and Problems

1. a. $V^U = \$10$ million/$0.10 = \$100$ million
   b. $V^L = V^U = \$100$ million, $D = \$35$ million and $E = \$65$ million

2. a. $V^U = \$20 \times 50$ million = $1 billion
   b. $V^L = V^U = \$1$ billion
   c. Share price = $1 billion/50 million = $20

   They will repurchase 500 million/$20 = 25 million shares.

3. a. $0.14 + 0.75(0.14 - 0.06) = 0.14 + 0.75(0.08) = 0.20 = 20\%$
   b. $0.14 + 1.25(0.14 - 0.09) = 0.14 + 1.25(0.05) = 0.2025 = 20.25\%$
   c. No, the capital structure with the highest expected return for stockholders should not necessarily be chosen. The capital structure in part (b) has a higher return for shareholders, but there is also an increased amount of risk.

4. a. $20 m $\times$ 0.08 $\times$ 0.30 = $480,000
   b. $480,000/(0.08) = $6,000,000

5. a. Value of equity today = $2 million/1.10 = $1.82 million; value of debt today $10 million/1.10 = $9.09 million.
   b. The present value of the increase in land value because of the improvement is ($36 m – $12 m)/1.10 = $21.82. Therefore, the NPV = –$18 m + $21.82 m = $3.82 million.
   c. With development the firm value will be $36 million/1.10 = $32.73 million today. The value of equity today would be $32.73 m – $9.09 m = $23.64 million; the value of the debt today would be $9.09 million.
   d. Yes, the equity holders would provide the money. The value of the equity would be $23.64 m. After subtracting out the initial equity of $1.82 m and the additional $18 m investment the equity holders make, they are $3.82 m ahead (which exactly equals the project's NPV of $3.82 m).

6. a. The debt financing provides a tax shield and the interest payments reduce the funds available for management to use at its discretion on wasteful spending.
   b. Medina's tax rate is 2.8 m/8 m = 0.35 = 35%. Therefore, each dollar spent on interest will reduce taxes by $0.35. As a result, $1 in interest would result in $0.65 less in dividends.

■ Self-Test Questions

1. Which of the following is NOT a characteristic of a perfect capital market?
   a. Investors can trade securities at competitive market prices equal to the present value of their future cash flows.
   b. Perfect information exists, so investors know that they will get an identical rate of return no matter what investment securities they choose.
   c. There are no tax consequences, transaction costs, or other issuance costs associated with financing decisions or security trading.
   d. A firm's financing decisions do not change the cash flows generated by its investments.

2. The term "unlevered equity" refers to:
   a. The equity in a firm in the absence of taxation and transaction costs.
   b. The equity in a firm with no debt.
   c. The portion of a firm's capital structure that is financed internally.
   d. The amount of Treasury stock a firm holds.

3. Modigliani and Miller argued that:
   a. The cash flows of levered equity should be discounted at the same discount rate used for unlevered equity.
   b. Because leverage does not change the overall value of the firm, which is based on the present value of the cash flows the assets generate, equity should be considered a risk-free security.
   c. Because the cash flows to the firm are the same, shareholders will require the same rate of return whether or not leverage is used.
   d. In a perfect capital market, the total value of a firm is equal to the market value of the free cash flows generated by its assets and is not affected by its choice of capital structure.

4. With perfect capital markets, as the amount of leverage increases
   a. the WACC remains constant.
   b. the WACC increases at an increasing rate.
   c. the WACC increases at a decreasing rate.
   d. the WACC falls.

5. Last year, Harmon Manufacturing paid $3 million in interest payments. Harmon is in the 30% tax bracket. Harmon's interest tax shield for the year was
   a. $630,000.
   b. $900,000.
   c. $1,200,000.
   d. $2,100,000.

6. In the presence of taxes, the total value of the levered firm:
   a. Equals the value of the firm without leverage.
   b. Exceeds the value of the firm without leverage due to the present value of the tax savings from debt.
   c. Is lower than the value of the firm without leverage due to the present value of the tax savings from debt.
   d. Is lower than the value of the firm without leverage due to the present value of the interest payments that must be made.

7. Trade-off theory
   a. measures the differences between the direct costs and indirect costs of financial distress.
   b. weighs the benefits of debt that result from shielding cash flows from taxes against the costs of financial distress associated with leverage.
   c. states that the total value of the levered firm is exactly equal to the total value of the unlevered firm.
   d. considers the costs of increased leverage but not the benefits of increased leverage.

8. Trident Technology just announced that it is selling 3 million new shares of stock. Which of the following would be the most reasonable for you to assume?
   a. Trident's managers think that the company's stock is currently overvalued.
   b. Trident's managers think that the company's stock is currently undervalued.
   c. Trident is signaling to the market that it has great projects because it is committing to large future debt payments.
   d. Agency problems must be significant for the firm for the managers to choose equity financing over debt financing.

9. According to the pecking order hypothesis, managers will have a preference to fund investment using:
   a. Debt, followed by retained earnings, and finally new equity.
   b. Debt, followed by new equity, and finally retained earnings.
   c. New equity, followed by retained earnings, and finally debt.
   d. Retained earnings, followed by debt, and finally new equity.

10. Simons Industries has just borrowed $1 million by issuing 20-year bonds. The company's cost of debt is 5%, so it will need to pay $50,000 in interest each year for the next 10 years and then repay the principal of $1 million in Year 20. The company's marginal tax rate is 30%. By how much does the interest tax shield increase the value of Simons?
    a. $186,933
    b. $563,823
    c. $623,111
    d. $1,623,111

11. Because bankruptcy is costly for managers, an increase in leverage is a signal that
    a. agency costs are significant.
    b. managers are willing to forego the interest tax shield in order to increase the risk and return of the company.
    c. managers are confident in the firm's ability to meet its debt obligations.
    d. managers are concerned that the company will not be profitable in the near future.

12. You hear a manager at Gulfdale Aeronautic Supplies say, "We are providing each of our managers with a new company car. The shareholders won't ever notice this expenditure we are making on ourselves." This comment is an example of
    a. management entrenchment.
    b. the pecking order hypothesis.
    c. the over-investment problem.
    d. the under-investment problem.

Answers to Self-Test Questions

1. b
2. b
3. d
4. a
5. b
6. b
7. b
8. a
9. d
10. a
11. c
12. a

Chapter 17
Payout Policy

■ Key Learning Objectives

- Identify the different ways in which corporations can make distributions to shareholders
- Understand why the way in which they distribute cash flow does not affect value absent market imperfections
- Demonstrate how taxes can create an advantage for share repurchases versus dividends
- Explain how increased payouts can reduce agency problems but potentially reduce financial flexibility
- Understand the role of payout policy in signaling information to the market
- Describe alternate non-cash methods for payouts

■ Notation

P_{cum}	cum-dividend stock price
P_{ex}	ex-dividend stock price
P_{rep}	stock price with share repurchase
PV	present value

■ Chapter Synopsis

17.1 Cash Distributions to Shareholders

A corporation's **payout policy** determines if and when it will distribute cash to its shareholders by issuing a **dividend** or undertaking a **stock repurchase**. To issue a dividend, the firm's board of directors must authorize the amount per share that will be paid on the **declaration date**. The firm pays the dividend to all shareholders of record on the **record date**. Because it takes 3 business days for shares to be registered, only shareholders who purchase the stock at least 3 days prior to the record date receive the dividend. As a result, the date that is 2 business days prior to the record date is know as the **ex-dividend date;** anyone who purchases the stock on or after the ex-dividend date will not receive the dividend. Finally, on the **payable (or distribution) date,** which is generally about a month after the record date, the firm pays the dividend.

Most dividend-paying corporations pay them at quarterly intervals. Companies typically increase the amount of their dividends gradually, with little variation. Occasionally, a firm may pay a one-time **special dividend** that is usually much larger than a **regular dividend.**

Dividends are a cash outflow for the firm and generally reduce the firm's retained earnings. However, in some cases a **return of capital dividend** or a **liquidating dividend** is attributed to other accounting sources, such as paid-in capital or the liquidation of assets.

An alternative way to pay cash to investors is through a share repurchase in which a firm uses cash to buy shares of its own outstanding stock. These shares are generally held in the corporate treasury, and they can be resold in the future. An **open market repurchase,** the most common way a firm repurchases shares, occurs when a firm buys its own shares in the open market. A firm can also use a **tender offer repurchase** in which it offers to buy shares at a prespecified price during a short time period at typically a 10% to 20% premium. In a **Dutch auction repurchase** a firm lists different prices at which it is prepared to buy shares, and shareholders indicate how many shares they are willing to sell at each price. The firm then pays the lowest price at which it can buy back its desired number of shares. A firm may also negotiate a purchase of shares directly from a major shareholder in a **targeted repurchase.**

17.2 Dividends Versus Share Repurchases in a Perfect Capital Market

In perfect capital markets, a stock's price will fall by the amount of the dividend when a dividend is paid and a share repurchase has no effect on the stock price. In addition, by selling shares or reinvesting dividends, an investor can effectively create any cash dividend desired and can sell stock in the open market without a share repurchase. As a result, investors are indifferent between the various payout methods the firm might employ.

The Modigliani and Miller irrelevance proposition states that in perfect capital markets holding fixed the investment policy of a firm, the firm's choice of dividend policy is irrelevant and does not affect the share value. The **MM Dividend Irrelevance** proposition can be stated as:

> *In perfect capital markets, holding fixed the investment policy of a firm, the firm's choice of dividend policy is irrelevant and does not affect the initial share price.*

17.3 The Tax Disadvantage of Dividends

Taxes are a market imperfection that influences a firm's decision to pay dividends or repurchase shares. When the tax rate on dividends exceeds the tax rate on capital gains, the optimal dividend policy is for firms to pay no dividends and use share repurchases for all payouts. Recent changes in the tax code have equalized the tax rates on dividends and capital gains. However, long-term investors can defer the capital gains tax until they sell, so there is still a tax advantage for share repurchases over dividends for most investors. The fact that firms continue to issue dividends despite their tax disadvantage is often referred to as the **dividend puzzle.**

17.4 Payout Versus Retention of Cash

With perfect capital markets, the Modigliani and Miller payout policy irrelevance holds that as long as a firm without positive NPV projects invests excess cash flows in financial securities, the firm's choice of payout versus retention is irrelevant and does not affect the value of the firm. However, in the presence of corporate taxes, it is generally costly for a firm to retain excess cash because the interest is taxable income for the corporation. Stockholders are better off if the corporation would pay the cash out so it can be invested by the investors before taxable interest is incurred.

Nevertheless, firms may want to hold cash balances in order to help minimize the transaction costs of raising new capital when they have future potential cash needs. However, there is no benefit to shareholders for firms to hold cash in excess of future investment needs.

In addition to the tax disadvantage of holding cash, agency costs may arise, as managers may be tempted to spend excess cash on inefficient investments and perks. Thus, dividends and share repurchases may help minimize the agency problem of wasteful spending when a firm has excess cash. Without pressure from shareholders, managers may also choose to horde cash in order to reduce the firm's leverage and increase their job security.

17.5 Signaling with Payout Policy

When managers have better information than investors regarding the future prospects of a firm, their payout decisions may signal this information. Firms typically undertake **dividend smoothing** by maintaining relatively constant dividends, and they increase dividends much more frequently than they cut them. If a firm uses dividend smoothing, its dividend choice may contain information regarding management's expectations of future earnings:

- When a firm increases its dividend, it sends a positive signal to investors that management expects to be able to afford the higher dividend for the foreseeable future.
- When a firm cuts its dividend, it may signal that it is necessary to reduce the dividend to save cash.

The idea that dividend changes reflect managers' views about a firm's future earnings prospects is called the **dividend signaling hypothesis.**

Share repurchases, like dividends, may also signal managers' information to the market. However, several important differences distinguish share repurchases and dividends.

1. Managers are much less committed to share repurchases than to dividend payments.

2. Unlike with dividends, firms do not smooth their repurchase activity from year to year.

3. The cost of a share repurchase depends on the market price of the stock. If managers believe the stock is currently overvalued, a share repurchase will be costly to the firm. Therefore, managers will clearly be more likely to repurchase shares if they believe the stock is undervalued.

17.6 Stock Dividends, Splits, and Spin-Offs

In a **stock split,** shareholders receive additional shares in the firm and the stock price generally falls proportionally with the size of the split. For example, in a 2-for-1 stock split the firm's stock price will fall by 1/2. The typical motivation for a stock split is to keep the share price in a range thought to be attractive to small investors. If the stock price is deemed too low, firms can use a **reverse stock split,** which decreases the number of shares outstanding resulting in a higher share price. Stock splits are generally accomplished using a **stock dividend.** When shareholders receive additional shares of stock in the firm itself, the stock dividend has the same effect as a stock split; when they receive shares of a subsidiary, it is called a **spin-off.**

17.7 Advice for the Financial Manager

Several important items the financial manager should consider when making payout decisions are:
- Try to maximize the after-tax payout to the shareholders for a given payout amount. Consider whether repurchases and dividends are taxed differently.
- If a large, infrequent distribution is to be made, consider repurchases and special dividends.
- Because starting and increasing a regular dividend payment is seen as an implicit commitment to maintain a regular dividend, only set regular dividend levels that you are confident the firm can maintain.
- Regular dividends send a stronger signal of financial strength to shareholders than do infrequent distributions, such as repurchases.
- Because of transaction costs, be mindful of future investment plans. Avoid making a large distribution followed by raising capital to fund a project.

■ Selected Concepts and Key Terms

Declaration Date
The date a corporation announces that it will pay dividends to all shareholders of record on the record date is the **declaration date.**

Dutch Auction
In a **Dutch auction** a firm lists the different prices at which it is prepared to buy shares, and shareholders indicate how many shares they are willing to sell at each price. The firm then pays the lowest price at which it can buy back its desired number of shares.

Greenmail
Greenmail is a targeted share repurchase, often at a premium, aimed at preventing a takeover.

Ex-Dividend Date
The **ex-dividend date** is the date 2 business days prior to the record date; anyone who purchases the stock on or after the ex-dividend date will not receive the dividend.

Open Market Repurchase
With an **open market repurchase** a firm announces its intention to buy its own shares in the open market just like any other investor.

Payable Date, Distribution Date
The **payable date** or **distribution date** is the date the firm mails dividend checks to the registered shareholders. Generally, this occurs about 1 month after the record date.

Payout Policy
Payout policy refers to the procedure a firm uses to distribute cash to its shareholders by either issuing a dividend or undertaking a stock repurchase.

Record Date
The **record date** is the date a stockholder must own a stock in order to receive the dividend.

Liquidating Dividend, Return of Capital
A **liquidating dividend** or **return of capital** is a dividend that is attributed to an accounting source other than retained earnings, such as paid-in capital or the liquidation of assets.

Special Dividend
A **special dividend** is a one-time dividend that is usually much larger than a regular dividend.

Targeted Repurchase
A firm negotiates the purchase of shares directly from a major shareholder in a **targeted repurchase.**

Tender Offer

In a **tender offer** a firm offers to buy shares at a prespecified price (usually a premium) during a short time period, generally within 20 days.

Cum-Dividend

Just before the ex-dividend date, a stock trades **cum-dividend** (meaning "with the dividend") because anyone who buys the stock will be entitled to the dividend.

Clientele Effect

The **clientele effect** is the idea that individuals in the highest tax brackets have a preference for stocks that pay no or low dividends whereas tax-free investors and corporations have a stronger preference for stocks with high dividends. Thus, a firm's dividend policy may be optimized for the tax preference of its investor clientele.

Dividend Puzzle

The **dividend puzzle** is the fact that firms continue to issue dividends despite their general tax disadvantage.

Dividend Signaling Hypothesis

The dividend signaling hypothesis is the idea that dividend changes reflect managers' views about a firm's future earnings prospects.

Dividend Smoothing

The practice of a firm maintaining relatively constant dividends, although earnings may be more volatile, is called **dividend smoothing.**

Spin-Off

A **spin-off** is the distribution of shares of stock in a subsidiary to existing shareholders on a pro rata basis as a stock dividend.

Stock Dividend

A **stock dividend** is a payment to shareholders in which each shareholder that owns the stock before it goes ex-dividend receives additional shares of stock of the firm itself or of a subsidiary.

Stock Split

A **stock split** is a transaction in which shareholders received additional shares in the firm. The stock price generally falls proportionally with the size of the split.

■ Concept Check Questions and Answers

1. How is a stock's ex-dividend date determined, and what is its significance?

    A stock's ex-dividend date is 2 business days prior to the record date. Anyone who purchases the stock on or after the ex-dividend date will not receive the dividend.

2. What is an open-market share repurchase?

   An open market share repurchase occurs when a firm buys shares of its own stock in the open market like any other investor.

3. Explain the misconception that when a firm repurchases its own shares, the price rises due to the decrease in the supply of shares outstanding.

   When a firm repurchases its own shares, the supply of shares is reduced but the value of the firm's assets declines when it spends its cash to buy the shares. If the firm repurchases its shares at their market prices, these two effects offset each other, and the share price is unchanged.

4. In a perfect capital market, how important is the firm's decision to pay dividends versus repurchase shares?

   As Modigliani and Miller make clear, the value of a firm, ultimately derives from its underlying free cash flow. A firm's free cash flow determines the level of payouts that it can make to its investors. In a perfect capital market, whether these payouts are made through dividends or share repurchases does not matter.

5. Under what conditions will investors have a tax preference for share repurchases rather than dividends?

   Investors will have a tax preference for share repurchases rather than dividends when the capital gains tax rate is lower than the tax rate on dividends.

6. What is the dividend puzzle?

   The dividend puzzle stems from the fact that the tax rate on dividends has been higher than the tax rate on capital gains. This tax disadvantage should lead firms to choose share repurchases over dividends, but some firms have paid and continue to pay dividends despite this disadvantage.

7. Is there an advantage for a firm to retain its cash instead of paying it out to shareholders in perfect capital markets?

   In perfect capital markets, the firm value is independent of the decision to pay out or retain capital.

8. How do corporate taxes affect the decision of a firm to retain excess cash?

   Corporate taxes make it costly for a firm to retain excess cash. When the firm receives interest from its investment in financial securities, it owes taxes on the interest. Thus, cash is equivalent to negative leverage, and the tax advantage of leverage implies a tax disadvantage to holding cash.

9. What possible signals does a firm give when it cuts its dividend?

   According to the dividend signaling hypothesis, when a firm cuts the dividend it gives a negative signal to investors that the firm does not expect that earnings will rebound in the near-term and it needs to reduce the dividend to save cash. Also, a firm might cut its dividend to exploit new positive-NPV investment opportunities. In this case, the dividend decrease might lead to a positive stock price reaction.

10. Would managers be more likely to repurchase shares if they believe the stock is under- or overvalued?

    If managers believe the stock is currently undervalued, a share repurchase is a positive-NPV investment. Managers will clearly be more likely to repurchase shares if they believe the stock to be undervalued.

11. What is the difference between a stock dividend and a stock split?

    There is not a substantial difference between a stock split and a stock dividend. Stock splits typically are stock dividends 50% or higher.

12. What are some advantages of a spin-off as opposed to selling the dividend and distributing the cash?

    The advantage of the spin-off is that the firm avoids transaction costs associated with the sale and investors are not subjected to an immediate tax effect of a special dividend.

■ Examples with Step-by-Step Solutions

Homemade Dividends

17.1 **Problem:** Del Sol Equipment is a manufacturer of swimming pool pumps and heaters. The company has no debt and expects to generate free cash flows of $5 million per year in the future. The company has 1 million shares of stock outstanding and $1 million in excess cash. The firm's unlevered cost of capital is 10%.

You currently own 3000 shares of Del Sol. The company is planning on paying a $1 dividend per share with its excess cash. You would prefer to receive a $2 per share dividend for a total of $6000 from your investment in Del Sol. Show how you can create a homemade dividend so that you receive the $6000.

Solution

Plan: If Del Sol pays a $1 dividend, you will receive $3000 in cash and still hold 3000 shares of stock. You can generate the additional $3000 you desire by selling shares of stock. First, you will need to determine the price of a share of stock. Then, you will be able to determine the number of shares you need to sell to generate the $3000 in cash.

Execute: The value of Del Sol's ongoing operations is $5 million/0.10 = $50 million. The company has 1 million shares outstanding; therefore, each share is worth $50 million/1 million = $50. To generate $3000 in cash you will need to sell $3000/$50 = 60 shares of stock. You then generate $3000 in dividends and $3000 in the stock sale, resulting in $6000 total.

Evaluate: If Del Sol had offered a $2 per share dividend, you would not have sold your shares, and you would have still owned 3000 shares. However, each share would have been worthless. By creating your homemade dividend, you own fewer shares, but the shares you own are still worth $50 a share. The policy that the firm chooses is irrelevant—you can transact in the market to create a homemade dividend policy that suits your preferences.

Payout Decisions in a Perfect Capital Market

17.2 **Problem:** Milton Pharmaceuticals has $200,000 in excess cash. Milton is considering investing the cash in 1-year Treasury bills paying 5% interest and then using the cash to pay a dividend next year. Alternatively, the firm can pay a dividend immediately and shareholders can invest the cash on their own. In a perfect capital market, which option would the shareholders prefer?

Solution

Plan: We need to compare what shareholders would receive from an immediate dividend of $200,000, to the present value of what they would receive in 1 year if Milton invested the cash.

Execute: If Milton retains the cash, at the end of 1 year the company will be able to pay a dividend of $200,000 × (1.05) = $210,000. Note that this payoff is the same as if shareholders had invested the $200,000 in Treasury bills themselves. In other words, the present value of this future dividend is exactly $210,000 ÷ (1.05) = $200,000, which is the same as the $200,000 shareholders would receive from an immediate dividend. Thus, shareholders are indifferent about whether the firm pays the dividend immediately or retains the cash.

Evaluate: Because Milton is not doing anything that the investors could not have done on their own, it does not create any value by retaining the cash and investing it for the shareholders versus simply paying it to them immediately.

Retaining Cash with Corporate Taxes

17.3 Problem: Suppose Milton from Example 17.2 must pay corporate taxes at a 30% rate on the interest it will earn from the 1-year Treasury bill paying 5% interest. Would pension fund investors (who do not pay taxes on their investment income) prefer that Milton use its excess cash to pay the $200,000 dividend immediately or retain the cash for 1 year?

Solution

Plan: As in the original example, the comparison is between what shareholders could generate on their own and what shareholders will receive if Milton retains and invests the funds for them. The key question then is: What is the difference between the after-tax return that Milton can earn and distribute to shareholders versus the pension fund's tax-free return on investing the $200,000?

Execute: Because the pension fund investors do not pay taxes on investment income, the results from the prior example still hold: They would get $200,000, invest it, and earn 5% to receive a total of $210,000 in 1 year.

If Milton retains the cash for 1 year, it will earn an after-tax return on the Treasury bills of

$$5\% \times (1 - 0.30) = 3.5\%$$

Thus, at the end of the year, Milton will pay a dividend of

$$\$200,000 \times (1.035) = \$207,000$$

Evaluate: This $207,000 that Milton will pay in 1 year if it invests in Treasury bills is less than the $210,000 the investors would have earned if they had invested the $200,000 in Treasury bills themselves. Because Milton must pay corporate taxes on the interest it earns, there is a tax disadvantage to retaining cash. Pension fund investors will therefore prefer that Milton pays the dividend now.

Cutting Negative-NPV Growth

17.4 Problem: Gani Drilling is an all-equity firm with 50 million shares outstanding. Gani has $100 million in cash and expects future free cash flows of $40 million per year. The company plans to use the cash to expand the firm's operations, which will in turn increase future free cash flows to $50 million per year. If the cost of capital of Gani's investments is 9%, how would a decision to use the $100 million in cash for a share repurchase rather than the expansion change the share price?

Solution

Plan: We can use the perpetuity formula to value Gani Drilling under the two scenarios: expansion and share repurchase. The repurchase will take place at market prices, so the repurchase itself will have no effect on Gani's share price.

Execute:
Expansion: Using the perpetuity formula, if Gani invests the $100 million to expand, its market value will be $50 million ÷ 0.09 = $555.55 million, or $11.11 per share with 50 million shares outstanding.

Share Repurchase: If Gani does not expand, the value of its future free cash flows will be $40 million ÷ 9% = $444.444 million. Adding the $100 million in cash it currently has, Gani's market value is $544.444 million, or $10.89 per share. If Gani repurchases shares, there will be no change to the share price: It will repurchase $100 million ÷ $10.89/share = 9.183 million shares, so it will have assets worth $444.444 million with 40.817 million shares outstanding, for a share price of $444.444 million ÷ 40.817 million shares = $10.89/share.

In this case, using the $100 million in cash to fund the new investment increases the share price by $0.22 per share ($11.11 − $10.89).

Evaluate: The share price is higher with the investment because the expansion has a positive NPV. It costs $100 million, but increases future free cash flows by $10 million, for an NPV of

$$-\$100 \text{ million} + \$10 \text{ million}/9\% = -\$100 \text{ million} + \$111.11 \text{ million}$$
$$= \$11.11 \text{ million or } \$0.22 \text{ per share}$$

■ Questions and Problems

1. An unlevered corporation has $100 million of excess cash and 50 million shares outstanding with a current market price of $20 per share. The board of directors has declared a special dividend of $100 million.
   a. What is the ex-dividend price of a share in a perfect capital market?
   b. If the board instead decided to use the cash to do a one-time share repurchase, what is the price of the shares once the repurchase is complete in a perfect capital market?
   c. What do stockholders want the firm to do?

2. How can firms use dividends to signal information about the firm's value?

3. Franks Mining has a market capitalization of $2 billion and 40 million shares outstanding. It plans to distribute $100 million through an open market repurchase. Assuming perfect capital markets:
   a. What will the price per share of Franks be right before the repurchase?
   b. How many shares will be repurchased?
   c. What will the price per share of Franks be right after the repurchase?

4. Blue Moon, Inc. will pay a constant dividend of $3 per share, per year, in perpetuity. Assume all investors pay a 20% tax on dividends and that there is no capital gains tax. The cost of capital for investing in Blue Moon stock is 11%.
   a. What is the price of a share of Blue Moon stock?
   b. Assume Blue Moon's management makes a surprise announcement that the company will no longer pay dividends but will use the cash to repurchase stock instead. What is the price of a share of Blue Moon stock now?

5. Williams International has $200,000 in excess cash. The company is considering investing the cash in 1-year Treasury bills paying 5% interest and then using the cash to pay a dividend next year. Alternatively, the firm can pay a dividend immediately and shareholders can invest the cash on their own.

   a. In a perfect capital market, which option will shareholders prefer?
   b. Suppose Williams must pay corporate taxes at a 30% rate on the interest it will earn from the 1-year Treasury bill. Would pension fund investors (who do not pay taxes on their investment income) prefer that Williams use its excess cash to pay dividends or retain the cash for 1 year?

■ Solutions to Questions and Problems

1. a. $P = \dfrac{\text{PV(Future Cash Flows)} + \text{Excess Cash}}{\text{Number of Shares}} = \$20 = \dfrac{\text{PV(Future Cash Flows)} + \$100 \text{ million}}{50 \text{ million}}$

   PV(Future Cash Flows) = $900 million

   The ex-dividend price is:

   $P = \$900 \text{ million} / 50 \text{ million} = \$18$

   b. Assuming the shares are repurchased at the current value of $20, the firm can repurchase $100 million/$20 = 5 million shares. The post-repurchase price = $900 million/45 million = $20.

   c. The firm's choice of dividend policy is irrelevant, and the value per share is $20 in any case.

2. The idea that dividend changes reflect managers' views about a firm's future earnings prospects is called the dividend signaling hypothesis. When a firm increases its dividend, it sends a positive signal to investors that management expects to be able to afford the higher dividend for the foreseeable future. When a firm cuts its dividend, it may signal that it is necessary to reduce the dividend to save cash.

3. a. $P_{before} = \$2 \text{ billion}/40 \text{ million shares} = \$50/\text{share}$
   b. $\$100 \text{ million}/\$50 = 2 \text{ million shares}$
   c. ($2 billion − $100 million)/38 million shares = $50/share

4. a. $P = \{\$3(1 - 0.20)\}/0.11 = \$21.82$
   b. $P = \$3/0.11 = \$27.27$

5. a. In a perfect capital market, the shareholders are indifferent. If they receive the cash today, they can invest in the T-bills and earn the same return.
   b. The pension fund investors would prefer to be paid the dividends today and invest the money to earn the 5% interest rate without paying taxes.

Self-Test Questions

1. Pear Computer Imaging announced that it will pay a $2.00 per share dividend. The firm will pay the dividend to all shareholders
   a. who owned the stock on the declaration date.
   b. who own the stock on the payable date.
   c. who purchase the stock on the ex-dividend date.
   d. of record on the record date.

2. What is the most common way for a firm to repurchase shares?
   a. A tender offer.
   b. An open market repurchase.
   c. A Dutch auction.
   d. A targeted repurchase.

3. In perfect capital markets, an open market share repurchase
   a. has no effect on the stock price.
   b. will reduce the price of the stock because the company's cash balance is lower.
   c. will increase the price of the stock because the supply of stock outstanding is lower.
   d. will increase the price of the stock because the demand for the stock has increased.

4. In perfect capital markets, investors
   a. prefer that the firm distribute funds via dividends rather than share repurchases.
   b. prefer that the firm distribute funds via share repurchases rather than dividends.
   c. are indifferent between the firm distributing funds via dividends or share repurchases.
   d. prefer that the firm retain funds rather than distribute them.

5. Which of the following is a TRUE statement?
   a. When dividends are paid, the share price drops by the amount of the dividend but when shares are repurchased, the share price is unaffected.
   b. When dividends are paid, the share price is unaffected but when shares are repurchased, the share price increases.
   c. When dividends are paid, the share price drops by the amount of the dividend but when shares are repurchased, the share price increases.
   d. When dividends are paid or shares are repurchased, the stock price will fall by the same amount.

6. The common practice of maintaining relatively constant dividends is known as:
   a. The bird in a hand theory.
   b. Modigliani and Miller hypothesis.
   c. Agency theory.
   d. Dividend smoothing.

7. The dividend signaling hypothesis would interpret a cut in dividends as:
   a. A positive signal that management expects to be able to afford higher dividends in the foreseeable future.
   b. A positive signal that the management is minimizing the tax consequences of its decisions.
   c. A signal that the firm's managers have given up hope that earnings will rebound in the near-term and so need to reduce the dividend to save cash.
   d. A sign that the company will be repurchasing shares.

8. A company might initiate a stock split
   a. to return funds to the investors.
   b. to keep the share price in a range thought to be attractive to small investors.
   c. as a signal that the company has many positive NPV projects.
   d. to alter its capital structure.

9. The dividend puzzle refers to:
   a. The inconsistent ways in which dividends are interpreted by investors.
   b. The fact that firms continue to issue dividends despite their tax disadvantage.
   c. Why firms would delay paying dividends when the present value exceeds the future value.
   d. A firm's attempt to minimize tax consequences in the complicated international environment of differential tax treatments depending on the income and location of investors.

10. Michael Kim owns 20% of the shares of Coastal Drilling, Inc. The company has negotiated to purchase 750,000 shares of Kim's stock at $32.20 a share. This agreement is known as a:
    a. Tender offer
    b. Open market purchase
    c. Dutch purchase
    d. Targeted repurchase

11. Regular dividends
    a. send a stronger signal of financial strength to shareholders than do infrequent distributions, such as repurchases.
    b. do not send as strong of a signal of financial strength to shareholders as do repurchases or other infrequent distributions.
    c. are not a consideration in a firm's capital structure.
    d. are always more advantageous than large, infrequent distributions to shareholders.

12. There is a _____ to holding cash because holding cash is like having a_____.
    a. negative tax consequence; negative leverage
    b. negative tax consequence; positive leverage
    c. positive tax consequence; positive leverage
    d. positive tax consequence; negative leverage

Answers to Self-Test Questions

1. d
2. b
3. a
4. c
5. a
6. d
7. c
8. b
9. b
10. d
11. a
12. a

Chapter 18
Financial Modeling and Pro Forma Analysis

■ Key Learning Objectives

- Understand the goals of long-term financial planning
- Create pro forma income statements and balance sheets using the *percent of sales method*
- Develop financial models of the firm by directly forecasting capital expenditures, working capital needs, and financing events
- Distinguish between the concepts of sustainable growth and value-increasing growth
- Use pro-forma analysis to model the value of the firm under different scenarios, such as expansion

■ Notation

FCF	free cash flow
PV	present value
ROA	return on assets
ROE	return on equity
SGR	sustainable growth rate

■ Chapter Synopsis

18.1 Goals of Long-Term Financial Planning

The goal of the financial manager is to maximize the value of the stockholders' stake in the firm. Long-term financial planning and modeling is a tool managers use to reach this goal. Long-term financial planning allows the financial manager to:

- Identify important linkages between sales, costs, capital investment, and financing.
- Analyze the impact of potential business plans on the firm's free cash flows and, hence, value.
- Plan for future funding needs.

18.2 Forecasting Financial Statements: The Percent of Sales Method

Let's look at an example of forecasting financial statements. An income statement and balance sheet for Pizza World are given below. Pizza World's primary target audience is families with elementary school-aged children. In addition to enjoying a salad, pizza, and dessert buffet, customers can play a variety of arcade style games. With over 100 restaurants, mainly in the western United States, Pizza World is looking at expanding to the east coast over the next few years. Pizza World's managers want to determine if and when the company will need external financing to fuel its growth.

	2010	
	($000s)	% of Sales
Income Statement		
1 Sales	83,254	
2 Costs Except Depr	−59,639	71.6%
3 **EBITDA**	23,615	28.4%
4 Depreciation	−6,122	7.4%
5 **EBIT**	17,493	21.0%
6 Interest Expense (net)	−450	
7 **Pretax Income**	17,043	20.5%
8 Income Tax	5,965	
9 **Net Income**	11,078	13.3%

Figure 18.1 Pizza World's Income Statement for 2010

	2010	% of Sales
Balance Sheet ($000s)		
Assets		
1 Cash and Equivalents	11,982	14.4%
2 Accounts Receivable	3,098	3.7%
3 Inventories	16,878	20.3%
4 **Total Current Assets**	31,958	38.4%
5 Property, Plant, and Equipment	75,987	91.3%
7 **Total Assets**	107,945	129.7%
Liabilities and Stockholders' Equity		
8 Accounts Payable	11,982	14.4%
9 Debt	4,500	NM
10 **Total Liabilities**	16,482	NM
11 **Stockholders' Equity**	91,463	NM
12 **Total Liabilities and Equity**	107,945	129.7%

Figure 18.2 Pizza World's Balance Sheet for 2010

Let's complete our forecast by using the **percent of sales method.** The percent of sales method assumes that as sales grow many income statement and balance sheet items will grow, remaining at the same percentage of sales. For example, Figure 18.1 shows that the company costs excluding depreciation for 2010 was 72% of sales. The percent of sales method assumes that if sales rise, these costs will remain at a level of 72% of sales. Essentially, we are assuming Pizza World will maintain its profit margins as its sales revenues grow. We can make similar assumptions about working capital items on the balance sheet such as cash, accounts receivable, inventory, and accounts payable in Figure 18.2. Some of the balance sheet items are marked "NM" for "Not Meaningful" in the "percent of sales" column. While assets and accounts payables might reasonably be expected to grow in line with sales, long-term debt and equity will not naturally grow in line with sales. Instead, the change in equity and debt will reflect choices management makes about dividends and new financing.

Let's create a pro forma income statement for 2011 based on the following assumptions:

- Sales growth will be 20% from 2010 to 2011
- Costs excluding depreciation will be 71.6% of sales in 2011
- Depreciation will be 7.4% of sales in 2011

- Pizza World pays a 35% tax rate
- Interest expense will remain at $450,000 (We will determine if our debt needs will change as part of the forecasting process.)

These assumptions lead to the pro forma income statement for 2011 in Figure 18.3 below. You will notice that, given these assumptions, net income is expected to rise to $13,195,000, a 20.83% increase from 2010.

		2010 ($000s)	% of Sales	Pro Forma 2011 ($000s)	% of Sales
	Income Statement				
1	Sales	83,254		99,905	
2	Costs Except Depr	−59,639	71.6%	−71,567	71.6%
3	**EBITDA**	23,615	28.4%	28,338	28.4%
4	Depreciation	−6,122	7.4%	−7,346	7.4%
5	**EBIT**	17,493	21.0%	20,992	21.0%
6	Interest Expense (net)	−450		−450	
7	**Pretax Income**	17,043	20.5%	20,542	20.6%
8	Income Tax	5,965		7,190	
9	**Net Income**	11,078	13.3%	13,352	13.4%

Figure 18.3 Pro Forma Income Statement

Now we need to forecast the balance sheet to see whether Pizza World needs any new financing in 2011 to fund its growth. Forecasting the balance sheet using the percent of sales method requires a few iterating steps. In Figure 18.4 we have our first iteration; assuming that all of our assets will increase as sales increase so that they will remain at the same percentage of sales. Accounts payable remains at 14% of sales. We will leave debt at $4.5 million because we have not yet decided to issue any new debt. The stockholders' equity will increase by the amount of retained earnings (since Pizza World is experiencing such fast growth, we will assume, for the time being, that the company is retaining all of its 2010 earnings and not paying out any dividends). With these assumptions, Pizza World will need $5,997,800 in **net new financing** to fund its growth.

		2010	% of Sales	Pro Forma 2011	Calculation
Balance Sheet ($000s)					
Assets					
1	Cash and Equivalents	11,982	14.4%	14,378	14.4% of sales
2	Accounts Receivable	3,098	3.7%	3,718	3.7% of sales
3	Inventories	16,878	20.3%	20,254	20.3% of sales
4	**Total Current Assets**	31,958	38.4%	38,350	Lines 1 + 2 + 3
5	Property, Plant, and Equipment	75,987	91.3%	91,185	91.3% of sales
6	**Total Assets**	107,945	129.7%	129,534	Lines 4 + 5
Liabilities and Stockholders' Equity					
7	Accounts Payable	11,982	14.4%	14,378	14.4% of sales
8	Debt	4,500	NM	4,500	No change
9	**Total Liabilities**	16,482	NM	18,878	Lines 8 + 9
10	**Stockholders' Equity**	91,463	NM	104,815	91,463 + retained earnings
11	**Total Liabilities and Equity**	107,945	129.7%	123,693	Lines 10 + 11
	Net New Financing			**5,841**	Line 7 − Line 12

Figure 18.4 Pro Forma Balance Sheet—First Iteration

The net new financing, $5,841,000 in this case is sometimes referred to as **the plug**—the amount we have to add to (plug into) the liabilities and equity side of the pro forma balance sheet to make it balance. To grow as expected, Pizza World has to secure almost $6 million in new financing from either new debt or new equity. Let's assume the company's financial managers decide that the best way to finance the growth is through additional debt; Figure 18.5 shows our second-pass pro forma balance sheet including the additional debt financing that brings the sheet into balance.

		2010	% of Sales	Pro Forma 2011	Calculation
	Balance Sheet ($000s)				
	Assets				
1	Cash and Equivalents	11,982	14.4%	14,378	14.4% of sales
2	Accounts Receivable	3,098	3.7%	3,718	3.7% of sales
3	Inventories	16,878	20.3%	20,254	20.3% of sales
4	**Total Current Assets**	31,958	38.4%	38,350	Lines 1 + 2 + 3
5	Property, Plant, and Equipment	75,987	91.3%	91,185	91.3% of sales
6	**Total Assets**	107,945	129.7%	129,534	Lines 4 + 5
	Liabilities and Stockholders' Equity				
7	Accounts Payable	11,982	14.4%	14,378	14.4% of sales
8	Debt	4,500	NM	10,341	4,500 + 5,841
9	**Total Liabilities**	16,482	NM	24,719	Lines 8 + 9
10	**Stockholders' Equity**	91,463	NM	104,815	91,463 + retained earnings
11	**Total Liabilities and Equity**	107,945	129.7%	129,534	Lines 10 + 11

Figure 18.5 Pro Forma Balance Sheet—Second Iteration

Pizza World's decision to take on additional debt in 2011 makes our initial assumption that the company's interest expense would remain constant in 2011 potentially incorrect. If the company takes on the debt before the end of the year, then there will be a partial-year interest expense from the debt. We would need to adjust the pro forma income statement and iterate the pro forma balance sheet to get the exact amount of new debt needed. However, we have achieved our primary objective: to identify a future funding need and determine approximately how much we will need and how we will fund it. We also note that debt has more than doubled, which justifies our original decision not to assume that it will increase in proportion to sales.

18.3 Forecasting a Planned Expansion

The percent of sales method is a useful starting point, but it is not useful in handling fast growth that requires "lumpy" investments in new capacity. The typical firm cannot add capacity smoothly in line with expected sales, but, instead, must occasionally make a large investment in new capacity. This kind of capacity expansion also implies that new funding will happen in large, infrequent financing rounds, rather than small increments each year as sales grow.

Let's address these realities in our long-term forecasting by modeling our capacity needs and capital expenditures directly by considering a planned expansion by Pizza World. By generating pro forma statements we can decide whether the expansion will increase the value of Pizza World. First, we identify capacity needs and how to finance that capacity. Next, we construct pro forma income statements and forecast future free cash flows. Finally, we use those forecasted free cash flows to assess the impact of the expansion on firm value.

Figure 18.6 details Pizza World's forecasted capital expenditures and depreciation over the next 5 years. In 2011, Pizza World will purchase and furnish several buildings on the East coast for their expansion; therefore, the company will make a $28 million capital investment in 2011. After the large expansion in 2011, the company will have recurring investments of $7.5 million a year.

	Year	2010	2011	2012	2013	2014	2015
Fixed Assets and Capital Investment ($000s)							
1	Opening Book Value	77,109	75,987	96,444	94,644	94,344	94,094
2	Capital Investment	5,000	28,000	7,500	7,500	7,500	7,500
3	Depreciation	−6,122	−7,543	−9,300	−7,800	−7,750	−7,600
4	Closing Book Value	75,987	96,444	94,644	94,344	94,094	93,994

Figure 18.6 Forecasted Capital Expenditures

Pizza World will be able to fund recurring investments from its operating cash flows, but it will seek external financing of the $28 million by issuing 10-year coupon bonds with a coupon rate of 7%. The company will only pay interest on the bonds until the repayment of principal in 10 years. Assuming that the principal on its outstanding debt of $4500 is not due in the next 5 years, Pizza World's planned debt and interest payments are shown in Figure 18.7.

	Year	2010	2011	2012	2013	2014	2015
Debt and Interest Table ($000s)							
Outstanding Debt		4,500	32,500	32,500	32,500	32,500	32,500
Net New Borrowing			28,000	0	0	0	0
Interest on Debt	7.00%	315	2,275	2,275	2,275	2,275	2,275

Figure 18.7 Planned Debt and Interest Payments

As with any investment opportunity, the value of Pizza World's investment arises from the future cash flows it will generate. To estimate the cash flows resulting from the expansion, let's begin by projecting the firm's future earnings. To build the pro forma income statement we need the estimated sales for Pizza World in the coming years. Management has included these sales projections in Figure 18.8. We will assume that costs except depreciation will continue to be 71.6% of sales, and we use the depreciation and interest estimates from Figures 18.6 and 18.7. We also assume that the income tax rate will remain at 35%.

	Year	2010	2011	2012	2013	2014	2015
Income Statement ($000s)							
1	Sales	83,254	99,905	119,886	131,874	142,424	153,818
2	Costs Except Depreciation	−59,639	−71,532	−85,838	−94,422	−101,976	−110,134
3	**EBITDA**	23,615	28,373	34,048	37,452	40,448	43,684
4	Depreciation	−6,122	−7,543	−9,300	−7,800	−7,750	−7,600
5	**EBIT**	17,493	20,830	24,748	29,652	32,698	36,084
6	Interest Expense (net)	−315	−2,275	−2,275	−2,275	−2,275	−2,275
7	**Pretax Income**	17,178	18,555	22,473	27,377	30,423	33,809
8	Income Tax	6,012	6,494	7,866	9,582	10,648	11,833
9	**Net Income**	**11,166**	**12,061**	**14,607**	**17,795**	**19,775**	**21,976**

Figure 18.8 Pizza World Pro Forma Income Statement for Expansion

Because increases in working capital reduce free cash flow, we estimate Pizza World's working capital needs in Figure 18.9. These estimates are based on cash, accounts receivable, inventory, and accounts payable, all remaining at a constant percentage of sales. With this planned expansion forecast, we will make the assumption that Pizza World distributes all cash in excess of the minimum required cash as dividends. If our forecast shows that the firm's cash flows will be insufficient to fund the minimum required cash, then we know we need to plan to finance those cash needs.

	Year	2010	2011	2012	2013	2014	2015
Working Capital ($000s)							
Assets							
1 Cash and Equivalents		11,982	14,378	17,254	18,980	20,498	22,138
2 Accounts Receivable		3,098	3,718	4,461	4,907	5,300	5,724
3 Inventories		16,878	20,254	24,304	26,735	28,874	31,183
4 Total Current Assets		31,958	38,350	46,020	50,622	54,671	59,045
Liabilities							
5 Accounts Payable		11,982	14,378	17,254	18,980	20,498	22,138
6 Total Current Liabilities		11,982	14,378	17,254	18,980	20,498	22,138
Net Working Capital							
7 Net Working Capital (Line 4 − Line 6)		19,976	23,971	28,765	31,642	34,173	36,907
8 Increase in Net Working Capital			3,995	4,794	2,877	2,531	2,734

Figure 18.9 Pizza World's Projected Working Capital Needs

18.4 Growth and Firm Value

A firm's **internal growth rate** is the maximum growth rate a firm can achieve without resorting to external financing. Intuitively, this is the growth that the firm can support by reinvesting its earnings. It is calculated using the formula:

$$\text{Internal Growth Rate} = \left(\frac{\text{Net Income}}{\text{Beginning Assets}}\right) \times (1 - \text{Payout Ratio})$$
$$= \text{ROA} \times \text{Plowback Ratio}$$

The **plowback ratio** is the fraction of net income retained to be reinvested in the firm.

A firm's **sustainable growth rate** is the maximum growth rate the firm can sustain without issuing new equity or increasing its debt-to-equity ratio. It tells us how fast the firm can grow by reinvesting its retained earnings and issuing only as much new debt as can be supported by those retained earnings. The formula for the sustainable growth rate is:

$$\text{Sustainable Growth Rate} = \left(\frac{\text{Net Income}}{\text{Beginning Equity}}\right) \times (1 - \text{Payout Ratio})$$
$$= \text{ROE} \times \text{Plowback Ratio}$$

Whenever you forecast growth greater than the internal growth rate, you will have to either reduce your payout ratio (increase your plowback ratio), plan to raise additional external financing, or both. If your forecasted growth is greater than your sustainable growth rate, you will have to increase your plowback ratio, raise additional equity financing, or increase your leverage (increasing your debt at a rate that increases your debt-to-equity ratio). Figure 18.10 compares internal and sustainable growth rates.

	Internal Growth Rate	Sustainable Growth Rate
Formula	ROA × Plowback Ratio	ROE × Plowback Ratio
Maximum growth financed only by	Retained Earnings	Retained Earnings and new debt that keeps D/E ratio constant
To grow faster, a firm must	Reduce payout, or raise external capital	Reduce payout, or raise new equity, or increase leverage

Figure 18.10 Summary of Internal Growth Rate versus Sustainable Growth Rate

While the internal and sustainable growth rates are useful in alerting you to the need to plan for external financing, they cannot tell you whether your planned growth increases or decreases the firm's value. The growth rates do not evaluate the future costs and benefits of the growth and the Valuation Principle tells us that the value implications of the growth can only be assessed by doing so. There is nothing inherently bad about growth at a rate greater than your sustainable growth rate as long as that growth is value increasing. Your firm will simply need to raise additional capital to finance the growth.

Remember, there are costs to seeking external financing—the flotation and issuance costs associated with issuing new equity or new bonds. Thus, the internal growth rate indicates the fastest growth possible without incurring any of these costs. The sustainable growth rate still assumes some new debt will be sought, so the company reduces, but does not eliminate entirely, its costs of external financing when growing at the sustainable growth rate.

18.5 Valuing the Expansion

We now have the data needed to forecast Pizza World's free cash flows over the next 5 years. To estimate free cash flows in Figure 18.11, we combine earnings, depreciation, and interest expense from Figure 18.8, capital expenditures are available from Figure 18.6, and changes in net working capital from Figure 18.9. The free cash flow on line 7 of Figure 18.11 shows the cash that the firm will generate for its investors, both debt and equity holders.

	Year	2010	2011	2012	2013	2014	2015
Free Cash Flow ($000s)							
1	Net Income		11,166	12,061	14,607	17,795	19,775	21,976
2	Plus: After-Tax Interest Expense		205	1,479	1,479	1,479	1,479	1,479
3	**Unlevered Net Income**		11,370	13,540	16,086	19,274	21,254	23,455
4	Plus: Depreciation		6,122	7,543	9,300	7,800	7,750	7,600
5	Less: Increases in NWC		0	3,995	4,794	2,877	2,531	2,734
6	Less: Capital Expenditures		5,000	28,000	7,500	7,500	7,500	7,500
7	**Free Cash Flow of Firm**		12,492	−10,913	13,092	16,697	18,972	20,821

Figure 18.11 Pizza World's Estimated Free Cash Flows

Now we can use these forecasts to determine whether the expansion plan is a good idea—does it increase the value of Pizza World? Remember that, absent distress costs, the value of a firm with debt is equal to the value of the firm without debt plus the present value of its interest tax shields. Therefore, to value Pizza World's expansion we compute the present value of the *unlevered* free cash flows and add to it the present value of the tax shields created by the planned interest payments. Because we have only forecasted cash flows out to 2013, we will need to account for the remaining value of the firm at that point.

Generally, we estimate a firm's continuation value (also called the terminal value) at the end of the forecast horizon using a valuation multiple. Because competition between firms should lead to a convergence of long-run expected growth rates, profitability, and risk of firms in the same industry, long-run expectations of multiples are likely to be relatively homogeneous across firms. Because distant cash flows are difficult to forecast accurately, estimating the firm's continuation or terminal value based on a long-run estimate of the valuation multiple for the industry is a common (and generally reliable) approach.

Of the different valuation multiples available, the EBITDA multiple is most often used in practice. We estimate the continuation value using an EBITDA multiple as follows:

Continuation Enterprise Value at Forecast Horizon = EBITDA at Horizon × EBITDA Multiple at Horizon

Pizza World's EBITDA in 2013 is forecast to be $43.684 million. If firms in Pizza World's industry are valued at an average EBITDA multiple of 9 and we assume that the appropriate EBITDA multiple will remain constant, then Pizza World's continuation value in 2013 is $43.684 million × 9 = $393.156 million.

Assume that Pizza World's financial managers have estimated that company's unlevered cost of capital to be 10%. To value Pizza World with the expansion we need to:

1. Compute the present value of the forecasted free cash flow of the firm over the next 5 years using the unlevered WACC as the discount rate.

2. Calculate the present value of the continuation value using the unlevered WACC.

3. Calculate the present value of the interest tax shield using the interest rate on the debt as the discount rate.

The total value of Pizza World with the expansion is the sum of the present values of the forecasted unlevered free cash flows, the continuation value of the firm, and the interest tax shields. As shown in Figure 18.12, the total firm value with the expansion is $286.5 billion.

		Year	2010	2011	2012	2013	2014	2015
1	Free Cash Flow of Firm			−10,913	13,092	16,697	18,972	20,821
2	PV Unlevered Free Cash Flow		39,330	—	—	—	—	—
3	Continuation Value		—	—	—	—	—	393,156
4	PV Continuation Value		244,119	—	—	—	—	—
5	Net Interest Expense		—	−2,275	−2,275	−2,275	−2,275	−2,275
6	Interest Tax Shield		—	796	796	796	796	796
7	PV Interest Tax Shield		3,018	—	—	—	—	—
8	Firm Value (Lines 2 + 4 + 7)		286,467	—	—	—	—	—

Figure 18.12 Calculation of Pizza World's Firm Value with Expansion

To determine whether the expansion is a good idea, we would need to compare Pizza World's value without the expansion to its value with the expansion. Without adding new locations, the majority of sales revenue growth over time will be due to price increases. We would need to complete the same process for forecasting the free cash flows of the firm without the expansion as we did for the firm with the expansion to see if the expansion is a good idea.

■ Selected Concepts and Key Terms

Percent of Sales Method

The percent of sales approach is a common approach to forecasting; it is where you assume that costs, working capital, and total assets will remain at a fixed percent of sales as sales grow.

Net New Financing, the Plug

When forecasting the impact that sales growth will have on a firm's balance sheet, the amount that equity and liabilities would fall short of the amount needed to finance the expected growth in assets is the **net new financing**. The net new financing indicates the total amount of financing needed from external sources and is sometimes referred to as **the plug**.

Internal Growth Rate

The internal growth rate identifies the maximum rate at which the firm can grow without external financing. The internal growth rate is calculated as:

$$\text{Internal Growth Rate} = \left(\frac{\text{Net Income}}{\text{Beginning Assets}}\right) \times (1 - \text{Payout Ratio})$$
$$= \text{ROA} \times \text{Plowback Ratio}$$

Sustainable Growth Rate

The sustainable growth rate identifies the maximum rate at which the firm can grow if it wants to keep its D/E ratio constant without any new equity financing. The sustainable growth rate is calculated as:

$$\text{Sustainable Growth Rate} = \left(\frac{\text{Net Income}}{\text{Beginning Equity}}\right) \times (1 - \text{Payout Ratio})$$
$$= \text{ROE} \times \text{Plowback Ratio}$$

Plowback Ratio

The plowback ratio is the percentage of net income that is retained within the company to finance growth. The plowback ratio plus the payout ratio sum to 1.

■ Concept Check Questions and Answers

1. How does long-term financial planning fit into the goal of the financial manager?

   Long-term financial planning is a tool to help financial managers maximize the value of the stockholders' stake in the firm.

2. What are the three main things that the financial manager can accomplish by building a long-term financial model of the firm?

   Building a long-term financial model of the firm allows the financial manager to (1) identify important linkages among the components of the firm's financial statements, (2) analyze the impact of a potential business plan, and (3) plan for future funding needs.

3. What is the basic idea behind the percent of sales method for forecasting?

   The basic idea behind the percent of sales forecasting method is that as sales grow many income statement and balance sheet items will grow, remaining the same percentage of sales.

4. How does the pro forma balance sheet help the financial manager forecast net new financing?

   An imbalance on the pro forma balance sheet will show the amount of net new financing that is needed to fund the firm's growth.

5. What is the advantage of forecasting capital expenditures, working capital, and financing events directly?

   Fast growth often requires "lumpy" investments in new capacity, rather than in the smooth manner that the percent of sales forecasting method assumes. Forecasting these items directly allows for the assumption that the firm will make large investments in capacity and will need new funding in large, infrequent financing rounds.

6. What role does minimum required cash play in working capital?

   The minimum required cash is the amount of cash a firm needs to keep the business running smoothly, given variations in the timing of income and expenses. Because these cash balances seldom earn interest, there is an opportunity cost of holding the cash balances. Due to the opportunity cost of holding the cash balance, the minimum required cash is included as working capital.

7. What is the difference between the internal growth rate and the sustainable growth rate?

   The internal growth rate identifies how much growth a firm can support using only its retained earnings. The sustainable growth rate tells us how fast the firm can grow by reinvesting retained earnings and issuing debt in an amount that maintains the firm's debt/equity ratio.

8. If a firm grows faster than its sustainable growth rate, is that growth value decreasing?

   No, growing faster than the sustainable growth rate is not necessarily value decreasing. If a company grows at a rate faster than the sustainable growth rate, it must incur flotation and issuance costs associated with the new financing. As long as the benefit of the growth is enough to cover these issuance costs, the growth can be value-enhancing.

9. What is the multiples approach to continuation value?

   Distant cash flows are difficult to estimate; therefore, a multiples approach is often used. Competition among firms within an industry will lead to long-term expectations of multiples to be the same across firms. Therefore, a long-term estimate of a valuation multiple for the industry is often used to estimate the continuation value of a firm.

10. How does forecasting help the financial manager decide whether to implement a new business plan?

    Forecasting gives the financial manager the variables needed to value the firm with the expansion and without the expansion.

Examples with Step-by-Step Solutions

Percent of Sales

18.1 Problem: In Figure 18.3, Pizza World had an expected sales growth rate of 20%. If a slowing economy causes the firm to revise its sales forecast downward, and Pizza World expects sales growth at only 12% between 2010 and 2011, what are its costs except for depreciation projected to be?

Solution

Plan: Forecasted 2011 sales will now be: 83,254 × (1.12) = 93,244. With this figure in hand and the information from Figure 18.3, we can use the percent of sales method to calculate its forecasted costs.

Execute: From Figure 18.3, we see that costs are 71.6% of sales. With forecasted sales of $93,244, this leads to forecasted costs except depreciation of $93,244 × (0.716) = $66,762.

Evaluate: Costs increase as sales increase. If costs remain a fixed percentage of sales, then the higher the sales growth rate, the higher the increase in costs.

Net New Financing

18.2 Problem: We assumed that Pizza World was not paying a dividend and retained all of its earnings. If instead, the company pays out 30% of earnings as dividends in 2011, how will its net new financing in Figure 18.4 change?

Solution

Plan: Pizza World currently pays out 0% of its net income as dividends, so rather than retaining $13,352 it will retain only $9346.4. This will decrease stockholders' equity, increasing the net new financing.

Execute: The new retained earnings will be $13,352 − $9346.4 = $4005.6 less. Therefore, stockholders' equity will be $100,809 and total liabilities and equity will only be $119,688. Net new financing needed, the imbalance between Pizza World's assets and liabilities and equity, will increase to $129,534 − $119,688 = $9846.

		2008	% of Sales	Pro Forma 2009	Calculation
Balance Sheet ($000s)					
Assets					
1	Cash and Equivalents	11,982	14.4%	14,378	14.4% of sales
2	Accounts Receivable	3,098	3.7%	3,718	3.7% of sales
3	Inventories	16,878	20.3%	20,254	20.3% of sales
4	**Total Current Assets**	31,958	38.4%	38,350	Lines 1 + 2 + 3
5	Property, Plant, and Equipment	75,987	91.3%	91,185	91.3% of sales
7	**Total Assets**	107,945	129.7%	129,534	Lines 4 + 5
Liabilities and Stockholders' Equity					
8	Accounts Payable	11,982	14.4%	14,378	14.4% of sales
9	Debt	4,500	NM	4,500	No change
10	**Total Liabilities**	16,482	NM	18,878	Lines 8 + 9
11	**Stockholders' Equity**	91,463	NM	100,809	91,463 + retained earnings
12	**Total Liabilities and Equity**	107,945	129.7%	119,688	Lines 10 + 11
	Net New Financing			9,846	Line 7 − Line 12

Evaluate: When a company is growing faster than it can finance internally, any distributions to shareholders will cause it to seek greater additional financing. The additional financing that is needed is equivalent to the dividends that are paid out to shareholders.

Internal and Sustainable Growth Rates and Payout Policy

18.3 **Problem:** Daisy Home Furnishings has $80 million in equity and $40 million in debt and forecasts $20 million in net income for the year. It currently pays dividends equal to 30% of its net income. What are Daisy's internal and sustainable growth rates? What would happen to each of these rates if the company decreased its dividend payout to 25%?

Solution

Plan: To calculate the internal growth rate we will multiply the ROA by the retention rate. To calculate the sustainable growth rate we will multiply the ROE by the retention rate. To calculate ROA we need to know the amount of assets the company has; if Daisy has $80 million in equity and $40 million in debt, then it has $120 million in assets. The company's ROA will be NI/Assets = $20 m/$120 m = 16.67%. Daisy's ROE will be NI/Equity = $20 m/$80 m = 25%. If the company retains 30% of its net income, its retention rate is 70%; if Daisy retains 25% of its net income, its retention rate is 75%.

Execute: Currently, with a 30% payout rate:

Internal growth rate = ROA × Retention rate = 16.67% × 0.7 = 11.67%
Sustainable growth rate = ROE × Retention rate = 25% × 0.7 = 17.5%

If the company decreases its payout rate to 25%:

Internal growth rate = 16.67% × 0.75 = 12.50%
Sustainable growth rate = 25% × 0.75 = 18.75%

Evaluate: If Daisy decreases its payout rate, it will be increasing the amount of retained earnings available to fund growth; a decrease in the payout ratio increases the company's internal and sustainable growth rates.

■ Questions and Problems

1. Bakeryland has sales of $200,000 this year and cost of goods sold of $130,000. You forecast sales to increase to $210,000 next year. Using the percent of sales method, forecast next year's cost of goods sold for Bakeryland.

2. For the upcoming fiscal year, you forecast the net income to be $80,000 and ending assets to be $400,000 for Green Thumb Gardening. The firm's payout ratio is 25%. Green Thumb's beginning stockholders' equity is $220,000 and its beginning total liabilities are $100,000. The company's non-debt liabilities, such as accounts payable, are forecasted to increase by $10,000. What is the firm's net new financing needed for next year?

Use the following income statement and balance sheet for Callie's Café for Problems 3–5:

Income Statement		Balance Sheet	
Sales	300,000	**Assets**	
Costs Except Depr	−120,000	Cash and Equivalents	20,000
EBITDA	180,000	Accounts Receivable	2,000
Depreciation	−9,000	Inventories	7,000
EBIT	171,000	Total Current Assets	29,000
Interest Expense (net)	−600	Property, Plant, and Equipment	15,000
Pretax Income	170,400	Total Assets	36,000
Income Tax	−51,120		
Net Income	119,280	**Liabilities and Equity**	
		Accounts Payable	2,000
		Debt	6,000
		Total Liabilities	8,000
		Stockholders' Equity	28,000
		Total Liabilities and Equity	36,000

3. Callie's expects sales to grow by 10% next year. Using the percent of sales method, forecast:
   a. Costs
   b. Depreciation
   c. Net Income
   d. Cash
   e. Accounts Receivable
   f. Inventory
   g. Property, Plant, and Equipment

4. Assume that Callie's pays out 50% of its net income. Use the percent of sales method to forecast:
   a. Stockholders' equity
   b. Accounts payable

5. What is the amount of net new financing needed for Callie's?

6. The information below is for Treasure Chest Toys.

Net Income	100,000
Beginning Total Assets	300,000
Beginning Stockholders' Equity	180,000
Payout Ratio	0%

   a. What is the firm's internal growth rate?
   b. What is the firm's sustainable growth rate?
   c. What would the firm's internal growth and sustainable growth rates be if it increased its payout ratio to 50%?

■ Solutions to Questions and Problems

1. Cost of goods sold were $130,000/$200,000 = 65% of sales. To maintain this ratio, if sales increase to $210,000, cost of goods sold will be $210,000 × 0.65 = $136,500.

2. The firm will need to finance $400,000 in assets. The beginning stockholders' equity is $220,000 and retained earnings will be $80,000 × .75 = $60,000. The firm expects to have liabilities of $110,000. The equity and liabilities will provide a total of $390,000 of financing. The firm will need $10,000 in additional financing.

3. Costs = $330,000 × 0.4 = $132,000; Depreciation = $330,000 × 0.03 = $9900; Net Income = $330,000 × 0.3976 = $131,208; Cash = $330,000 × 0.0667 = $22,000; Accounts Receivable = $330,000 × 0.00667 = $2200; Inventory = $330,000 × 2.333% = $7700; Property, Plant, and Equipment = $330,000 × 0.05 = $16,500.

4. a. $28,000 + (0.5 × 131,250) = $93,625
   b. $2200

5. Callie's net new financing needed is –$62,225. Because of the large net income and the company retaining 50% of the net income, the stockholders' equity rises significantly. Without a large increase in assets that need to be financed, the company will be in a position of having negative net new financing needed.

6. a. ROA × Retention rate = (100,000/300,000) × 100% = 33.33%
   b. ROE × Retention rate = (100,000/180,000) × 100% = 55.55%
   c. 16.67%; 27.78%

■ Self-Test Questions

1. In 2010, Garcia Food Supply had sales of $300,000 and costs excluding depreciation of $200,000. Using the percent of sales forecasting method, if Garcia's sales are $315,000 in 2011, you would estimate that the costs excluding depreciation in 2011 will be:
   a. $206,666
   b. $210,000
   c. $216,666
   d. $215,000

2. When constructing a pro forma balance sheet, the term "net new financing" refers to:
   a. The amount of retained earnings that the company is using to finance its assets.
   b. The amount of debt the firm issued during the year to finance new assets.
   c. The amount of additional external financing the company will have to secure to pay for a planned increase in assets.
   d. The difference between current assets and current liabilities.

3. Multiplying a firm's return on assets by its retention rate calculates the firm's
   a. sustainable growth rate.
   b. internal growth rate.
   c. net new financing.
   d. net present value.

4. Pride Paper Products wants to maintain its debt/equity ratio at its current level and does not want to issue any more debt. They have asked the company's CEO, Cynthia Stimmons, how quickly the company can grow with these constraints. Cynthia should calculate the firm's
   a. internal growth rate.
   b. sustainable growth rate.
   c. leveraged growth rate.
   d. pro forma growth rate.

5. A company's sustainable growth rate will increase if
   a. its ROE increases.
   b. its plowback rate decreases.
   c. its payout ratio increases.
   d. All of the above.

6. Which of the following would be the most reasonable way to forecast a company's continuation value?
   a. Multiply the firm's EBITDA by the industry's EBITDA multiple.
   b. Divide the firm's EBITDA by the firm's cost of capital.
   c. Divide the firm's net income by the firm's unlevered cost of capital.
   d. Multiply the firm's net income by the firm's cost of capital.

7. Williams Office Supply wants to know the maximum growth rate it can have without using any external financing. The firm should calculate its
   a. sustainable growth rate.
   b. internal growth rate.
   c. EBITDA multiple.
   d. unlevered cost of capital.

8. Tony's Cereal Co. has an ROA of 25% and an ROE of 16%. The company pays 25% of its net income in dividends. The company's sustainable growth rate is:
   a. 4.00%
   b. 6.25%
   c. 12.00%
   d. 18.75%

9. The basic idea behind the percent of sales method of forecasting is that:
   a. As sales grow, many income statement and balance sheet items will grow, remaining the same percent of sales.
   b. As sales grow, many income statement and balance sheet items will grow by the same dollar amount.
   c. As sales grow, many assets grow in a "lumpy" manner.
   d. As sales grow, many income statement items grow by the same percent of sales, but many balance sheet items remain constant.

10. Park Enterprises has created a pro forma balance sheet for next year. The pro form balance sheet shows assets of $5.5 million and liabilities and equity of $5.2 million. The difference between these two numbers represents
    a. the firm's retained earnings.
    b. the firm's projected net income.
    c. net working capital.
    d. net new financing needed.

11. Letty is a financial manager at Century Computer Concepts (CCC). In evaluating a possible expansion, she has forecasted cash flows for the first 4 years after the expansion. She has used the industry average EBITDA multiple to estimate CCC's continuation value after those first 4 years. Using this valuation multiple
    a. is a reasonable approach because competition leads long-term growth rates and profitability of firms within an industry toward one another.
    b. is an unreasonable approach because the EBITDA valuation multiple is extremely sensitive to leverage differences across firms.
    c. will lead to an upwardly biased estimation due to the fact that taxes and depreciation are ignored in the model.
    d. will lead to an underestimation of firm value because competition among firms will ensure that all firms are profitable in the long run.

12. Bernstein Bakeries is considering expanding into the frozen pie business. Bernstein Bakeries should expand if
    a. the value of the firm with the new expansion is positive.
    b. the terminal value of the expansion project is positive.
    c. the value of the firm with the expansion exceeds the value of the firm without the expansion.
    d. the expansion generates positive cash flows.

Answers to Self-Test Questions

1. b
2. c
3. b
4. b
5. a
6. a
7. b
8. c
9. a
10. d
11. a
12. c

Appendix: The Balance Sheet and Statement of Cash Flows

The information we have calculated so far can be used to project Pizza World's balance sheet and statement of cash flows through 2013 as shown in Figure 18.13 and Figure 18.14. While these statements are not critical for our valuation of the expansion, they often prove helpful in providing a more complete picture of how a firm will grow during the forecast period.

	Year	2010	2011	2012	2013	2014	2015
Balance Sheet ($000s)							
Assets							
1	Cash and Cash Equivalents	11,982.0	14,378.4	17,254.1	18,979.5	20,497.8	22,137.7
2	Accounts Receivable	3,098.0	3,717.6	4,461.1	4,907.2	5,299.8	5,723.8
3	Inventories	16,878.0	20,253.6	24,304.3	26,734.8	28,873.5	31,183.4
4	**Total Current Assets**	31,958.0	38,349.6	46,019.5	50,621.5	54,671.1	59,044.9
5	Property, Plant, and Equipment	75,987.0	96,444.0	94,644.0	94,344.0	94,094.0	93,994.0
6	Goodwill	—	—	—	—	—	—
7	**Total Assets**	107,945.0	134,793.6	140,663.5	144,965.5	148,765.1	153,038.9

Continued

	Year	2010	2011	2012	2013	2014	2015
Liabilities							
8	Accounts Payable	11,982.0	14,378.4	17,254.1	18,979.5	20,497.8	22,137.7
9	Debt	4,500.0	32,500.0	32,500.0	32,500.0	32,500.0	32,500.0
10	**Total Liabilities**	16,482.0	46,878.4	49,754.1	51,479.5	52,997.8	54,637.7
Stockholders' Equity							
11	Starting Stockholders' Equity	80,297.0	91,463.0	87,915.2	90,909.4	93,486.0	95,767.3
12	Net Income	11,166.0	12,060.8	14,607.5	17,795.1	19,775.0	21,975.9
13	Dividends		0.0	−15,608.6	−11,613.3	−15,218.5	−17,493.7	−19,342.0
14	Capital Contributions	—	—	—	—	—	—
15	**Stockholders' Equity**	91,463.0	87,915.2	90,909.4	93,486.0	95,767.3	98,401.2
16	**Total Liabilities and Equity**	107,945.0	134,793.6	140,663.5	144,965.5	148,765.1	153,038.9

Figure 18.13 Pro Forma Balance Sheet for Pizza World

	Year	2011	2012	2013	2014	2015
Statement of Cash Flows ($000s)						
1	**Net Income**	12,060.8	14,607.5	17,795.1	19,775.0	21,975.9
2	Depreciation	7,543.0	9,300.0	7,800.0	7,750.0	7,600.0
3	Changes in Working Capital	—	—	—	—	—
4	Accounts Receivable	619.6	743.5	446.1	392.6	424.0
5	Inventory	3,375.6	4,050.7	2,430.5	2,138.7	2,309.9
6	Accounts Payable	2,396.4	2,875.7	1,725.4	1,518.3	1,639.9
7	**Cash from Operating Activities**	18,005.0	21,989.0	24,443.9	26,512.0	28,481.9
8	Capital Expenditures	28,000.0	7,500.0	7,500.0	7,500.0	7,500.0

(*Continue*)

	Year	2011	2012	2013	2014	2015
Statement of Cash Flows ($000s)						
9 Other Investment		—	—	—	—	—
10 **Cash from Investing Activities**		−28,000.0	−7,500.0	−7,500.0	−7,500.0	−7,500.0
11 Net Borrowing		28,000.0	0.0	0.0	0.0	0.0
12 Dividends		−15,608.6	−11,613.3	−15,218.5	−17,493.7	−19,342.0
13 Capital Contributions		—	—	—	—	—
14 **Cash from Financing Activities**		12,391.5	−11,613.3	−15,218.5	−17,493.7	−19,342.0
15 **Change in Cash (Lines 7 + 10 + 14)**		**2,396.4**	**2,875.7**	**1,725.4**	**1,518.3**	**1,639.9**

Figure 18.14 Pro Forma Statement of Cash Flow for Pizza World

On the pro forma balance sheet, current assets and liabilities come from the net working capital spreadsheet (Figure 18.9). The inventory entry on the balance sheet includes both raw materials and finished goods. Property, plant, and equipment information comes from the capital expenditure spreadsheet (Figure 18.6) and the debt comes from Figure 18.7.

Pizza World's debt will jump from $4500 to $32,500 in 2011 when it finances its expansion. The company's accounts payable will grow steadily with sales. In 2010, Pizza World's debt-equity ratio is 4500/91,463 = 4.92%. It increases to 32,500/87,915 = 36.97% and then steadily drops to 32,500/98,401.2 = 33.03%.

The statement of cash flows in Figure 18.14 starts with net income. Cash from operating activities includes depreciation as well as changes to working capital items (other than cash), and cash from investing activities includes the capital expenditures. Cash from financing activities includes net borrowing. We assume Pizza World pays out all excess cash in dividends. Because Pizza World is not planning to raise any additional equity financing, there are no capital contributions on the cash flow statement. As a final check on the calculations, note that the change in cash and cash equivalents on line 15 equals the change in the minimum cash balance shown on the balance sheet in Figure 18.13.

Chapter 19
Working Capital Management

■ Key Learning Objectives

- Understand the cash cycle of the firm and why managing working capital is important
- Use trade credit to the firm's advantage
- Make decisions on extending credit and adjusting credit terms
- Manage accounts payable
- Know the costs and benefits of holding additional inventory
- Contrast the different instruments available to a financial manager for investing cash balances

■ Notation

CCC	cash conversion cycle
EAR	effective annual rate
g	perpetuity growth rate
NPV	net present value
PV	present value
r	discount rate

■ Chapter Synopsis

19.1 Overview of Working Capital

The main components of net working capital are cash, inventory, receivables, and payables. Working capital includes the cash that is needed to run the firm on a day-to-day basis, but does not include excess cash. Working capital alters a firm's value by affecting its free cash flow. Let's look at the components of net working capital and their effect on the firm's value.

The Cash Cycle

The level of working capital reflects the length of time between when cash goes out of a firm at the beginning of the production process and when it comes back in. A firm's **operating cycle** is the average length of time between when a firm originally purchases its inventory and when it receives the cash back from selling its product. A firm's **cash cycle** is the length of time between when the firm pays cash to purchase its initial inventory and when it receives cash from the sale of the output produced from that inventory. The cash cycle can be measured by calculating the **cash conversion cycle (CCC)**:

$$CCC = \text{Inventory Days} + \text{Accounts Receivable Days} - \text{Accounts Payable Days}$$

where

$$\text{Inventory Days} = \frac{\text{Inventory}}{\text{Average Daily Cost of Goods Sold}}$$

$$\text{Accounts Receivable Days} = \frac{\text{Accounts Receivable}}{\text{Average Daily Sales}}$$

$$\text{Accounts Payable Days} = \frac{\text{Accounts Payable}}{\text{Average Daily Cost of Goods Sold}}$$

The longer a firm's cash cycle, the more working capital it has, and the more cash it needs to carry to conduct its daily operations.

Because of the characteristics of the different industries, working capital levels vary significantly. For example, a retail grocery store typically sells on a cash-only basis, so you would expect accounts receivable to be a very small percentage of its sales.

Any reduction in working capital requirements generates a positive free cash flow that the firm can distribute immediately to shareholders. For example, if a firm is able to reduce its required net working capital by $50,000, it will be able to distribute this $50,000 as a dividend to its shareholders immediately. Recall that the Valuation Principle implies that the value of the firm is the present value of its free cash flows. Managing working capital efficiently will increase those free cash flows, allowing a manager to maximize firm value. We now turn our attention to some specific working capital accounts.

19.2 Trade Credit

When a firm allows a customer to pay for goods at some date later than the date of purchase, it creates an account receivable for the firm and an account payable for the customer. The credit that the firm is extending to its customer is known as **trade credit.** If a supplier offers its customers terms of "net 30," payment is not due until 30 days from the date of the invoice, and the supplier is effectively letting the customer use its money for an extra 30 days.

The selling firm may also offer the buying firm a discount if payment is made early. The terms "2/10, net 30" mean that the buying firm will receive a 2% discount if it pays for the goods within 10 days; otherwise, the full amount is due in 30 days. The cash discount is the percentage discount offered if the buyer pays early, and the discount period is the number of days that the buyer has to take advantage of the cash discount. The credit period is the total length of time that credit is extended to the buyer—the total amount of time they have to pay. Firms offer discounts to encourage customers to pay early so that the selling firm gets cash from the sale sooner. However, the amount of the discount also represents a cost to the selling firm because it does not receive the full selling price for the product.

Trade credit is like a loan from the selling firm to the customer. If a firm sells a product for $100 but offers its customer terms of 2/10, net 30, the customer can take advantage of the discount and pay $98 within the 10-day period. The customer has the option to use the $98 for an additional 20 days (30 – 10 × 20). The interest rate for the 20-day term of the loan is $2/$98 × 2.04%. With a 365-day year, this rate over 20 days corresponds to an effective annual rate of

$$\text{EAR} = (1.0204)^{365/20} - 1$$
$$= 44.6\%$$

If the firm can obtain a bank loan at a lower interest rate, it would be better off borrowing at the lower rate and using the cash proceeds of the loan to take advantage of the discount offered by the supplier.

One factor that contributes to the length of a firm's receivables and payables is the delay between the time a bill is paid and the cash is actually received. **Collection float** is the amount of time it takes for a firm to be able to use funds after a customer has paid for its goods. Firms can reduce their working capital needs by reducing their collection float. Collection float is determined by three factors:

1. *Mail float:* How long it takes the firm to receive the check after the customer has mailed it.

2. *Processing float:* How long it takes the firm to process the check and deposit it in the bank.

3. *Availability float:* How long it takes before the bank gives the firm credit for the funds.

Disbursement float is the amount of time it takes before payments to suppliers actually result in a cash outflow for the firm. Like collection float, it is a function of mail time, processing time, and check-clearing time. Although a firm may try to extend its disbursement float in order to lengthen its payables and reduce its working capital needs, it risks making late payments to suppliers. The **Check Clearing for the 21st Century Act (Check 21),** which became effective on October 28, 2004, eliminated the part of the disbursement float due to the check-clearing process. Under the act, banks can process check information electronically, and the funds are deducted from a firm's checking account on the same day that the firm's supplier deposits the check in its bank in most cases. Unfortunately, even though the funds are taken out of the check writer's account almost immediately under Check 21, the check recipient's account is not credited as quickly. As a result, the act does not serve to reduce collection float.

19.3 Receivables Management

Establishing a credit policy involves three steps:

1. Establishing credit standards

    Large firms perform this analysis in-house with their own credit departments, while small firms purchase credit reports from credit rating agencies such as Dun & Bradstreet. The decision of how much credit risk to assume plays a large role in determining how much money a firm ties up in accounts receivables. While a restrictive policy can result in a lower sales volume, the firm will have a smaller investment in receivables.

2. Establishing credit terms

    The firm decides on the length of the period before payment must be made (the "net" period) and chooses whether to offer a discount to encourage early payments. If it offers a discount, it must also determine the discount percentage and the discount period. If the firm is relatively small, it will probably follow the lead of other firms in the industry in establishing these terms.

3. Establishing a collection policy

    The content of this policy can range from doing nothing if a customer is paying late, to sending a polite letter of inquiry, to charging interest on payments extending beyond a specified period, to threatening legal action at the first late payment.

The **accounts receivable days** is the average number of days that it takes a firm to collect on its sales. A firm can compare this number to the payment policy specified in its credit terms to judge the effectiveness of its credit policy. An **aging schedule** categorizes accounts by the number of days they have been on the firm's books. It can be prepared using either the number of accounts or the dollar amount of the accounts receivable outstanding. The aging schedule is sometimes augmented by analysis of the **payments pattern,** which provides information on the percentage of monthly sales that the firm collects in each month after the sale.

19.4 Payables Management

A firm should choose to borrow using accounts payable only if trade credit is the cheapest source of funding. When a company has a choice between trade credit from two different suppliers, it should take the least expensive alternative. Also, a firm should always pay on the latest day allowed. Some firms ignore the payment due period and pay the amount owed later, in a practice referred to as **stretching the accounts payable.**

19.5 Inventory Management

A firm needs its inventory to operate for several reasons. Inventory helps minimize the risk that the firm will not be able to obtain an input it needs for production. If a firm holds too little inventory, **stock-outs,** the situation when a firm runs out of inventory, may occur, leading to lost sales. Disappointed customers may switch to one of the firm's competitors. Firms may hold inventory because factors such as seasonality in demand mean that customer purchases do not perfectly match the most efficient production cycle.

Tying up capital in inventory is costly for a firm. We can classify the direct costs associated with inventory into three categories:

1. Acquisition costs are the costs of the inventory itself over the period being analyzed (usually 1 year).

2. Order costs are the total costs of placing an order over the period being analyzed.

3. Carrying costs include storage costs, insurance, taxes, spoilage, obsolescence, and the opportunity cost of the funds tied up in the inventory.

Minimizing these total costs involves some tradeoffs. For example, if we assume no quantity discounts are available, the lower the level of inventory a firm carries, the lower its carrying cost, but the higher its annual order costs because it needs to place more orders during the year. With **"just-in-time" (JIT) inventory management,** a firm acquires inventory precisely when needed so that its inventory balance is always zero, or very close to it. This technique requires exceptional coordination with suppliers as well as a predictable demand for the firm's products.

19.6 Cash Management

Firms hold cash to meet day-to-day needs, to compensate for the uncertainty associated with its cash flows, and to satisfy bank requirements. The amount of cash a firm needs to be able to pay its bills is sometimes referred to as a **transactions balance.** The amount of cash a firm holds to counter the uncertainty surrounding its future cash needs is known as a **precautionary balance.** A firm's bank may require it to hold a **compensating balance** in an account at the bank as compensation for services that the bank performs. Compensating balances are typically deposited in accounts that either earn no interest or pay a very low interest rate.

■ Selected Concepts and Key Terms

Cash Cycle

The **cash cycle** is the length of time between when the firm pays cash to purchase its initial inventory and when it receives cash from the sale of the output produced from that inventory. The longer a firm's cash cycle, the more cash it needs to carry, to conduct its daily operations, and the more working capital it has. The **cash conversion cycle** equals Inventory Days + Accounts Receivable Days − Accounts Payable Days.

Operating Cycle

A firm's **operating cycle** is the average length of time between when it originally purchases its inventory and when it receives the cash back from selling its product. If the firm pays cash for its inventory, this period is identical to the firm's cash cycle.

Collection Float

Collection float is the amount of time it takes for a firm to be able to use funds after a customer has paid for its goods. **Mail float** is how long it takes the firm to receive the check after the customer has mailed it. The time it takes the firm to process the check and deposit it in the bank is called the **processing float**. **Availability float** is the time it takes before the bank gives the firm credit for the funds after the firm deposits a check.

Disbursement Float

Disbursement float is the amount of time it takes before payments to suppliers actually result in a cash outflow for the firm.

Check Clearing for the 21st Century Act (Check 21)

The **Check Clearing for the 21st Century Act (Check 21)** eliminated the check-clearing process part of the disbursement float. Under the act, banks can process check information electronically, and the funds are deducted from a firm's checking account on the same day that the firm's supplier deposits the check in its bank in most cases. Unfortunately, even though the funds are taken out of the check writer's account almost immediately under Check 21, the check recipient's account is not credited as quickly. As a result, the act does not serve to reduce collection float.

Trade Credit

Trade Credit is the credit that a firm extends to its customers when a firm allows a customer to pay for goods at **some** date later than the date of purchase. This creates an account receivable for the firm and an account payable for the customer. The **cash discount** is the percentage discount offered if the buyer pays early, and the **discount period** is the number of days the buyer has to take advantage of the cash discount. The **credit period** is the total length of time credit is extended to the buyer; it is the total amount of time they have to pay.

Aging Schedule

An **aging schedule** categorizes accounts receivable by the number of days they have been on the firm's books. It can be prepared using either the number of accounts or the dollar amount of the accounts receivable outstanding. The aging schedule can be augmented by an analysis of the payments pattern, which provides information on the percent of monthly sales the firm collects in each month after the sale.

Stretching the Accounts Payable

When a firm ignores the payment due period and pays the amount owed later, the practice is referred to as **stretching the accounts payable.**

"Just-In-Time" (JIT) Inventory Management

With **"just-in-time" (JIT) inventory management,** a firm acquires inventory precisely when needed so that its inventory balance is always zero, or very close to it.

Stock-Out

A **stock-out** occurs when a firm runs out of inventory, resulting in lost sales.

Compensating Balance

A **compensating balance** is a minimum balance required by a bank as compensation for services that the bank performs. Compensating balances are typically deposited in accounts that either earn no interest or pay a very low interest rate.

Precautionary Balance

The amount of cash a firm holds due to the uncertainty regarding its future cash needs is its **precautionary balance**.

Transactions Balance

The amount of cash a firm needs to hold to be able to pay its bills is known as its **transactions balance**.

■ Concept Check Questions and Answers

1. What is the difference between a firm's cash cycle and operating cycle?

    A firm's cash cycle is the length of time between when the firm pays cash to purchase its inventory and when it receives cash from the sale of the output produced from the inventory. The operating cycle is the average length of time between when a firm originally purchases its inventory and when it receives the cash back from selling its products.

2. How does working capital impact a firm's value?

    Working capital impacts a firm's value by affecting its free cash flows.

3. What does the term "2/10, net 30" mean?

    The term "2/10, net 30" means that the buying firm will receive a 2% discount if it pays for the goods within 10 days; otherwise, the full amount is due in 30 days.

4. List three factors that determine collection float.

    The three factors that determine collection float are the mail float, processing float, and the availability float. Mail float is how long it takes the firm to receive the check after the customer has mailed it. The time it takes the firm to process the check and deposit it in the bank is called the processing float. Availability float is the time it takes before the bank gives the firm credit for the funds after the firm deposits a check.

5. Describe three steps in establishing a credit policy.

    Establishing a credit policy involves three steps: establishing credit standards (whom the firm will extend credit to), establishing credit terms (the length of the period before payment must be made), and establishing a collection policy to deal with late payments.

6. What is the difference between accounts receivable days and an aging schedule?

    Accounts receivable days are the average number of days that it takes a firm to collect on its sales. An aging schedule categorizes accounts by the number of days they have been on the firm's books.

7. What is the optimal time for a firm to pay its accounts payable?

   The optimal time for a firm to pay its accounts payable is on the latest day allowed. For example, if the terms are 2/10, net 30, and the firm is taking the discount, payment should be made on day 10. If the discount is not taken, then payment should be made on day 30. The firm should pay on day 10 and take the discount unless this is the cheapest source of funding for the firm.

8. What do the terms COD and CBD mean?

   COD means cash on delivery and CBD means cash before delivery.

9. What are the direct costs of holding inventory?

   The direct costs of holding inventory are acquisition costs, order costs, and carrying costs.

10. Describe "just-in-time" inventory management.

    With "just-in-time" inventory management, the firm acquires inventory precisely when needed so that its inventory balance is always zero, or very close to it.

11. List three reasons why a firm holds cash.

    A firm holds cash to meet its day-to-day needs, to compensate for the uncertainty associated with its cash flows, and to satisfy bank requirements.

12. What tradeoff does a firm face when choosing how to invest its cash?

    When choosing how to invest its cash, a firm faces a risk-return tradeoff. In fact, the firm may choose from a variety of short-term securities that differ somewhat with regard to their default risk and liquidity risk: the greater the risk, the higher the expected return on the investment. The financial manager must decide how much risk she is willing to accept in return for a higher yield.

■ Examples with Step-by-Step Solutions

Computing the Cash Conversion Cycle

19.1 **Problem:** The following information is from Travis Cement's 2008 Income Statement and Balance Sheet (numbers are in millions of dollars). Use it to compute Travis's cash conversion cycle (CCC).

Sales	5900
Cost of Goods Sold	4958
Accounts Receivable	489
Inventory	56
Accounts Payable	540

Solution

Plan: The CCC is defined above as Inventory Days + Accounts Receivable Days − Accounts Payable Days. Thus, we need to compute each of the three ratios in the CCC. In order to do this, we need to convert Sales and COGS into their average daily amounts simply by dividing the total given for the year by 365 days in a year.

Execute:

$$\text{Average Daily Sales} = \text{Sales}/365 \text{ Days} = 5900/365 = 16.16$$

$$\text{Average Daily COGS} = \text{COGS}/365 \text{ Days} = 4958/365 = 13.58$$

$$\text{Inventory Days} = \frac{\text{Inventory}}{\text{Average Daily Cost of Goods Sold}}$$

$$= \frac{56}{13.58}$$

$$= 4.12$$

$$\text{Accounts Receivable Days} = \frac{\text{Accounts Receivable}}{\text{Average Daily Sales}}$$

$$= \frac{489}{16.16}$$

$$= 30.26$$

$$\text{Accounts Payable Days} = \frac{\text{Accounts Payable}}{\text{Average Daily Cost of Goods Sold}}$$

$$= \frac{540}{13.58}$$

$$= 39.76$$

So, Travis Cement's CCC = 4.12 + 30.26 – 39.76 = –5.38.

Evaluate: Travis Cement's CCC is –5.38 days. This means that generally the company receives cash for its products 5.38 days before it pays its supplier for the materials used to produce the products.

The Value of Working Capital Management

19.2 **Problem:** Outdoor Outfitters' projected net income and free cash flow next year are given in the following table in thousands of dollars.

Net Income	300,000
+ Depreciation	55,000
– Capital Expenditures	–55,000
– Increase in Working Capital	–12,000
= Free Cash Flow	288,000

The company expects capital expenditures and depreciation to continue to offset each other and for both net income and increase in working capital to grow at 4% per year. Outdoor Outfitters' cost of capital is 11%. Given these assumptions, what is the value of the company? If Outdoor Outfitters were able to reduce its increase in working capital for next year to $8 million by managing its working capital more efficiently without adversely affecting any other part of the business, what would be the effect on the company's value?

Solution

Plan: The value of Outdoor Outfitters is the present value of the future free cash flows. We can use the formula for a growing perpetuity (PV = CF$_1$/r – g) to calculate the value of the company. With the current assumptions, the free cash flow in 1 year is $288 million; the required rate of return is equal to the cost of capital of 11%, and the growth rate is 4%. If the company manages its working capital more efficiently, then free cash flow next year will be $292 million. This free cash flow will still grow at a rate of 4% a year.

Execute: With the current assumptions, Outdoor Outfitters' value is:

$$PV = \frac{CF_1}{r-g}$$
$$= \frac{288 \text{ m}}{0.11 - 0.04}$$
$$= \$4.11 \text{ billion}$$

If Outdoor Outfitters is able to manage its working capital more efficiently, the company's value will be:

$$PV = \frac{CF_1}{r-g}$$
$$= \frac{292}{0.11 - 0.04}$$
$$= \$4.17 \text{ billion}$$

Evaluate: Although the change will not affect Outdoor Outfitters' earnings (net income), it will increase the free cash flow available to shareholders, increasing the value of the firm by $60 million.

Estimating the Effective Cost of Trade Credit

19.3 Problem: Your firm purchases goods from its supplier on terms of 1/15, net 30. What is the effective annual cost to your firm if it chooses not to take advantage of the trade discount offered?

Solution

Plan: Using a $100 purchase as an example: 1/15, net 30, means that you get a 1% discount if you pay within 15 days, or you can pay the full amount within 30 days. 1% of $100 is a $1 discount, so you can either pay $99 in 15 days, or $100 in 30 days. The difference is 15 days, so you need to compute the interest rate over the 15 days and then compute the EAR associated with that 15-day interest rate.

Execute: $1/$99 = 0.0101, or 1.01% interest for 15 days. There are 365/15 = 24.3, 15-day periods in a year. Thus, your effective annual rate is $(1.0101)^{24.3} - 1 = 0.2766\% = 27.66\%$.

Evaluate: Your supplier is effectively charging you 27.66% interest. If you really need to take the full 30 days to produce the cash to pay and you can borrow from the bank at a rate lower than 27.66%, you would be better off borrowing the $99 from the bank and taking advantage of the discount.

Evaluating a Change in Credit Policy

19.4 **Problem:** Your company currently extends credit terms of net 30 to your customers. You currently sell 1000 units per month at $200 each. Your variable cost is $150 per unit. All customers currently pay on day 30. You are considering changing your credit terms so that customers who pay immediately receive a 1% discount; otherwise, the balance is due in 30 days. You estimate that 25% of your existing customers will pay immediately and take the 1% discount. You also estimate that you will sell an additional 200 units per month to new customers, all of whom will pay immediately and take the discount. If your required rate of return is 0.75% per month, should you switch your policy?

Solution

Plan: To decide whether to change your policy, you need to compute the NPV of the change. It costs you $150,000 to make the 1000 units you currently sell. You receive $200,000 from your customers 30 days later. At that point you are starting over with the next set of your product. Thus, you can think of your cash flows in the 30-day period as:

	Now	30 days
Produce first set of 1000 units at $150 each	−150,000	
Customers pay for 1000 units at $200 each		+200000
Produce next set of 1000 units at $150 each		−150,000
Total	−150,000	'+200,000−150,000

Under the new policy, your cash flows would become:

	Now	30 days
Produce first set of 1200 units at $150 each	−180,000	
Customers pay for 450 units at $198	+89,100	
Customers pay for 750 units at $200 each		+150,000
Produce next set of 1200 units at $150 each		−180,000
Customers pay for 450 units at $198		89,100
Total	−90,900	'+150,000−90,900

With these cash flows, you are ready to compute the NPV of the policy change.

Execute:

$$NPV_{current} = -150,000 + \frac{200,000 - 150,000}{1.0075} = -150,000 + 49,625.33 = 100,374.67$$

$$NPV_{new} = -90,900 + \frac{150,000 - 90,900}{1.0075} = -90,900 + 58,660.05 = 123,139.95$$

So, the NPV of the change in policy will be $123,139.95−$100,374.67 = $22,765.28.

Evaluate: You should make the switch because the NPV of the change is positive. Although you will be receiving only $198 from 250 customers who had paid $200 previously, you will receive this money 30 days earlier and you will gain new customers. The present value of these benefits outweighs the present value of the costs.

Aging Schedules

19.5 Problem: Your company has the following accounts receivable:

Customer	Accounts Receivable	Age in Days
1	$50,000	25
2	70,000	55
3	90,000	3
4	110,000	2
5	40,000	22
6	20,000	22
7	80,000	44
8	30,000	76

Your company extends credit terms of 1/15, net 45. Prepare an aging schedule for your company using 15-day increments.

Solution

Plan: To begin, we want to sort the accounts receivable customers by the age of their receivables. We also want to add the total amount of receivables so that we can calculate each category as a percentage of the total amount outstanding.

Execute: Sorting the accounts receivable by age gives us:

Customer	Accounts Receivable	Age in Days
4	$110,000	2
3	90,000	3
5	40,000	22
6	20,000	22
1	50,000	25
7	80,000	44
2	70,000	55
8	30,000	76
Total	490,000	

Now, we group them into 15-day increments to determine the aging schedule:

Days Outstanding	Accounts Receivable	Percent of Accounts Receivable
0–15	200,000	40.82%
16–30	110,000	22.45%
31–45	80,000	16.33%
46–60	70,000	14.29%
over 60	30,000	6.12%
	490,000	100.00%

Evaluate: The aging schedule lets you see what percentage of your accounts receivable is not being paid within the 45-day period of your credit terms. From the aging schedule above, you can see that the majority of your accounts receivable falls within the 0 to 45-day time period. However, over 20% of the accounts receivable extends beyond the 45-day period of your credit terms.

Accounts Payable Management

19.6 **Problem:** You have just purchased $30,000 worth of components from a supplier that offers credit terms of 3/10, net 30. If you pay today how much would you pay? Should you pay today? What is the effective cost of the trade credit if you pay on day 30?

Solution

Plan: If you pay today, you are paying within the first 10 days and receive a 3% discount off of the $30,000 price. To calculate the cost of the trade credit, we need to calculate how much more we would pay on day 30 than we would pay on day 10. Paying on day 30 allows you to use the money for 20 extra days. There are 365/20 = 19.25 20-day periods in a year. The effect cost of the trade credit is the EAR.

Execute: If you pay today, you will pay $30,000 − 0.03 × ($30,000) = $29,100. Since you would pay the same amount if you waited until day 10 to pay, you should wait 10 days if you chose to take advantage of the discount.

If you wait until day 30, you will need to pay the entire $30,000. Thus, you are paying $900 in interest for a 20-day loan (from day 10 to day 30). The interest rate over this period is:

$$\frac{\$900}{\$29,100} = 0.031$$
$$= 3.1\%$$

So, the effective annual cost of the trade credit is:

$$\text{EAR} = (1.031)^{18.25} - 1 = 74.57\%$$

Evaluate: You should not pay today. You will pay $29,100 whether you pay on day 1 or day 10. If you are going to take the discount, wait until day 10. If you do not pay by day 10 and take the discount, then wait until day 30. If you pay any time between day 11 and day 30, you will have to pay $30,000. If you do not pay by day 10, there is no advantage of paying before day 30.

Cost of Trade Credit with Stretched Accounts Payable

19.7 **Problem:** What is the effective annual cost of credit terms of 1/10, net 30, if the firm stretches the accounts payable to 45 days?

Solution

Plan: First, we need to compute the interest rate per period. The 1% discount means that on a $100 purchase, you can either pay $99 in the discount period, or keep the $99 and pay $100 later. Thus, you pay $1 interest on the $99. If you pay on time, then this $1 in interest is over the 20 day period between the 10th day and the 30th day. If you stretch, then this $1 in interest is over the 35-day period between the 10th day and the 45th day.

Execute: The interest rate per period is $1/$99 = 1.01%. If the firm delays payment until the 45th day, it has use of the funds for 35 days beyond the discount period. There are 365/35 = 10.43 45-day periods in 1 year. Thus, the effective annual cost is $(1.0101)^{10.43} - 1 = 0.1105$, or 11.05%.

Evaluate: Paying on time corresponds to a 20-day credit period and there are 365/20 = 19.25 20-day periods in a year. Thus, if it pays on the 30th day, the effective annual cost is $(1.0101)^{18.25} - 1 = 0.2013$ or 20.13%. By stretching its payables, the firm substantially reduces its effective cost of credit.

■ Questions and Problems

1. Last year, Crocodile Dock, Inc. had sales of $170 million, cost of goods sold of $140 million, and the following end of year balance sheet:

Crocodile Dock, Inc.
Balance Sheet (millions of dollars)

Assets		Liabilities and Equity	
Cash	$ 21.0	Accounts Payable	$ 25.0
Accounts Receivable	20.0	Notes Payable	15.5
Inventory	10.0	Accruals	7.5
Total Current Assets	$ 51.0	Total Current Liabilities	48.0
Net Plant, Property,		Long-Term Debt	210.0
and Equipment	$219.0	Total Liabilities	258.0
Total Assets	$270.0	Common Equity	12.0
		Total Liabilities and Equity	$270.0

   a. How much does Crocodile Dock have invested in working capital?
   b. How long is the company's cash cycle?

2. You have just purchased inventory for a supplier that offered credit terms of 1/10, net 45. What is the effective cost of the trade credit if you pay on day 45?

3. What is the effective annual cost of credit terms of 1/15, net 45, if the firm stretches the accounts payable to 60 days?

4. Your company has the following accounts receivable:

Customer	Accounts Receivable	Age in Days
1	100,000	22
2	170,000	33
3	170,000	29
4	10,000	56
5	80,000	8
6	220,000	6
7	40,000	14
8	20,000	21
9	70,000	88

   Develop an aging schedule using 15-day increments through 60 days.

5. Millennium Telecommunications had $16 million in sales in 2008. Its cost of goods sold was $10 million, and its average inventory balance was $500,000.
   a. What was Millennium's inventory days ratio? What does it mean?
   b. Coastal Telecommunications turns over its inventory every 4 days. By how much would Millennium need to reduce its investment in inventory to match Coastal's inventory turnover ratio?

6. Explain how it would be possible for a firm to have a *negative* cash cycle.

■ Solutions to Questions and Problems

1. a. Net working capital is current assets minus current liabilities, so Crocodile Dock's investment in net working capital is $51 – $48 = $3 million.

   b. The cash conversion cycle (CCC) is equal to the inventory days plus the accounts receivable days minus the accounts payable days. Crocodile Dock's CCC is:

   $$CCC = \frac{\text{Inventory}}{\text{Average Daily COGS}} + \frac{\text{Accounts Receivable}}{\text{Average Daily Sales}} - \frac{\text{Accounts Payable}}{\text{Average Daily COGS}}$$

   $$= \frac{\$10}{\left(\frac{\$140}{365}\right)} + \frac{\$20}{\left(\frac{\$170}{365}\right)} - \frac{\$25}{\left(\frac{\$140}{365}\right)}$$

   $$= 26.07 \text{ days} + 42.94 \text{ days} - 65.18 \text{ days}$$

   $$= 3.83 \text{ days}$$

2. The terms offer a 1% discount if you pay within 10 days. Thus, you would pay $(1 - 0.01) \times \$X$ if you pay within the first 10 days. If you wait until day 45, you will owe $X. Thus, you are paying $(0.01) \times \$X$ in interest for a 35-day loan (from day 10 to day 45). The interest rate over this period is:

   $$\frac{(0.01) \times \$X}{(0.99) \times \$X} = 0.0101$$

   $$= 1.01\%$$

   The number of 35-day periods in a year is 365/35 = 10.429. So, the effective annual cost of the trade credit is:

   $$EAR = (1.0101)^{10.429} - 1 = 11.05\%$$

3. If they wait until day 60, they will owe $X. Thus, they are paying $(0.01) \times \$X$ in interest for a 45-day loan (from day 15 to day 60). The interest rate over this period is:

   $$\frac{(0.01) \times \$X}{(0.99) \times \$X} = 0.0101$$

   $$= 1.01\%$$

   The number of 45-day periods in a year is 365/45 = 8.11. So, the effective annual cost of the trade credit is:

   $$EAR = (1.0101)^{8.11} - 1 = 8.49\%$$

4. The Aging Schedule is:

Days Outstanding	Accounts Receivable	Percent of Accounts Receivable
0–15	340,000	38.64%
16–30	290,000	32.95%
31–45	170,000	19.32%
46–60	10,000	1.14%
over 60	70,000	7.95%
	880,000	100.00%

5. a. The inventory days ratio is equal to the inventory divided by average daily cost of goods sold.

$$\text{Inventory Days} = \frac{\text{Inventory}}{\text{Average Daily COGS}}$$

$$= \frac{\$500,000}{\left(\dfrac{\$10,000,000}{365}\right)}$$

$$= 18.25 \text{ days}$$

This implies that, on average, Millennium's inventory is around for about 18 days.

b. Millennium's inventory days would be equal to 4 days if it reduced its inventory to:

$$\text{Inventory Days} = \frac{\text{Inventory}}{\text{Average Daily COGS}}$$

$$= \frac{\$X}{\left(\dfrac{\$10,000,000}{365}\right)}$$

$$= 4 \text{ days} \Rightarrow X = \$109,589$$

Thus, the company would need to reduce its inventory by $500,000 − $109,589 = $390,411.

6. A firm can have a negative cash cycle if it gets paid for a product before it has to pay for the cost of producing it. Suppose, for example, a fruit market purchases fruit from the grower, promising to pay within 30 days. The fruit market sells the fruit to its customer on the day it is purchased from the grower. The fruit market would have a negative cash cycle because it is receiving the money from selling the fruit before the grower (its supplier) is being paid.

■ Self-Test Questions

1. Which of the following would cause a company's cash cycle to increase?
   a. An increase in inventory days.
   b. An increase in accounts payable days.
   c. A decrease in accounts receivables days.
   d. All of the above.

2. Campbell Corporation sells products to its customers with the terms 2/10, net 45. This means that:
   a. The customer must pay 2% of the bill in 10 days and the remaining balance within 45 days.
   b. The customer must pay 10% of the bill in 2 days and the remaining balance within 45 days.
   c. The customer gets a 2% discount if paying within the first 10 days and the total amount is due by day 45.
   d. The customer gets a 10% discount if paying within the first 2 days and the total amount is due by day 45.

3. The suppliers of Southern Soda Company offer a trade credit of 2/10, net 30. Southern Soda routinely pays its suppliers on day 35. This practice is referred to as:
   a. Just-in-time payment
   b. Float management
   c. Increasing collection float
   d. Stretching the accounts payable

4. Adkins Autos can borrow on a line of credit at its local bank at a rate of 6.5%. The company is purchasing supplies from Terrence Tires. Terrence Tires is offering a trade credit with terms of 3/10, net 30. Of the strategies below, which is the best for Adkins to follow?
   a. Pay on day 3, borrowing money from the bank if necessary.
   b. Pay on day 10, borrowing money from the bank if necessary.
   c. If the company cannot pay by day 3 without borrowing money from the bank, wait and pay on day 11.
   d. If the company cannot pay by day 10 without borrowing money from the bank, wait and pay on day 30.

5. A firm practicing _____ acquires inventory precisely when needed so that its inventory balance is always zero, or very close to it.
   a. acquisition cost minimization
   b. compensating balance management
   c. stock-out management
   d. just-in-time inventory management

6. Which of the following is a reason a firm might hold cash?
   a. To meet its day-to-day transactions needs.
   b. To compensate for uncertainty associated with its cash flows.
   c. To satisfy bank requirements.
   d. All of the above.

7. Your company is purchasing supplies from Elizondo Electrical. Elizondo is offering you a trade credit with the terms of 2/10, net 30. The effective annual rate of this trade credit is:
   a. 2.04%
   b. 20.4%
   c. 27.87%
   d. 44.6%

8. Any reduction in working capital requirements
   a. reduces the value of the firm by the present value of the capital requirements.
   b. generates a positive free cash flow that the firm can distribute immediately to shareholders.
   c. requires the firm to seek additional outside financing.
   d. generates a reduction in net income and, thus, a decrease in firm value.

9. Clarkson, Intl. wants to analyze whether its credit policy is working effectively. Which of the following combination of tools might Clarkson use to do this?
   a. Accounts receivable days and the aging schedule.
   b. Average collection period and inventory turnover.
   c. Accounts payable days and the EAR.
   d. Inventory days and accounts payable days.

10. Jeju Resort Clothing just decreased its inventory days from 60 to 45. This would cause
    a. the company's working capital to increase.
    b. an increase in the cash needs of the company.
    c. a decrease in the company's cash conversion cycle.
    d. a decrease in the company's accounts receivable.

11. Uniforms Unlimited owes has ordered $5000 worth of fabric from each of two vendors. Vendor A has trade terms of 2/10 net 30. Vendor B has trade terms of 2/10 net 45. Uniforms Unlimited has determined that it will have only $5000 in cash to pay its vendors within the next 10 days. Uniforms Unlimited should:
    a. Pay $2500 to Vendor A and $2500 to Vendor B.
    b. Pay $5000 to Vendor A because Vendor B's trade credit is cheaper.
    c. Pay $5000 to Vendor B because Vendor A's trade credit is cheaper.
    d. Flip a coin to see which vendor should be paid.

12. Which of the following is NOT a direct cost associated with inventory that a firm needs to consider when determining its optimal inventory level?
    a. Acquisition costs
    b. Compensating balance costs
    c. Order costs
    d. Carrying costs

Answers to Self-Test Questions

1. a
2. c
3. d
4. b
5. d
6. d
7. d
8. b
9. a
10. c
11. b
12. b

Chapter 20
Short-Term Financial Planning

■ Key Learning Objectives

- Forecast cash flows and short-term financing needs
- Understand the principle of matching short-term needs to short-term funding sources
- Know the types of different bank loans and their tradeoffs
- Understand the use of commercial paper as an alternative to bank financing
- Use financing secured by accounts receivable or inventory
- Know how to create a short-term financial plan

■ Notation

APR	annual percentage rate
EAR	effective annual rate

■ Chapter Synopsis

20.1 Forecasting Short-Term Financing Needs

The first step in short-term financial planning is to forecast the company's future cash flows. This exercise has two distinct objectives. First, a company forecasts its cash flows to determine whether it will have surplus cash or a cash deficit for each period. Second, management needs to decide whether that surplus or deficit is temporary or permanent.

When sales are concentrated during a few months, sources and uses of cash are likely to be seasonal. Firms in this position may find themselves with a surplus of cash during some months that is sufficient to compensate for a shortfall during other months. Occasionally, a company will encounter a negative or a positive cash flow shock in which cash flows are temporarily positive or negative for an unexpected reason.

20.2 The Matching Principle

In a perfect capital market, the choice of financing is irrelevant; thus, how the firm chooses to finance its short-term cash needs cannot affect the firm's value. In reality, important market frictions exist, such as the opportunity cost of holding cash in accounts that pay little or no interest and transactions costs from obtaining a loan to cover a cash shortfall. A firm can increase its value by adopting a policy that minimizes these kinds of costs.

The **matching principle** states that short-term needs should be financed with short-term debt and long-term needs should be financed with long-term sources of funds. Following the matching principle should, in the long run, help minimize a firm's transaction costs.

Permanent working capital is the amount that a firm must keep invested in its short-term assets to support its continuing operations. Because this investment in working capital is required so long as the firm remains in business, it constitutes a long-term investment. The matching principle indicates that the firm should finance this permanent investment in working capital with long-term sources of funds.

Temporary working capital is the difference between the actual level of investment in short-term assets and the permanent working capital investment. Because temporary working capital represents a short-term need, the firm should finance this portion of its investment with short-term financing.

Financing part or all of the permanent working capital with short-term debt is known as an **aggressive financing policy.** By relying on short-term debt the firm exposes itself to **funding risk,** which is the risk of incurring financial distress costs should the firm not be able to refinance its debt in a timely manner or at a reasonable rate. Financing short-term needs with long-term debt is known as a **conservative financing policy.**

20.3 Short-Term Financing with Bank Loans

Bank loans are typically initiated with a **promissory note,** which is a written statement that indicates the amount of the loan, the date payment is due, and the interest rate.

The most straightforward type of bank loan is a single, end-of-period-payment loan which requires that the firm pay interest on the loan and pay back the principal in one lump sum at the end of the loan. The interest rate may be fixed or variable. The **prime rate** is the rate banks charge their most creditworthy customers.

However, large corporations can often negotiate bank loans at an interest rate that is *below* the prime rate. Another common benchmark rate is the **London Inter-Bank Offered Rate, or LIBOR,** which is the rate of interest at which banks borrow funds from each other in the London inter-bank market. It is quoted for maturities of 1 day to 1 year for 10 major currencies. As it is a rate paid by banks with the highest credit quality, most firms will borrow at a rate that exceeds LIBOR.

Another common type of bank loan arrangement is a **line of credit,** in which a bank agrees to lend a firm any amount up to a stated maximum. This flexible agreement allows the firm to draw upon the line of credit whenever it chooses.

An **uncommitted line of credit** is an informal agreement that does not legally bind the bank to provide the funds. A **committed line of credit** consists of a written, legally binding agreement that obligates the bank to provide the funds regardless of the financial condition of the firm (unless the firm is bankrupt) as long as the firm satisfies any restrictions in the agreement. A **revolving line of credit** is a committed line of credit that involves a solid commitment from the bank for a longer period of time, typically 2 to 3 years. A revolving line of credit with no fixed maturity is called **evergreen credit.** These arrangements are typically accompanied by a **compensating balance** requirement and restrictions regarding the level of the firm's working capital.

A **bridge loan** is another type of short-term bank loan that is often used to "bridge the gap" until a firm can arrange for long-term financing. Bridge loans are often quoted as discount loans with fixed interest rates. With a **discount loan,** the borrower is required to pay the interest at the *beginning* of the loan period. The lender deducts interest from the loan proceeds when the loan is made.

Various loan fees charged by banks affect the effective interest rate that the borrower pays. A **loan origination fee,** which is a fee the firm pays when the loan is initiated, reduces the amount of usable proceeds that the firm receives. A **compensating balance** requirement in the loan agreement reduces the usable loan proceeds. Firms also pay a **commitment fee** of 1/4% to 1/2% of the unused portion of the line of credit.

20.4 Short-Term Financing with Commercial Paper

Commercial paper is short-term, unsecured debt used by large corporations that is usually a cheaper source of funds than a short-term bank loan. With **direct paper,** the firm sells the security directly to investors. With **dealer paper,** dealers sell the commercial paper to investors in exchange for a spread (or fee) for their services. The spread decreases the proceeds that the issuing firm receives, thereby increasing the effective cost of the paper. Like long-term debt, commercial paper is rated by credit rating agencies. The average maturity of commercial paper is 30 days and the maximum maturity is 270 days. Extending the maturity beyond 270 days triggers a registration requirement with the Securities & Exchange Commission (SEC).

20.5 Short-Term Financing with Secured Financing

Businesses can also obtain short-term financing by using **secured loans,** which are loans collateralized with short-term assets—most typically the firm's accounts receivables or inventory. Commercial banks, finance companies, and **factors,** which are firms that purchase the receivables of other companies, are the most common sources for secured short-term loans.

In a **pledging of accounts receivable** agreement, the lender reviews the invoices that represent the credit sales of the borrowing firm and decides which credit accounts it will accept as collateral for the loan, based on its own credit standards. The lender then typically lends the borrower some percentage of the value of the accepted invoices—say, 75%. If the borrowing firm's customers default on their bills, the firm is still responsible to the lender for the money.

In a **factoring of accounts receivable** arrangement, the firm sells receivables to the lender (i.e., the factor), and the lender agrees to pay the firm the amount due from its customers at the end of the firm's payment period. A factoring arrangement may be **with recourse,** meaning that the lender can seek payment from the borrower should the borrower's customers default on their bills. Alternatively, the financing arrangement may be **without recourse,** in which case the lender bears the risk of bad debt losses.

In a **floating lien, general lien,** or **blanket lien** arrangement, a firm's entire inventory is used to secure the loan. This arrangement is the riskiest setup from the standpoint of the lender because the value of the collateral used to secure the loan dwindles as inventory is sold. With a **trust receipts loan,** or **floor planning,** distinguishable inventory items are held in a trust as security for the loan. As these items are sold, the firm remits the proceeds from their sale to the lender in repayment of the loan. In a **warehouse arrangement,** the inventory that serves as collateral for the loan is stored in a warehouse. The arrangement may call for a **public warehouse,** which is a business that exists for the sole purpose of storing and tracking the inflow and outflow of the inventory or a **field warehouse,** which is on the borrower's premises but operated by a third party.

20.6 Putting It All Together: Creating a Short-Term Financial Plan

A financial manager plans for how to deal with a seasonal cash flow swing. In particular, the manager must plan how to finance any shortfalls. Preparing a spreadsheet tracking a company's cash balance and short-term financing assists the financial manager in anticipating upcoming shortfalls, allowing them enough time to investigate the least costly way to finance them.

■ Selected Concepts and Key Terms

Matching Principle

The **matching principle** is the notion that short-term needs should be financed with short-term debt and long-term needs should be financed with long-term debt. Financing part or all of the permanent working capital with short-term debt is known as an **aggressive financing policy.** By relying on short-term debt, the firm exposes itself to **funding risk,** which is the risk of incurring financial distress costs should the firm not be able to refinance its debt in a timely manner or at a reasonable rate. Financing short-term needs with long-term debt is known as a **conservative financing** policy.

Permanent Working Capital

Permanent working capital is the amount that a firm must keep invested in its short-term assets to support its continuing operations.

Temporary Working Capital

Temporary working capital is the difference between the actual level of investment in short-term assets and the permanent working capital investment.

Bridge Loan

A **bridge loan** is a short-term bank loan that is often used to bridge the gap until a firm can arrange for long-term financing.

Line of Credit

With a **line of credit,** a bank agrees to lend a firm any amount up to a stated maximum, allowing the firm to draw upon the line of credit whenever it chooses. An **uncommitted line of credit** is an informal agreement that does not legally bind the bank to provide the funds. A **committed line of credit** consists of a written, legally binding agreement that obligates the bank to provide the funds regardless of the financial condition of the firm (unless the firm is bankrupt) as long as the firm satisfies any restrictions in the agreement. A **revolving line of credit** is a committed line of credit that involves a solid commitment from the bank for a longer period of time, typically two to three years. A revolving line of credit with no fixed maturity is called **evergreen credit.**

Promissory Note

Bank loans are typically initiated with a **promissory note,** which is a written statement that indicates the amount of the loan, the date payment is due, and the interest rate.

Discount Loan

With a **discount loan,** the borrower is required to pay the interest at the *beginning* of the loan period. The lender deducts interest from the loan proceeds when the loan is made.

Loan Origination Fee

A **loan origination fee,** which is a fee the firm pays when the loan is initiated, reduces the amount of usable proceeds that the firm receives.

London Inter-Bank Offered Rate (LIBOR)

The **London Inter-Bank Offered Rate (LIBOR)** is the interest rate at which banks borrow funds from each other in the London inter-bank market that is quoted for maturities of one day to one year for 10 major currencies. It is a common benchmark rate used for floating-rate loans.

Prime Rate

Prime rate is the interest rate that banks charge their most creditworthy customers.

Commercial Paper

Commercial paper is short-term, unsecured debt used by large corporations that is usually a cheaper source of funds than a short-term bank loan. With **direct paper,** the firm sells the security directly to investors. With **dealer paper** dealers sell the commercial paper to investors in exchange for a spread.

Blanket Lien, Floating Lien, General Lien

With a **blanket, floating,** or **general lien,** a firm's entire inventory is used to secure a loan.

Trust Receipts Loan, Floor Planning

With a **trust receipts loan,** or **floor planning,** distinguishable inventory items are held in a trust as security for the loan. As these items are sold, the firm remits the proceeds from their sale to the lender in repayment of the loan.

Factoring of Accounts Receivable

Factoring of accounts receivable is a form of short-term financing in which a firm sells receivables to the lender (i.e., the **factor**), and the lender agrees to pay the firm the amount due from its customers at the end of the firm's payment period. A factoring arrangement may be **with recourse,** meaning that the lender can seek payment from the borrower should the borrower's customers default on their bills. Alternatively, the financing arrangement may be **without recourse,** in which case the lender bears the risk of bad debt losses.

Pledging of Accounts Receivable

The **pledging of accounts receivable** is a method of securing a loan in which the lender reviews the invoices that represent the credit sales of the borrowing firm and decides which credit accounts it will accept as collateral for the loan, based on its own credit standards. The lender then typically lends the borrower some percentage of the value of the accepted invoices.

Secured Loans

Secured loans are loans collateralized with short-term assets—most typically the firm's accounts receivables or inventory.

Warehouse Arrangement

A **warehouse arrangement** is a method of securing a loan in which the inventory that serves as collateral for the loan is stored in a warehouse. The arrangement may call for a **public warehouse,** which is a business that exists for the sole purpose of storing inventory, or a **field warehouse,** which is operated by a third party but set up on the borrower's premises.

Concept Check Questions and Answers

1. How do we forecast the firm's future cash requirements?

   The first step in short-term financial planning is to forecast the company's future cash flows. When we analyze the firm's short-term cash financing needs, we typically examine its cash flows at quarterly intervals.

2. What is the effect of seasonalities on short-term cash flows?

   Seasonal sales create large short-term cash flow deficits and surpluses. Therefore, firms need short-term financing to fund seasonal working capital requirements.

3. What is the matching principle?

   The matching principle specifies that short-term needs for funds should be financed with short-term sources of funds and long-term needs with long-term sources of funds.

4. What is the difference between temporary and permanent working capital?

   Permanent working capital is the amount that a firm must keep invested in its short-term assets to support its continuous operations. Temporary working capital is the difference between the actual level of investment in short-term assets and the permanent working capital investment.

5. What is the difference between an uncommitted line of credit and a committed line of credit?

   An uncommitted line of credit is an informal agreement that does not legally bind the bank to provide the funds. A committed line of credit consists of a written, legally binding agreement that obligates the bank to provide the funds regardless of the financial condition of the firm (unless the firm is bankrupt) as long as the firm satisfies any restrictions in the agreement.

6. Describe common loan stipulations and fees.

   Common loan stipulations and fees include loan commitment fees, loan origination fees, and compensating balance requirements. A loan commitment fee is interest charged on the unused portion of a committed line of credit. A loan origination fee is a fee that a bank charges to cover credit checks and legal fees. A compensating balance requirement means that the firm must hold a certain percent of the principal of the loan in an account at the bank.

7. What is commercial paper?

   Commercial paper is short-term, unsecured debt used by large corporations that is usually a cheaper source of funds than a short-term bank loan.

8. What is the maximum maturity of commercial paper?

   Due to SEC registration requirements, the maximum maturity of commercial paper is 270 days.

9. What is factoring of accounts receivable?

   Factoring of accounts receivables means the firm sells receivables to the lender (i.e., the factor) and the lender agrees to pay the firm the amount due from its customers at the end of the firm's payment period.

10. What is the difference between a floating lien and a trust receipt?

   In a floating lien arrangement, the entire inventory is used to secure the loan. This arrangement is risky to the lender because the value of the collateral securing the loan is reduced as inventory is sold. With a trust receipt loan, distinguishable inventory items are held in a trust as security for the loan. As these items are sold, the firm remits the proceeds from the sale to the lender in repayment of the loan.

■ Examples with Step-by-Step Solutions

Compensating Balance Requirements and the Effective Annual Rate

20.1 **Problem:** Clayton Construction needs to borrow $1 million. First State Bank will make a 1-month loan with an APR of 8% to the company; however, First State Bank requires that Clayton maintain a compensating balance of 2% of the loan at the bank. This compensating balance will earn no interest. What is the effective interest rate on this loan?

Solution

Plan: Clayton will need to borrow more than $1 million to have the $1 million it needs and to maintain the compensating balance the bank is requiring. The company needs to borrow $1,000,000/(1 − 0.02) = $1,020,408. At 8% APR, the interest expense for the 1-month loan will be (0.08/12) × $1,020,408 = $6802.72. We can use this information to determine the EAR.

Execute: The actual 1-month interest rate paid is $6802.72/$1,000,000 = 0.006802. Expressing this as an EAR gives $1.006802^{12} - 1 = 8.475\%$.

Evaluate: Because the bank requires Clayton to maintain a compensating balance, the effective interest rate is higher than the 8% APR.

The Effective Annual Rate of Commercial Paper

20.2 **Problem:** A firm issues 6 month commercial paper with a $100,000 face value and receives $97,000. What effective annual rate is the firm paying for its funds?

Solution

Plan: The firm receives $97,000 today and must pay $100,000 in 6 months. This can be thought of as the company paying $3000 to borrow $97,000 for 6 months. First, we calculate the 6-month interest rate paid, and then we covert it to an EAR using the equation $EAR = (1 + r)^n - 1$. In this case, $n = 2$ because there are two 6-month periods in a year.

Execute: The actual 6-month interest rate paid is

$$\$3000/\$97,000 = 0.0309$$

$$= 3.09\%$$

Expressing this as an EAR gives

$$EAR = (1 + 0.0309)^2 - 1$$

$$= 1.0628 - 1$$

$$= 6.28\%$$

Evaluate: The financial manager needs to know the EAR of the entire firm's funding sources to be able to make comparisons across them and choose the least costly way to finance the firm's short-term needs.

Calculating the Effective Annual Cost of Warehouse Financing

20.3 **Problem:** Honeysmoked Hams wants to borrow $1 million for 1 month. Using its inventory as collateral it can obtain a 9% (APR) loan. The lender requires that a warehouse arrangement be used. The warehouse fee is $5000 payable at the end of the month. Calculate the effective annual rate of this loan for Honeysmoked Hams.

Solution

Plan: The monthly interest rate is 9%/12 = 0.75%. We need to compute the total cash flows Honeysmoked will owe at the end of the month (including interest and warehouse fee). By scaling those cash flows by the amount of the loan, we will have a total monthly cost for the loan, which we can then convert to an EAR.

Execute: At the end of the month, Honeysmoked will owe $1,000,000 × 1.0075 = $1,007,500 plus the warehouse fee of $5000. Putting the cash flows on a timeline gives:

The actual 1 month interest rate paid is

$$\$12,500/\$1,000,000 = 0.0125$$

$$= 1.25\%$$

Expressing this as an EAR gives

$$(1 + 0.0125)^{12} - 1 = 0.1608$$

$$= 16.08\%$$

Evaluate: The warehouse arrangement is quite costly: the EAR on the loan itself is $(1.0075)^{12} - 1 = 0.0938$, or 9.38%, but the warehouse arrangement raises it to 16.08%!

■ Questions and Problems

1. Your firm wants to borrow $1 million for 1 month. Using its inventory as collateral, it can obtain a 9% APR loan. The lender requires that a warehouse arrangement be used. The warehouse fee is $3000 payable at the end of the month. What is the effective annual rate of this loan?

2. A firm issues 3-month commercial paper with a $100,000 face value and receives $98,200. What is the effective annual rate of this loan?

3. You are considering borrowing $1 million for 1 month at an APR of 12%. The bank will require a (no-interest) compensating balance of 5% of the face value of the loan and will charge a $3000 loan origination fee. What is your effective annual borrowing rate?

4. Your candy company experiences surges in demand during the holidays and around Valentine's Day. The following table contains financial forecasts in millions from November through April.

	Oct	Nov	Dec	Jan	Feb	Mar	Apr
Net Income		$ 2	$21	$ 2	$80	$ 2	$ 2
Depreciation		2	2	2	2	2	2
Capital Expenditures		2	2	2	2	2	2
Levels of Working Capital							
Cash	1	1	1	1	1	1	1
Accounts Receivable	2	2	20	10	70	10	2
Inventory	2	12	15	40	50	2	2
Accounts Payable	2	20	20	10	40	10	2

During which months are the firm's seasonal working capital needs the greatest? When does it have surplus cash?

5. What are the permanent working capital needs of the company in Problem 4? What are the temporary needs?

■ Solutions to Questions and Problems

1. The monthly rate is 9%/12 = 0.75%. At the end of the month, you will owe $1 million × 0.0075 = $7500. Thus, with the warehouse fee of $3000 you will pay $10,500 and the 1-month rate is ($10,500/$1,000,000) = 1.05%. The effective annual rate is $1.0105^{12} - 1 = 13.4\%$.

2. The amount of interest paid is $1800. The 3-month rate is ($1800/$98,200) = 1.84%. The effective annual rate is $1.0184^4 - 1 = 7.6\%$.

3. You will need to borrow $1,003,000 to cover the loan origination fee. You also need to have enough to meet the compensating balance requirement. So, the total amount that you must borrow is $1,003,000/(1 − 0.05) = $1,055,789. At a 12% APR, the interest expense for the 1-month loan will be (0.12/12)($1,0055,789) = $10,558. Since the loan origination fee is simply additional interest, the total interest on the 1-month loan is $10,558 + $3000 + $13,558. The firm can use $1,000,000 from the loan. So, the interest rate for 1 month is $13,558/$1,000,000 = 0.0136. The effective annual rate is thus $1.0136^{12} - 1 = 17.5\%$.

4. To determine the firm's seasonal working capital needs, calculate the changes in net working capital for the firm:

Changes in Working Capital	Nov	Dec	Jan	Feb	Mar	Apr
Cash	0	0	0	0	0	0
Accounts Receivable	0	18	−10	60	−60	−8
Inventory	10	3	25	10	−48	0
Accounts Payable	18	0	−10	30	−30	−8
Change in Net Working Capital	−8	21	25	40	−78	0

Next, determine the cash position each month:

	Nov	Dec	Jan	Feb	Mar	Apr
Net Income	$ 2	$21	$ 2	$80	$ 2	$ 2
+Depreciation	2	2	2	2	2	2
−Changes in Net Working Capital	−8	21	25	40	−78	0
Cash Flow from Operations	12	2	−21	42	82	4
−Capital Expenditures	2	2	2	2	2	2
Change in Cash	10	0	−23	40	80	2

The company has a large need for cash in January and a surplus of cash in February and March.

5.

	Oct	Nov	Dec	Jan	Feb	Mar	Apr
Cash	1	1	1	1	1	1	1
Accounts Receivable	2	2	20	10	70	10	2
Inventory	2	12	15	40	50	2	2
Accounts Payable	2	20	20	10	40	10	2
Net Working Capital	3	−5	16	41	81	3	3

The permanent level of working capital is likely to be about $3 million. This is the level in October, March, and April. The firm's temporary working capital needs are very large, especially in January and February as its inventory rises significantly.

■ Self-Test Questions

1. Which of the following would be considered an aggressive financing policy?
    a. Financing permanent working capital with long-term debt and temporary working capital with short-term debt.
    b. Financing permanent working capital and temporary working capital with long-term debt.
    c. Financing permanent working capital and a portion of temporary working capital with long-term debt.
    d. Financing temporary working capital and a portion of permanent working capital with short-term debt.

2. A _____ consists of a legally binding agreement that obligates a bank to provide funds to a firm regardless of the financial condition of the firm as long as the firm satisfies any restrictions in the agreement.
    a. committed line of credit
    b. trust receipt
    c. secured loan
    d. permanent working capital loan

3. The maximum maturity for commercial paper is:
   a. 90 days
   b. 180 days
   c. 270 days
   d. 360 days

4. A firm issues $100,000 of 3-month commercial paper and receives $96,000. What is the effective rate on this paper?
   a. 4.25%
   b. 12.99%
   c. 14.25%
   d. 17.74%

5. A floating lien arrangement
   a. is a risky setup from the standpoint of the lender because the value of the collateral used to secure the loan dwindles as inventory is sold.
   b. is less risky than a floor planning arrangement from the standpoint of the lender because a firm's entire inventory is sued to secure the loan.
   c. is less risky than a floor planning arrangement from the standpoint of the lender because a firm's accounts receivables are used to secure the loan rather than the firm's inventory.
   d. is the financing of permanent working capital with short-term debt.

6. The net working capital for Sandia Skiwear averages $2 million in the months April through September. The net working capital rises during the fall and reaches a peak of $7 million in December. The net working capital of $2 million would be considered
   a. permanent working capital.
   b. temporary working capital.
   c. floor planning working capital.
   d. compensating working capital.

7. The interest rate a bank charges its most creditworthy customers is known as the
   a. commercial paper rate.
   b. prime rate.
   c. discount rate.
   d. committed line rate.

8. Which of the following is referred to as the "matching principle?"
   a. Short-term needs for funds should be financed with short-term sources of funds and long-term needs should be funded with long-term sources of funds.
   b. Temporary working capital should be financed with long-term debt and permanent working capital should be financed with short-term debt.
   c. Firms should finance inventory with long-term debt and accounts receivables with short-term debt.
   d. Internal projects should be financed using bank loans and external projects should be financed with commercial paper.

9. Secured loans
   a. are legally binding agreements that obligate a bank to provide funds to a firm regardless of the financial condition of the firm as long as the firm satisfies any restrictions in the agreement.
   b. are loans that finance permanent working capital.
   c. are loans collateralized with short-term assets—most typically the firm's accounts receivables or inventory.
   d. are loans collateralized with accounts payable.

10. Which of the following is usually the cheapest way for a large, creditworthy company to borrow?
    a. Issuing commercial paper.
    b. Borrowing at prime rate.
    c. Taking out a loan that requires a compensating balance.
    d. Factoring accounts receivable.

11. A lender has reviewed Pinewood Furniture's accounts receivable and has agreed to lend Pinewood 75% of the value of its accounts receivable, with the accounts receivable serving as collateral for the loan. This process is known as:
    a. Issuing commercial paper.
    b. Financing permanent working capital.
    c. Committing a line of credit.
    d. The pledging of accounts receivable.

12. Wildflower Seed Co. needs to borrow $100,000 for 1 month. First National Bank has offered to make a loan to Wildflower at 6% APR. The bank will also require that Wildflower maintain a 2% compensating balance at the bank, and this balance will earn no interest. How large of a loan will Wildflower need to take out to have $100,000 to use?
    a. $102,040.82
    b. $106,382.98
    c. $108,423.80
    d. $125,000.00

Answers to Self-Test Questions

1. d
2. a
3. c
4. d
5. a
6. a
7. b
8. a
9. c
10. a
11. d
12. a

Chapter 21
Option Applications and Corporate Finance

■ Key Learning Objectives

- Understand basic option terminology
- Explain the difference between *calls* and *puts*, how they pay off, and the profit to holding each to expiration
- Analyze the factors that affect option prices
- Become familiar with the Black-Scholes option pricing formula
- Describe the relationship that must hold between the prices of similar *calls* and *puts* on the same stock
- Demonstrate how options are applied in corporate finance

■ Notation

NPV	net present value
PV	present value

■ Chapter Synopsis

21.1 Option Basics

The owner of a **financial option** contract has the right (but not the obligation) to purchase or sell an asset at a fixed price at some future date. A **call option** gives the owner the right to buy the asset; a **put option** gives the owner the right to sell the asset. The **option writer** is the person who takes the side of the contract opposite of the contract owner. Options are considered **derivatives** because they derive their value solely from the price of another asset. A **warrant** is a call option written by a firm whereby new stock will be issued if the warrant is exercised.

When a holder of an option enforces the agreement by buying or selling a share of stock at the agreed-upon price, she is **exercising** the option. The price at which the stock is bought or sold when the option is exercised is called the **strike price** or the **exercise price.**

American options allow the holder to exercise the option on any date up to and including the **expiration date. European options** can only be exercised on the expiration date. **Open interest** refers to the total number of contracts of a particular option that have been written and not yet closed.

When the exercise price of an option is equal to the current price of the stock, the option is said to be **at-the-money.** If the payoff from exercising an option immediately is positive, the option is said to be **in-the-money.** Call options are in-the-money when the strike price is below the current stock price, and put options are in-the-money when the strike price is above the current stock price. If the payoff from exercising the option immediately is negative, the option is **out-of-the-money.** If the strike price and the stock price are very far apart, an option is referred to as **deep-in-the-money** or **deep-out-of-the-money.**

Using an option to reduce risk is called **hedging.** Options also allow investors to **speculate,** or place a bet on the direction in which they believe the underlying security is likely to move.

21.2 Option Payoffs at Expiration

The owner of a call option will exercise the option if the stock price is greater than the strike price at expiration. The holder's payoff is the difference between the stock price and the strike price. If the stock price is less than the strike price, the call will not be exercised and has no value.

The owner of a put option will exercise the option if the stock price is below the strike price at expiration. The holder receives the strike price when the stock is worth less than the strike price; the holder's gain is equal to the strike price minus the stock price.

Remember that the owner of an option has the right, but not the obligation, to exercise the option; the owner of an option is said to be in a long position and will only exercise the option when it is in her best interest to do so. On the other hand, the writer of the option has an obligation should the holder choose to exercise it; thus, the option writer is said to be in a short position. If the option holder does not exercise the option, the option writer loses nothing. If you are the writer of a call option that is exercised, you lose the difference between the stock price and the strike price. If you are the writer of a put option that is exercised, you lose the strike price and the stock price.

When calculating the profits from an option position, the initial cost of the option must be considered. For example, although the payout on a long position in an option will never be negative, the profit from purchasing an option can be negative; the payout at expiration might be less than the initial cost of the option.

21.3 Factors Affecting Option Prices

The value of an otherwise identical call option is higher if the strike price that the holder must pay to buy the stock is lower. For a given strike price, the value of a call option is higher if the current price of the stock is higher.

The value of an otherwise identical put option is higher if the strike price at which the holder is able to sell the stock is higher. For a given strike price, the value of a put option is higher if the current price of the stock is lower.

For American options, the longer the time to exercise the option, the more valuable the option. Because the holder of an American option can exercise the option at any time before the expiration date, the longer-term option holder has all of the rights of the shorter-term option holder and more. However, European options with a later expiration date are not necessarily more valuable because European options can only be exercised on the expiration date.

The value of an option generally increases with the volatility of the underlying stock. An increase in volatility increases the likelihood of very high and very low returns for the stock.

21.4 The Black-Scholes Option Pricing Formula

Professors Fischer Black and Myron Scholes derived a formula for the price of a European-style call option for a non dividend-paying stock which serves as the basis of pricing for options contracts. This formula is:

$$\text{Call Price} = \text{Stock Price} \times N(d_1) - \text{PV(Strike Price)} \times N(d_2)$$

The present value is calculated using the risk-free rate. The expressions for d_1 and d_2, while complicated, contain only the stock price, strike price, risk-free rate, time to expiration of the option, and the volatility of the stock. These are the five factors that are relevant in valuing an option.

21.5 Put-Call Parity

We can use combinations of options to insure a stock against a loss. You can form a **protective put** by purchasing a put option while still holding the stock. You can also use this strategy to ensure against a loss on an entire portfolio of stocks by using put options on the portfolio of stocks as a hold; this is known as **portfolio insurance.**

Another way to achieve portfolio insurance is to purchase a bond and a call option. Because of the Valuation Principle, these two ways of insuring against a loss must have the same price:

$$\text{Stock Price} + \text{Put Price} = \text{PV(Strike Price)} + \text{Call Price}$$

The left side of the equation is the cost of buying the stock and the put. The right side is the cost of buying a zero-coupon bond with a face value equal to the strike price of the put and a call option (with the same strike price as the put). Rearranging the terms in the equation gives the following expression for the price of a European call option for a non dividend-paying stock:

$$\text{Call Price} = \text{Put Price} + \text{Stock Price} - \text{PV(Strike Price)}$$

This relationship between the value of the stock, the bond, and call and put options is known as **put-call parity.**

For a dividend-paying stock, we need to add the present value of future dividends to the combination of the bond and the call:

$$\text{Stock Price} + \text{Put Price} = \text{PV(Strike Price)} + \text{PV(Dividends)} + \text{Call Price}$$

Rearranging the terms in this equation gives us:

$$\text{Call Price} = \text{Put Price} + \text{Stock Price} - \text{PV(Strike Price)} - \text{PV(Dividends)}$$

21.6 Options and Corporate Finance

A share of stock can be thought of as a call option on the assets of the firm with a strike price equal to the value of debt outstanding. Debt holders can be thought of as owning the firm by having written a call option on the firm's assets to the equity holders with a strike price equal to the required debt payments. Remember that the price of an option increases with the volatility level of the underlying security. This suggests that equity holders benefit from a zero-NPV project that increases the volatility of the firm's assets. Because debt holders, as lenders to the firm, do not benefit from an increase in the risk of the firm's assets, a conflict of interest between equity holders and debt holders is created.

■ Selected Concepts and Key Terms

Financial Option

A **financial option** gives the holder the right, but not the obligation, to buy or sell a security. A **call option** gives the holder the right to purchase an asset at some future date. A **put option** gives the holder the right to sell an asset at some future date. When a holder of an option enforces the agreement and buys or sells the asset, the holder is **exercising** the option. The price at which the holder agrees to buy or sell the share of stock when the option is exercised is called the **strike price** or **exercise price.** The last date on which the holder has the right to exercise the option is called the **expiration date.**

American and European Options

An **American option** can be exercised on any date up to, and including, the expiration date. A **European option** can be exercised only on the expiration date.

Derivatives

Options are considered **derivatives** because they derive their value solely from the price of another asset.

Warrant

A **warrant** is a call option written by a firm whereby new stock will be issued if the warrant is exercised.

At-the-Money

When the exercise price of an option is equal to the current price of the stock, the option is said to be **at-the-money.**

In-the-Money

If you would make money by exercising the option immediately, the option is **in-the-money.** If the stock price and the strike price are far apart, resulting in a large payoff, the option is **deep-in-the-money.**

Out-of-the-Money

If you would lose money by exercising an option immediately, the option is **out-of-the-money.** If there would be a large negative payoff, the option is **deep-out-of-the-money.**

Hedging

Using an option to reduce risk is called **hedging.** For example, a **protective put** protects the owner of a stock from the risk of the price of the stock falling.

Speculate

Investors can use options to **speculate,** or place a bet on the direction in which they believe the market is likely to move.

Open Interest

The total number of contracts of a particular option that have been written and not yet closed is referred to as **open interest.**

Option Writer

The **option writer** is the one who sells the option and takes the opposite side of the contract of the option holder.

Portfolio Insurance

Portfolio insurance is the strategy of insuring against a loss on an entire portfolio of stocks by using put options on the portfolio of stocks.

Put-Call Parity

Put-call parity relates the value of the European call to the value of the European put and the stock as:

$$\text{Call Price} = \text{Put Price} + \text{Stock Price} - \text{PV(Strike Price)} - \text{PV(Dividends)}$$

■ Concept Check Questions and Answers

1. Does the holder of an option have to exercise it?

   No, the holder has the right, but not the obligation to exercise the option. Therefore, a holder of an option will exercise the option only when it is beneficial to the holder.

2. What is the difference between an American option and a European option?

   An American option allows the holder to exercise the option on any date up to and including the expiration date, while a European option allows the holder to exercise the option only on the expiration date.

3. How are the profits from buying an option different from the payoff to the option at expiration?

   The payout on a long position in an option contract is never negative; the profit from purchasing an option and holding it to expiration could be negative.

4. How are the payoffs to buying a call option related to the payoffs from writing a call option?

   Because the option is a contract between the writer of the option and the buyer of the option, the losses of one party are the gains of the other.

5. Can a European option with a later exercise date be worth less than an identical European option with an earlier exercise date?

   Yes, a European option with a later exercise date can trade for less than an identical European option with an earlier exercise date. For example, suppose the stock price of XYZ goes to zero due to bankruptcy, the 1-month European put is worth more than the 1-year European put because you can exercise and get your money sooner.

6. Why are options more valuable when there is increased uncertainty about the value of the stock?

   An increase in volatility increases the likelihood of a very high or very low return on the stock. The greater the stock price move when the option is in-the-money, the greater the option payoff. However, if the option is out-of-the money, the payoff is zero regardless of how large the stock price change is.

7. What factors are used in the Black-Scholes formula to price a call option?

   The five factors that are relevant to valuing an option: the stock price, the strike price, the risk-free rate, time to expiration of the option, and the volatility of the stock, are the factors in the Black-Scholes formula.

8. How can the Black-Scholes formula not include the expected return on the stock?

   The expected return on the stock is not included as a factor in the Black-Scholes formula because the expected return of the stock is already incorporated into the current stock price, which is a factor in the formula.

9. Explain put-call parity.

   Put-call parity relates the value of a call to the value of the stock, the bond, and the put with the same strike price and the same maturity date. It says that the price of a European call equals the price of the stock plus an otherwise identical put minus the price of a bond that matures on the exercise date of the option.

10. If a put option trades at a higher price from the value indicated by the put-call parity equation, what action should you take?

    If a put trades at a higher price from the value indicated by the put-call parity, you can arbitrage by selling the overvalued put and stock and simultaneously buying the call option. You are guaranteed to make a profit while taking no risk.

11. Explain how equity can be viewed as a call option on the firm.

    A share of stock can be thought of as a call option on the assets of the firm with the strike price equal to the debt outstanding.

12. Under what circumstances would equity holders have a possible incentive to take on negative-NPV investments?

    The debt holders can be viewed as owning the firm and having sold a call option with a strike price equal to the required debt payment. Remember that the value of an option increases as the volatility of the underlying security increases. Therefore, shareholders benefit from high-volatility investments. Because the price of the equity is increasing with the volatility of the firm's assets, the shareholders can benefit from negative-NPV investments that increase the volatility of the value of the firm's assets.

■ Examples with Step-by-Step Solutions

Purchasing Options

21.1 **Problem:** It is October 13, 2010, and you have decided to purchase 20 November call contracts on Apple's stock with an exercise price of $320. You find the quotes from the CBOE in the chart below. Because you are buying, you must pay the ask price. How much money will this purchase cost you? Is this option in-the-money or out-of-the-money?

AAPL (APPLE INC) **300.14** +1.60
Oct 13, 2010 @ 21:32 ET   Bid 300.20 Ask 300.21 Size 1x1 Vol 22503227

Calls	Last Sale	Net	Bid	Ask	Vol	Open Int		Puts	Last Sale	Net	Bid	Ask	Vol	Open Int
AAPL1016J290-E	10.40	+1.20	10.25	10.50	3067	32019	10 Oct 290.00	AAPL1016V290-E	0.23	-0.32	0.20	0.23	3465	24436
AAPL1016J300-E	2.35	+0.08	2.24	2.38	10390	44923	10 Oct 300.00	AAPL1016V300-E	2.11	-1.59	2.05	2.17	3758	9729
AAPL1016J310-E	0.22	-0.14	0.20	0.22	3650	33185	10 Oct 310.00	AAPL1016V310-E	10.10	-1.60	9.90	10.10	715	2105
AAPL1016J320-E	0.05	-0.02	0.03	0.06	986	22906	10 Oct 320.00	AAPL1016V320-E	19.52	-3.78	19.70	20.00	41	490
AAPL1020K290-E	18.30	+0.67	18.30	18.50	1223	20504	10 Nov 290.00	AAPL1020W290-E	8.05	-0.74	7.95	8.10	1002	10116
AAPL1020K300-E	12.75	+0.65	12.65	12.80	2546	22204	10 Nov 300.00	AAPL1020W300-E	12.40	-0.92	12.30	12.45	1524	7215
AAPL1020K310-E	8.45	+0.45	8.35	8.50	5382	17852	10 Nov 310.00	AAPL1020W310-E	18.15	-0.99	17.95	18.15	409	2409
AAPL1020K320-E	5.39	+0.29	5.35	5.45	1998	10054	10 Nov 320.00	AAPL1020W320-E	25.15	-2.55	24.90	25.10	90	539

Source: Chicago Board Options Exchange at www.cboe.com.

Solution

Plan: From the table, you see that the ask price of this option is $5.45. Remember that the price quoted is per share and that each contract is for 100 shares. You want to buy 20 contracts.

Execute: You are purchasing 20 contracts and each contract is on 100 shares, so the transaction will cost 5.45 × 20 × 100 = $10,900 (ignoring any commission fees). Because this is a call option and the exercise price ($320) is above the current stock price ($300.14), the option is currently out-of-the-money.

Evaluate: Even though the option is currently out-of-the-money, it still has value. During the time left to expiration, the stock could rise above the exercise (strike) price of $320.

Payoff of a Call Option at Maturity

21.2 Problem: You own a call option on Trident Technologies stock with an exercise price of $15 that expires today. Plot the value of this option as a function of the stock price.

Solution

Plan: You will exercise the option only if the stock price is greater than $15. If you exercise the option, the payoff is the stock price minus the strike price. If the price is less than or equal to $15, the payoff is zero.

Execute:

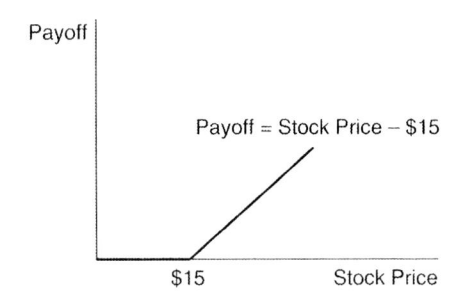

[Graph: Payoff vs. Stock Price. Horizontal line at zero up to $15, then line with slope 1 labeled "Payoff = Stock Price − $15" beyond $15.]

Evaluate: Because it allows you to force the call writer to sell the stock to you for $15, regardless of the market price, the payoff of the call option increases as Trident's stock price increases. For example, if Trident's price were $20, you could exercise the option and then immediately sell the stock in the market for $20, resulting in a $5 payoff.

Payoff of a Short Position in a Call Option

21.3 Problem: You are short a call option on Trident Technologies stock with an exercise price of $15 that expires today. What is your payoff at expiration as a function of the stock price?

Solution

Plan: If the holder of the option chooses to exercise the option, you are obligated to sell the stock for $15. The holder of the option will not exercise the option if the stock price is $15 or lower. If the stock price rises above $15, the holder will exercise the option, and your payoff will be $15 minus the stock price.

Execute:

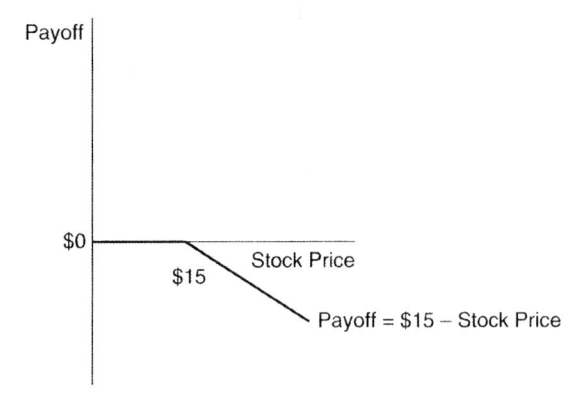

[Graph: Payoff vs Stock Price. Payoff is $0 for stock price ≤ $15, then declines linearly as Payoff = $15 − Stock Price for stock price > $15.]

Evaluate: If the stock price rises above $15, the option will be exercised and you will have a negative payoff. As the stock price rises, your loss becomes larger and larger. Because there is no limit to how high a stock price can rise, there is no limit to the downside you face.

Profit on Holding a Position in a Call Option Until Expiration

21.4 Problem: You are the owner of the Trident Technologies call option in Example 21.2. You paid $3 for the option. Plot the profit of the position as a function of the stock price on expiration.

Solution

Plan: If you do not exercise the option, your profit will be −$3, the cost of the option. If you do exercise the option, your profit will be the stock price minus the strike price minus $3. Remember that you will exercise the option if the price of Trident's stock rises above $15.

Execute:

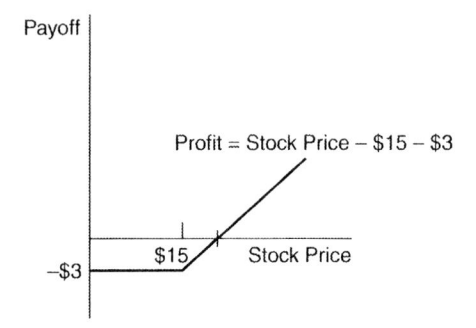

[Graph: Payoff vs Stock Price. Profit is −$3 for stock price ≤ $15, then rises linearly as Profit = Stock Price − $15 − $3 for stock price > $15.]

Evaluate: Even if the payoff is positive, if it is not enough to offset the premium you paid to acquire the option, your profit will be negative. For example, if Trident's stock price is $17, you will exercise the option and your profit will be $17 − $15 − $3 = −$1. You exercise the option even though your profit is negative because you would prefer to have a loss of $1 rather than a loss of $3.

Option Value and Volatility

21.5 Problem: Two European call options with a strike price of $40 are written on two different stocks—a high volatility stock and a low volatility stock. Suppose that the low volatility stock will have a price of $40 tomorrow for certain. The high volatility stock will be worth either $30 or $50, with each price having equal probability. If the exercise date of both options is tomorrow, which option will be worth more today?

Solution

Plan: The value of the options will depend on the value of the stocks at expiration. The value of the options at expiration will be the stock price minus $40 if the stock price is greater than $40 and $0 otherwise.

Execute: Because the low volatility stock will be worth $40 tomorrow, its option will be worth $0. The high volatility stock will be worth either $30 or $50, so its option will pay off either $0 or $50 − $40 = $10. Because options have no chance of a negative payoff, the one that has a 50% chance of a positive payoff has to be worth more than the option on the low volatility stock.

Evaluate: Because the volatility increases the chance that an option will pay off, the options have different values even though the expected value of both stocks tomorrow is $40.

Using Put-Call Parity

21.6 Problem: You are an options dealer who deals in option contracts that are not publicly traded. One of your clients wants to purchase a 1-year European call option on Ogden Oil with a strike price of $60. Another dealer is willing to write a 1-year European put option on Ogden Oil stock with a strike price of $60 and sell you the put option for a price of $3.00 a share. Ogden Oil is currently trading for $55 per share and pays no dividends. If the risk-free interest rate is 4%, what is the lowest price you can charge your client for the call option and guarantee yourself a profit?

Solution

Plan: We can use put-call parity to determine the price of the option:

$$\text{Call Price} = \text{Put Price} + \text{Stock Price} - \text{PV(Strike Price)}$$

In order to price a 1-year European call with a strike price of $60, we need to know the price of a 1-year European put with the same strike price, the current stock price, and the risk-free interest rate. All of this information is given in the problem.

Execute:

$$\text{Call Price} = \text{Put Price} + \text{Stock Price} - \text{PV(Strike Price)}$$
$$= \$3.00 + \$55 - \$60/1.04$$
$$= \$0.31$$

Questions and Problems

1. You own a call option on Bauer Pharmaceuticals with a strike price of $75. The option will expire in exactly 1 month.
   a. If the stock is trading at $60 in 1 month, what will be the payoff of the call?
   b. If the stock is trading at $80 in 1 month, what will be the payoff of the call?
   c. Draw a payoff diagram showing the value of the call at expiration as a function of the stock price at expiration.

2. Assume that you have shorted the call option in Problem 1.
   a. If the stock is trading at $60 in 1 month, what will you owe?
   b. If the stock is trading at $80 in 1 month, what will you owe?
   c. Draw a payoff diagram showing the amount you owe at expiration as a function of the stock price at expiration.

3. You own a put option on Fossil Oil with a strike price of $100. The option will expire in exactly 3 months.
   a. If the stock is trading at $80 in 3 months, what will the payoff of the put be?
   b. If the stock is trading at $120 in 3 months, what will the payoff of the put be?
   c. Draw a payoff diagram showing the value of the put at expiration as a function of the stock price at expiration.

4. Assume that you have shorted the put option in Problem 3.
   a. If the stock is trading at $80 in 3 months, what will you owe?
   b. If the stock is trading at $120 in 3 months, what will you owe?
   c. Draw a payoff diagram showing the amount you owe at expiration as a function of the stock price at expiration.

5. Butterfly Beauty Supply stock is currently trading for $45 a share. The stock pays no dividends. A 1-year European put option on Butterfly with a strike price of $50 is currently trading for $3.25. If the risk-free rate is 5%, what is the price of a 1-year European call option on Butterfly with a strike price of $50?

■ Solutions to Questions and Problems

1. a. 0
   b. $80 − $75 = $5
   c.

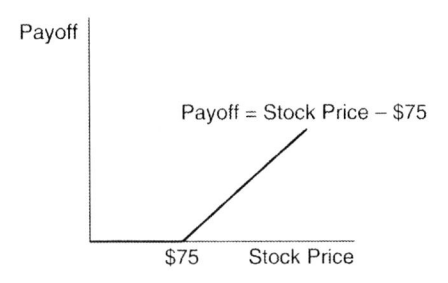

   [Payoff graph: Payoff = Stock Price − $75, kink at $75]

2. a. 0
   b. $75 − $80 = −$5
   c.

   [Payoff graph: Payoff = $75 − Stock Price, kink at $75, downward sloping below]

3. a. $100 − $80 = $20
   b. 0
   c.

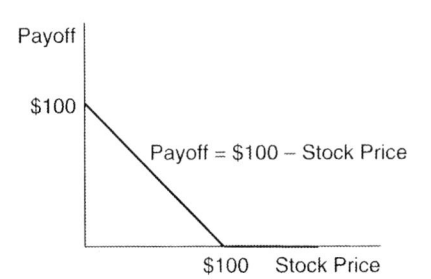

   [Payoff graph: Payoff = $100 − Stock Price, starts at $100, reaches 0 at $100]

4. a. −$100 + $80 = −$20
    b. 0
    c.

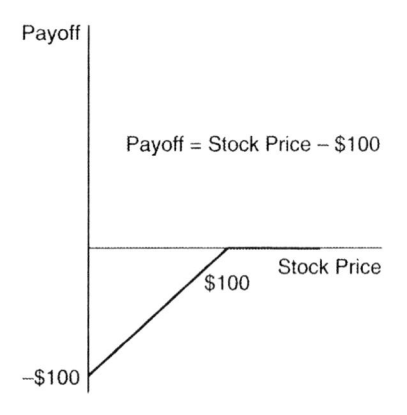

    Payoff

    Payoff = Stock Price − $100

    $100   Stock Price

    −$100

5. Call Price = $3.25 + $45 − ($50/1.05) = $0.63.

■ Self-Test Questions

1. Margie has the right to buy 100 shares of ABC stock at a price of $32 a share any time in the next 3 months. Margie is a
    a. call option holder.
    b. call option writer.
    c. put option holder.
    d. put option writer.

2. The $32 price in Question 1 is known as the
    a. option price.
    b. expiration price.
    c. strike price.
    d. warrant price.

3. A European option
    a. has no expiration date.
    b. can only be exercised on the expiration date.
    c. is a call option written by the firm whereby new stock will be issued if the call is exercised.
    d. is used for hedging while an American option is used for speculating.

4. A put option is in-the-money when:
    a. The strike price is above the current stock price.
    b. The strike price is below the current stock price.
    c. The exercise price is equal to the current stock price.
    d. The exercise price is below the current stock price.

5. Which of the following is a TRUE statement?
   a. Payoffs on a long position in an option contract are never negative, but the profit from purchasing an option and holding it to expiration could be negative.
   b. Both the payoff on a long position in an option contract and the profit from purchasing an option and holding it to expiration could be negative.
   c. Payoffs on a long position in an option contract may be negative, but the profit from purchasing an option and holding it to expiration could never be negative.
   d. Both the payoff on a long position in an option contract and the profit from purchasing an option and holding it to expiration can never be negative.

6. A share of stock can be thought of as a
   a. put option on the assets of the firm with a strike price equal to the value of the debt outstanding.
   b. put option on the assets of the firm with a strike price equal to the value of the assets of the firm.
   c. put option on the debt of the firm with a strike price equal to the value of the assets of the firm.
   d. call option on the assets of the firm with a strike price equal to the value of the debt outstanding.

7. Anthony owns Apple stock. He is concerned that the stock might decline in value, but does not want to give up the possibility of making money if the stock price increases, Anthony can insure against a loss by:
   a. Purchasing a call option.
   b. Purchasing a put option.
   c. Writing a call option.
   d. Writing a put option.

8. Which of the following factors will increase the value of a call option?
   a. A decrease in the stock price.
   b. An increase in the strike price.
   c. A decrease in the risk-free rate.
   d. An increase in volatility in the underlying stock.

9. Which of the following factors will increase the value of a put option?
   a. A decrease in the stock price.
   b. A decrease in the strike price.
   c. An increase in the risk-free rate.
   d. A decrease in the volatility in the underlying stock.

10. For an American option, an increase in the time to expiration will
    a. increase the value of a call option and decrease the value of a put option.
    b. increase the value of a call option and a put option.
    c. decrease the value of a call option and a put option.
    d. decrease the value of a call option and increase the value of a put option.

11. An investor who uses options to protect against risk is _____, while an investor who uses options to bet which direction the market will move is _____.
    a. calling; hedging
    b. striking; calling
    c. hedging; speculating
    d. speculating; striking

12. Marvelle Money Management is insuring against a loss on its entire portfolio of stocks by using put options on the portfolio of stocks. This strategy is known as:
    a. Speculation
    b. Put-call parity
    c. Portfolio insurance
    d. Expiring options

Answers to Self-Test Questions

1. a
2. c
3. b
4. a
5. a
6. d
7. b
8. d
9. a
10. b
11. c
12. c

Chapter 22
Mergers and Acquisitions

■ Key Learning Objectives

- Discuss the types of mergers and trends in merger activity
- Understand the stock price reactions to takeover announcements
- Critically evaluate the different reasons to acquire
- Follow the major steps in the takeover process
- Discuss the main takeover defenses
- Identify factors that determine who gets the value-added in a merger

■ Notation

A	premerger total value of target
EPS	earnings per share
N_A	premerger number of shares of acquirer outstanding
N_T	premerger number of shares of target outstanding
P/E	price-earnings ratio
P_A	premerger share price of acquirer
P_T	premerger share price of target
S	value of all synergies
T	premerger total value of target
x	number of new shares issued by acquirer to pay for target

■ Chapter Synopsis

22.1 Background and Historical Trends

When one firm acquires another, the buyer is known as the **acquirer** or **bidder.** The selling firm is referred to as the **target** firm. In a **takeover** another firm or a group of individuals and acquire the target firm, or the target firm can merge with another firm. More mergers occur during economic expansions than during contractions, resulting in **merger waves.**

A **horizontal merger** occurs when the target and acquirer are in the same industry. **Vertical mergers** occur between an acquiring firm and a target firm in an industry that buys from or sells to the acquiring firm. **Conglomerate mergers** occur between target firms and acquiring firms in unrelated industries.

Shareholders of the target firm typically receive stock, cash, or a mix of the two. When they receive stock, the deal is often called a **stock swap.** A **term sheet** summarizes the structure of a merger transaction.

© 2012 Pearson Education, Inc. Publishing as Prentice Hall

22.2 Market Reaction to a Takeover

Usually, an acquiring firm pays an **acquisition premium.** The acquisition premium is calculated as the percentage difference between the acquisition price and the premerger price of the target firm. On average the premium paid over the pre merger price is 43%. On the announcement of a merger, the target firm's stock price increases, on average, 15%, and the acquiring firm's stock price increases, on average, 1%.

22.3 Reasons to Acquire

An acquiring firm would be willing to pay an acquisition premium if it could add economic value that an individual investor could not. Either cost-reducing or revenue-enhancing synergies may exist. If a large company and produce goods in high volume at a lower average cost than a smaller company, **economics of scale** are said to exist. **Economies of scope** exist when a firm can benefit from combining the marketing and distribution of related products. A company might find that it can benefit from **vertical integration** because it will have more direct control of the inputs required to make the product. Sometimes, a company may acquire another company to purchase labor talent, skill, and expertise. However, companies must balance any of these gains with the costs associated with managing a larger company.

If merged firms are able to substantially reduce competition in an industry, monopoly power could be used to increase profits. Because society as a whole bears the cost of monopoly strategies, most countries limit such activity through antitrust laws.

If a target company is being run by inefficient managers, an acquirer can purchase the shares at a discounted price to take control of the corporation, replacing the inefficient management. Conglomerates may also face some tax advantages over a single-product firm.

Three benefits of diversification that a merger brings about are often cited: direct risk reduction, lower cost of debt or increased debt capacity, and liquidity enhancement. While a large firm does bear less idiosyncratic risk, investors can achieve this benefit by holding a diversified portfolio. Because a larger, more diversified firm has a lower probability of bankruptcy given the same degree of financial leverage, a larger firm can increase leverage, enjoying the tax benefits, without incurring significant costs of financial distress. Because shareholders of private companies are often under diversified, when a private target is acquired, the owners can cash out their investment and invest in a more diversified portfolio.

In addition to economic reasons, managers may have personal reasons for merging. For example, a manager might benefit from additional pay and prestige that can come with managing a bigger company. If managers are overconfident in their abilities, they will think that their ability to create value from a merger is higher than it really is.

22.4 The Takeover Process

Takeover synergies refer to the value obtained from an acquisition that could not be obtained if the target remained an independent firm. For a bidder, a takeover is a positive NPV project if the premium it pays does not exceed the takeover synergies.

The acquiring firm makes a tender offer which is a public announcement of its intention to purchase a large block of shares for a specified price. The bidder can pay for the target using either cash or stock. The **exchange ratio** refers to the number of bidder shares received in exchange for each target share.

A stock-swap merger adds value for the acquiring shareholders if the share price of the merged firm exceeds the premerger price of the acquiring firm. This can be expressed as:

$$\frac{A+T+S}{N_A+x} > \frac{A}{N_A}$$

Where: A is the premerger value of the acquiring firm

T is the premerger value of the target firm

S is the value of the synergies created by the firm

N_A is the acquirer's shares outstanding before the merger

x is the new shares issued to pay for the target

There is no guarantee that a takeover will take place after a tender offer is announced. **Risk arbitrageurs** speculate on the outcome of the deal. These traders can potentially benefit from the difference between the target's stock price and the implied offer price, known as the **merger-arbitrage spread.** Although the term *arbitrage* is used, this is not an arbitrage opportunity in the strict sense of the word because there is a risk that the deal will not go through, leaving the trader with a loss.

The manner in which the acquirer pays for the target affects the taxes of both the target shareholders and the combined firm. Any cash received is an immediate tax liability for the target shareholders. If the target shareholders receive stock, then the tax liability is deferred until the target shareholders actually sell their new shares of stock. If the acquirer purchases the target assets directly, then it can **step up** the book value of the target's assets to the purchase price, reducing future taxes through larger depreciation charges.

Both the target and acquiring board of directors must approve a merger deal and put the question to a vote of the shareholders of the target. In some cases, the shareholders of the acquiring firm must also vote. In a **friendly takeover** the target board of directors supports the merger, negotiates with potential acquirer, and agrees on a price that is presented to the shareholders for a vote. A **hostile takeover** is a takeover in which the board of directors fights the takeover attempt. In this case, the acquirer, often called a **raider,** must garner enough shares to take control of the target and replace the board of directors.

22.5 Takeover Defenses

For a hostile takeover to succeed, the acquirer must appeal directly to the target shareholders. In a **proxy fight** the acquirer attempts to convince the target shareholders to unseat the target board by using their proxy votes to support the acquirers' candidates for election to the target board.

A **poison pill** is a takeover defense that makes the takeover so expensive that acquiring shareholders choose to pass on the deal. The poison pill is a rights offering that gives the existing target shareholders the right to buy shares in the target at a deeply discounted price. Because target shareholders can purchase shares at less than the market price, the rights offering dilutes the value of any shares held by the acquirer.

Companies often have a **staggered** (or **classified**) board to prevent a determined bidder from getting its own slate of directors elected to the target board. With only one-third of the directors up for election each year, the bidder cannot win control of the board in one election.

When a target company is facing a hostile takeover, it might look for a friendly company, known as a **white knight,** to come to its rescue and acquire it. A **white squire** is a large, passive investor or firm that agrees to purchase a substantial block of shares in a target with special voting rights. A **golden parachute** is an extremely lucrative severance package that is guaranteed to a firm's senior managers in the event that the firm is taken over and the managers are let go.

Firms may recapitalize as a defense against a takeover. A company with a lot of cash might choose to pay out a large dividend. A company without a lot of cash might instead choose to issue debt and then use the proceeds to pay a dividend or repurchase stock. A corporation's charter may forestall a takeover by requiring a supermajority of votes to approve a merger or by restricting the voting rights of very large shareholders. Also, a firm can require that a "fair" price, determined by the board of directors or senior management, be paid for the company.

Regulators must approve all mergers. Antitrust enforcement in the United States is governed by three main statutes: the Sherman Act of 1890, the Clayton Act of 1914, and the Hart-Scott-Rodino Act of 1976. The European Commission has also established a process that imposes restrictions on a combined firm's operations and sales in Europe.

22.6 Who Gets the Value Added from a Takeover?

Who profits from the valued created by a merger? It might seem as if the people who do the work of acquiring the corporation and replacing its management would capture this value. However, based on the average stock price reaction it appears that the premium the acquirer pays is approximately equal to the value it adds. This means that the target shareholders, rather than the acquirer, capture the value added.

Shareholders of a target firm can benefit from selling their shares to an acquirer at a higher price than the pre merger announcement price. However, if an individual shareholder holds out and does not sell to the acquirer, that shareholder will have shares worth even more if the merger adds value beyond what has accrued to the target shareholders. This is a "free-rider problem" in that an individual shareholder can share in the acquirer's gains without doing the work that the acquirer did. An acquirer might try to minimize this free-rider problem by acquiring an initial stake in the company, known as a **toehold.**

In a leveraged buyout (LBO), an investor announces a tender offer for outstanding shares, but instead of using his own cash to purchase the shares, money is borrowed through a shell corporation by pledging the shares themselves as collateral on the loan. If a leveraged buyout involves the current management of the company, it is called a **management buyout (MBO).** In a **freezeout merger** an acquiring company is able to freeze existing shareholders out of the gains from merging by forcing nontendering shareholders to sell their share for the tender offer price.

■ Selected Concepts and Key Terms

Mergers

A **takeover** involves on firm, the **acquirer** or **bidder,** taking over another firm, known as the **target** firm. **Merger waves** form as more mergers occur during economic expansions than during contractions. **Horizontal mergers** occur between firms in the same industry. **Vertical mergers** occur between an acquiring firm and a target firm in an industry that buys from or sells to the acquiring firm. **Conglomerate mergers** occur between firms in unrelated industries.

Term Sheet

A **term sheet** summarizes the structure of a merger transaction. Shareholders of the target firm typically receive stock, cash, or a mix of the two. When they receive stock, the deal is often called a **stock swap.**

Acquisition Premium

The **acquisition premium** is calculated as the percentage difference between the acquisition price and the premerger price of the target firm.

Economies of Scale and Scope

Economies of scale exist when a larger firm can produce a product at a lower average cost than a smaller firm can. **Economies of scope** exist when a firm can benefit from combining the marketing and distribution of related products.

Takeover Synergies

Takeover synergies refer to the value obtained from an acquisition that could not be obtained if the target remained an independent firm. An example would be the gains that come from **vertical integration** in a vertical merger.

Tender Offer

A **tender offer** is a public announcement of an intention to purchase a large block of shares for a specified price. The bidder can pay for the target using either cash or stock. The **exchange ratio** refers to the number of bidder shares received in exchange for each target share. If the acquirer purchases the target assets directly, then it can **step up** the book value of the target's assets to the purchase price, reducing future taxes through larger depreciation charges.

Friendly and Hostile Takeovers

In a **friendly takeover,** the target board of directors supports the merger, negotiates with potential acquirer, and agrees on a price that is presented to the shareholders for a vote. In a **hostile takeover,** the board of directors fights the takeover attempt. In this case, the acquirer, or **raider,** must garner enough shares to take control of the target and replace the board of directors.

Risk Arbitrageurs

Because there is no guarantee that a takeover will take place after a tender offer is announced, **risk arbitrageurs** speculate on the outcome of the deal. These traders can potentially benefit from the difference between the target's stock price and the implied offer price, known as the **merger-arbitrage spread.**

Takeover Defenses

In a **proxy fight,** the acquirer attempts to convince the target shareholders to unseat the target board by using their proxy votes to support the acquirers' candidates for election to the target board. A **staggered board** is a defense strategy which prevents a bidder from acquiring control over the board in a short period of time by having only a portion of board members up for election each year. A **poison pill** gives target shareholders the right to buy shares in either the target or the acquirer at a deeply discounted price.

A target company may look for a friendly company, known as a **white knight,** to come to its rescue and acquire it. A **white squire** is a large, passive investor or firm that agrees to purchase a substantial block of shares in a target with special voting rights. A **golden parachute** is an extremely lucrative severance package that is guaranteed to a firm's senior managers in the event that the firm is taken over and the managers are let go.

Toehold

If an acquirer purchases an initial stake in a company before a tender offer is made, it is known as a **toehold.**

Management Buyout (MBO)

A leveraged buyout that involves the current management of a company is called a **management buyout (MBO).**

Freezout Merger

In a **freezout merger,** an acquiring company is able to freeze existing shareholders out of the gains from merging by forcing nontendering shareholders to sell their share for the tender offer price.

Concept Check Questions and Answers

1. What are merger waves?

    Merger waves are periods when a large number of mergers occur (generally during an economic expansion), followed by a trough in merger activity (generally during slow economic times).

2. What is the difference between a horizontal and vertical merger?

    A horizontal merger would be a merger between two companies in the same industry. A vertical merger occurs when an acquiring firm merges with another firm in an industry that is either a supplier to or a purchaser from the acquiring firm's industry.

3. On average, what happens to the target share price on the announcement of a takeover?

    The target share price increases an average of 15% on the announcement of a takeover.

4. On average, what happens to the acquirer share price on the announcement of a takeover?

    On average, the share price of the acquirer increases 1% on the announcement of a takeover.

5. What are the reasons most often cited for a takeover?

    The most common reasons given for acquiring a firm are the synergies that can be gained through an acquisition. These synergies include economies of scale and scope, the control provided by vertical integration, monopolistic power gains, expertise gains, improvements in operating efficiency, and benefits related to diversification such as increased borrowing capacity and tax savings.

6. Explain why risk diversification benefits and earnings growth are not good justifications for a takeover intended to increase shareholder wealth.

    Risk diversification benefits are not a good justification for a takeover because investors can achieve the benefits of diversification themselves by purchasing shares in the two separate firms themselves; because most stockholders already hold a well-diversified portfolio, they get no further gains from diversifying through acquisition. Earnings growth is not a justification for a takeover because a high-growth company can combine with a low-growth company and increase the earnings per share, but lower the overall growth rate of the earnings.

7. What are the steps in the takeover process?

    A tender offer, which is a public announcement of an intention to purchase a large block of shares for a specified price, is made. Both the target and the acquiring board of directors must approve the merger and put the question to a vote of the target shareholders (and, in some cases, the acquiring shareholders, also).

8. What do arbitrageurs do?

    Risk arbitrageurs are traders who, once a takeover is announced, speculate on the outcome of the deal.

9. What defensive strategies are available to help target companies resist an unwanted takeover?

   A poison pill, which gives target shareholders the right to buy shares in the target at a deeply discounted price, can be used as a defensive strategy because it makes the takeover very expensive. Having a staggered board can also be used as a defense because it prevents a bidder from acquiring control over the board in a short period of time. Other defenses include finding a friendly bidder (a white knight), making it expensive to replace management through the use of golden parachutes, and changing the capital structure of the firm.

10. How can a hostile acquirer get around a poison pill?

    A hostile acquirer can try to get around a poison pill by using a proxy fight to gain control over the board at the next annual shareholders' meeting.

11. What mechanisms allow corporate raiders to get around the free-rider problem in takeovers?

    Corporate raiders overcome the free-rider problem by acquiring a toehold in the target, attempting a leveraged buyout, or by offering a freezeout merger.

12. Based on the empirical evidence, who gets the value added from a takeover? What is the most likely explanation of this fact?

    The evidence suggests that most of the value added accrues to the target shareholders. This is most likely due to competition that exists in the takeover market. Once an acquirer starts bidding on a target company and it is clear that a significant gain exists, other potential acquirers begin bidding and competing the profits away.

■ Examples with Step-by-Step Solutions

Taxes for a Merged Corporation

22.1 **Problem:** Consider two firms, American League Sportswear (ALS) and National League Sportswear (NLS). ALS will either make $60 million or lose $30 million every year with equal probability. NLS will either make $50 million or lose $20 million every year with equal probability. Also, the firms' profits are perfectly negatively correlated. That is, in a year that ALS makes $60 million, NLS loses $20 million. In a year that ALS has a loss of $30 million, NLS will have a gain of $50 million. Assume that the corporate tax rate is 25%. What is the total expected after-tax profits of both firms when they are two separate firms? What are the expected after-tax profits if the two firms merge into one firm but are run as two independent divisions? (Assume it is not possible to carry back or carry forward any losses.)

Solution

Plan: We need to calculate the after-tax profits of each firm in the good and bad states by multiplying profits by (1 − tax rate). We can then compute the expected after-tax profits as the weighted average of the after-tax profits in the good and bad states. If the firms are combined, their total profits would be either ($60 million − $20 million)/2 or (−$30 million + $50 million)/2 with equal probability.

Execute: Let's start with ALS. In the profitable state, the firm must pay corporate taxes, so after-tax profits are $60 million × (1 − 0.25) = $45 million. When the firm reports losses, no taxes are owed; so the after-tax profits in those years is −$30 million. Thus, ALS's expected after-tax profits are .5 × $45 million + 0.5 × −$30 million = $7.5 million.

When ALS is in a profitable state, NLS will have a loss of $20 million; because NLS will owe no taxes in those years, it will report an after-tax profit of −$20 million. When ALS has a loss, NLS will make $50 million. NLS will have an after-tax profit of $50 million × (1 − 0.25) = $37.5 in those years. Thus, the expected after-tax profits for NLS are .5 × −$20 million + 0.5 × $37.5 = $8.75 million.

The total expected after-tax profit of both companies operated separately is $7.5 million + $8.75 million = $16.25 million.

The merged company would have profits of $60 million + − $20 million = $40 million half of the time and −$30 million + $50 million = $20 million half of the time. Thus, the expected after-tax profits for the combined company would be (0.5 × $40 million + 0.5 × $20 million) × (1 − 0.25) = $22.5 million.

Evaluate: The combined company would have an expected after-tax profit of $22.5 million per year which is significantly greater than the $16.25 million expected after-tax profit of both companies operated separately. There is no change in the before-tax incomes of the companies when combined. The sole advantage is the tax advantage of having the losses of one division reduce the taxes on the other division's profits.

Mergers and Earnings per Share

22.2 Problem: Consider two corporations that both have earnings of $4 per share. The first firm, Arkansas Enterprises (AE) is a mature company with few growth opportunities. It has 10 million shares outstanding and the shares are currently priced at $40 per share. The second company, Mississippi Manufacturing (MM) has many more growth opportunities than AE does. Although it also has 10 million shares outstanding, its shares are trading for $80 per share. Assume MM acquires AE using its own stock. If this takeover adds no value, what is the value of MM after the acquisition in a perfect market? At current market prices, how many shares must MM offer AE's shareholders in exchange for their shares? What will MM's earnings per share be after the acquisition?

Solution

Plan: Because the merger adds no value, the post-takeover value of MM will equal the pre-takeover value of the separate two companies; AE's pre-takeover value is 10 million × $40 = $400 million. MM's pre-takeover value is 10 million × $80 = $800 million. To acquire AE, MM must pay $400 million. First, we must calculate how many shares MM must issue to pay AE shareholders $400 million. The ratio of MM shares issued to AE shares will give us the exchange ratio. Once we know how many new shares will be issued, we can divide the total earnings of the combined company by the new total number of shares outstanding to get the earnings per share.

Execute:

At its pre-takover stock price of $80 a share, MM will need to issue $400 million/$80 = 5 million shares of stock. As a group, AE's stockholders will then exchange their 10 million outstanding shares in AIE for the 5 million shares in MM. The exchange ratio is the ratio of issued shares to exchanged shares, or 5 million/10 million = 0.5. So, AE shareholders will receive 0.5 share of MM for each 1 share of AE they held.

Notice that the price per share of MM stock is the same after the takeover. The post-takevoer value of MM is $1.2 billion, and there are 15 million shares outstanding. This gives a stock price of $1.2 billion/15 million = $80. However, MM's earnings per share have changed. Before the takeover, both companies earned $4 per share × 10 million shares = $40 million. Therefore, the combined company now earns $80 million. Because there are 15 million shares outstanding, the earnings per share are now calculated as:

$$\text{EPS} = \frac{\$80 \text{ million}}{15 \text{ million shares}} = \$5.33 \text{ per share}$$

Thus, by taking over AE, MM has raised its earnings per share by $1.33, from $4.00 to $5.33.

Evaluate: No value was created by the merger; therefore, we can think of the combined company as simply a portfolio of AE and MM. Although the portfolio has a higher total earnings per share, it also has lower growth rate than the pre-takeover that MM had because we have combined the low growth of AE with the high growth of MM. The higher current earnings per share has come at a price—lower earnings per share growth. Therefore, we would expect the P/E multiple for MM to drop.

Mergers and the Price-Earnings Ratio

22.3 Problem: Calculate MM's price-earnings ratio, before and after the takeover described in Example 22.2.

Solution

Plan: The price-earnings ratio is price per share divided by the earnings per share. MM's price per share is $80 before and after the takeover. Its earnings per share are $4 before the takeover and $5.33 after the takeover.

Execute:

Before the takeover, MM's price-earnings ratio is

$$\text{P/E} = \frac{\$80 \text{ per share}}{\$4 \text{ per share}} = 20$$

After the takeover, MM's price-earnings ratio is

$$\text{P/E} = \frac{\$80 \text{ per share}}{\$5.33 \text{ per share}} = 15$$

Evaluate: The price-earnings ratio has dropped to reflect the fact that after taking over AE, more of the value of MM comes from earnings from current projects than from future growth.

Maximum Exchange Ratio in a Stock Takeover

22.4 Problem: Gulf Oil announces that it plans to acquire Star Oil. At the time of the announcement, Gulf's stock was trading for $60 a share and the company had 500 million shares outstanding. Star's stock was trading for $50 a share and the company had 100 million shares outstanding. If the projected synergies were $2 billion, what is the maximum exchange ratio that Gulf could offer in a stock swap and still generate a positive NPV? What is the maximum cash offer Gulf can make?

Solution

Plan: We can use the following equation to compute the maximum shares Gulf could offer and still have a positive NPV:

$$\text{Exchange ratio} < \frac{P_T}{P_A}\left(1 + \frac{S}{T}\right)$$

To compute the maximum cash offer we can calculate the synergies per share and add that to Star's current share price.

Execute: The exchange ratio would be:

$$\text{Exchange ratio} < \frac{P_T}{P_A}\left(1+\frac{S}{T}\right) = \frac{50}{60}\left(1+\frac{2}{5}\right) = 1.167$$

Gulf could offer up to 1.167 shares of Gulf stock for each share of Star's stock and generate a positive NPV.

For a cash offer, given synergies of $2 billion/100 million shares = $20 per share, Gulf could offer up to $50 + $20 = $70 per share.

Evaluate: Offering 1.167 shares of Gulf stock which is worth $60 a share is equivalent to $70 per share. Both the cash amount and the exchange offer have the same value. If Gulf pays $70 per share for Star, it is paying full price for the existing company plus paying Star shareholders for all of the synergy gains created, leaving no gain for Gulf shareholders. Thus, at $70 a share, Gulf's takeover of Star is a zero-NPV project.

Leveraged Buyout

22.5 Problem: Swift International stock is currently trading at $30 a share. There are 30 million shares outstanding and the company has no debt. Your firm specializes in leveraged buyouts. You think that the management of Swift could be improved considerably. If the current managers were replaced with more competent managers, your analysis suggests that the value of the company would increase by 40%. You decide to initiate a leveraged buyout and issue a tender offer for at least a controlling interest—50% of the outstanding shares. What is the maximum amount of value you can extract and still complete the deal?

Solution

Plan: Currently, the value of Swift is $30 × 30 million = $900 million, and you estimate that you can add an additional 40%, or $360 million. If you borrow $450 million and the tender offer succeeds, you will take control of the company and install new management. The total value of the company will increase by $360 million to $1.26 billion. You will also attach the $450 million in debt to the company. You can then compute the value of the post-takeover equity and your gain.

Execute:
The value of the equity once the deal is done is the total value minus the debt outstanding, or $1.26 billion − $450 million = $810 million. The value of the equity is less than the pre merger value. In the United States, existing shareholders must be offered at least the premerger price for their shares. Therefore, you will need to pay $900 million to complete the deal. Because you borrowed $450 million, you will need to pay for $900 million − $450 million = $450 million out of your own pocket. You will own all of the equity, which is worth $810 million. You paid $450 million for the equity, so your profit is $360 million.

Evaluate: The most you can gain is the $360 million in value you add by taking over Swift. Thus, you cannot extract more value than the value you add to the company by taking it over.

Questions and Problems

1. Consider two firms, Aggie Engineering and Longhorn Engineering. Aggie and Longhorn will each either make $60 million or lose $30 million every year with equal probability. Also, the firms' profits are perfectly negatively correlated. That is, in a year that Aggie makes $60 million, Longhorn loses $30 million. In a year that Aggie has a loss of $30 million, Longhorn will have a gain of $60 million. Assume that the corporate tax rate is 30%. What is the total expected after-tax profits of both firms when they are two separate firms? What are the expected after-tax profits if the two firms merge into one firm but are run as two independent divisions? (Assume it is not possible to carry back or carry forward any losses.)

2. Consider two corporations that both have earnings of $5 per share. The first firm, Alpha Corp. is a mature company with few growth opportunities. It has 10 million shares outstanding and the shares are currently priced at $50 per share. The second company, Beta Corp. has many more growth opportunities than Alpha does. Although it also has 10 million shares outstanding, its shares are trading for $80 per share. Assume Beta acquires Alpha using its own stock.
   a. If this takeover adds no value, what is the value of Beta after the acquisition in a perfect market?
   b. At current market prices, how many shares must Beta offer Alpha's shareholders in exchange for their shares?
   c. What will Beta's earnings per share be after the acquisition?

3. Calculate Beta's price-earnings ratio before and after the takeover described in Question 2 above.

4. International Food Services (IFS) announces that it plans to acquire Kimchi International. At the time of the announcement, IFS's stock was trading for $50 a share and the company had 500 million shares outstanding. Kimchi's stock was trading for $10 a share and the company had 10 million shares outstanding.
   a. If the projected synergies were $20 million, what is the maximum exchange ratio IFS could offer in a stock swap and still generate a positive NPV?
   b. Given $20 million in synergies, what is the maximum cash offer Gulf can make?
   c. Is there any difference in how much IFS can pay if it pays in cash or offers a stock swap?

Solutions to Questions and Problems

1. Separately, the expected after-tax profits for Aggie would be $60 million × (1 − 0.30) = $42 million or a loss of $30 million with equal probability of occurring. This is an expected after-tax profit of ($42 million − $30 million)/2 = $6 million. Longhorn's expected after-tax profit will also be $6 million. As a merged firm, expected earnings would be $60 million + (−$30 million) = $30 million. After-tax profits would be $30 million × (1 − 0.30) = $21 million.

2. a. Beta's after-acquisition value = pre-takeover value of Alpha + pre-takeover value of Beta = $500 million + $800 million.
   b. Beta must offer Alpha $500 million worth of shares or $500 million/$80 shares = 6.25 million shares. The exchange ratio would be 6.25 million/10 million = 0.625 shares of Beta for each share of Alpha owned.
   c. EPS = ($5 × 20 million)/16.25 million = $6.15 per share.

3. Before the merger, the P/E ratio is $80/$5 = 16. After the merger the P/E ratio is $80/$6.15 = 13.

4. a. The exchange ratio would be:

    $$\text{Exchange ratio} < \frac{P_T}{P_A}\left(1+\frac{S}{T}\right) = \frac{10}{50}\left(1+\frac{20}{100}\right) = 0.24$$

    IFS offers up to 0.24 shares of IFS stock for each share of Kimchi's stock and generate a positive NPV.
    b. For a cash offer, given synergies of $20 million/10 million shares = $2 per share, IFS could offer up to $10 + $2 = $12 per share.
    c. No, IFS would be willing to pay $12 per share for Kimchi. Or, IFS would be willing to give Kimchi shareholders 0.24 shares of IFS stock for each share of Kimchi they currently hold. This is worth 0.24 × $50 = $12.

■ Self-Test Questions

1. Simply Soft Drinks acquires Real Cola. This is a _____ merger.
    a. horizontal
    b. vertical
    c. conglomerate
    d. wave

2. Which of the following mergers would be the best example of a vertical merger?
    a. United Airlines merges with Continental Airlines
    b. Fossil Oil acquires Ancient Ages Publishing
    c. Toyota acquires Whitewall Tires
    d. North Pole Ice Company merges with South Pole Penguin Tours

3. Eastern Engines is attempting a takeover of Midway Motors. The board of Midway does not want to have Eastern Engines acquire it, so Midway approaches International Instruments to see if International Instruments would be willing to acquire it. International Instruments would be known as a(n):
    a. White knight
    b. Raider
    c. Arbitrageur
    d. Golden parachute

4. Premerger, Tri Delta Pharmaceuticals was trading for $10 a share. When Tri Delta was acquired by Delaware Drug Co., Delaware paid $14 a share, or 40% more than the premerger price. This 40% is known as the
    a. carry-forward premium.
    b. economies of scope value.
    c. synergy value.
    d. acquisition premium.

5. Which of the following is the best example of a golden parachute?
    a. Management at Golden Auto Parts approaches Central Auto Manufacturers to acquire Golden because Golden does not want to be acquired by Detroit Automobile Manufacturing.
    b. Senior management at LGI will receive a severance package averaging $7 million each in the event that the firm is taken over and the managers are let go.

c. The management of Coastal Packaging purchases the company through a leveraged buyout.
d. Toronto Tools pays out a large dividend when it has a lot of cash to make itself less attractive as a target.

6. Which of the following is TRUE?
   a. Based on the average stock price reaction, target shareholders, on average, ultimately capture the value added by the acquirer in a merger.
   b. On average, the stock price of a target firm increases by 1% and the stock price of an acquiring firm increases by 45% when a merger is announced.
   c. On average, the gains from synergy provided by a merger are split equally between the acquiring firm and the target firm.
   d. The stock price of a target firm tends to decrease when a merger is announced, while the stock price of an acquiring firm tends to increase.

7. Gordon Greedo announces a tender offer for half of the outstanding shares of Holiday Cruise Line for $35 a share. He borrows money through a shell corporation by pledging the shares themselves as collateral on the loan. This is known as a
   a. horizontal merger.
   b. white Squire.
   c. toehold.
   d. leveraged buyout.

8. Caroline owns 500 shares of Trident Tools which was trading at $42 a share when an acquiring company made a tender offer of $47 a share. If the firms merge and Caroline is a non tendering shareholder, she will be forced to sell her shares for the $47 tender offer price. This is known as a
   a. vertical merger.
   b. freezeout merger.
   c. leveraged buyout.
   d. management buyout.

9. The most common justifications given for acquiring a firm are:
   a. The synergies that can be gained through acquisition.
   b. The gains that come from switching to a less liquid investment.
   c. The gains that come from reduced government regulation.
   d. The benefits that come from an increased P/E ratio due to the fact that investors prefer large companies.

10. Bidders can pay for a target
    a. only using cash.
    b. only using stock.
    c. using cash, stock, or a combination of the two.
    d. using cash or debt.

11. The acquirer in a hostile takeover is often called a
    a. white knight.
    b. white squire.
    c. risk-arbitrageur.
    d. raider.

12. A proxy fight exists when
    a. a white knight and a white squire duel for control of a company.
    b. government regulators challenge the legality of a merger on the basis of antitrust laws.
    c. an acquirer attempts to convince the target's shareholders to unseat the target's board by using their proxy votes to support the acquirer's candidates for election to the target's board.
    d. a target firm gives the existing target shareholders the right to buy shares in the target at a deeply discounted price, diluting the value of any shares held by the acquirer.

Answers to Self-Test Questions

1. a
2. c
3. a
4. d
5. b
6. a
7. d
8. b
9. a
10. c
11. d
12. c

Chapter 23
International Corporate Finance

■ Key Learning Objectives

- Explain the basics of foreign exchange
- Identify and hedge exchange rate risk
- Understand integrated capital markets and their implication for prices
- Determine how to handle cash flows in foreign currencies in capital budgeting
- Analyze the impact of different countries' tax rates on investment decisions and firm value
- Show how to exploit opportunities from segmented international markets
- Demonstrate how to address exchange rate risk in your capital budgeting approach

■ Notation

C_{FC}	foreign currency cash flow
D	market value of debt
E	market value of equity
F	forward exchange rate
$r_\$$	dollar risk-free interest rate
$r_\$^*$	dollar cost of capital
r_{FC}	foreign currency risk-free interest rate
r_{FC}^*	foreign currency cost of capital
r_D	required return on debt
r_E	required return on equity
r_{wacc}	weighted average cost of capital
S	spot exchange rate

■ Chapter Synopsis

23.1 Foreign Exchange

A **foreign exchange rate** is a price for a currency denominated in another currency. Currencies are traded in the **foreign exchange (FX or forex) market.** The foreign exchange market is open around the clock, has no central physical location, and experiences daily turnover of over $3 trillion. The U.S. dollar and the euro account for more than half of this trading volume.

23.2 Exchange Rate Risk

Multinational firms face the risk of currency exchange rate fluctuations. Most exchange rates are **floating rates** and change constantly depending on the quantity supplied and demanded for each currency in the market. The supply and demand for each currency is driven by the activity of firms trading goods, trading by currency market investors, and actions of central banks in each country.

Fluctuating exchange rates cause a problem known as the **importer-exporter dilemma** for firms doing business in international markets. If neither party in an international transaction will accept exchange rate risk, the transaction may be difficult or impossible to negotiate.

A **currency forward contract** is a contract that sets the exchange rate in advance. It is usually written between a firm and a bank; however, the bank will generally enter into a second forward contract with offsetting exposure to eliminate its risk.

A currency forward contract specifies: (1) an exchange rate, (2) an amount of currency to exchange, and (3) a delivery date on which the exchange will take place. The exchange rate set in the contract is referred to as the **forward exchange rate.** By entering into a currency forward contract a firm can lock in an exchange rate in advance and reduce or eliminate its exposure to fluctuations in a currency's value.

An alternative method to accomplish the same objective is to use a **cash-and-carry strategy** which, for a dollars-to-euros contract, consists of the following three simultaneous trades:

1. Borrow euros today using a 1-year loan with the interest rate, $r_€$.

2. Exchange the euros for dollars today at the current exchange rate, also referred to as the **spot exchange rate.**

3. Invest the dollars today for 1 year at the interest rate, $r_\$$.

In 1 year, you will owe euros (from the loan in Transaction 1) and receive dollars (from the investment in Transaction 3). Thus, you have converted euros in 1 year to dollars in 1 year, just as with the forward contract.

Because the forward contract and the cash-and-carry strategy accomplish the same conversion, by the Law of One Price they must do so at the same rate. Combining the rates used in the cash-and-carry strategy leads to the following no-arbitrage formula for the forward exchange rate called **covered interest parity:**

$$\underbrace{\text{Forward Rate}}_{\substack{\text{€ in one year} \\ \text{\$ in one year}}} = \underbrace{\text{Spot Rate}}_{\substack{\text{€ today} \\ \text{\$ today}}} \times \underbrace{\frac{1+r_€}{1+r_\$}}_{\substack{\text{€ in one year/€ today} \\ \text{\$ in one year/\$ today}}}$$

The **covered interest parity equation** above states that the difference between the forward and spot exchange rates is related to the interest rate differential between the currencies.

Currency options are another method that firms commonly use to manage exchange rate risk. Currency options give the holder the right, but not the obligation, to exchange currency at a given exchange rate.

23.3 Internationally Integrated Capital Markets

In **internationally integrated capital markets,** in which any investor can exchange either currency in any amount at the spot rate or forward rates and is free to purchase or sell any security in any amount in either country at their current market prices, the value of an investment does not depend on the currency we use in the analysis.

23.4 Valuation of Foreign Currency Cash Flows

In an internationally integrated capital market, two equivalent methods can be used for calculating the NPV of a foreign project:

1. Calculate the NPV in the foreign country and convert it to the local currency at the spot rate.

2. Convert the cash flows of the foreign project into the local currency and then calculate the NPV of these cash flows.

When using the second method, the foreign cost of capital in terms of the domestic cost of capital and interest rate is:

$$r_{FC}^* = \frac{1+r_{FC}}{1+r_\$}(1+r_\$^*) - 1$$

23.5 Valuation and International Taxation

Determining the corporate tax rate on foreign income is complicated because corporate income taxes must be paid to two national governments: the host government and the home government. If the foreign project is a separately incorporated subsidiary of the parent, the amount of taxes a firm pays generally depends on the amount of profits **repatriated** and brought back to the home country.

U.S. tax policy requires U.S. corporations to pay taxes on their foreign income at the same rate as profits earned in the United States. However, a full tax credit is given for foreign taxes paid up to the amount of the U.S. tax liability. If the foreign tax rate exceeds the U.S. tax rate, companies must pay this higher rate on foreign earnings.

Under U.S. tax law, multinational corporations may use any excess tax credits generated in high-tax foreign countries to offset their net U.S. tax liabilities on earnings in low-tax foreign countries. Thus, if the U.S. tax rate exceeds the combined tax rate on all foreign income, it is valid to assume that the firm pays the same tax rate on all income no matter where it is earned. Otherwise, the firm must pay a higher tax rate on its foreign income.

When the foreign tax rate is less than the U.S. tax rate, deferring the repatriation lowers the overall tax burden in much the same way as deferring capital gains lowers the tax burden imposed by the capital gains tax.

23.6 Internationally Segmented Capital Markets

Segmented capital markets occur when all investors do not have equal access to financial securities in different capital markets. In some cases, a country's risk-free securities are internationally integrated but markets for a specific firm's securities are not. Firms may face differential access to markets if there is any kind of asymmetry with respect to information about them. Using a **currency swap**, a firm can borrow in the market where it has the best access to capital, and then "swap" the coupon and principal payments to whichever currency it would prefer to make its payment in. Thus, swaps allow firms to mitigate their exchange rate risk exposure between assets and liabilities, while still making investments and raising funds in the most attractive locales.

When capital markets are internationally segmented, the important implication is that one country or currency has a higher cost of capital than another country or currency when the two are compared in the same currency. If the return difference results from a market friction such as capital controls, corporations can exploit this friction by setting up projects in the high-return country/currency and raising capital in the low-return country/currency.

23.7 Capital Budgeting with Exchange Rate Risk

Many firms use imported inputs in their production processes or export some of their output to foreign countries. These scenarios alter the nature of a project's foreign exchange risk and, in turn, change the valuation of the foreign currency cash flows.

Whenever a project has cash flows that depend on the values of multiple currencies, the most convenient approach is to separate the cash flows according to the currency they depend on. To correctly value such projects, the foreign and domestic cash flows should be valued separately.

■ Selected Concepts and Key Terms

Foreign Exchange Market

The **foreign exchange market** is a very high volume market, operating around the clock, where currencies are traded.

Foreign Exchange Rate

A **foreign exchange rate** is a price for one currency denominated in another currency. A **floating rate** is an exchange rate that changes depending on supply and demand in the market. The **spot exchange rate** is the current foreign exchange rate; the **forward exchange rate** applies to an exchange that will occur in the future and is set in a currency forward contract.

Cash-and-Carry Strategy

The **cash-and-carry strategy** is a strategy used to lock in the future cost of an asset by buying the asset for cash today and storing (or "carrying") it until a future date.

Covered Interest Parity Equation

The **covered interest parity equation** states the difference between the forward and spot exchange rates is related to the interest rate differential between the currencies.

Currency Forward Contract

A **currency forward contract** sets a currency exchange rate, and an amount to exchange, in advance.

Currency Timeline

A **currency timeline** indicates time horizontally by dates (as in a standard timeline) and currencies vertically.

Internationally Integrated Capital Markets

Internationally integrated capital markets exist when any investor can exchange currencies in any amount at the spot or forward rates and is free to purchase or sell any security in any amount in any country at its current market price.

Repatriated

Repatriated profits are a firm's profits that are brought back to the home country from a foreign country.

Currency Swaps

Currency swaps are arrangements in which the holder receives coupons in one currency and pays coupons and the final face value denominated in a different currency. Using a currency swap, a firm can borrow in the market where it has the best access to capital, and then "swap" the coupon and principal payment to whichever currency it would prefer to make payments in. Thus, swaps allow firms to mitigate their exchange rate risk exposure between assets and liabilities, while still making investments and raising funds in the most attractive locales.

Segmented Capital Markets

International markets in which all investors do not have equal access to financial securities are **segmented capital markets.**

■ Concept Check Questions and Answers

1. What is an exchange rate?

   An exchange rate is the price for a currency denominated in another currency.

2. Why would multinational companies need to exchange currencies?

   U.S. companies that collect revenue in other countries with different currencies need to exchange their profits in the foreign currencies into dollars. Also, these firms might need to pay for parts and labor in other currencies.

3. How can firms hedge exchange rate risk?

   Firms can hedge exchange rate risk in financial markets by using currency forward contracts to lock in an exchange rate in advance and by using currency option contracts to protect against an exchange rate moving beyond a certain level.

4. Why may a firm prefer to hedge exchange rate risk with options rather than forward contracts?

   A firm prefers options to forward contracts when there is a chance that the transaction it is hedging will not take place. In this case, a forward contract requires the firm to make an exchange at an unfavorable rate for the currency it does not need, whereas an option allows the firm to walk away from the exchange.

5. What assumptions are needed to have internationally integrated capital markets?

   We make the following assumptions: any investor can exchange either currency in any amount at the spot rate or forward rate and is free to purchase or sell any security in any amount in either country at their current market price.

6. What implication does internationally integrated capital markets have for the value of the same asset in different countries?

   The implication of internationally integrated capital markets is that the value of a foreign investment does not depend on the currency (home or foreign) we use in the analysis.

7. Explain two methods we use to calculate the NPV of a foreign project.

   One, we can calculate the NPV in the foreign country and convert it to local currency at the spot rate. Two, we can convert the cash flows of the foreign project into local currency and then calculate the NPV of these cash flows.

8. When do these two methods give the same NPV of the foreign project?

   The two methods give the same NPV of a foreign project when markets are internationally integrated and uncertainty in spot exchange rates are uncorrelated with the foreign currency cash flows.

9. What tax rate should we use to value a foreign project?

   Because a U.S. corporation pays the higher of the foreign or domestic tax rate on its foreign project, we should use the higher of these two rates to value a foreign project.

10. How can a U.S. firm lower its taxes on foreign projects?

    A U.S. firm can lower its taxes by having foreign projects in other countries that can be pooled with the new project or by deferring the repatriation of earnings.

11. What are the reasons for segmentation of the capital markets?

    Market segmentation can exist when a country's risk-free securities are internationally integrated but markets for a specific firm's securities are not. Also, some countries impose capital controls or foreign exchange controls that create barriers to international capital flows.

12. What is the main implication for international corporate finance of a segmented financial market?

    The implication for international corporate finance of a segmented financial market is that one country or currency has a higher rate of return than another, when compared in the same currency.

13. What conditions cause the cash flows of a foreign project to be affected by exchange rate risk?

    To value projects that have inputs and outputs in different currencies correctly, the foreign and domestic cash flows should be valued separately.

14. How do we make adjustments when a project has inputs and outputs in different countries?

    When a project has inputs and outputs in different currencies, the foreign-denominated cash flows are likely to be correlated with changes in spot rates.

■ Examples with Step-by-Step Solutions

The Effect of Exchange Rate Risk

23.1 **Problem:** On the first day of 2004, Espresso Parts Northwest (EPNW) ordered 2 million euro worth of Mazzer espresso grinders from the Italian manufacturer, Mazzer Luigi S.r.l. The payment in euros was due when the grinders were delivered in one year. The exchange rate at the beginning of the year was $1.05 per euro. On the last day of 2004, the exchange rate was $1.24 per euro. What was the actual cost in dollars for EPNW when the payment was due? If the price was set in dollars at the current exchange rate how much would Mazzer receive when the payment was due in euros?

Solution

Plan: The price was set in euros, but the $/€ exchange rate will fluctuate over time and the problem asks us to consider what would happen if it goes to $1.24/euro, which means that dollars are worth less because it takes more dollars to buy one euro. We can always convert between dollars and euros at the going exchange rate by multiplying the $/€ exchange rate by the number of euros or by dividing the number of dollars by the $/€ exchange rate.

Execute: With the price set at 2 million euro, EPNW had to pay:

$$(\$1.24/\text{euro}) \times (2 \text{ million euros}) = \$2.48 \text{ million}$$

If the price had been set in dollars, EPNW would have paid:

$$(\$1.05/\text{euro}) \times (2 \text{ million euros}) = \$2.1 \text{ million}$$

which would have been worth only $2.1 million/($1.24/euro) = 1.694 euros to Mazzer.

Evaluate: Whether the price was set in euros or dollars, one of the parties would have suffered a substantial loss. Neither party knows which will suffer the loss ahead of time, so each has an incentive to hedge.

Using a Forward Contract to Lock in an Exchange Rate

23.2 Problem: At the beginning of 2004, banks were offering 1-year currency forward contracts with a forward exchange rate of $1.03 per euro. Suppose that, when EPNW placed the order with Mazzer in Example 23.1, it simultaneously hedged by entering into a forward contract to purchase 2 million euros at the forward exchange rate. What payment would EPNW be required to make when the payment was due?

Solution

Plan: If EPNW entered into a forward contract, locking in an exchange rate of $1.03/euro, then it does not matter what the actual exchange rate is at the end of the year. The company will be able to buy 2 million euros at a price of $1.03 per euro.

Execute: EPNW must pay 2 million euros × $1.03/euro = $2.06 million at the end of the year. EPNW would pay $2.06 million to the bank in exchange for 2 million euros, which are then paid to Mazzer.

Evaluate: Given the way exchange rates moved, the forward contract would have been a good deal for EPNW. Without the hedge, it would have had to exchange dollars for euros at the prevailing rate of $1.24/euro, raising its cost to $2.48 million. However, the exchange rate could have moved the other way. If euros had become cheaper, rather than more expensive, Mazzer would have been committed to paying $1.03/euro with the forward contract. Thus, the forward contract locks in the exchange rate and eliminates risk, whether the movement of the exchange rate is favorable or unfavorable.

Computing the No-Arbitrage Forward Exchange Rate

23.3 Problem: Assume that the spot exchange rate for the South Korean won is 1030 won/$. Also, assume that the 1-year interest rate in the United States is 4.0% and the 1-year interest rate in South Korea is 4.5%. Based on these rates, what forward exchange rate is consistent with no arbitrage?

Solution

Plan: We can compute the forward exchange rate using the formula:

$$\text{Forward Rate}_{won/\$} = \text{Spot Rate}_{won/\$} \times \frac{1+r_{won}}{1+r_\$}$$

Because the exchange rate is expressed in terms of won/$, we need to make sure that we have the formula arranged so that we are dividing 1 plus the won rate by 1 plus the dollar rate.

Execute:

$$\text{Forward Rate}_{won/\$} = \text{Spot Rate}_{won/\$} \times \frac{1+r_{won}}{1+r_\$}$$

$$= \text{won } 1030/\$ \times \frac{1.045}{1.040} = \text{won } 1034.95/\$ \text{ in 1 year}$$

Evaluate: The forward exchange rate is higher than the spot exchange rate, offsetting the higher interest rate on won investments. If the forward exchange rate were anything other than won 1034.95/$, arbitrage profits would be available.

Present Values and Internationally Integrated Capital Markets

23.4 **Problem:** The spot yen-dollar exchange rate is ¥110/$ and the 1-year forward rate is ¥106.8571/$. The appropriate dollar cost of capital is $r_\$ = 5\%$ and the appropriate yen cost of capital is $r_¥ = 2\%$. What is the present value of ¥20 million cash flow to a Japanese corporation in 1 year? What is the present value of a ¥20 million cash flow for a U.S. corporation who first converts the ¥20 million into dollars and then applies the dollar discount rate?

Solution

Plan: For the Japanese corporation, we can compute the present value of the future yen cash flow at the yen discount rate and use the spot exchange rate to convert that amount to dollars. For the U.S. corporation, we can convert the future yen cash flow to dollars at the forward rate and compute the present value using the dollar discount rate.

Execute: The present value of the yen cash flow to the Japanese corporation is:

$$¥20 \text{ m}/1.02 = ¥19,607,843$$

To find the dollar equivalent, we use the current spot rate of ¥110/$; the dollar equivalent is:

$$(\$1/¥110) \times ¥19,607,843 = \$178,253$$

For the U.S. corporation, we first convert the ¥20 m to dollars using the forward rate; the dollar equivalent is:

$$¥20 \text{ m}/106.8571 = \$187.166$$

Then, using the dollar cost of capital, the present value is:

$$\$187.166/1.05 = \$178,253$$

Evaluate: Because the U.S. and Japanese capital markets are internationally integrated, both methods produce the same result.

Internationalizing the Cost of Capital

23.5 Problem: Your company is considering an investment in Japan. Your dollar cost of equity is 10%, and you are trying to determine the comparable cost of equity in Japanese yen for a project with free cash flows that are uncorrelated with spot exchange rates. The risk-free interest rate in the United States is 6% and the risk-free interest rate in Japanese yen is 2%. You believe that, in this case, capital markets are internationally integrated. What is the yen cost of equity?

Solution

Plan: The foreign cost of capital in terms of the domestic cost of capital and interest rates can be found using the following equation:

$$r_{FC}^* = \frac{1+r_{FC}}{1+r_\$}(1+r_\$^*) - 1$$

We know that $r_{FC} = 2\%$, $r_\$ = 6\%$, and $r_\$^* = 10\%$.

Execute:

$$r_Y^* = \frac{1+0.02}{1+0.06} \times (1+0.10) - 1 = 5.85\%$$

Evaluate: Your company's yen cost of capital is 5.85%. If you have the project's free cash flows in yen, you can use this yen cost of capital to calculate the present value of the yen free cash flows.

Valuing a Foreign Acquisition in a Segmented Market

23.6 Problem: Jetset Jewelry, a U.S. company, is considering expanding by acquiring Tyrolia Crystals, a company in Austria. The acquisition is expected to increase Jetset's free cash flows by 50 million euros the first year. The free cash flow is expected to grow at a rate of 4% per year from then on. The acquisition would cost $1 billion euros and the current exchange rate is $1.25 per euro. Jetset believes that the appropriate after-tax euro WACC is 10% and that its after-tax dollar WACC for this expansion is 8%. Assume that the markets for risk-free securities are integrated and that the yield curve in both countries is flat. U.S. risk-free interest rates are 5%, and euro risk-free interest rates are 7%. What is the value of Tyrolia Crystals to Jetset Jewelry in terms of euro cash flows? What is the value of Tyrolia Crystals to Jetset Jewelry in terms of dollar cash flows?

Solution

Plan: The expected free cash flows are a growing perpetuity. We can calculate the NPV of the expansion in euros and convert the result into dollars at the spot rate. We can also compute the NPV in dollars by converting the expected cash flows into dollars using forward rates. We calculate the forward rate using the equation:

$$\underbrace{\text{Forward Rate}}_{\substack{\$ \text{ in } N \text{ years} \\ \euro \text{ in } N \text{ years}}} = \underbrace{\text{Spot Rate}}_{\substack{\$ \text{ today} \\ \euro \text{ today}}} \times \underbrace{\frac{(1+r_\$)^N}{(1+r_\euro)^N}}_{\substack{\$ \text{ in } N \text{ years}/\$ \text{ today} \\ \euro \text{ in } N \text{ years}/\euro \text{ today}}}$$

Execute: To calculate the value of the deal in euros:

The cash flow in Year 1 will be 50 million euros. Because the cash flow is expected to increase at a rate of 4% a year, the present value of this growing perpetuity is:

$$\text{Value}_{\text{euros}} = \frac{50 \text{ m}}{0.10 - 0.04} = 833 \text{ million euros}$$

So, the NPV = −1 billion + 833 million = −167 million euros.

The NPV converted to dollars at the spot rate is −167 million euros × $1.25/1 euro = −$209 million.

To calculate the value of the deal in dollars:

First, we calculate the N-year forward rate:

$$\underbrace{\text{Forward Rate}}_{\substack{\$ \text{ in } N \text{ years} \\ \text{€ in } N \text{ years}}} = \underbrace{\text{Spot Rate}}_{\substack{\$ \text{ today} \\ \text{€ today}}} \times \underbrace{\frac{(1+r_\$)^N}{(1+r_\text{€})^N}}_{\substack{\$ \text{ in } N \text{ years}/\$ \text{ today} \\ \text{€ in } N \text{ years}/\text{€ today}}}$$

$$= 1.25 \times \left(\frac{1.05}{1.07}\right)^N$$

$$= 1.25 \times 0.9813^N$$

$$= 1.2266 \times 0.9813^{N-1}$$

Thus, the dollar expected cash flows are:

$$C_\$^N \times F_N = 50(1.04)^{N-1} \times (1.2266 \times 0.9813^{N-1})$$

$$= 61.33 \times 1.0206^{N-1}$$

So, the dollar cash flows are expected to grow at 2.06% a year.

The present value of the future dollar cash flows is 61.33/(0.08 − 0.026) = $1.032 billion.

The upfront investment cost in dollars is 1 billion euros × ($1.25/1 euro) = $1.25 billion.

So, the NPV is −$1.25 billion + $1.032 billion = −$218 million.

Evaluate: The dollar NPV calculated with dollar cash flows is a bit lower than with the euro cash flows. Both methods have potential sources of estimation error. To compute the dollar expected cash flows by converting the euro expected cash flows at the forward rate, we are making the implicit assumption that spot rates and the project cash flows are uncorrelated. The difference might simply reflect that this assumption failed to hold. Another possibility is that the difference reflects estimation error in the respective WACC estimates. Or, the difference may occur because the U.S. and Austrian capital markets are not integrated. In any case, the NPV is negative using either approach, which indicates that this is not a good deal for Jetset.

■ Questions and Problems

1. You are going to attend a month-long study abroad program in France. The dormitory housing at the French university costs 600 euros for the month. If the exchange rate is $1 = 0.77 euros, how much will the housing cost you in dollars?

2. It will be 3 months before you begin your study abroad program in Question 1 and you will pay for your housing when you arrive. You are on a tight budget and have decided that you cannot afford to take the trip if the housing will cost you more than $850. What would the exchange rate have to be for you not to be able to afford the trip? What might you do to mitigate this risk?

3. SDB Enterprises is considering an investment in Mexico. The company's dollar cost of equity is 10%. The risk-free interest rate in the United States is 5% and the risk-free interest rate in Mexican pesos is 8%. The financial managers for SDB believe that capital markets are internationally integrated. What is the peso cost of equity for a project with free cash flows that are uncorrelated with spot exchange rates.

4. Joseph's Textiles has a subsidiary in China. This year, the subsidiary reported and repatriated earnings before interest and taxes (EBIT) of 1 billion Chinese yuan. The current fixed exchange rate is $7.896 per yuan. The Chinese tax rate on this activity is 33%. U.S. tax law requires Joseph's to pay taxes on the Chinese earnings at the same rate as profits earned in the United States, which is currently 35%. However, the U.S. gives a full tax credit for foreign taxes paid up to the amount of the U.S. tax liability. What is Joseph's U.S. tax liability on its Chinese subsidiary?

5. The spot dollar Argentine peso exchange rate is $3.095 per peso and the 1-year forward exchange rate is $3.025 per peso. The yield on short-term Argentine government bonds is 9%, while the comparable 1-year yield on U.S. Treasury securities is 3%.
   a. Using the covered interest parity relation, calculate the implied 1-year forward rate.
   b. Compare this rate to the actual forward rate, and explain why the two rates may differ.

6. Your U.S. firm is considering a new project in Spain with expected free cash flows in euros of:

Year	Free Cash Flow in Millions of Euros
0	−100
1	20
2	70
3	40

   The spot exchange rate is $1.26 per euro, the risk-free interest rate in dollars is 5%, and the risk-free interest rate on euros is 7%. Assume that these markets are internationally integrated and the uncertainty in the free cash flows is not correlated with uncertainty in the exchange rate. The dollar WACC for these cash flows is 10%. What is the dollar present value of the project?

■ Solutions to Questions and Problems

1. $1 = 0.77 euros; so 1 euro = $1.2987. You will need $1.2987 × 600 = $779.22 to buy 600 euros.

2. 600 euros × (? dollars/euro) = $850 dollars; if the value of the dollar drops so that it costs more than $1.4166667 to buy a euro (or if $1 is less than 0.70588 euros); the cost of the housing will be more than $850 when you arrive in 3 months. To mitigate your risk, you could purchase 600 euros at today's spot rate and hold the euros until you need them; or you could enter into a 3-month forward contract or an option contract. The forward contract would lock-in your exchange rate, so you will know exactly what you will pay, but the trade-off is that you may be paying more than the spot rate in 3 months.

3. $r_{FC} = \dfrac{1+0.08}{1+0.05} \times (1+0.10) - 1 = 13.14\%$

4. With earnings of 1 billion yuan and the Chinese tax rate of 33%, the tax paid in China is 330 million yuan. With an exchange rate of $7.896 per yuan, the earnings are $127 million and the Chinese taxes amount to $42 million. With a tax rate of 35%, the U.S. tax on Joseph's Chinese income would be $44 million. However, Joseph's is able to claim a tax credit of $42 million, for a net tax liability of $2 million.

5. a. $F + (1.03/1.09) \times 3.095 = $2.925 per peso
    b. Since the U.S. bonds have virtually zero probability of default, the difference in the exchange rates likely indicates that the Argentine government bonds have some default risk. Otherwise, an investor could convert the pesos to dollars, invest in U.S. Treasuries, and convert the proceeds back to pesos at a rate locked in with a forward contract.

6. First, calculate the forward rates:

$$F_1 = (\$1.26/€)(1.05/1.07) = \$1.2364/€$$
$$F_2 = (\$1.26/€)(1.05^2/1.07^2) = \$1.2133/€$$
$$F_3 = (\$1.26/€)(1.05^3/1.07^3) = \$1.1907/€$$

Next, convert euro cash flows into dollars:

Year	Euro Cash Flow	Exchange Rate	Dollar Cash Flow
0	−100	1.2600	−79.37
1	20	1.2364	16.18
2	70	1.2133	57.69
3	40	1.1907	33.59

Finally, the net present value is:

$$NPV = -79.37 + (16.18/1.10) + (57.69/1.10^2) + (33.59/1.10^3) = \$8.25 \text{ million.}$$

Self-Test Questions

1. A _____ is an exchange rate that changes constantly depending on the quantity supplied and demanded for each currency in the market.
   a. flexible rate
   b. forward rate
   c. fundamental rate
   d. floating rate

2. A currency forward contract specifies
   a. an exchange rate.
   b. an amount of currency to exchange.
   c. a delivery date on which currency exchange will take place.
   d. All of the above.

3. The covered interest parity equation
   a. states that the difference between the forward and spot exchange rates is related to the interest rate differential between the two currencies.
   b. states that the difference between the forward and spot exchange rates is equal to the sum of the interest rates in the two countries.
   c. states that if the markets are internationally integrated, then the interest rates in the two countries will be identical.
   d. equates the NPV of cash flows from two different currencies.

4. Hedging with an option
   a. locks in an exchange rate that the firm must pay, regardless of the directional movement of the exchange rate.
   b. leaves a firm fully exposed to exchange rate risk.
   c. allows a firm to benefit if the exchange rate falls and protects the firm from a very large increase in the exchange rate.
   d. obligates a firm to trade the currency at the future date whether the firm needs the currency for a transaction or not.

5. With internationally integrated capital markets
   a. interest rates are the same in all countries.
   b. the value of an investment does not depend on the currency we use in the analysis.
   c. exchange rates are stable and do not change.
   d. the spot exchange rate and the forward exchange rate are equivalent.

6. The term "repatriation" refers to:
   a. Two parties agreeing to exchange coupon payments and a final face value payment that are in different currencies.
   b. A firm bringing the profits from a foreign project back to its home country.
   c. Using the domestic WACC to discount cash flows from a foreign project.
   d. Using the forward exchange rate to value the future cash flows from a foreign project.

7. A floating exchange rate
   a. is an exchange rate that is agreed upon in advance for a transaction to take place at a future date.
   b. is the difference between the spot rate and the forward rate.
   c. is determined by supply and demand of the currencies in the market.
   d. is determined by the governments of the two countries.

8. Annette will be traveling to Italy in 6 months and she has booked a hotel that will cost a total of 1000 euros for 10 nights. Currently, the exchange rate is $1 = 0.88 euros. Annette is concerned that the value of the dollar may decrease, increasing the cost of her hotel room. Therefore, she goes to her bank today and enters into a contract to purchase 1000 euro at a rate of $1 = 0.85 euros in six months. Annette has
   a. entered into a forward contract.
   b. followed a cash-and-carry strategy.
   c. practiced covered interest rate parity.
   d. entered into a currency swap.

9. The supply and demand for a currency is driven by:
   a. Firms trading goods.
   b. Investors trading securities.
   c. The actions of central banks in each country.
   d. All of the above.

10. Assume that the spot exchange rate for the euro is €0.80/$. Also assume that the 1-year interest rate in the United States is 5% and the 1-year euro interest rate is 3%. Based on these numbers, what forward exchange rate is consistent with no arbitrage?
    a. 0.7500€/$
    b. 0.7848€/$
    c. 1.2743€/$
    d. 1.3333€/$

11. IntelVision wants to use a cash-and-carry strategy for a dollars-to-euros contract. The company borrows euros today, exchanges the euros for dollars today at the current exchange rate, and invests the dollars today for 1 year. The company has essentially
    a. converted euros in 1 year to dollars in 1 year.
    b. increased its exposure to changes in foreign exchange rates over the next year.
    c. converted a currency forward contract into a floating exchange contract.
    d. created a floating currency option contract.

12. Currency swaps allow
    a. countries to issue currency for another country's central bank.
    b. firms to make investments and raise funds only in their home country.
    c. residents of a country to trade currency, but not goods, with residents of other countries.
    d. firms to mitigate their exchange rate risk exposure between assets and liabilities, while still making investments and raising funds in the most attractive locales.

Answers to Self-Test Questions

1. d
2. d
3. a
4. c
5. b
6. b
7. c
8. a
9. d
10. b
11. a
12. d